BRITISH BARRACKS
1600 – 1914

For Rosa

BRITISH BARRACKS
1600 – 1914

Their Architecture and Role in Society

James Douet

With an opening chapter by Andrew Saunders

© English Heritage 1998

All Rights Reserved. No part of this publication may be reproduced, stored in a retrieval system, or transmitted in any form or by any means, electronic, mechanical, photocopying, recording or otherwise without the permission of The Stationery Office, St. Crispins, Duke Street, Norwich, Norfolk, NR3 1PD.

ISBN 0 11 772482 3

Catalogue in Publication Data
A CIP catalogue record for this book is available from the British Library
A Library of Congress CIP catalogue record has been applied for

First published 1998

Themes in Military Architecture and Archaeology series editor: Jeremy Lake

Designer Richard Jones

Published by The Stationery Office and available from:

The Publications Centre
(mail, telephone and fax orders only)
PO Box 276, London SW8 5DT
General enquiries 0171 873 0011
Telephone orders 0171 873 9090
Fax orders 0171 873 8200

The Stationery Office Bookshops
59–60 Holborn Viaduct, London EC1A 2FD
temporary until mid 1998
(counter service and fax orders only)
Fax 0171 831 1326
68–69 Bull Street, Birmingham B4 6AD
0121 236 9696   Fax 0121 236 9699
33 Wine Street, Bristol BS1 2BQ
0117 9264306   Fax 0117 9294515
9–21 Princess Street, Manchester M60 8AS
0161 834 7201   Fax 0161 833 0634
16 Arthur Street, Belfast BT1 4GD
01232 238451   Fax 01232 235401
The Stationery Office Oriel Bookshop
The Friary, Cardiff CF1 4AA
01222 395548   Fax 01222 384347
71 Lothian Road, Edinburgh EH3 9AZ
(counter service only)

Customers in Scotland may
mail, telephone or fax their orders to:
Scottish Publications Sales
South Gyle Crescent, Edinburgh EH12 9EB
0131 228 4181 Fax 0131 622 7017

The Stationery Office's Accredited Agents
(see Yellow Pages)

and through good booksellers

Front cover: Clarence Marines Barracks, Portsmouth (see Figure 40 in the colour section)

Back cover: The officers' quarters, Clarence Barracks, Portsmouth (see Figure 164 in the colour section)

Left flap: Plan of Fort George (see Figure 34 in the colour section)

Right flap: The dockyard at Plymouth in 1756 (see Figure 38 in the colour section)

Printed in the United Kingdom for The Stationery Office
J22516   2/98   C8   072435

Contents

Contributors' Details		vii
Foreword		ix
List of Abbreviations		x
Introduction		xi
Chapter One	1600–1750: Early Evolution *Andrew Saunders*	1
Chapter Two	1714–1750: 'No Standing Armies	29
Chapter Three	1750–1792: 'Out of Reach of Revolutionary Contagion'	43
Chapter Four	1792–1815: 'No Barns, No Pigstyes'	67
Chapter Five	1815–1852: 'No Better Military School for Officers and Privates'	103
Chapter Six	1852–1872: 'Old, Gloomy and Bad'	127
Chapter Seven	1847–1869: 'The Three Panics'	151
Chapter Eight	1872–1914: Localization and the 'Great Camps'	167
Postscript		195
Appendix A	Departments and Senior Officers Responsible for Barracks	199
Appendix B	Ranks and Roles in Infantry, Cavalry and Horse Artillery Units in 1857	201
Acknowledgements		203
Select Bibliography		207
Index		211

Colour plates

These appear on pages 95 – 101

Maps

Map 1   Barracks and Garrisons in the early eighteenth century   15

Map 2   Barracks in Britain before 1792   61

Map 3   Barracks in the Revolutionary and Napoleonic Wars   70

Map 4   South-east England from Devon to the Wash: temporary camps
        built between 1803 and 1805   75

Map 5   Barracks in the United Kingdom before the Crimean War   117

Map 6   Cardwell localization depots in 1880   168

Map 7   Barracks built with the Military and Naval Loans before
        the First World War   178

Tables

Table 1 Comparative dimensions of barrack rooms, number of beds per room
        (each for two men) and an estimate of the cubic space allotted to the
        individual private soldier   28

Table 2 Ordnance Board accommodation on the eve of the Revolutionary
        War, showing the official capacity of each region   68

Contributors' Details

James Douet

James Douet worked as a builder and stonemason for a number of years, before advising English Heritage on updating the registers of listed buildings in Bristol and other West Country towns. English Heritage's emphasis changed from settlements to thematic studies of particular building types, when he produced reports and recommendations for protecting water pumping stations, silk mills and, finally, barracks. His main area of historical interest has been industrial buildings, including a book on industrial chimneys with the Victorian Society, *Going up in Smoke* (London 1990), and a report for SAVE on pumping station architecture, *Temples of Steam* (Bristol 1992). He moved to live with his Catalan wife in Barcelona in 1996. He is now studying the European development of barracks, and the architecture of the Catalan Industrial Revolution.

Jeremy Lake

Series Editor Jeremy Lake has worked as an Inspector of Historic Buildings with English Heritage since 1988. His work reflects a wide-ranging interest in historic building types. He edits the *Journal of the Historic Farm Buildings Group*, and previous publications include *The Great Fire of Nantwich* (Nantwich 1983), a detailed account of life in an Elizabethan town based around its destruction by fire in 1588, and *Historic Farm Buildings: An Introduction and Guide* (London 1989), published in association with the National Trust.

Andrew Saunders

During a career in the Ancient Monuments Inspectorate (Ministry of Works – Department of the Environment), Andrew Saunders came to specialize in military architecture, both early medieval castles and later artillery fortification. He is a Fellow of the Society of Antiquaries and of the Royal Historical Society, and a former President of the Royal Archaeological Institute. Since retiring as Chief Inspector of Ancient Monuments and Historic Buildings at English Heritage in 1989, his publications include *Fortress Britain: Artillery Fortification in the British Isles and Ireland* (Liphook 1989) and *Channel Defences* (London 1997), as well as numerous articles in specialist journals, and guidebooks to ancient monuments. He was editor of the castles and fortifications quarterly, *Fortress* (1989–93). He is currently Chairman of the Fortress Study Group. He lives in Blackheath, South-East London, with his wife and younger daughter.

Foreword

This book is the first in a series of studies which have arisen out of the first comprehensive 'Thematic Study' by English Heritage into aspects of our military heritage, in partnership with the Ministry of Defence. Barracks comprise an important but neglected part of the nation's social, political and military history, providing witness to domestic instability as much as the threat of foreign invasion. Some are now very rare. The last surviving pair of brick huts at Aldershot, for example, provide examples of the living conditions experienced by thousands of soldiers from nineteenth century volunteers to post-war servicemen.

Whilst many sites have a history of unbroken military use, others are in the process of being transferred to new occupiers. The launch of this publication now is particularly relevant in the light of the changes facing the Defence Estate.

The public are increasingly drawn to military buildings and the distinguished service traditions they embody. Accordingly, we commend this book as an authoritative addition to the already extensive body of knowledge on the subject. We believe that it will generate a greater interest and understanding of military barracks and help to inform proposals to secure their viable future.

John Spellar MP
Under Secretary of State for Defence

Sir Jocelyn Stevens
Chairman of English Heritage

Abbreviations

BL	British Library
CMI	Commissioners of Military Inquiry
EH	English Heritage
JSAHR	*Journal of the Society of Army Historical Research*
NAM	National Army Museum
NMM	National Maritime Museum
PRO	Public Record Office
PRONI	Public Record Office Northern Ireland
RCHME	Royal Commission on the Historical Monuments of England
RCHMS	Royal Commission on the Ancient and Historical Monuments of Scotland
RE	Royal Engineers
RE Library	Royal Engineers Library, Chatham
SRO	Stafford Record Office

Introduction

'Aldershot. All-der-shot; *how did such closely fitting sounds come to be invented for this either bleak or burning capital of English militarism? The syllables* Alder *suggest, almost as if by magic formula, the universality of boredom – while* shot *puts* finis *to the word with the emblematic crack, as well as the meaning, of a rifle bullet.*'[1]

It must be admitted from the outset that few topics are burdened with such connotations of dullness as barracks, especially in terms of architecture. Barracks usually provide a metaphor for buildings which are unimaginative, oppressive, cheerless or cold. As a consequence of this prejudice, long after many more marginal or specialized building types have been analysed and recorded, this large and complex subject – overlapping many other areas of military, urban, social and architectural history – has remained unexplored.

Barracks are an instrument of war. They are built because they make better soldiers, and better soldiers form more effective armies. No less than good generals, strong forts, efficient suppliers or a productive economy, barracks confer a clear military advantage on states which have them over those which do not.

Barracks made their first appearance as quarters for elite units like the Roman Praetorian Guard, the Varangian Guard of the Byzantine emperors, the Papal Swiss Guard or the Household Guard of the English sovereigns. They became more widely used in the early modern period as battlefield tactics underwent a revolution which required highly trained and disciplined soldiers for whole armies.

Too valuable to be lost at the end of the campaigning season, such men formed the first permanent or standing armies since classical times. As these armies became too large for civilian society to sustain through the traditional means of scavenging, looting and free quartering, so States had to provide permanent accommodation for them.

The evolution of barracks since the seventeenth century has continued to be driven by competition between States to raise the quality of their fighting men. Living conditions slowly improved, then wider opportunities for exercise and education were provided, because healthier, fitter, better-informed soldiers were more effective than malnourished, feeble or illiterate ones. In the early nineteenth century, large, permanent camps were established across Europe because greater armies of mixed regulars and auxiliaries needed to practise co-ordinated, combined manoeuvres. Later in the century, barracks became more comfortable, barrack life became less austere, and even barrack architecture became more attractive, as better economic conditions forced armies to compete for recruits.

In addition to this role, which one writer has called 'a kind of discipline factory' for soldiers,[2] barracks perform a more specific military function as low-level strongholds. In this capacity, they have been used to hold and stabilize captured territory – as they were, for example, by Spain's Army of Flanders in the Low Countries, or by the British Army in Ireland. On a smaller scale, barracks have been built as part of counter-insurgency campaigns where mountainous terrain gave irregular forces an

---

[1] Osbert Sitwell, *Great Morning* (London 1949), p.127.

[2] Jones (1980), p.162.

advantage, such as in the Highlands of Scotland. They have also been applied extensively in a policing role during periods of domestic unrest, when the State felt itself to be under threat. The barracks built in the north-west of England during the Chartist disturbances are an instance of this (see Chapter Five). These complexes drew on fortification theory for their design, and there are many crossovers between barracks and forts, particularly during the 1860s, when the distinction between the two became completely blurred (see Chapter Seven).

The evolution of barracks in the British Isles has been uneven in terms of their architecture, planning and geography, but it has always been propelled by the State's perception of its need for coercion to apply its policies, at home or abroad, and to protect itself against the policies of rival powers.

The roles and responsibilities of British forces

Britain has traditionally maintained forces for three principal duties: foreign war, defence of the realm and upholding the civil order. When the army was fighting overseas, there was usually a backwash effect on barracks at home, which benefited from the increased funding which Parliament allocated in wartime estimates. Popular enthusiasm when a war was going well inhibited the ever present tendency in Parliament towards retrenchment, and sustained the advocates of stronger national defence. For example, at the start of the Crimean War, Prince Albert pressed the Government to embark on the construction of the first permanent training camp at Aldershot before popular enthusiasm for the army waned. Later in the nineteenth century, a series of triumphs against technologically inferior forces, and the Pyrrhic victory over the Boers, helped channel money into better accommodation. Conversely, periods of peace or military security, as in the late twentieth century, led to barracks assuming a lower priority or being abandoned altogether.

The defence of the realm has been a more passive role, and the demands it has made on stationing and accommodating the forces have been more consistent than those generated by foreign expeditions. Troops have always been garrisoned in London, for instance, as well as around the strategically vital royal dockyards. The orientation of Britain's defences has changed only slowly, in response to the perceived source of the threat. Fear of invasion has been a constant in the geography of barrack construction, however, and invasion scares have frequently set the timing of building campaigns. Support for the authority of the Government was the main role of the army during peacetime, from the passing of the Riot Act in 1715 until the gradual extension of a civilian police force during Queen Victoria's reign, and troops continued to be used to control political – and, increasingly, industrial – unrest into the twentieth century, culminating in the 1926 General Strike. Their deployment in Northern Ireland is a modern instance of this enduring role, and the security of the barracks has again been an important issue. Apart from occasional invasion scares, the need to station forces to quell revolt, protest or riot, to deter smuggling or to defend the authority of the Crown was the predominant influence on new barrack construction in peacetime until the police took on more of these tasks in the mid-nineteenth century. Even then, the Chartist disturbances provoked a Government set on military retrenchment into a campaign to build barracks in the centres of unrest and agitation.

Political control of the armed forces was effectively lost by the Crown to Parliament in the settlement of 1688. But the army and the navy maintained effective control over their own internal affairs for much longer, and only began to submit themselves to closer Government control in the late nineteenth century. Following the Cardwell reforms of the 1870s, there was a period in which the old, aristocratic army hierarchy struggled against demands for reform and greater professionalism. A General Staff was finally established in 1905, creating the structure that was to last through both world wars.

Introduction

Permanent military quarters in the British Isles

The formation of a standing army in the mid-seventeenth century provided a new role for many semi-obsolete castles such as Stirling and Edinburgh, which were adapted and given a new role as military quarters. As Andrew Saunders explains in Chapter One, the earliest purpose-built military lodgings were called 'barracks' after the temporary shelters which soldiers built for themselves in the field. The same word was subsequently used when the first detached, enclosed complexes, including 'barracks', evolved in Britain and Ireland from the early seventeenth century. The distinction between the individual building and the larger complex is more precisely expressed in Spain and France, whose languages reflect a longer familiarity with a standing army, and in which separate words distinguish between the two: buildings in which soldiers live are known as *cuarteles* or *quartiers*, and the enclosed complex is called a *caseron* or *caserne*. The English word 'barracks' has to convey both these meanings, but it is important to be aware of the difference between them.

From the establishment of the standing army, and particularly after the Glorious Revolution of 1688, constitutional objections were raised to the construction of barracks complexes. A standing army isolated within barracks was thought to pose a greater potential threat to parliamentary independence than one dispersed among the populace, and was associated with the absolutist regimes of the Bourbons and the Hapsburgs. (This connection between barracks and a politically unreliable army is made explicit in Spanish, in which *cuartelado* is the word for a *coup d'état* or military uprising.) As the century progressed, such constitutional objections became anachronistic, but they accounted for the rarity of barracks complexes in England before the French Revolutionary War.[3]

Barracks continued to be a 'political' issue long after the 1688 settlement, however, and their major constructional phases have resulted from political rather than purely military decisions. The high capital cost of construction has always been a significant factor in the annual army estimates, and new building works had to be sanctioned by Parliament before they could be undertaken. The alternative to a costly network of barracks was the billeting system, whereby soldiers were lodged and fed in inns and public houses, where the terms of the licence obliged the licensee to take them at a price fixed by the State.

As we shall see, barracks only came to be more widely built in England through a deliberate deception of Parliament. In the 1790s, civil unrest followed by national emergency swept away the old constitutional objections. Whilst it had been acceptable during the eighteenth century for Britain to forswear the military benefits which barracks conferred, it was no longer possible to put up with the inefficiencies of billeting under the intense demands of national defence, and a hasty campaign of barracks construction had to be undertaken during the 1790s. By the end of the war, the great majority of British troops at home lived in barracks. A restricted amount of billeting continued for troops on the march, or away from the main garrisons, until it was brought back again for Kitchener's huge New Armies late in 1914.

By the middle of the nineteenth century, objections were no longer directed against barracks themselves, but the appalling conditions endured by their inhabitants. The scandal provoked by the high levels of disease and mortality exposed by the commissions of inquiry after the Crimean débâcle forced the Government to begin a programme of improvements. However, the debate over military accommodation in Britain was influenced by opposing views of the character of the British soldier: what responsibility the army or the State had for his well-being or betterment, and how far in any case his behaviour could be affected by his environment. Traditionalists believed the rank and file to be irremediably bad and only controllable by violence. Reformers hoped to raise the 'moral tone' of soldiers by improving their living conditions, and

---

[3] Perhaps the only instance of barracks-fermented political involvement in Britain was the Curragh Incident of 1914, when a number of cavalry officers at the camp near Dublin indicated that they would resign rather than march north to Ulster to enforce the proposed Home Rule on fellow Protestants.

through education, primarily religious. Some officers claimed better barracks would in themselves attract a higher quality of recruit, whilst others thought the army should continue to offer a useful purpose and a means of betterment to society's dregs and scum. Each in turn considered that barracks should serve as prisons, schools or potential reformatories, which influenced both their layout and design.

The pressure to improve barracks conditions was reinforced by the army's continuing recruitment problems during a period of full employment and expanding imperial commitments. A significant part of the Cardwell reforms in the 1870s focused on this issue of recruitment, and they included an extensive and costly barracks construction programme partly intended to make military life more appealing. Meanwhile, the increasing complexity and sophistication of naval warships obliged the Admiralty to introduce Long Term Service, and as a consequence, to build permanent naval barracks for the first time.

Better housing failed to resolve the shortfall in both regular and reserve forces, however, which resulted from more profound structural factors in both society and the army. Uncertainty over the organization and the use of the army continued into the early-twentieth century until the major administrative reforms carried out by Richard Haldane. The establishment of large, permanent camps, into which the army increasingly moved in the latter part of the nineteenth century, was indicative of both the new type of wars which the army anticipated fighting and the scale of the forces which they intended to deploy. This was the situation in 1914, when the army's new, large camps, as well as its old estate of barracks dating back to the Glorious Revolution, were overwhelmed by the arrival of Kitchener's New Armies.

Military society and barracks planning

An important consideration in an examination of military barracks is how their planning and architecture were affected by the structure of human relationships and the pattern of social behaviour within the armed forces. After all, the erection and planning of the buildings was intended to facilitate the effective working of the military 'organism'. The military routine of drill and training, and the daily rhythm of eating, washing and sleeping were obviously overriding influences, but they were overlain by concepts of the integrity of the unit, of the relationship between the officers and the other ranks, and between the military and civilian worlds.

Social customs could translate directly into planning. Religious sensitivities might be catered for, but mess and recreational facilities were not generally provided for ordinary soldiers until late in the Victorian period. Officers' messes were small or non-existent until the French Revolutionary War, because officers customarily dined outside the barracks. The appearance of distinct and clearly differentiated quarters with mess and ante-rooms at the end of the eighteenth century coincided with pressure from the Commander-in-Chief, the Prince of Wales, for officers to spend more time with their regiments to foster unity and cohesiveness. In London, where Guards officers played an active role in metropolitan social life, the barracks had no mess rooms until much later. The dining room and ante-room at Regent's Park Barracks were added in the 1860s, and there was still no mess at the Guards' Wellington Barracks in Westminster before the First World War.

The ways in which other social structures are transposed into material ones and manifested in planning and architecture are not always obvious, and are beyond the scope of this book; moreover, these considerations seem rarely to have been discussed or analysed by barracks designers themselves. Nevertheless, other modes of communal life have similarities with military service. One obvious parallel, for instance, is with the monastic system, also highly structured, disciplined, and composed of a single-gender population – one eighteenth-century military training manual even

Introduction

aimed to produce 'the perfection of the cloister'.[4] Correlations can be drawn between barracks and other closed institutions such as monasteries and convents, colleges, boarding schools, prisons, hospitals or asylums. All of these have frequently engendered strong and clear planning typologies, arising directly from the structure of their social group and from the organization of its activities.

During the late eighteenth and early nineteenth centuries, the idea that there was an association between the design of space and the behaviour of individuals had a strong influence on social policy, most notably in the area of prison reform. With Jeremy Bentham's panopticon as an exemplar, social reformers in Britain and on the Continent felt that the spatial planning of institutions could help to bring about moral improvements in the criminals, paupers and delinquents who found their way into prisons, workhouses and asylums. Such an intellectual approach seems not to have interested barracks designers. No professional authority on barracks emerged from within the Royal Engineers who had the vision of Joshua Jebb on prison design or of Douglas Galton on hospitals, though both expressed views on the housing of soldiers. In the heyday of the model planning of artisan housing, factories, industrial colonies, prisons, schools and farms, no model barracks was ever proposed.[5] There has also been little curiosity in recent times about the way in which military society translates itself into architectural space.

In this context, before examining individual buildings in greater detail, it is necessary to examine some of the aspects of the social organization of communal military life, and the ways these have influenced the architecture and planning of barracks.

As a social system, the primary characteristics of military barracks are gender, class and hierarchy. The army discouraged women from living in barracks because of the cost and fears about their effect on martial ardour, and excluded all but a small number of wives. Granting permission to marry provided senior officers with an additional means of control, and created an incentive for good behaviour, whilst the wives' labour could be exploited as cooks, laundresses or cleaners. No special arrangements were made to accommodate them. This changed later in the Victorian period, partly as a result of external disapproval at the way families of married soldiers lived among single men, and partly through a realization of how the army could benefit by encouraging the 'service family'. Separate married quarters were built which concentrated the soldiers' families together, away from the barracks of the single men.

Always a highly class-conscious organization, the army polarized into a soldier proletariat and an officer aristocracy. The proletariat was traditionally recruited from unskilled labourers – mostly agricultural until the early nineteenth century, increasingly urban thereafter. The officer class was made up of men from the nobility and the landed gentry, who were entrusted with running the nation's army because of their interest in maintaining the *status quo*, long after their inadequacies as soldiers were generally acknowledged. This dichotomy was reflected in the hierarchy of rank, from the regimental colonel through the officers in one class, and non-commissioned officers and privates in the other. Exceptions were very limited, even when combat accelerated the promotion of NCOs or national emergency widened the pool of recruits to include 'gentleman rankers'. The scope to move through the ranks was very limited, as it was between classes; this was clearly the case under the purchase system, and altered very little after purchase was abolished in 1871.

A third significant structure within the army was its hierarchical subdivision into operational units (see Appendix B). The most important of these was the regiment. As the troops were moved about by regiment, the larger barracks were organized to accommodate that number of men. An infantry regiment was divided into sections or companies, and a cavalry regiment into troops, and these units

---

[4] Quoted by Jones (1980), p.162.
[5] A certain amount of interest was expressed through *The Builder* at the time of the 1856 London barracks competition, but the winning designs were selected for their architectural quality, in consideration of the status of the Guards regiments and the social aspirations of their neighbours in Knightsbridge and Chelsea, rather than their resolution of the spatial needs of the occupants.

usually formed the basis for the internal divisions of barracks, to encourage members to develop ties of loyalty and mutual dependence – one of the attractions of barracks for Europe's armies.

The civilian world outside the barracks also exerted a strong influence on their planning. Barrack plans generally aimed to exclude it, since the harmful effects of lax or hostile civilian life on discipline, loyalty and security were in part what prompted States to provide specialized quarters in the first place. The first national construction programme in England was embarked on primarily to separate soldiers from the seditious influences to which billeting in public houses exposed them. The orderly layout of the barracks in contrast to the apparent disorder of the surrounding streets can be seen in the map of Portsmouth in the late nineteenth century (see fig. 163, page 184). This perception was reinforced by the desire of officers to improve corps solidarity and cohesiveness through isolation. The tall perimeter wall protected the soldiers when their safety was threatened by mobs or rioters, and also prevented soldiers from returning to the civilian world by deserting.

If these are some of the fundamental social aspects of military barracks, there are also several basic and recurrent patterns in their planning and layout. The most obvious is the formal regularity of the site plan. In British barracks up to the 1870s, the fundamental components of the officers' and soldiers' blocks were disposed symmetrically about the communal space of the parade square. The following analysis of the way in which the rebuilt Aldershot Camp was planned in the 1880s could be applied to most of these earlier complexes, with the proviso that before the middle of the eighteenth century, officers' quarters were attached to those of the men:

'The hierarchy of barracks were typically emphasised by linking officers' quarters symmetrically about a major axis ... and soldiers' barracks and stables facing each other across a minor axis ... The model usually took the form of ... a pivotal position generally occupied by officers' quarters and subsidiary wings grouped around 3 or 4 sides of a courtyard or parade ground. The parade ground was a common area, and [the] physical and ceremonial focus for the whole barracks. The primacy of this relationship and the image of self containment and independence which it generated was reinforced by a paucity of architectural display to the surrounding community. This tended also to confirm the perception of barracks as functional and utilitarian habitations.' [6]

The square or parade ground formed an important ceremonial space, and the area necessary for assembling and drilling was a primary consideration when planning the rest of the barracks. Within it, the whole community could be assembled for instruction or the dissemination of information; training, drill and manoeuvres were practised there, and it was the scene of disciplinary actions, exemplary floggings or other punishments. The parade ground formed a rectilinear space, overlooked by the principal accommodation buildings built along its sides.

The closed, claustral plan or quadrangle, common in the architecture of other communal organizations and widely used by European military engineers, is rare in British barracks, however. Perhaps it gave too little emphasis to military rank and social position. The architectural differentiation of the officers' accommodation from that of the rank and file was a second general characteristic of barracks, both in their planning – when separate, officers' quarters were almost invariably at the head of the square – and as a vehicle for whatever decorative elaboration was provided.

The concept of the bilaterally symmetrical, inward-looking, parade ground-centred plan was maintained until the middle of the nineteenth century. From then on, more varied typologies developed, associated with a decline in the hostile circumstances under which barracks for civil order had been built and an increase in the complexity of military society, as sergeants and other NCOs

---

[6] Aldershot Military Historical Trust, *Report on the Development of Aldershot Camp* (London 1994), p.13.

acquired their own messes or quarters, and as the army took on responsibility for soldiers' welfare with the provision of married quarters, schools, churches, sports and recreational facilities. These are some of the underlying considerations which have played a part in generating the buildings and complexes examined in this book.

The background to the book

The recent contraction of Britain's armed forces has led to a reassessment of the Ministry of Defence's real estate and the historic buildings in its ownership and care. In 1993, an exhibition was mounted by SAVE Britain's Heritage called 'Deserted Bastions',[7] which highlighted the losses of valuable, historic military buildings and the threatened condition or uncertain future of many more. Increasing national awareness of what was becoming known as the 'defence heritage' led to the realization that the long neglect of barracks by both military and architectural historians provided no basis for judging which were of historical significance, if any. A disparity in statutory protection existed between what the army calls 'the Teeth and the Tail' – in other words, the structures of the combat formations, forts or castles, which tended to be well understood compared to those of the support formations, like munitions works, magazines, dockyards, hospitals or barracks, which were not.

These circumstances, coupled with an awareness that barracks – especially those outside historic fortifications – were among the most threatened and least understood categories of buildings, prompted English Heritage to commission a report on barracks in 1994. As a result, all new recommendations for the protection of the best and most representative examples are now based upon a thorough understanding of a hithero unexplored subject, taking into account the results of both fieldwork and focused documentary research. The discovery of so much new material, combined with a desire on the part of English Heritage and the Ministry of Defence to foster a broader understanding of the subject, led to the decision to publish the survey results more widely. The earlier research has now been supplemented by further primary and illustrative material, and Andrew Saunders has contributed an opening chapter which explores Continental precedents and the early history of barracks.

Because this is the first general account of barracks, it concentrates on providing an overview of their architectural and archaeological history, focusing on the buildings, their arrangement and internal planning, their purpose and how barracks and architecture are related. It also examines the history of how the State has used barracks in ruling the country, as well as touching upon other important issues which influenced planning and design, such as the development of fortifications, the relationship between the army and society, the position of women within the army, and soldiers' health and schooling.

Remarkably few detailed studies of individual barracks have been published – Rowe's examination of Barnstaple is a rare exception[8] – and no barracks complex has enjoyed a rigorous, modern analysis of its planning or construction. It has not been possible here to delve far into detailed primary sources for individual buildings, with the exception of the Cirencester militia store because so little was known about this unique type of building. The view of the European scene has also been limited by the lack of accessible research, but an international comparative study is much needed. The influence of other European countries was of greatest significance in Britain in the early developmental stage, during the seventeenth century, as Chapter One makes clear, but as in all areas of military development, European States observed their neighbours' innovations with interest, and applied what they learned when they thought it to their advantage. This is no less true today, as countries reassess their legacy of barracks in the post-Cold War era, and consider how best to deal with it.

The original report was limited by English Heritage's geographical remit, although it was realized that a proper understanding of the subject,

---

[7] See Watson-Smyth et al. (1993).
[8] Rowe (1988).

never mind a book claiming to be a history of barracks, demanded inclusion of the other countries which were occupied by the home forces. Time and resources – the usual suspects – have meant that Irish barracks are dealt with in less depth than those in England, Scotland and Wales. However, the great majority of British barracks in Ireland were built in the eighteenth century, so it has been possible to concentrate on this earlier and more significant period. Furthermore, with the Act of Union in 1801, the independent, Dublin-based barracks organization was abolished and the British Ordnance Board replaced it. As a result, even though a detailed history of later Irish barracks remains to be written, in general policy and design terms there was little variation from mainland British experience during this period. The construction of the 1870s localization depots is an obvious example, in which both countries were dealt with by the same London War Office department.

Similar restrictions have also imposed the exclusion of colonial barracks. Starting with isolated forts on the eastern seaboard of North America, then in Malta and Gibraltar, the Royal Engineers were sent to build barracks all over the globe as colonies were acquired and territory annexed to the expanding British Empire. Home experience was applied abroad, and lessons learned in the colonies were in turn brought back – a process illustrated by the tropical-style verandas attached to many mid-nineteenth-century barracks in Britain. This fascinating aspect of the colonizing process remains to be examined.

The connection between barracks and urban planning is another intriguing area which merits more study. Personal experiences of barracks life have varied, as might be expected given the wide cross-section of the population which has passed through these institutions. The references and bibliography direct the reader to works where many of these matters have been considered more fully.

This book will show barracks to be a more complex and interesting subject than their common image would suggest. Osbert Sitwell thought the very name of his barracks in Aldershot conjured up the feeling of misery and tedium which he experienced living there. Yet even he had to admit that the word did not evoke the same images in everyone:

'for when some years later, during the season of Russian Ballet, which opened in October 1918 at the Coliseum, my brother continually had to leave the theatre early, explaining, as he got up, to Diaghilev, by whose side we sometimes sat in the stalls, that he had "to return to Aldershot by midnight", the great impresario eventually asked "Qu'est que c'est cette Aldershot – c'est une femme?"' [9]

---

[9] Osbert Sitwell, *Great Morning* (London 1949), p.127.

Chapter One
1600–1750: Early Evolution

The word 'barracks' seems only to have come into the English language during the late seventeenth century, although purpose-built, permanent accommodation for soldiers in Britain and elsewhere had existed much earlier. The origin of the word goes back to the improvised campaign shelter of the late medieval and early modern soldier (*barraca* in Spanish and *baraque* in French). This was normally a hut, constructed of materials immediately to hand, often taken from deserted buildings rather than from standing timber, and then destroyed or burnt as the army moved on. As the need to accommodate permanent garrisons evolved, and eventually, as States acquired standing armies, the same term, 'barrack', was employed in English for the specialized buildings housing military personnel.

Barracks were more than buildings for housing soldiers: they were also a means for imposing discipline upon a large body of men by keeping it concentrated in one place and under supervision. Close association led to a sense of identity and camaraderie, particularly at company, and later, regimental level. Barracks also separated the military from the civilian. This was understandably appreciated by the vulnerable civilians traditionally held in contempt by the licentious soldiery. Separation was also seen by commanders as a means to avoid the softening influences of civil life at a time when irregular pay made soldiers in regular garrisons eke out a living by following trades and becoming part of civilian life as well as forming local family relationships. In the eighteenth century, the authorities sought to detach soldiers from wider society and dedicate them to stern military ideals. This was reflected in the sheer bulk and formal architectural composition of barracks, which could attain a dominant position within a community, recalling the oppressive symbolism of the medieval castle.

Barracks have their origins in antiquity wherever permanent armies existed. These buildings are a familiar feature of Roman forts, such as those which have been excavated and displayed in the hinterland of Hadrian's Wall and elsewhere in Britain. They follow a pattern which can be seen in the rest of the Roman Empire.[1] The regular Roman barracks were long, narrow ranges usually intended to house a century of around 80 men and subdivided by timber partitions into barrack rooms, normally nine or ten in number. Over time, there was a certain amount of adaptation in their use, depending upon the nature of the unit, and by the fourth century at Wallsend, near Newcastle upon Tyne, for example, the accommodation arrangements changed to separate and irregular huts or 'chalets', possibly for individual occupancy by a soldier and his family. From classical times, it had been considered that permanent accommodation was essential for the good order and discipline of a standing army. The maxims and treatises on military life and organization by classical writers bear this out, and were to have a fundamental influence on the military theory textbooks compiled during the sixteenth and seventeenth centuries in Western Europe.

After the collapse of the Roman Western Empire, regular armies ceased to exist, so there was no longer a need to house soldiers over prolonged periods. Military forces were raised on the basis of seasonal war bands, local levies for self-defence, feudal obligations for military service over a fixed time-scale, and recruitment of mercenary bands whose captains were responsible for their

---

[1] The Latin term was *contubernium*, literally 'tent companionship', illustrating again that the permanent barrack block had its origins in the tented accommodation of the marching camp.

maintenance. Armies during the Middle Ages were raised in the short term for the summer campaigning season, usually living off the country before dispersing. More regular forces and long-term garrisons began to appear during the fifteenth century, when armies needed to be kept together in winter quarters in preparation for the coming campaigning season. The *Ordonnances* of Charles VII led to an elaboration of monarchial control, and historians have attributed the birth of the French standing army to 1449.[2]

At the close of the Middle Ages, the emergence of gunpowder weapons coincided with greater military professionalism and a growth of national identity, and ways had to be found to accommodate soldiers on a regular basis. Throughout Western Europe, the easy and cheap solution was to billet soldiers on householders in town and country. Whilst payment was usually intended for such accommodation, the system was much abused and caused deep resentment. However, the Venetian State began to organize the housing of troops within fixed garrisons during the fifteenth century.[3] A Venetian barracks of the fifteenth century remains in use today within the fortress of S. Nicolò on the Lido. It has a square, claustral plan of two storeys with a colonnaded ground floor. A similar structure from the same period, located near the Bastion di Spagnia at Verona, is rectangular and has three storeys.[4]

The gradual emergence of standing armies in the sixteenth century, maintained year after year and engaged in regular seasons of warfare, for example in Italy or in the Netherlands, required something more permanent than the campaign tent or hut, and if it was to retain the support of its subjects, it was in a government's interest to find an alternative to the hated imposition of billeting on householders. The building of specific garrison accommodation to separate the civil and military was one solution but, as this was costly, the creation of barracks was a slow and piecemeal process.

The development of standing armies nevertheless spread beyond the areas of perennial conflict. It went hand in hand with the emergence of the centralized nation State, whether this was a republic like Venice or the United Provinces, or a monarchy imbued with the Renaissance concepts of political power set out in Machiavelli's *The Prince*. As kings achieved absolute power in much of Europe by the end of the seventeenth century, the existence of a professional standing army was an essential prop to their political security, and grandiose barrack buildings became an expression of this aspect of royal authority. Wherever there was a prospect of rebellion and political opposition within a State, governments erected barracks as a policing measure. This practice was to be adopted in Ireland by Cromwell, and to counter Jacobite insurgency in Scotland in the early eighteenth century. In contrast, those concerned with attaining or retaining *constitutional* monarchy saw barracks as symbols of oppression, and this was especially true of popular opinion in eighteenth-century Britain. (The constitutional objections to barracks are discussed more fully in Chapter Two.)

This growth of standing armies in Western Europe during the sixteenth century, together with technical improvements in gunpowder artillery and an increasingly standardized, geometrically based system for defending forts and towns which took into account more effective firepower, was accompanied by a more theoretical and scientific approach to most military matters. Arms drill and military training techniques were formalized, largely through the efforts of Prince Maurice of Nassau in the Netherlands, and were widely published. The organization of armies in the field and on the march was also set out in textbooks and treatises which owed much to writers of the classical world such as Vegetius, Polybius and even Xenophon. The organization of an army for battle was complemented by the ordering of the marching camp or siegework, where ranks had their place and the separation of parts within the camp was distinguished in terms of space and symmetry. Prince Maurice's mentor, Simon Stevin, laid out rules for encampment in the field for the quartermasters whose responsibility it was to arrange lodgings for an army. It was necessary to be

---

[2] Dallemagne (1990), p.9.
[3] M.E. Mallett and J.R. Hale, *The Military Organisation of a Renaissance State. Venice c.1400 to 1617* (Cambridge 1984), pp.131–6.
[4] Information from Professor Gianni Perbellini.

a good 'arithmetician and geometrician', for the quarters were first drawn on paper and then marked out on site by the 'camp measurer'.

Laying out the camp's streets, the quarters for each regiment and the space for the army huts was a precise task (see Figure 1). Each company was allotted two rows of 20 huts, each row being 200 feet (61 metres) long and 8 feet (2.4 metres) wide, with a street 8 feet (2.4 metres) wide between the rows. Facing the street were a quadrangle for the captain and another for the sutlers (vendors of provisions), together with cooking pits for the soldiers at the opposite end of the street. The distribution of the soldiers' huts along the rows was staked out by each company sergeant.[5]

Similar examples of planned encampments occur in English textbooks of military theory of the mid-seventeenth century. Robert Ward illustrates a defended enclosure with the huts and tents of the captains and colonels in an even line, with the double and single rows of huts for the soldiers along streets at right angles both to the officers' accommodation and to the houses of sutlers, butchers and the like, which are in a parallel line at the opposite side of the plan. Ward stipulates that the streets between the rows of huts should be 10 feet (3 metres) broad, and the huts themselves, 50 per row, should be 8 feet (2.4 metres) square, each housing two soldiers.[6] This regimentation of the temporary camp had a continuing influence when more permanent quarters came to be established.

The earliest barracks in France and the Low Countries

During the latter half of the fifteenth century in France, as in the Venetian State, formal arrangements governed the long-term lodging of garrisons, and particularly winter quarters. Especially in areas adjacent to the borders of France, *gîtes d'étape* (staging posts) and special housing were defined, but during wartime the troops camped as usual.[7] The officers lodged in tents, whereas the troops built huts (*baraques*), usually for two or three men.

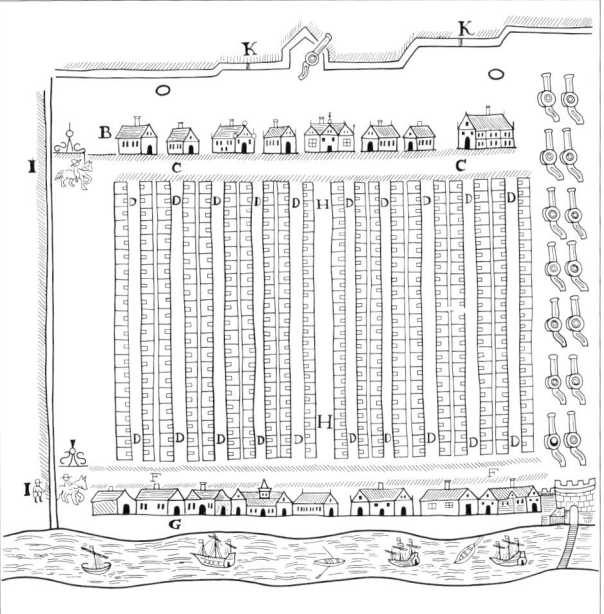

Figure 1 Woodcut of the planning of an enclosed encampment containing rows of soldiers' huts, with houses for officers across the top, sutlers' and store buildings along the bottom and the artillery park on the right. From Robert Ward, *Animadversions of Warre* (London 1639), Book 2, p.33.

The initiative for creating permanent quarters – barracks – for long-standing garrisons seems to have come from the authorities in the Spanish Netherlands during the protracted war with the Dutch, where the need to find a solution for the problem of maintaining the health of the troops while avoiding public antagonism was recognized by the end of the sixteenth century. Philip II's decision to make the archdukes independent rulers of the Netherlands also contributed to this change. Following 1598, the Archduke Albert, in his position as both a sovereign prince and captain general, had to balance civil and military interests. An ambitious programme of barrack construction in brick and timber began in 's-Hertogenbosch, Geldern, Grol and other military strongholds, and was apparently inspired as much by the need to regularize relations between the military and civil society as it was dictated by the Spanish policy of maintaining garrisons in the Low Countries.[8] This need was recognized as early as 1586 by Sir Philip Sidney while in command of Vlissingen (Flushing) in support of the Dutch. The frequent clashes between townsmen and the unpaid English companies

---

[5] Simon Stevin, *Castrimetatio, dat is Legermeting* (Rotterdam 1617); W.H. Schukking (ed.), *The Principal Works of Simon Stevin: Vol.4, The Art of War* (Amsterdam 1964).
[6] Robert Ward, *Animadversions of Warre* (London 1639).

[7] Dallemagne (1990), p.28.
[8] Jonathan Israel, *The Dutch Republic: Its Rise, Greatness, and Fall 1477–1806* (Oxford 1995), p.270.

caused Sir Philip to write to the Privy Council urging the erection of barracks. Queen Elizabeth approved but was not prepared to meet the cost, and she thought that the burghers should be persuaded to build new houses or rent vacant ones for the garrison.[9] The hostility between garrisons and townspeople in the United Provinces was such that Prince Maurice adopted measures within the military code to instil respect for the civil population. Action to separate soldiers from the civil population and to make them subject to the law became politically necessary, and formed an important element in the rules and organization of the Dutch armies towards the end of the sixteenth century. The appearance of barracks in the Low Countries reflects this increased formality.

It is acknowledged that the earliest barracks in France existed in the former Spanish provinces that had been ceded to France in 1659 by the King of Spain. The Spaniards had constructed important barracks in Roussillon as well as in Flanders, at Montmédy, Lille, Port Vendres and Valenciennes. In most cases, these barracks were detached, two-storey buildings with rooms sometimes measuring 82 by 65 feet (25 by 19.8 metres). At Fort de Bescou, Agde, built in 1598–1600, there were two ranges of lodgings, one with a bakehouse at one end. The oldest known French barracks dates fom 1593 within the citadel of Grenoble, with single and double ranges on two floors. Individual rooms measured 20 by 13 feet (6.1 by 4 metres). At Le Havre, early in the seventeenth century, there was a double tenement with stairs against the partitions and rooms measuring roughly 20 by 19 feet (6.1 by 5.8 metres). Barracks also appeared at Port Louis (1617), Brest (1620), Montpellier (1624) and Bethune (1645).[10]

As permanent barracks began to be built, a degree of standardization of plan seems to emerge, with rows of small rooms in two storeys, each room housing about four or six men, sometimes more. At the same time, rules for the conduct of barrack life emerged. The first barracks were clearly influenced by the pattern of the rows of huts in temporary camps, which may explain the transference of the term 'barrack' into English. They were also modelled on row houses in towns and the pattern of rooms in almshouses. The long, parallel rows of houses of Nybodn, Copenhagen, built in the early years of the seventeenth century by royal initiative to accommodate naval personnel and dockyard workers, still remain today. Similar rows of 'houses' for accommodating garrisons can be seen in plans of contemporary Dutch fortresses such as at Fort Oranje, near Bergen op Zoom. This fort was built after 1615, and a plan of its interior remains from c.1630. Single rows with fireplaces set in the partitions between 'houses' are shown on a similar but undated plan of the Kasteel of Breda.[11] Indeed, stone and timber structures sprang up across the Low Countries: at 's Hertogenbosch (1609),[12] Dunkirk (1611), Maastricht and Damme (1616) and thereafter in most other military centres. In the citadels of the Spanish Netherlands – Ghent, Antwerp, Cambrai – the barracks were somewhat larger than those within towns.[13] Barracks were built at Breda after its capture by Spinola in 1625. These were called De Blokken ('The Blocks') and also Hooge Barakken ('High Barracks') because they possessed an upper storey. The Antwerpse Barakken were built in 1640 after Breda had been recaptured by Frederik Hendrik.[14]

In some French and Danish garrisons, each room of the barrack 'houses' contained two or three beds, each shared by three men. In England, the practice was two men to a bed. This probably reflects the earlier ratio of men to huts and bivouacs. Whereas cooking was carried out in the vicinity of the sutlers' quarters in camp because of the fire risk to the soldiers' huts, in permanent barracks each room had its own fireplace for cooking and heating. However, in this early period it was never possible to lodge a large garrison entirely in barracks – most troops still had to be quartered on the population. Barracks also varied in quality. In 1678, the poor 'barraques' at Nieuport were causing sickness among the English troops.[15]

---

[9] M.W. Wallace, *The Life of Sir Philip Sidney* (Cambridge 1915), p.356.
[10] Dallemagne (1990), pp.31–7.
[11] J. Sneep, J.P.C.M. van Hoof, G.J.L. Koolhof and S.H. Poppema (eds) *Atlas van historische vestingwerken in Nederland: Noord-Brabant* (Utrecht 1996), pp.80 and 117.
[12] C.J. Gudde, *Vier eewen geschiedenis van het garnizoen 's Hertogenbosch'* ('s Hertogenbosch, 1958), p.31.
[13] Geoffrey Parker, *The Army of Flanders and the Spanish Road 1567–1659* (Cambridge 1972), pp.166–7.
[14] G.G. Van Der Hoeven, *Geschiedenis der Vesting Breda* (Breda 1868), p.150; E.M. Dolne, 'Kazernegebouwen in Nederland: Bouw, ontwikkeling en kunsthistorische aspecten', *Parade* (1993), pp.6–24.
[15] Calendar of State Papers Domestic, Charles II (1678), p.323.

Soldiers' lodgings in sixteenth- and early seventeenth-century Britain and Ireland

There was no permanent army in Britain during the early sixteenth century, only the Yeomen of the Guard to protect the sovereign's person, and garrisons in Ireland and Calais. Under Elizabeth I, the militia (local auxiliary forces raised and organized by counties) was the basis of a military force. Traditionally, English armies were only assembled for overseas expeditions, and then dispersed upon their withdrawal, so there was no need for barrack accommodation. The permanent military institutions that arose in Henry VIII's time owed their existence to home defence. The invasion crisis of 1539/40 led to the construction of many forts and blockhouses which protected the main anchorages along the south coast and the approaches to London from the Thames. Their design included purpose-built accommodation for the small resident garrisons of gunners and porters whose ranks and names in the individual forts are identified, together with their rates of pay.[16] These garrisons were little more than caretakers, however, and the extent of the accommodation available did not allow anything resembling the common perception of a barracks. Nevertheless, it is still possible to identify residential functions within the Henrician castles: kitchens and mess rooms for the gunners at places such as Deal and Pendennis Castles, where evidence of planning and partitions survives, as well as the quarters for the captain or governor. The arrangement of Pendennis Castle, as it appears in Colonel Christian Lilly's survey of 1715, shows how the interior of one of Henry VIII's castles could be subdivided to provide barrack accommodation (see Figure 2).[17]

Troops could also be housed at the more substantial English and Scottish royal fortresses, such as the Tower of London and Edinburgh Castle. There was a permanent garrison at Calais until its loss to the French in 1558, but there is no evidence of how Henry VIII's troops were housed there; presumably, they were billeted in the town, as was customary. The Elizabethan garrison of 500 men at Berwick-upon-Tweed was certainly billeted on the townspeople. The Statutes of Berwick, as defined in 1560, set out the regulations pertaining to garrison life there.[18] Individual barrack-like structures were nevertheless appearing by the late sixteenth century. A plan of Tynemouth Castle, probably from 1588, indicates separate buildings for men's lodgings.[19] Lodgings for soldiers in forts in Ireland and Scotland emerged earlier, since there were long-standing policing duties for the English forces. There are indications of specific buildings for housing troops in the plans of the new forts of occupation constructed in the Scottish Lowlands during the War of the Rough Wooing: at Broughty and Lauder in 1548 in particular. At Roxburgh Castle, there was a supply centre which contained 441 men. A plan shows 'The Captayn's Logynge', a

Plans of the upper and lower Story's of PENDENNIS CASTLE by C: Lilly 1715
A. dining room. **B.** Governor's bedchamber. **C.** other bedchambers. **D.** closets. **E. and F.** staircases. **G.** parlour. **H.** little kitchen. **I.** passage. **K.** soldiers' lodgings. **L.** entries. **M.** bridge. **N.** lodging room. **O.** brewhouse. **P.** noted by Lilly as 'a Breastwork where formerly Gunns was placed'. **Q.** passage. **R.** noted by Lilly as 'part of the counterscarpe of a ditch which formerly surrounded ye Castle'.

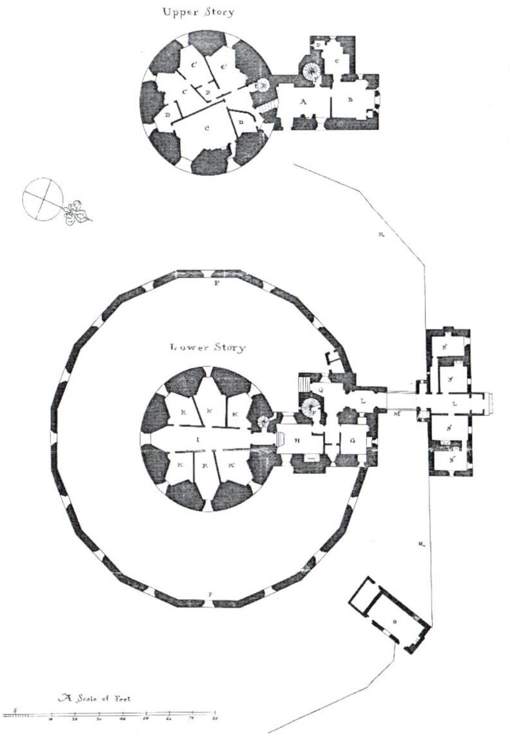

Figure 2 A scheme for the adaptation of the interior of Henry VIII's Pendennis Castle for barrack purposes as well as accommodation for the governor – by Colonel Christian Lilly RE, 1715.

16 BL Cotton MS, App. XXVII, f.19.
17 BL King's MS 45, f.23.
18 BL Egerton MS 2790, f.43.
19 BL Cotton MS Aug.I ii, f.6.

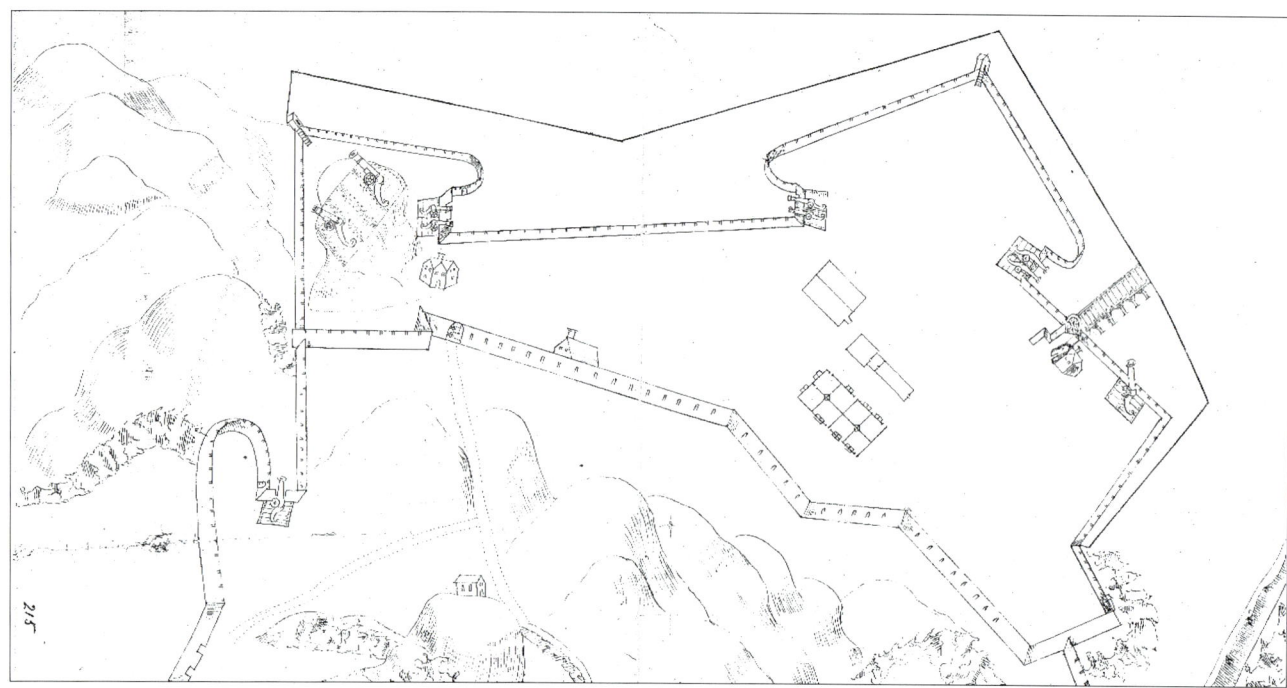

Figure 3 Part of Plymouth Fort in 1596, with a barrack block of eight rooms (four rooms back to back) within the fort. Each room has a corner fireplace and a porch in front of each door.

brewhouse and bakehouse, a storehouse, two ranges of lodgings along the Tweedside wall and another irregular, five-chambered building near the entrance.[20] In Ireland, a plan of Corkbeg in 1569 shows two ranges of lodgings parallel to the ramparts.[21]

At about the same time as purpose-built barracks in garrison towns were appearing on the Continent, distinct barracks were becoming recognizable, first in England at the newly built Plymouth Fort (1596), and then within forts in Ireland following the end of the war with Spain in 1603. The plan of Plymouth Fort endorsed by Ferdinando Gorges depicts a double-depth block totalling eight rooms back to back, each with a fireplace grouped in the angles against the dividing wall and served by two chimneys with porches to each doorway (see Figure 3).[22] There is no mistaking the function of this building.

At Duncannon Fort in Ireland, Sir Josias Bodley's bird's-eye view of 1595–1600 shows a long building for a constable, lieutenant and 30 'warders',[23] but in 1624 Captain Nicholas Pynnar noted that Duncannon was 'much out of repair'. Within the fort was a timber-framed house, 100 feet (30.5 metres) long to accommodate a hundred men, now unroofed and in poor condition. At St Augustine's Fort, Galway, built by Bodley in 1611, there was a house for the commandant and officers, and separate lodgings for soldiers. These were in two rows set at right angles, containing eight square rooms in each row, with individual fireplaces placed in alternate partitions, and with doors opposite the partitions.[24] These quarters have some of the characteristics which were to become more common in the Netherlands later in the century. There was a similar right-angled range of soldiers' lodgings at Castle Park Fort at Kinsale.[25] The fort at Banagher was completed in 1624 and contained a long, narrow building which was probably a barracks. Following the Cromwellian conquest of Ireland, a number of citadels were constructed supplementing the already numerous garrisons across the country. Outside the towns, the troops would have had to be housed in special buildings, often in forts. For example, a square, bastioned fort was built at

---

[20] Colvin (1982), **4**, part 2, pp.694–726.
[21] PRO MPF85.
[22] PRO MPF262 (SP 12/262); Elisabeth Stuart, *Lost Landscapes of Plymouth: Maps, Charts and Plans to 1800* (Stroud 1991), p.82.
[23] BL Cotton MS Aug.I ii, f.31.
[24] Ibid., f.34.
[25] Ibid., f.35.

Bantry at the time of the First Dutch War (1652–4). A perspective view of 1685 shows it with two large buildings in the interior. The recommended garrison in 1659 amounted to a hundred men. By 1677 there was accommodation for 200 soldiers in the fort, but by then the barracks were in poor repair.[26]

The emergence of barracks and a standing army in England

Leaving aside the traditional guards and garrisons, when a true standing army in England was created out of the New Model Army by the Commonwealth in the aftermath of the Civil Wars, billeting was still the normal practice, and was subsequently one of the causes of popular resentment of the army. Yet there are references in David Papillon's treatise on fortification of 1645, written from a Parliamentarian perspective, to suggest that barracks of a kind did exist within redoubts and fortifications during the English Civil War, since he stresses that the ramparts of forts should be sufficiently high to mask the ridge of the soldiers' lodgings.[27] Presumably, these were always temporary structures of timber, akin to the huts of encampments. However, permanent structures had already been built on the Isles of Scilly, but whether by the previous Royalist garrison or subsequently by the Commonwealth forces is unclear. A survey taken in October 1661 distinguishes the soldiers' lodgings (called 'the Folly') from those quarters in Star Castle on St Mary's whose roofs and floors were in need of repair.[28] There was also a barracks on Tresco, where the walls needed to be built up and 13 new stone chimneys made. This was probably a reuse of the mid-sixteenth-century King Charles's Castle above the anchorage of New Grimsby. The same south-western survey of 1661 proposed the building of two houses for soldiers lodgings – one 100 feet (30.5 metres) long, the other 72 feet (22 metres) long and 12 feet (3.7 metres) broad – at Plymouth Fort. Each of the 18 rooms to be provided was to have a chimney. Opposite, on St Nicholas Island, only the walls of the existing soldiers' lodgings were standing.

In Scotland after 1652, the Protectorate's four citadels, intended as a policing measure, were planned for permanent garrisons of cavalry and infantry, and may be claimed as the first examples of distinct, fortified barracks intended for control of the civil population on the British mainland. The Cromwellian citadels were deliberately destroyed following the Restoration, so detailed information on the internal buildings is scarce. At Ayr and Inverness, there was a four-storey block for accommodation. The basic arrangement for the soldiers' lodgings was that of a collegiate stair serving four separate rooms on each floor. Each room had its own window and fireplace. Leith had 'a good capacious chapel ... the piazza ... as large as Trinity College [Cambridge] great court ...', with 'very pleasant, convenient and well-built houses for the governor, officers and soldiers'. Plans of Ayr and Inverness show a central parade corresponding to the geometrical figure of the citadel's enceinte (principal fortified enclosure), with parallel rows of buildings broken by streets on the axis of the bastions' salients. At Inverlochy, the internal buildings, which included barracks for named companies and store buildings, were set out in double rows parallel to the ramparts, leaving a parade in the centre, with the governor's house at the head and the main guard inside the gate (see Figure 4).[29] This suggests that formality was expected, and that certain conventions, doubtless influenced by experience of Continental conditions, were in force.

The reorganization of the army following the disbandment of the Cromwellian New Model Army at the Restoration established the nucleus of royal standing forces. Despite the resurrection of the militia as a measure of political expediency, two regiments of Foot Guards (Grenadier and Coldstream) and two troops of Horse Guards (Life Guards and Royal Horse Guards) were formed. The garrison of Tangier formed another regiment, and during the recurring wars with the Dutch during Charles II's reign, additional forces were recruited and mostly later disbanded. The needs of the Guards regiments, combined with Charles's fortification programme at Plymouth, Portsmouth, Sheerness and Tilbury, led to the construction of a

---

[26] Kerrigan (1995), pp. 81 and 99.
[27] David Papillon, *A Practical Abstract of the Arts of Fortification and Assailing* (London 1645), ch.10.
[28] PRO WO55/1697.

[29] A.A. Tait, 'The Protectorate Citadels of Scotland', *Architectural History*, **8** (1965), pp.9–24.

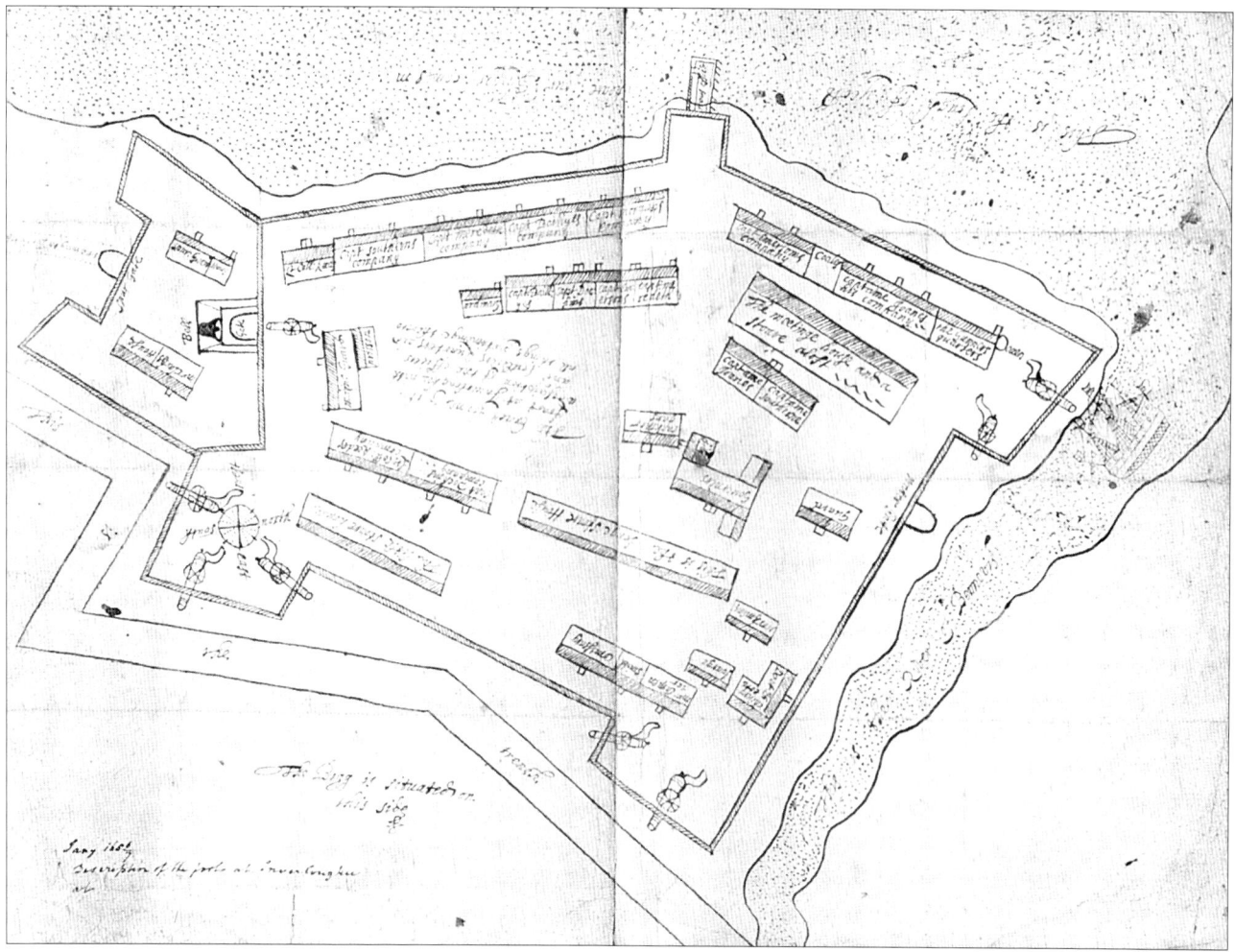

Figure 4 The Cromwellian citadel of Inverlochy, 1656, with its internal buildings which included a governor's house, and barracks for named companies and the main guard inside the gate.

few substantial barracks at the main garrisons and at some of the royal palaces. The Ordnance Office, since the Middle Ages responsible for the supply of guns and ammunition to both the army and navy, was also responsible for constructing and maintaining fortifications (see Appendix A). Concurrent with this activity was the design and furnishing by the Ordnance of such barracks as there were. Soldiers were occasionally permanently stationed elsewhere than in the coastal forts and garrison towns. On the fringe of the City of London was the Royal Palace of the Tower of London, where the need for soldiers' accommodation had been expressed in 1667. Preparations were made two years later, when the 'Irish Barracks' were begun according to the pattern set out by the Assistant Surveyor of the Ordnance, Sir Jonas Moore.[30] To the west of the City, the Savoy was fitted up for a regiment of foot in 1681, and there were other barracks in Southwark and Whitehall. Temporary barracks had been built in Hyde Park during the time of the Great Plague in 1665.[31] The first use of the word 'barracks' (as opposed to the term 'soldiers' lodgings') recorded in the English language comes in 1670, and applied to the 'Irish Barracks' just completed in the Tower of London.[32] These barracks were timber-framed and weatherboarded houses built against the outside of the East Curtain,

---

[30] Parnell (1993), pg.76; PRO WO49/112
[31] Calendar of State Papers Venetian (1664–6), p.178.
[32] PRO WO47/19A, f.70.

originally providing 30 rooms. There were other permanent garrisons beyond London at Windsor Castle and at the Foot Guards' barracks at Hampton Court.

Sir Bernard de Gomme

Ordnance Office building practices developed and were formalized during the period when Sir Bernard de Gomme was Chief Engineer (1661–85) as well as Surveyor General of the Ordnance (1682–5). De Gomme had been recruited by Prince Rupert at the start of the Civil Wars and became the Royalists' chief engineer. He returned to royal service at the Restoration and was responsible for the design and construction of Charles II's south coast fortifications. He became a dominant figure in the Ordnance Office, which encouraged standardization of designs for the main Ordnance building types, including barracks. The basic military unit determining the size of barracks at the time was the company (sixty or so men). Barrack rooms in England were to provide accommodation for four men in two beds. Each room was properly lit and provided with a fireplace for cooking as well as heating. Fixed schedules were laid down for equipping barrack rooms with beds and bedding, and these items were also supplied by the Ordnance Office. It would appear from surviving fort plans that there was a developmental stage taking place in England during the 1660s and early 1670s, undoubtedly deriving from Continental influences, and that the early forms of soldiers' accommodation were first conceived as single rows of individual houses or 'lodgings'.

The detailed process of late-seventeenth century barrack planning in England can be followed in the successive plans prepared by de Gomme for Plymouth Citadel and Tilbury Fort, Essex. In the preliminary proposals of the mid-1660s, rows of individual 'houses' were arranged along 'streets' and around courtyards at both forts. Similar single rows of soldiers' lodgings are to be seen in some early seventeenth-century Dutch forts, such as the fort of Oranje near Bergen op Zoom.[33] They were a feature with which de Gomme was familiar and, while employed in the Netherlands in 1651, he recorded rows of such houses inside Forts Frederick Henderick and Blaugaret on the bank of the Scheldt near Lillo.[34] At Plymouth, the 1665 plan shows the barracks placed in blocks opposite the curtains, with a street 24 feet (7.3 metres) wide between them and the rampart.[35] De Gomme's second plan of 1666–7 and another of 1668 show three irregular plots with single rows of lodgings around the edge of a central courtyard.[36] A proposal for Tilbury, dated 1668, envisaged small, square lodgings lining the sides of three rectangular blocks. An alternative plan of the same date places the barracks around the sides of four blocks cut by axial streets leading to the bastions.[37] One range consists of three rows of ten small, square rooms. The 1670 design, which in broad terms represents the eventual shape of the Tilbury Fort, has the barracks set around three unequal courtyards with a total of 36 single houses.[38] This ambiguity suggests an uncertain attempt on the one hand to develop a radial plan reminiscent of Renaissance ideal fortress towns, and on the other, to adopt the parallel rows of barracks of mid-seventeenth-century Dutch type, examples of which still survive at the Copenhagen citadel (Kastellet) designed by the Dutch engineer Hendrik Ruse in 1663–5 (see Figure 5, page 95). By this date, double-depth rows of two storeys had appeared, with individual rooms about 15 feet (4.6 metres) square and each containing two three-man beds. Eventually, during the 1670s, at both Plymouth and Tilbury, de Gomme's plans show double-depth rows of ten rooms on each side (assuming much the same pattern as his specification and drawing for barracks at Portsmouth in 1679), which were placed parallel to the curtains of the bastioned figure. Elevational drawings of 1715 show that these barrack ranges at Plymouth and Tilbury were of two storeys with an 'M' gable.[39] Another characteristic detail of de Gomme's barrack design was the provision of cisterns ('rain banks') at the gable ends, fed from the roof gutters.

An important distinction, confirmed at both Plymouth and Tilbury, was made between the main barrack blocks for transient foot companies of the

---

[33] J. Sneep, J.P.C.M. van Hoof, G.J.L. Koolhof and S.H. Poppema (eds) *Atlas van historische vestingwerken in Nederland: Noord-Brabant* (Utrecht 1996), p.80.
[34] BL King's Top. Coll. Cii 21 4 Tab 48, f.22.
[35] BL Add. MS 16371, ff.42–3.
[36] NMM P/45; BL Add. MS 16371 D.
[37] BL Add. MS 16370, ff.7 and 9.
[38] Ibid., f.5.
[39] BL King's MS 45, f.36.

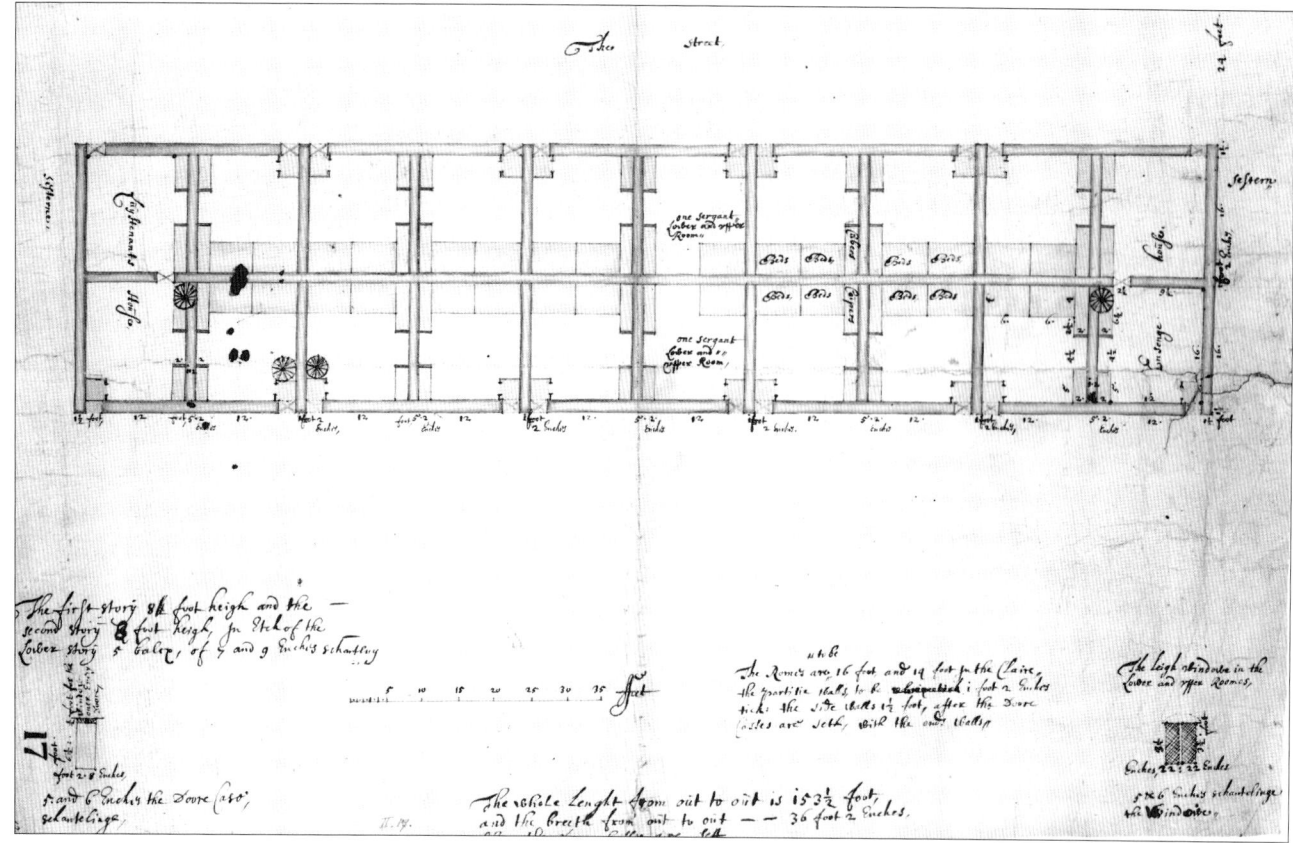

Figure 6 Ground-floor plan of a barracks at Portsmouth by Sir Bernard de Gomme, c.1679. There is a marked similarity to the Kastellet plan by Hendrik Ruse (see fig. 5, p. 95).

army, and the quarters for the resident gunners who were on the 'civil' establishment of the Ordnance. At Plymouth, the gunners' quarters were attached to the pair of houses allotted to the governor and the lieutenant governor and set at right angles to them. These helped to form an enclosed courtyard with gardens to the rear. At Tilbury, the gunners' quarters were also separate from the main barracks. In 1673 at Tilbury, soon after construction was under way, soldiers were housed in timber-framed lodgings until more permanent brick-built barracks were erected. As many as 84 bedsteads, 40 tables and 80 forms were made, suggesting a garrison of more than two companies.[40] By 1679, the barrack accommodation had been increased to cater for 220 soldiers.[41] Similar solutions were adopted at Sheerness Fort. In 1676, de Gomme was specifying two rows of double-depth, two-storeyed 'huts' for lodgings. By 1681, more permanent accommodation for two companies had still not been started, but seems to have been built shortly afterwards.[42] Alongside barracks, and as a concomitant of garrison life, there were chapels, storehouses and sutlers' houses as well as the houses for the governor and other officers.

The detailed plan and specifications for free-standing barracks within the town of Portsmouth, designed by Sir Bernard de Gomme and built in 1679, survive among the Dartmouth papers in the National Maritime Museum (see Figure 6).[43] This plan represents the earliest known detailed drawing of barracks in England. The long, double-depth range in ten bays was to accommodate 120 men (or two companies), four to a room in two beds. The building also included rooms on two floors for officers at either end of the block, with two sergeants' rooms on the ground floor in the centre. The overall length of the barracks was 153 feet 6 inches (46.8 metres), and it was 36 feet 2 inches (11

[40] PRO WO53/530 16 May 1673.
[41] PRO WO49/181.
[42] PRO WO49/180; SRO D(W)1788 v/32; NMM CAD/C/9, f.44.
[43] NMM P42, f.17.

1600–1750: Early Evolution

Figure 7 Foundations of the soldiers' barracks, Tilbury Fort, c.1680, which have identical dimensions to those in the contemporary Portsmouth barrack plan.

metres) wide. Each room had a fireplace, and the stacks were grouped in alternate partition walls, producing an elevation of five pairs of chimneys. Newel stairs seem to have been positioned against the back of the enclosed lobby behind each external door. The rooms were nearly square, 16 long by 14 feet wide (4.9 by 4.3 metres), and 8 feet (2.4 metres) high. The proposed newel stairs in the Portsmouth plan may have parrallels with those constructed behind the external doors and against the partitions in the barracks at Kastellet, Copenhagen, in 1664.[44]

The Portsmouth drawing is probably a preliminary sketch – certainly the newel stairs seem to be an afterthought – because there are distinct differences in the barracks as described in the building contract.[45] The overall dimensions of the building are similar to the drawing, but internally there were two 'double stairs', and on the upper floor there was a 'long gallery' or corridor giving access to the rooms, thereby superseding the proposal for newel stairs, at any rate for the soldiers' rooms. The upper floor was lit by 40 'Lanthorne lights' or dormers, two to a room and provided with 'ornaments'. The elevation had also been changed. Instead of ten doors on each side, there were a total of 14 large doors and doorcases with lights above. Each ground-floor room had two transomed windows of four lights. The original generous provision of two beds to each room had changed to five beds, allowing space for 280 soldiers, presumably because of practical considerations. In 1684, the number of beds in each room was reduced to four. Associated with the barracks were two wells with pumps, two washhouses, which were two-storeyed structures with furnaces or coppers with provision for four beds on the upper floors, together with a 'Necessary house for the soldiers'. These barracks were in the vicinity of Pembroke Mount on the eastern side of the town defences. There were other barracks in Portsmouth, a two-storey structure near the Landport and another at the Round Tower, which were in use in 1684 and were provided with furniture and bedding.[46]

The soldiers' brick-built barracks on the western side of the parade at Tilbury Fort, damaged by bombing in the Second World War and considered in too bad a condition to be repaired, now only remain as foundations (see Figure 7). Nevertheless, these foundations are physical confirmation of the Portsmouth pattern. They are identical to the

[44] Plan, cross-section and elevation of Barrack No.1 (Stjernestok) (1664) by Quartermaster General Samuel Christoph Geddes for Kastellet in 1754 (Forsvarets Bygningstjenestes Historiske Tegningsarchiv, Copenhagen).
[45] PRO WO51/23, ff.105–7.
[46] PRO WO49/111.

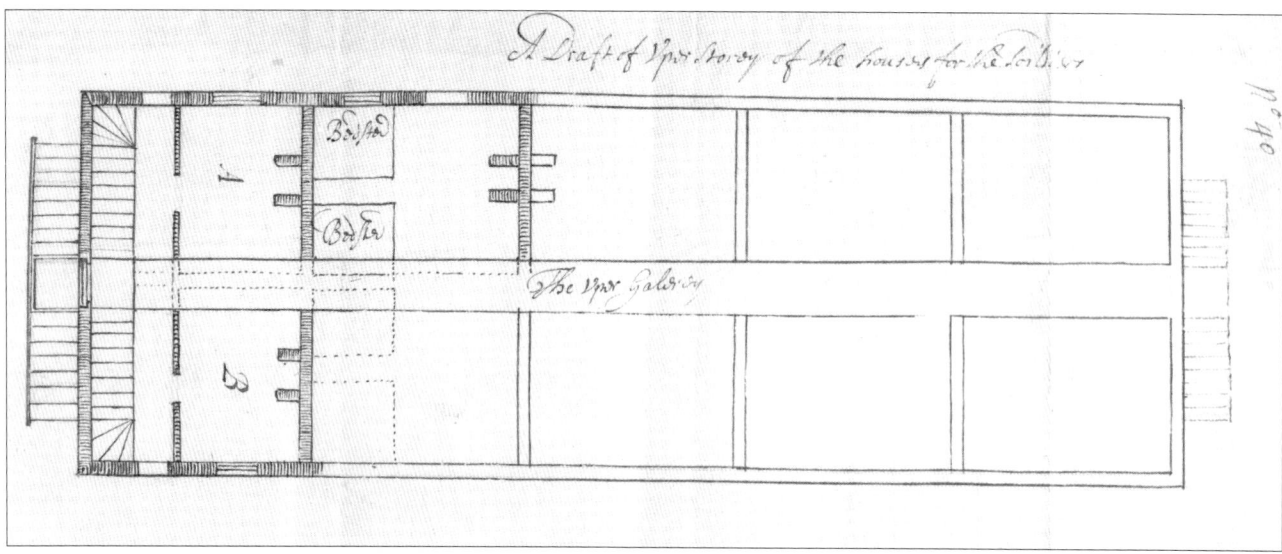

Figure 8 Sketch plan in de Gomme's hand of the upper floor of a barracks intended for Sheerness, c.1680. On the reverse is an elevation of a gable and external stair with the caption:
'A Draft of the Stayercase ...'.
The central passage represents an informed understanding of the latest developments in domestic planning, although it was not found in other double-depth barrack blocks of the period.

Portsmouth plan in the numbers of rooms, their size and the overall dimensions of the range. The main walls are two bricks (18 inches/46 centimetres) wide, and the partitions are a brick and a half (14 inches/36 centimetres) wide. There is now no evidence for the positions of stairs and doors. In the modified officers' range on the opposite side of the parade, the height of the ground-floor rooms is 8 feet (2.4 metres), and this is likely to have been followed in the soldiers' rooms, as in the Portsmouth specifications.

There is another surviving drawing of a barracks of this period in de Gomme's hand, intended for Sheerness (see Figure 8).[47] This plan represents the upper floor of a double-depth row, with five rooms on each side. Here, there are external stairs at the gable end to the upper floor leading to a central corridor between the rooms. Again, two beds are indicated in the soldiers' rooms, and there seem to be officers' or sergeants' quarters at the end, where the size of the room was reduced by the internal stairs and landing. On the reverse of the plan and entitled 'Draught of Barracque' is another unsigned sketch in de Gomme's hand with the caption, 'A Draft of the Stayercase how it will be ... go up the outside of the Houses'. This shows the gable end with its pitched roof springing from first-floor level, with dormer windows lighting the upper floor. A double stair and landing serves the first-floor entrance, with the upright posts capped with ball finials. In addition to the fort at Sheerness, de Gomme was intended to provide accommodation for the officers of the Navy Yard, as well as storage buildings and a common hall for the workmen.

[47] Rochester, Guildhall Museum.

1600–1750: Early Evolution

Figure 9 The Foot Guards' barracks and guardroom at Hampton Court Palace, built in 1689, are the earliest purpose-built barracks to have survived in England.

These proposals appear in a bird's-eye view of 1677 which shows the building for the officers of the yard as long, rectangular ranges with a courtyard separating them and closed by two-storey houses with attics.[48] The soldiers' lodging is shown as a single-storey, double-depth range with attics, having shutters on the lower windows.

The mixture of officers, sergeants and soldiers within the same building was not frequently repeated outside de Gomme's barracks at Portsmouth, Plymouth and perhaps, originally, at Tilbury. Greater separation of ranks became normal in the eighteenth century, whether in distinct buildings for officers and private soldiers – which can be identified eventually at Tilbury Fort and at Dover Castle – or in officers' quarters in pavilions at the end of soldiers' barracks, as at Berwick-upon-Tweed.

The Plymouth Citadel barracks of the early 1670s were surveyed in 1715. This shows them to be of two storeys, with the upper floor lit by dormer windows, and in this respect similar to the Portsmouth model.[49] Officers still had quarters at the end of the four ranges, with newel stairs to the upper floor. The main stairs were on either side of the party walls between the soldiers' rooms and opposite the external doors. Fireplaces were in the gable walls or in the central party wall. In 1679, the intended barracks in Guernsey was to have a similar plan to that at Portsmouth.[50] It was somewhat smaller, with a double row of six rooms on the ground floor and one straight double staircase of the eventual Portsmouth model. There were four bedsteads in the lower rooms and three in the rooms on the upper floor.

Elsewhere, in addition to the large establishments at major forts, and garrisons at dockyards and naval bases which were vulnerable to attack by the Dutch, formal accommodation for military garrisons was being built in the wider limits of the kingdom. To protect Bressay Sound, near Lerwick in Shetland, from the Dutch, a fort was begun in 1665. Inside was a two-storey barrack block for a hundred men. When the Dutch landed in 1673, during the Third Dutch War, they burnt the barracks in the now abandoned fort.[51] The most substantial fortress to be constructed in Ireland at this time (1678–83) was Ringcurran (or Fort Charles, as it became known), at Kinsale. The earliest barracks in the fort formed a continuous line of buildings following the inner side of the rampart containing the sea batteries. By the mid-eighteenth century, most of them had been removed and new accommodation provided by a new square of barracks in the eastern half of the fort.[52]

[48] PRO MPI155; ADM/3548, f.595.
[49] BL King's MS 45, f.36.
[50] PRO WO55/1785, f.38.
[51] Tabraham and Grove (1995), p.27.
[52] Kerrigan (1995), p.113.

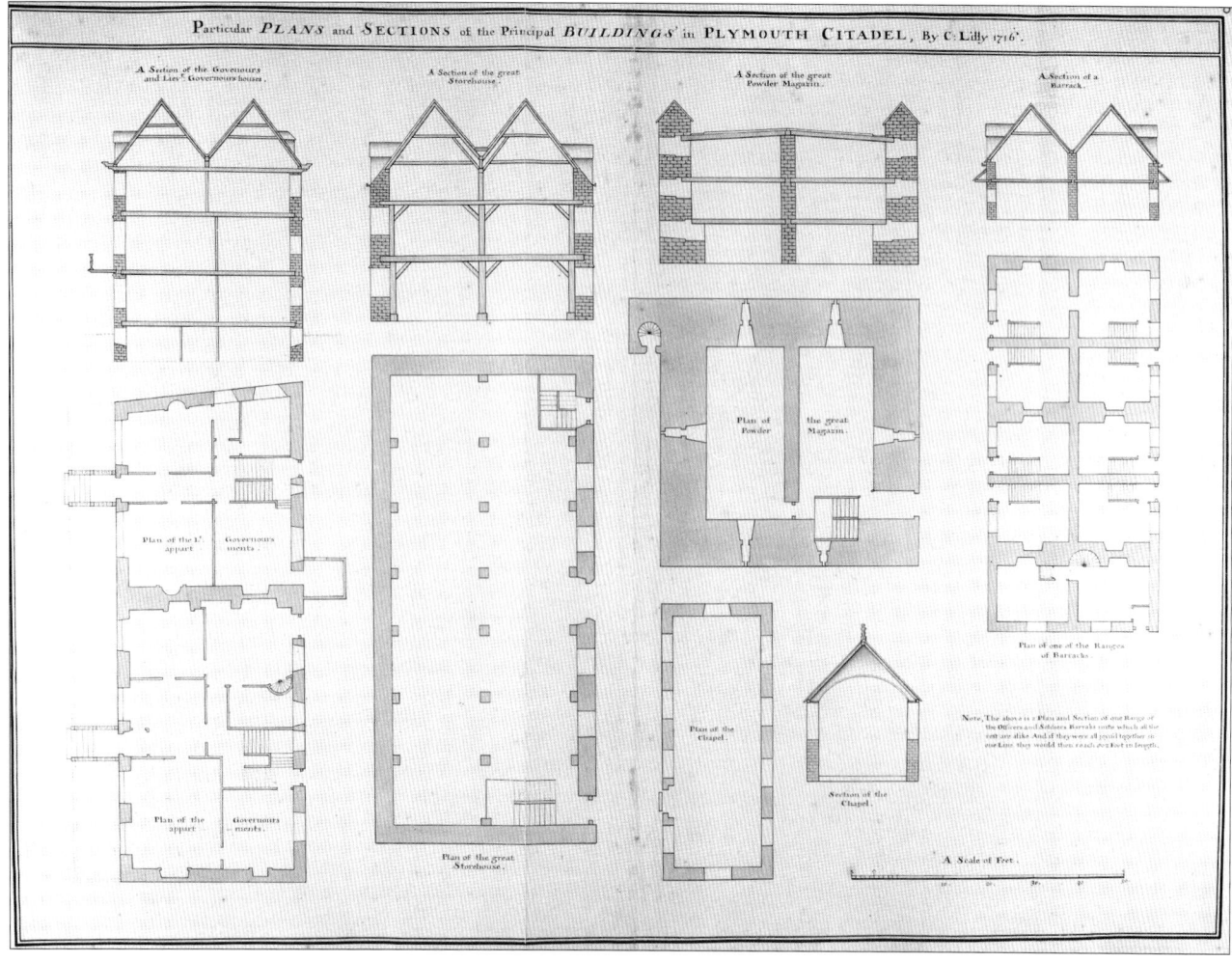

Figure 10 Plymouth Citadel. Some internal buildings surveyed in 1715 by Colonel Christian Lilly RE, which include on the right-hand side a cross-section and plan of a barrack range as built by de Gomme.

Billeting and absolute monarchy

For Britain in the late seventeenth century, a standing army was regarded as an instrument of absolute monarchy, and consequently dangerous to the liberty of the subject. There were abiding memories of army rule during the Commonwealth, and despite regulations against compulsory billeting on private citizens, all these fears became justified during the reign of James II, when the size of the army was substantially increased.

At James's accession, the English Army numbered 8,865 men, of whom 1,393 were permanently attached to various garrisons.[53] Barrack structures were still extremely rare, and the problem of billeting was highly contentious. The Disbanding Act of 1679 held that no private householders could be 'compelled against their wills to receive soldiers into their houses ... without [their] consent', and any subject was entitled 'to refuse to soujourn or quarter any soldier or soldiers notwithstanding any command, order, or billeting whatever'. Given the almost total absence of barracks for the soldiery outside some forts or dockyard towns, owners of inns and taverns were in no position to refuse to quarter troops. Through his desire to extend the power of the army all over England and by

[53] Childs (1980), p.1.

1600–1750: Early Evolution

Map 1 Barracks and Garrisons in Britain and Ireland in the early eighteenth century

■ Infantry Barracks
▶ Cavalry Barracks

Berwick-upon-Tweed
Calshot Castle
Carlisle
Chester
Cinque Ports – Dover Castle, Archliffe, Motes Bulwark, Sandown,
　Deal, Walmer
Clifford's Fort
Dartmouth
Gravesend and Tilbury ('and the Barrack')
Guernsey
Holy Island
Hull and the Blockhouse ('and the Barrack')
Hurst Castle
Isle of Wight – Yarmouth, Carisbrooke Castle
Jersey
Landguard Fort
North Yarmouth
Pendennis Castle
Plymouth, St Nicholas Island, The Citadel
Portland Castle
Scarborough
Scilly
Sheerness ('and the Barrack')
St James's Park
St Mawes Castle
Tower of London
Tynemouth
Upnor, Cockham Wood, Gillingham, Howness
Windsor Castle

North Britain:
Blackness
Dumbarton
Edinburgh
Fort William (containing a regiment of foot)
Stirling

Ireland:
Arklow
Armagh
Athenry
Athlone
Athy
Ballyshannon
Banagher
Bantry
Belfast
Belturbet
Boyle
Bray
Callan
Cappoquin
Carlingford
Carlow
Carrick-on-Shannon
Carrick-on-Suir
Carrickfergus
Castlebar
Cavan
Charieville
Charlemont
Clare Castle
Clonmel
Coleraine
Collooney
Cork
Cullmore
Derry
Dingle
Downpatrick
Drogheda
Dublin
Duncannon
Dungannon
Dungarvan
Enniscorthy
Enniskillen
Galway
Headford
Jamestown
Kilkenny
Kilmacthomas
Kinsale
Lanesborough
Lifford
Limavady
Limerick
Longford
Loughrea
Macroom
Mallow
Maryborough
Navan
Nenagh
New Ross
Newmarket
Newry
O'Brien's Bridge
Philipstown
Portumna
Roscrea
Rosecommon
Ross Castle
Sligo
Thurles
Tralee
Trim
Tullow
Waterford
Wexford
Wicklow
Youghal

Sources: England and Scotland list of 1708 – PRO WO24/45; Ireland list 1704 – Kerrigan (1995), p.130–2.

Figure 11 An eighteenth-century view of Plymouth Citadel showing the internal buildings. The storehouse (see fig. 117, page 141), the Governor's and Lieutenant Governor's House have survived from the original layout. Soldiers were accommodated in vaulted casemates in the south flank (see fig. 47, page 55) as well as the two main barracks ranges.

increasing its numbers substantially, James created enormous difficulties in accommodating his men: Hull had a garrison which was never less than 500 soldiers; Portsmouth had a garrison of over 700 men, but was said to have public accommodation for just 164. It was claimed that James formulated plans to convert Whitehall into an armed citadel by constructing barracks, stables and fortifications, and by building a new bridge across the Thames from the Palace of Whitehall to avoid having to depend upon London Bridge.[54]

With the accession of William and Mary, greater attention was given to Hampton Court as a royal residence, and 'guard-houses' for the Horse Guards and Foot Guards were erected there in the summer of 1689 (see Figure 9).[55] They are the earliest barracks in Britain to survive, although with their own particular characteristics. They differ from the Ordnance Office standard plan. A plan dated 1710–13 shows the ground floor of the Horse Guards' range as given over to stables. The ground floor of the Foot Guards' range is divided into two very long rooms with smaller rooms at either end, perhaps for officers.[56] This arrangement probably represents the form of the guardrooms, with the likelihood of more conventional barrack rooms on the upper floor.

As a consequence of the Glorious Revolution of 1688, the first of the Mutiny Acts ensured that no standing force could be maintained unless Parliament approved, had voted supplies for its cost, agreed its size, and passed annually an Act for its discipline – an arrangement which, in essence, survives to this day. The Mutiny Act of 1689 declared that it was illegal to quarter any soldier upon a private citizen, and empowered local magistrates to fix their own county and borough rates for providing billets in public houses. Even a large garrison town such as Berwick-upon-Tweed was not equipped with barracks, though the corporation was to petition for one in 1705.[57] Quarter could be used for political purposes – a factor which increased public hatred of the army. As a result, during the first half of the eighteenth century, when purpose-built barracks were scarce, the army was scattered all over the country in minute detachments, for inns were the only

---

[54] Ibid., pp.104–5.
[55] Colvin (1976), **5**, p.156; plan showing the original internal layout of the guardhouses, All Souls iv, 2.
[56] Soane Museum Folio II, no.40.

[57] MacIvor (1967), p.19.

quarters permitted by the Mutiny Act. In 1697, it was calculated that there was sufficient barrack accommodation for 5,000 infantry, and in that year an estimate was submitted to Parliament on this basis for furniture, as well as provision for tents for a further 6,000 infantry and 4,000 horse.[58] Map 1 shows the accommodation for the Guards and the garrisons of England and Scotland in 1708, and for the Irish garrison in 1704.

By contrast, in France, where an absolute monarchy was well established, there was a dramatic expansion of barracks under the supervision of the great military engineer Sébastien le Prestre de Vauban, during 1680–1705, when his fortification of the country's borders was under way. Under Louis XIV, the French standing army had reached a total of 200,000 men, and drastic measures were necessary to accommodate it. By 1710, it is claimed that 160 barracks had been constructed in France. Some very large complexes were later built during the first half of the eighteenth century. The Vauban-style barracks still contained comparatively small rooms, often arranged on three floors with attics, and with officers housed in attached pavilions. The double-depth soldiers' barracks, often with a corridor running down the centre, marked them out as a more sophisticated, double-pile type of plan, with stairs taking up narrow bays at right angles to the corridor along the range. All rooms had a fireplace, for the troops were still expected to cook for themselves. In some Vauban barracks, there were internal latrines. By 1695 at Montpellier, there were extensive ranges built around large, quadrangular courtyards.[59]

The Duke of Marlborough

The appointment of the Duke of Marlborough as Master General of the Ordnance (1702–12 and 1714–22) did much to reorganize the British Army and acted as a stimulus for the construction of barracks. The condition of the various forts and garrisons was surveyed (see Figures 10, 12 and 15). Colonel Christian Lilly, 'one of His Majesties engineers', carried out the survey of the Plymouth Division in 1714–17.[60] In it he refers to and shows the situation of the 'old' barracks (presumably 'the Folly' surveyed in 1661) on St Mary's, Isles of Scilly, and at the same time presented a plan for a proposed new barracks to accommodate two companies (see Figure 12). The design, which is dated 1715, is not dissimilar to those constructed by de Gomme at Portsmouth and Plymouth, but lacks the provision for a mixture of officers and private soldiers. There are differences of detail. The arrangement of chimney stacks differs from that at Portsmouth, though each room had its own fireplace. The planning of the stairs is simplified and set against the room partitions. The overall size of the barracks for St Mary's was 100 by 32 feet (30.5 by 9.8 metres), divided into six rooms to contain four men in two beds. Therefore, the lower two floors were to contain 48 men each, with a further 24 men, two to a room, in the attics, which were lit with 'Lutheran lights' (dormer windows). The windows throughout now had sash frames.

In the same year, Lilly also provided drawings for a new barracks building for Pendennis Castle (see Figure 13). This was initially planned for 64 men (company strength), but with the possibility for it to be enlarged threefold. The building was to be 68 feet (20.7 metres) long by 32 feet (9.8 metres) broad and 20 feet (6.1 metres) high. As was now standard, it

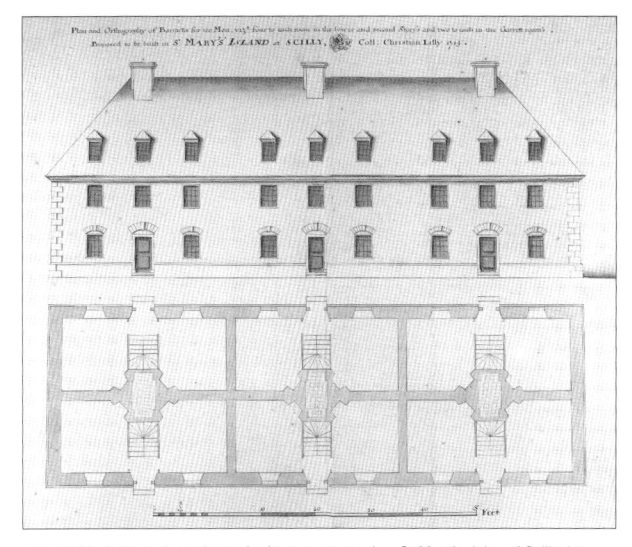

Figure 12 Proposed new barracks for two companies, St Mary's, Isles of Scilly, by Colonel Christian Lilly RE, 1715.

---
[58] Clode (1869), p.221.
[59] Dallemagne (1990), pp.42–58.
[60] BL King's MS 45.

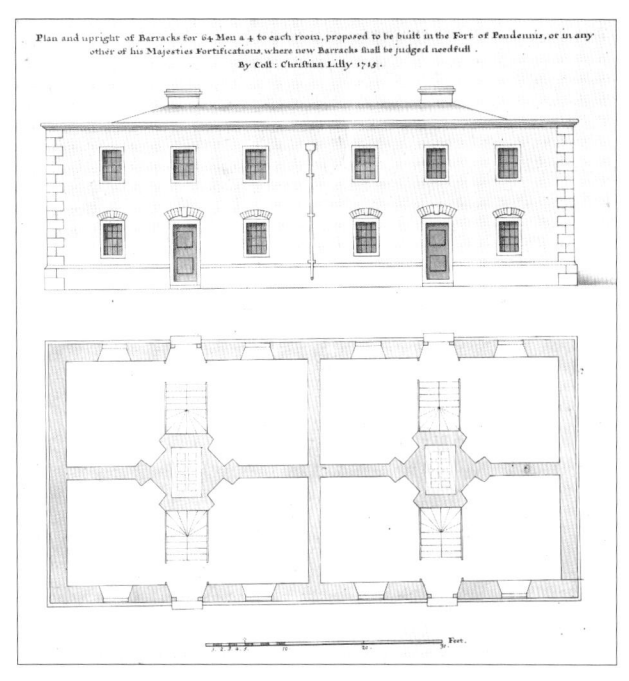

Figure 13 Proposed new barracks for 64 men in the fort of Pendennis, Cornwall, by Colonel Christian Lilly RE, 1715.

Figure 14 Kilchurn Castle, Loch Awe, from the north. The regular windows on the right lit the barrack rooms of the 1690s.

was intended for four men in each room. There were 16-light sash windows, a fielded, two-panel door, and segmental arches with keystones over each opening to provide the architectural niceties. Lilly's south-western survey provides a valuable point of comparison with the practice a generation earlier.

The military situation in Scotland following the replacement on the throne of James II by William of Orange required a different kind of garrisoning to that emerging in England, and was to some extent different from that adopted in Ireland, where, as we shall see in Chapter Two, as well as accommodation for horse and foot in barracks in towns across the country, there were many smaller, defensible barracks or redoubts in strategic locations. In Scotland, measures were confined to counteracting Jacobite insurgency and providing a form of policing system in the Highlands. It is in Scotland that the physical evidence of early barrack construction is most visible in the British Isles today.[61] A new garrison fortress was constructed at Inverlochy (Fort William) in 1690, on the site of a Cromwellian citadel, but this does not survive. For the first few months, the soldiers there lived in tents, but then timber barracks were constructed. However, an unusual contemporary development for what seems to have been a private army of the Campbell, Lord Breadalbane, survives at Kilchurn Castle at the northern end of Loch Awe (see Figure 14). An earlier castle was substantially remodelled to accommodate three companies of soldiers in an L-shaped block of three storeys, each housing a company, above a vaulted basement. Each floor of the longer wing was divided into four rooms, and the shorter arm was divided into two. Each room had a fireplace and at least two windows. There were latrines at the junction of the two ranges. Kilchurn should not necessarily be regarded as typical, and it does not comply with the pattern already established by the Ordnance Office, but it does demonstrate that the concept of formal barrack buildings was accepted in mainland Britain by the end of the seventeenth century.

Edinburgh Castle was the main garrison for Scotland, and its site contains a succession of barrack buildings surviving from the eighteenth century. Accommodation in the late seventeenth century was contrived in the medieval Great Hall, where broad, timber galleries carrying rows of beds were constructed against the walls. More conventional was the officers' barracks (Queen Anne's Building) begun on the west side of the principal courtyard by Captain Theodore Drury in

---

[61] Tabraham and Grove (1995), pp.39–45.

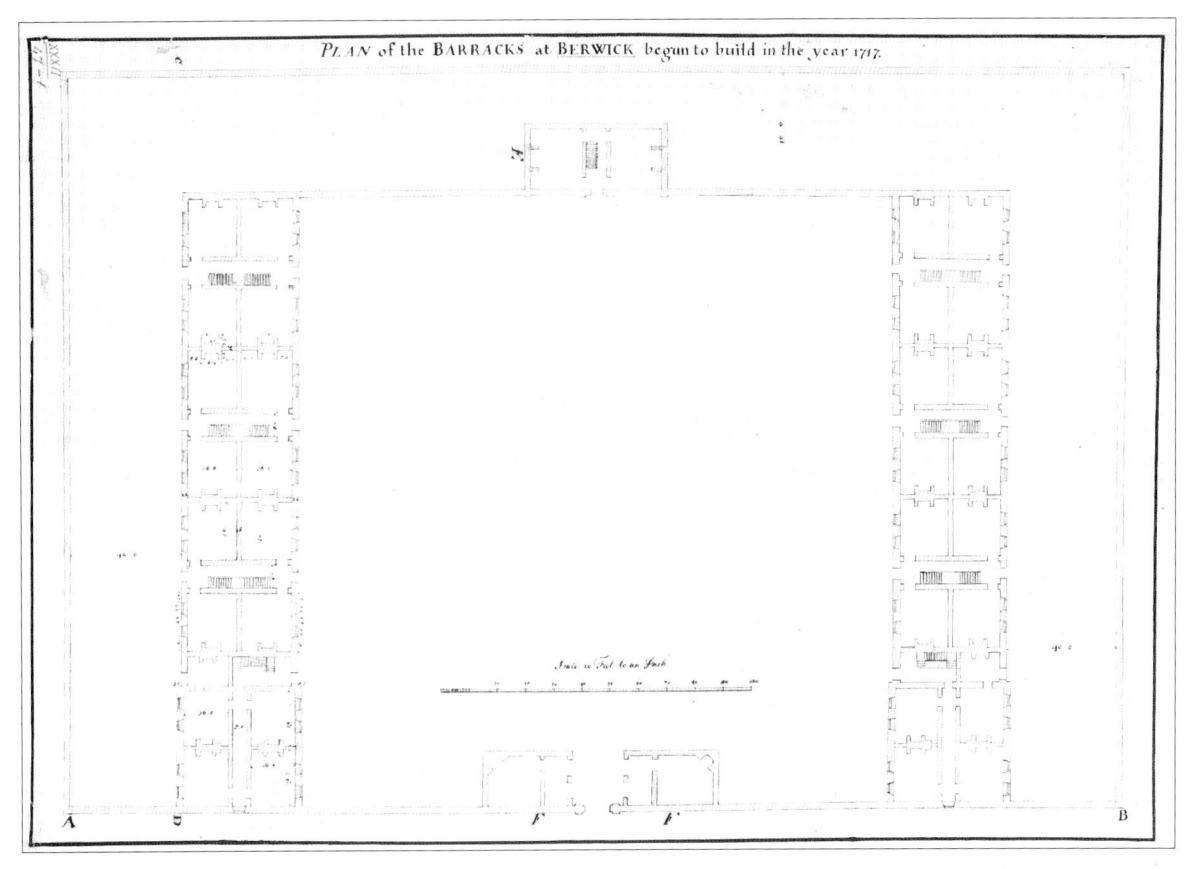

Figure 15 Berwick-upon-Tweed, plan of the barracks, 1717. The similarity to other collegiate plans of the period can be seen in the double-depth blocks with their stair passages.

Figure 16 Berwick-upon-Tweed Barracks, showing the east barrack range (left) and the barracks from the north (right).

1708. In 1737, the interior of the Great Hall was again altered to give six large barrack rooms for 310 men. This must have precluded barrack-room cooking. The Governor's House of 1740–2 is a fine example of Ordnance Office design. More barracks were to follow later in the century.[62] Stirling Castle was another of the traditional fortresses where barrack accommodation was contrived in the Great Hall. Elsewhere in Scotland, there were plans in 1711 for a new barracks at Fort William in place of the timber structures of Inverlochy. This was to be one long barrack pile, 'about 200 feet [61 metres]

[62] MacIvor (1993), pp.92–5.

Figure 17 Upnor Castle, showing the barrack block from the east.

long [giving] room for 9 chambers on one side and as many on the other, is 18 Chambers the first story and 18 above maketh 36 in all, and reckoning 12 men in each room this will lodge 432 men'.[63]

It is in the context of the Jacobite threat in Scotland that the most extensive and monumental set of barracks of early eighteenth-century England was begun at Berwick-upon-Tweed in 1717 (see Figures 15 and 16). The influence of Nicholas Hawksmoor upon the design has been established from a surviving preliminary sketch plan.[64] The engineer responsible for the ultimate structure was Thomas Phillips. The barracks were intended for 600 men and 36 officers. As first built, they consisted of two double ranges facing each other across a wide parade. A screen wall pierced by a gateway linked the two at the front; later, in 1742, a large store building blocked the fourth side. Each barrack range had three common stairs with four rooms off them on each of the three floors. There was a

[63] Tabraham and Grove (1995), pp.50–1.
[64] Hewlings (1993).
[65] BL King's Top. Coll. XXXII 47-f.

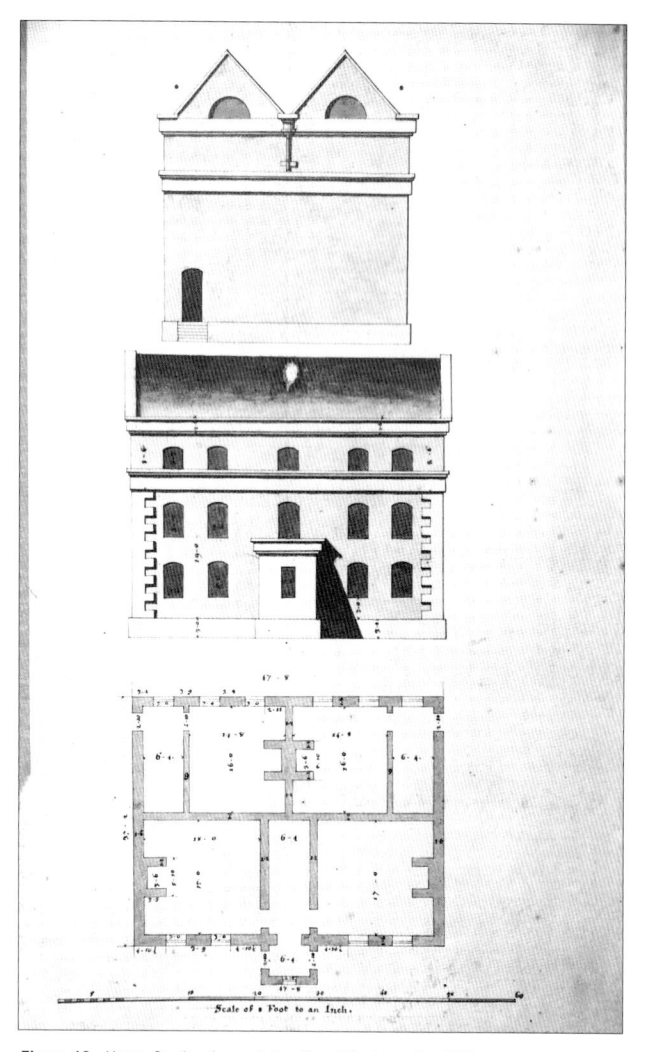

Figure 18 Upnor Castle, plan and elevation of the barracks, 1719.

further stair at the north end of each range, serving the officers' quarters in a pavilion stepped forward from each main façade (see Figure 16). Each barrack room was designed to accommodate eight men in four beds, and there was a fireplace for cooking and heating in each room, but no latrines were provided in the barrack blocks. In the arrangement of individual rooms to stairs there was a marked change from the de Gomme pattern of the previous generation.[65] Architecturally, this was the most distinguished composition in the Baroque idiom so far attempted by the Ordnance Office. Significantly, it was an enclosed establishment separated from the town.

Almost contemporary with Berwick-upon-Tweed was a small barrack block built in 1719 alongside Upnor Castle, Kent, opposite Chatham Dockyard (see Figures 17 and 18). The sixteenth-century fort on the bank of the Medway had been converted into a magazine after the Dutch Raid of 1667. This barracks for two officers and 64 men follows the Ordnance Office formula, with a central stair providing access to rooms in the three-storey block. These vary in size from 18 by 17 feet (5.5 by 5.2 metres) for private soldiers to 16 feet by 14 feet 8 inches (4.9 by 4.5 metres) for the officers' rooms at the rear, with separate access. This suggests soldiers' rooms with four beds. Externally, the block is well proportioned, with a plat band distinguishing the level of the attics, and a cornice. There are semicircular windows in the gables (see Figure 18).[66]

Jacobite insurgency in the Highlands

The Jacobite rebellion of 1715 instigated a particular form of defensible barracks which were built in the Highlands as part of a counter-insurgency policy. A similar policy involving the construction of secure 'redoubts' had already been adopted on a larger scale in Ireland since the Williamite War. Individual barrack rooms and their arrangement remained much the same as in earlier Ordnance Office barracks. The difference lay in the fact that the barracks complex now had to be self-defensible, and the whole exterior of the enclosure capable of being covered by flanking musketry fire from bastion-like angle towers, sometimes at each corner, sometimes at alternate angles. Four locations were chosen: Bernera in the valley of the Spey; Inversnaid, Stirlingshire; Kiliwhimen in the Great Glen, and Ruthven in Badenock (see Figure 19). Ruthven Barracks is the best-preserved (see Figure 20). It was intended for two companies, or about 120 men. Here, as at the other defensible barracks, the blocks consisted of three storeys, with basements and attics. The rooms were almost square, and 18 feet (5.5 metres) long. Each room had a fireplace and space for five double beds, and unlike Berwick-upon-Tweed, there were separate latrines for both officers and men. A barracks was also proposed at Inverness in 1716 which would have been 326 feet (99.4 metres) long and capable of lodging 500 men and their officers on two floors, with additional space in the garrets. There were to be two end pavilions for officers.[67]

New barracks continued to be built at long-established Scottish garrisons. Grandiose proposals were made for Kiliwhimen in 1726.[68] Three new blocks matching the earlier ones in height, with three floors and attics, were to be added. The distinction lay in the adoption of a central corridor more familiar in France, running the length of the ranges and connecting the wings, instead of the more space-consuming stairs separating the barrack rooms. However, an entirely new Fort Augustus was built beside Loch Ness instead, to serve as the headquarters for the army in the Highlands. Within the square, bastioned fort, the barrack buildings were set around a central parade (see Figure 21). The governor's and captain's houses occupied one side and possessed considerable architectural pretension, having a Venetian window above a rusticated door with circular attic windows. Opposite was a soldiers' barracks with pavilions at each end for eight subalterns' rooms. The main soldiers' barracks faced the entrance range as a double pile. In all there were 30 soldiers' rooms, each entered off the stairs. With an intended garrison of five companies (about 300 men), each room could accommodate five double beds.[69] On a different scale, the tower-house of Corgarff in western Aberdeenshire was adapted in 1748 to provide two main barrack rooms which could contain up to eight beds each. Within its star-trace and loopholed enclosing wall, the tower-house served as a 'police' post from which patrols were sent out into the countryside.[70]

Elsewhere in Britain, barrack accommodation was becoming more common in the major forts during the eighteenth century, and older castles were being adapted for the purpose, particularly during the 1745 crisis when the medieval hall at Carlisle was brought into use. At Chester in 1725, two long 'barrack' rooms were set against the medieval curtain wall west of the Outer Gate, with gunners' dwellings in the gatehouse.[71] On the Kent coast, a

---

[66] Ibid., XVIII 58c.
[67] Stell (1973) PP.20–30.
[68] BL King's Top. Coll. L 11.
[69] Ibid., L 19.
[70] Iain MacIvor and Chris Tabraham, *Corgarff Castle* (Edinburgh 1995).
[71] BL King's Top. Coll. IX 8.

British Barracks 1600–1914

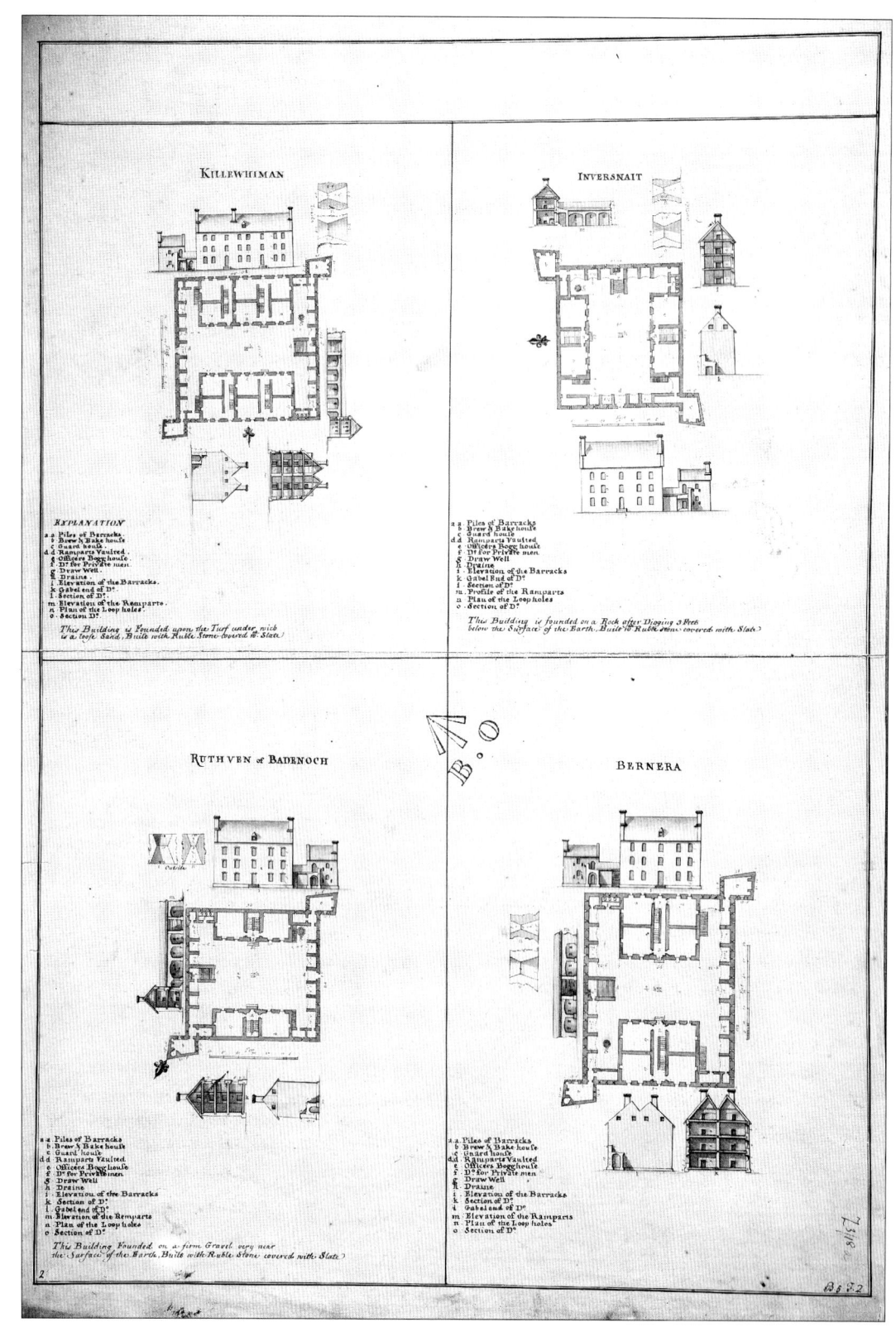

Figure 19 These drawings of 1717 by the Board of Ordnance's surveyor show all the barracks proposed after the 1715 Rising.

Figure 20 Ruthven Barracks, completed in 1724.

small, two-storey, weatherboarded gunners' house of the early eighteenth century remains embedded in Walmer Castle, across the back of one of the large Henrician bastions (see Figure 22). The former gunners' barrack on the Gun Wharf at Portsmouth, built in 1717,[72] was a three-storey block over a basement with attics. In the following year, there were proposals for a grandiose scheme for barracks at Portsmouth which, if built, would have eclipsed in architectural magnificence those at Berwick-upon-Tweed.

At Dover Castle, more prosaically, three-storey blocks were built against the medieval curtain wall in the keep yard in 1745, and these still remain (see Figure 23).[73] Here, officers and men were separated into distinct houses. The distinction was applied architecturally: the soldiers' barracks had square-headed windows, the windows of the officers' accommodation were round-headed. These were the last in the tradition which had evolved in the Ordnance Office from the time of Sir Bernard de Gomme.

There was already a move towards larger, dormitory-type barrack rooms at Edinburgh Castle. It followed a pattern emerging in British barrack rooms, where more and more men were accommodated in each room, with a resultant decline in the space available for each man. In Fort Augustus of 1747, however,

casemates (bomb-proof vaulted chambers within the ramparts) for ten men were provided, and casemates 30 feet (9.1 metres) long by 12 feet (3.7 metres) wide and 12 feet (3.7 metres) high, also for ten men, were planned for Inverness.[74] This was a form to be commonly applied in the new fortifications of the latter half of the eighteenth century, and offered an improvement in space per man. In this respect, it was to bring the standards of accommodation closer to those achieved by de Gomme in his Portsmouth prototype of 1679.

Barrack furniture and fittings

Construction and maintenance of barracks were the responsibility of the Ordnance Office in England, but not in Ireland, where there was a separate Ordnance organization.[75] The garrisons established their barrack masters to oversee the use of the accommodation and organize local contracts for the periodic washing of bedding and for the supply of fuel. The furnishing complements of barrack rooms had become defined at an early stage. Beds and bedding were sent to Tynemouth Castle and Landguard Fort in 1664.[76] By 1679, beds and their furniture had become an ordinary charge to the Ordnance Office.[77] Lilly includes in his south-western survey of 1715–17 a scale drawing of a two-man barrack bed 6 feet (1.8 metres) long by 4 feet (1.2 metres) wide (see Figure 24).[78] De Gomme had

[72] Ibid., XIV 42y.
[73] Coad (1995), pp.60–1.
[74] BL King's Top. Coll. L 9e.
[75] Barker (1993).
[76] PRO WO49/111.
[77] Walton (1894), p.717; BL Harl MS 4251.
[78] BL King's MS 45, f.49.

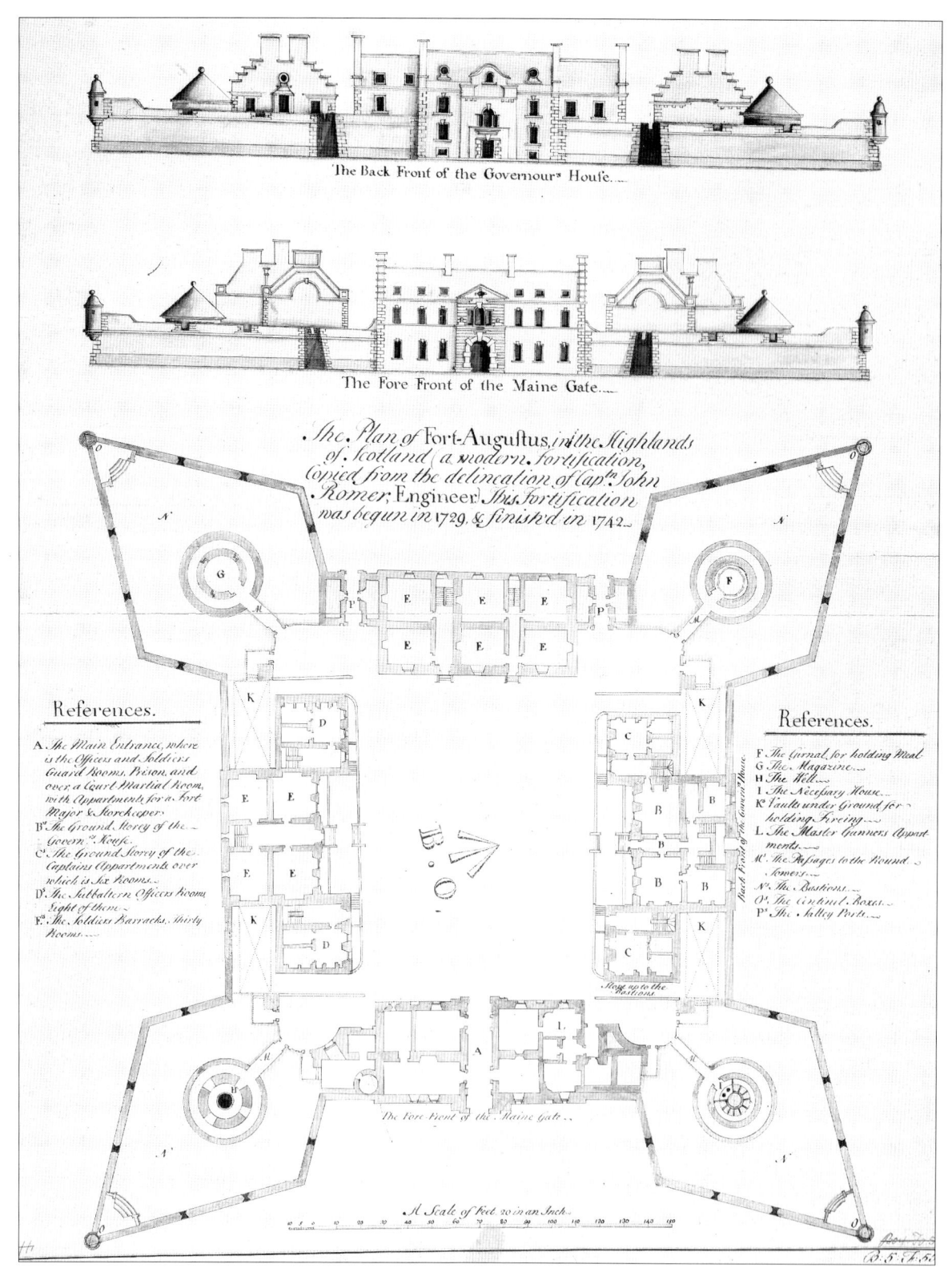

Figure 21 Fort Augustus, 1729–42, showing John Romer's scheme arranged on four sides of a square.

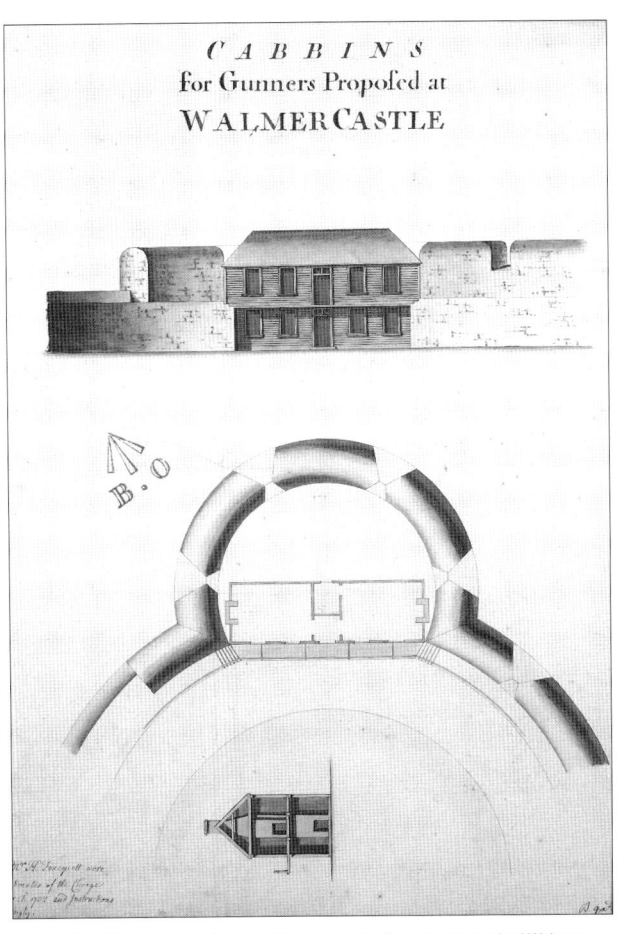

Figure 22 This two-storeyed gunners' house was built across the back of Walmer Castle's south bastion in the early eighteenth century. It was built in timber and weatherboarded.

specified a bed 3 inches (7.6 centimetres) longer for the hospital at Portsmouth in 1681, but the smaller bed seemed to be general for barracks.[79] For his barrack beds, de Gomme had specified bedsteads 'with sacking bottoms and well corded'; by Lilly's day, the beds were boarded. The plan, elevation and section of a 'Guard-Bed' for the New Guard Room in the Tower of London dates from 1717.[80] The standard furniture – a bed shared by two men, a table, two wooden forms or benches and sometimes cupboards – all complied to fixed specifications. In fact, the barrack furniture with which the National Serviceman of the late 1940s and 1950s was familiar, and the regulations governing it, had not altered essentially from those which had been established in the 1670s.

Figure 23 Barrack blocks in the keep yard of Dover Castle, 1745.

The basic equipment and utensils for cooking – from iron grates and fenders, fire shovels and tongs to four-gallon iron pots, flesh forks and buckets, together with fuel, iron candlesticks and lighting – were also provided by the Ordnance Office. The charges for fire and candles were set out in 1708 for all the 44 garrisons in Britain.[81] The allocation of coal per room in the early eighteenth century was 1½ pecks from 29 September to 25 March, and half a peck during the spring and summer.[82] De Gomme made provision for storing coal beneath the staircases at Portsmouth. There was a set allocation of mattress, bolster, sheets, rug and blankets for each bed. These had been established by the time Sir Bernard de Gomme had succeeded to the post of Surveyor General, and such chores as checking barrack inventories were added to his existing responsibilities of Chief Engineer. He signed the appropriate allocations of bedding to be sent to Tilbury Fort, Portsmouth and elsewhere.[83] An inkling of barrack conditions of the time can be obtained from the printed pro forma setting out the schedule for beds, bedding and barrack furniture for soldiers of a foot company: a surviving example contains the articles of agreement made between the Overseers of the Barracks in Ireland on 3 December 1715, whereby William Thompson of Clonmel in County Tipperary maintained the bedding and utensils for the barracks in Waterford and neighbourhood according to the schedule: he had to deliver one pair of clean sheets every 15 days

[79] PRO WO55/1785, f.14.
[80] BL King's Top. Coll. XXIV 23o.
[81] PRO WO24/45.

[82] R.E. Scouller, *The Armies of Queen Anne* (Oxford 1966), p.167.
[83] PRO WO49/111.

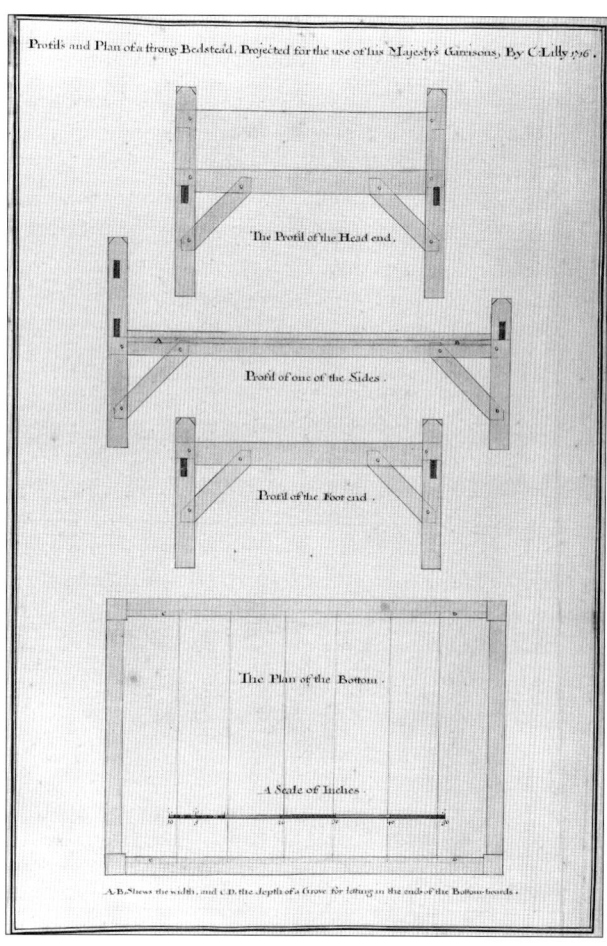

Figure 24 Design for a barrack bedstead, by Colonel Christian Lilly RE, 1715.

for officers and one pair every 30 days for the soldiers' beds. Foul sheets were to be handed in, and a charge of 2d per pair was levied for washing.[84] As standard schedules of furniture and bedding were established, so there arose the concept of 'barrack damages' to counter the mistreatment they suffered at the hands of garrison soldiers.[85] An order of 1685 stated that the garrison commander was to take a particular indent of barrack stores from the captain of every company, who was to give satisfaction for any embezzlements and breakages.[86] In 1715, Lilly drew attention to the amount of destruction of barrack furniture and damage to buildings at Plymouth Citadel that was due to the absence of a barrack master in the garrison. Lilly provided a detailed appreciation of the number and condition of the bedsteads, and arranged for iron numbers and the broad arrow symbol of the Ordnance to be fixed to each item. Articles such as 'bellows, wooden dishes, trenchers, cans, ladles, or chamber pots are liable to be broken without due care', and storekeepers were therefore to allow £2 per year, and no more, to furnish these to NCOs and private soldiers.[87] 'Rules, Orders and Regulations for the good government and preservation of the barracks in several garrisons, towns, forts and castles etc in Great Britain and the foreign garrisons' were drawn up in 1737.[88]

Ordnance Office style

Throughout the early development of British barracks, the Ordnance Office had a crucial role in design and the establishment of formulae which could be applied across the country.[89] A number of engineer architects can be identified, as well as the outstanding architectural figure of Nicholas Hawksmoor – de Gomme, Lilly, Phillips, Jelf, Romer and Rudolph Corneille being among the most prominent. The barracks of the second half of the seventeenth century tended to be domestic in style, essentially double-depth rows of small houses, of a kind which would have been familiar in an urban context in London and the Low Countries, and which had become common in Dutch fortifications. The composition of the elevation of the Foot Guards' barracks at Hampton Court suggests the possibility that barracks and the terraced house might have a common source, although their internal layouts are more clearly related to collegiate than domestic planning of the period. The more substantial storehouses and governor's houses were given more architectural distinction, but ostentation was left principally to the gatehouses of forts.

The beginning of the eighteenth century, during Marlborough's second term of office as Master General of the Ordnance, brought a more self confident vision of barracks as architecture. Hawksmoor's Baroque composition for Berwick-upon-Tweed and the proposed design for Portsmouth show respectively what was and what might have been achieved. Apart from the grand schemes for large garrisons, the evidence from

---

[84] NAM Military MS, vol.133, 21, *Articles of Agreement ... between the Overseers of the Barracks ... and Wiliam Thompson ...*, 3/2/1715.
[85] Clode (1869), p.228.
[86] Tomlinson (1979), p.155.
[87] BL King's MS 45.
[88] Clode (1869), p.229.
[89] Barker (1993).

Upnor and the drawings for barracks in Scilly and Pendennis Fort show a restrained style with few decorative features, and were still essentially buildings of domestic proportions. By the 1740s, the barracks being built in Scotland were more than devices for housing troops: they were political statements. Architectural details were usually applied to distinguish levels of rank at most barracks.

In terms of spatial planning within garrisons, there is little on which to comment. Where seventeenth-century barracks and other garrison structures were built inside forts, their arrangement was dictated by the geometrical figure of the defensive enceinte. This would usually allow a central parade. Elsewhere, the earliest barracks were free-standing, whether along a street or outside a palace gate. This is probably due to their size, generally limited to housing only one or two companies. When garrison strength was on a greater scale in the eighteenth century, as at Berwick-upon-Tweed or Fort Augustus, there were sufficient ranges to fit round a more formal square. The other essential ingredients of garrison life – the governors' houses, chapels, storehouses and sutlers' houses – must be considered together with the barrack ranges. During the early eighteenth century, they became more closely integrated into an overall scheme. Some barrack structures were more ephemeral. The addition of a timber shed to the sutler's house at Plymouth Citadel in 1672 is perhaps the first recorded example of a soldiers' canteen, and illustrates some of the realities of seventeenth-century barrack life.[90] It can be no coincidence that the communal 'bog houses' were sited just behind it within James Bastion.

Whilst there were no consistent standards for internal barrack design which can be used for comparative purposes, certain trends in room size and space per man can be recognized from Table 1. These can be set against the recommendations of the Royal Commission on Barracks, which in 1861 pressed for improved cubic footage of space per man. It is clear from this report that in some contemporary barracks, conditions were as poor as those that have been identified in the early eighteenth century.[91] De Gomme's Portsmouth Barracks of 1679 established a benchmark where the norm appears to be a two-bed room with comparatively generous space per man. In the early eighteenth century, while externally the buildings were on a grander and more architectural scale, on the inside, small, four-bedded rooms were characteristic, with a correspondingly reduced allocation of space per man. In Scotland during the first half of the eighteenth century, either through necessity or by intention, more men were packed into smaller spaces. Indeed, the Ordnance Office wrote to the Duke of Roxburgh in 1718 in respect of the Highland defensible barracks: 'Your Grace will be pleased to observe that we have calculated five beds for ten men in so little room as can be well allowed ...'.[92] There was subsequently a marked progression towards putting more men into larger barrack rooms, and in consequence a move away from the more domestic standards set by Charles II's Chief Engineer.

[90] PRO E357/3609.
[91] Watson (1954), p.153.
[92] Clode (1869), p.222.

Table 1 Comparative dimensions of barrack rooms, number of beds per room (each for two men) and an estimate of the cubic space allotted to the individual private soldier

	Date	Room size	Beds per room	Space per soldier
Irish Barracks, Tower	1669	25×c.25×8 ft (7.6×c.6.6×2.4 m)	?	?
Plymouth Citadel	1675	15.75×12×8 ft (4.8×3.7×2.4 m)	2	378 cu. ft (10.7 m^3)
Portsmouth	1679	16×14×8 ft (4.9×4.3×2.4 m)	2	448 cu. ft (12.7 m^3)
Tilbury Fort	1680	16×14×?8 ft (4.9×4.3×?2.4 m)	2	448 cu. ft (12.7 m^3)
St Mary's, Scilly (proposed)	1715	13×12.5×7.5 ft (4×3.8×2.3 m)	2	305 cu. ft (8.6 m^3)
Pendennis Castle (proposed)	1715	12.75×12.75×8 ft (3.9×3.9×2.4 m)	2	325 cu. ft (9.2 m^3)
Inverness (proposed)	1716	14×14×?8 ft (4.3×4.3×?2.4 m)	4	196 cu. ft (5.6 m^3)
Berwick	1717	20×18×?9 ft (6.1×5.5×?2.7 m)	4	405 cu. ft (11.5 m^3)
Portsmouth (proposed)	1718	18×17×?9 ft (5.5×5.2×?2.7 m)	?4	344 cu. ft (9.7 m^3)
Upnor	1719	18×17×?9 ft (5.5×5.2×?2.7 m)	?4	344 cu. ft (9.7 m^3)
Bernera/Ruthven	1720	18×17×9 ft (5.5×5.2×2.7 m)	5	275 cu. ft (7.8 m^3)
Dover Castle	1745	18×c.16×? ft (5.5×c.4.9×? m)	?	?
Inverness (proposed)	1747	25×15×8 ft (7.6×4.6×2.4 m)	6	250 cu. ft (7.1 m^3)
Inverness casemates (proposed)	1747	30×12×12 ft (9.1×3.7×3.7 m)	5	432 cu. ft (12.2 m^3)

Note: The Report of the Royal Commission on Barracks of 1861 recommended that each soldier should have 600 cu. ft (17 m^3) of space, but found that this amount of accommodation was quite exceptional. It was admitted that many soldiers had less than 400 cu. ft (11.3 m^3), while in some contemporary barracks the figure was less than 250 cu. ft (7.1 m^3).

Chapter Two
1714–1750: 'No Standing Armies'

In October 1691, the besieged Jacobite army in the citadel at Limerick finally surrendered to King William's army, thus ending formal resistance to English Protestant rule. The Dutch commander, Baron van Ginkel, immediately asked for barracks and stables to be built without loss of time.[1] The need to take control of the island, inhibit local risings and protect the Protestant capital at Dublin required a substantial standing army to be kept on. Unhindered by the ideological objections to barracks which existed in England, William continued the practice begun in Ireland by Cromwell, and ordered a network of barracks connecting the six main Irish garrisons.

The King had a study made of where they would most usefully be located, and in 1697 the Dublin Parliament voted the first of a series of Acts authorizing and funding their construction. The early work was undertaken by Sir William Robinson, who held the patents of Engineer General and Surveyor General until 1700. In that year, a completely new administrative structure was created to oversee the task. Two barracks commissions were established by patents from the King. The first held the legal title to the barracks, as the Irish Board of Ordnance did to the island's forts and castles. Overriding any objections which the Catholic majority might have had to the presence of an English standing army of occupation, the patent cheerfully announced:

'Whereas, for the ease of our subjects of our Kingdom of Ireland from the charge and trouble of quartering the several troops and companies of our army there, and for the lodging and receiving such troops and companies, and securing the dangerous passages and fastnesses from Toryes and Rapparees, we have directed the building of convenient barracks and houses in our Kingdom of Ireland.' [2]

The second and much larger commission became known as the Barracks Board and consisted of 20 Overseers of Barracks. It was responsible for new construction, as well as the maintenance of the new network. This body included members of the legal and military establishment of Protestant Dublin, including the three Lord Justices, the Lord Chancellor and Attorney General as well as the holders of all the key military administrative posts. But the man responsible for the design and construction of the barracks was Robinson's successor, the Chief Engineer, Captain Thomas Burgh. After the Irish war, Burgh had served as a member of the Irish Establishment of Engineers in Flanders between 1692 and 1695. He had therefore experienced French, Dutch and Spanish military engineering at first hand, and had apparently worked closely with one of the two great military engineers of the age, the Dutch Baron van Coehorn.[3] In 1700, aged 30, Burgh combined the posts of Surveyor General for the King's Works and Chief Engineer and Director General of Fortifications for the Irish Board of Ordnance, as well as architect of the new Overseers of Barracks.

In the year of Burgh's appointment, 1700, the Irish Parliament approved the erection of an enormous new barracks in Dublin. This was unprecedented in character, comparable only in its sense of style and ambition to the royal military hospitals of the late seventeenth century (see Figures 25 and 26). The strong Dutch connection provides support for the theory that there was a direct transfer of Continental experience from the Low Countries to Ireland, for although individual barrack complexes

---

[1] Van Ginkel wrote to Lord Coningsby requesting barracks be built at Athlone, and for 300 infantrymen at Banagher. PRONI D608/12/104A.

[2] Quoted in Watson (1954), p.135. 'Toryes' were Roman Catholic outlaws who attacked Protestant settlers. 'Rapparees' were irregular Irish looters and plunderers.

Figure 25 The Royal Hospital, Kilmainham, Dublin (1680–84), designed by Sir William Robinson to house veterans after the example of Louis XIV's Hôtel des Invalides (1670) in Paris.

Figure 26 Chelsea Hospital, London (1682–91). Wren's plan follows the claustral or collegiate approach of Kilmainham, though one side was open to the river. The royal military hospitals were built on a scale and magnificence never approached by barracks.

were already under construction, the new work broke new ground in its size and planning. It became known as the Grand Barracks c.1750, as the Royal Barracks from c.1803, and the Collins Barracks in 1922, when, along with all the other British barracks taken over by the Irish Free State, it was given a new name free of past associations.

The site chosen was triangular, defined by the north bank of the River Liffey and a road, between the built-up part of Dublin and Phoenix Park.[4] A large, open-sided quadrangle, Royal Square, was laid out, followed by matching, half-size quadrangles: Little Square (later Brunswick Square) to the east in 1704 and Horse Square (later Cavalry Square) to the west in 1706 (see Figure 27). In July 1706, Burgh wrote to the Secretary of State, Lord Southwell, saying: 'he was glad the Duke of Ormond [the landowner] was pleased with his design for the barracks and he wished to know if he should go ahead with the work for another Infantry regiment, as the stone cutters were collected from all parts of Ireland'.[5] To the rear of Little Square, a further half-quadrangle occupied the deep part of the triangle facing Oxmantown Green to the east, called New Square (later Palatine Square).

The barracks was indeed palatial, the largest single building built by the State during King William's reign. The three main elevations to the front squares, each with a central pediment, made up a spectacular palace front, which remained one of the standard views published by Dublin engravers throughout the eighteenth century (see Figures 28–30). When it was completed by 1709, at a cost of £22,863, 'it was regarded as the largest and most complete barracks in Europe'.[6]

The starting point for Burgh's grand new project would have been the intended capacity of the new buildings: two regiments of infantry and three troops of cavalry. At this time, an infantry regiment and a battalion were more or less synonymous, with an establishment of ten or twelve companies of some fifty privates each with a captain, lieutenant, two sergeants and three corporals, plus a company of grenadiers, making a full complement of about 600 men. The cavalry regiment was a smaller unit, made up of six troops, each of 36 troopers with a captain, lieutenant, cornet, quartermaster, two corporals, a trumpeter, and their horses. The smallest divisions, a troop of cavalry and a company of infantry, were both commanded by a captain. A troop of dragoons was of the same strength and organization, but with a sergeant instead of the quartermaster, and an hautboy (a piper) instead of a drummer. Field and staff officers (for whom there were quarters in the larger barracks, although they

---

[3] In a letter to Edward Southwell, Archbishop William King described Burgh as 'Cohorns [sic] Disciple who had great value for him'. Trinity College Dublin, King to Southwell, 11 March 1711/12, MS 750/4/30v. I am indebted to Dr Edward McParland for this and the previous reference on Burgh's Dutch connections.

[4] Hefferson (1968), p.129; O'Donnell (1973), p.48.

[5] BL Add. MS 9717, ff. 97 and 98.

[6] Watson (1954), p.137. For a garrison of about 1,400 men and horses, this was a per capita expenditure of just over £16 – cheap, at least by the standards established during the major building campaigns of the Napoleonic Wars (PRO Dublin t1/100/184, 185).

1714–1750: 'No Standing Armies'

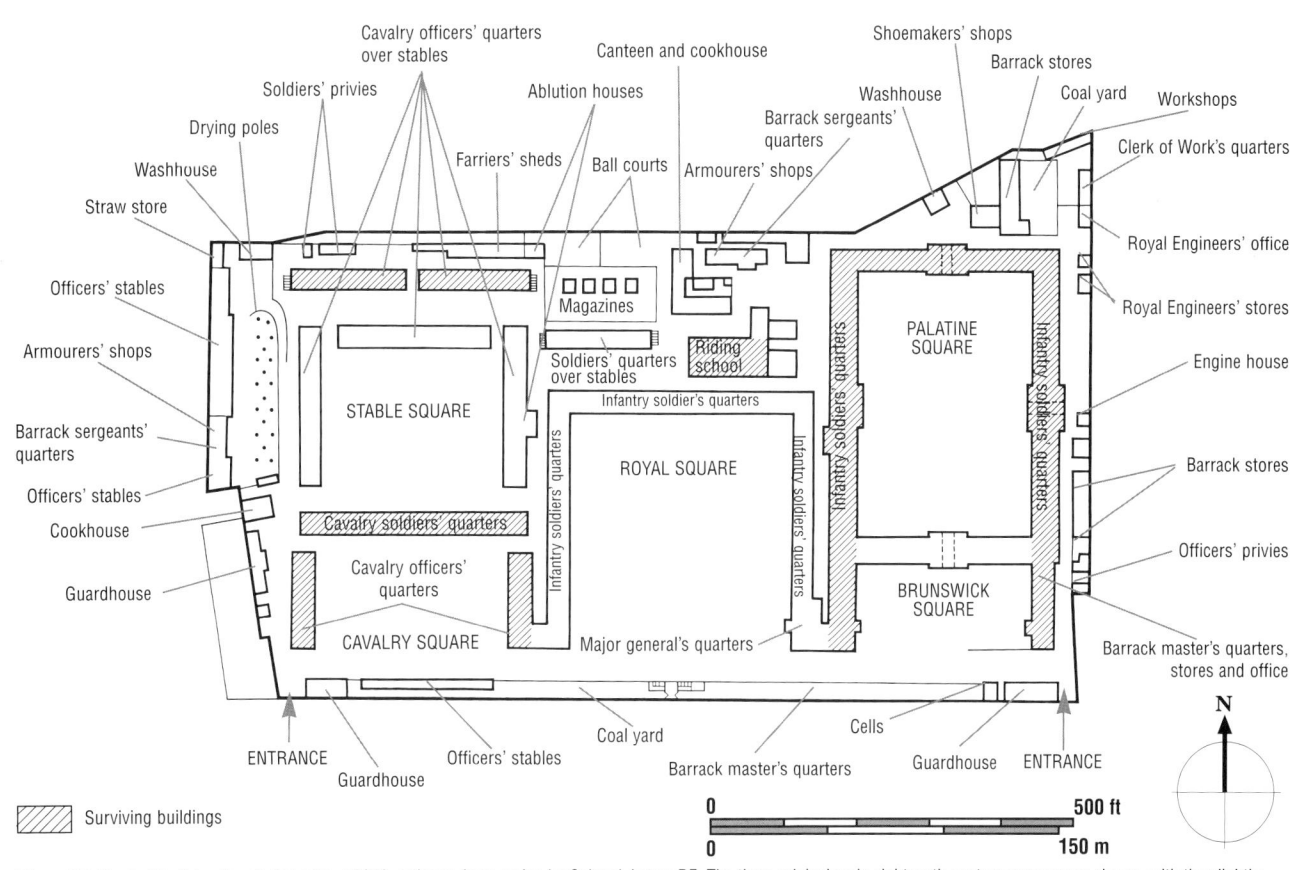

Figure 27 The Dublin (later Royal) Barracks, c.1860, redrawn from a plan by Colonel James RE. The three original early eighteenth-century squares are shown, with the slightly later east side of Palatine Square, and the late eighteenth-century cavalry accommodation and Stable Square to the north-west.

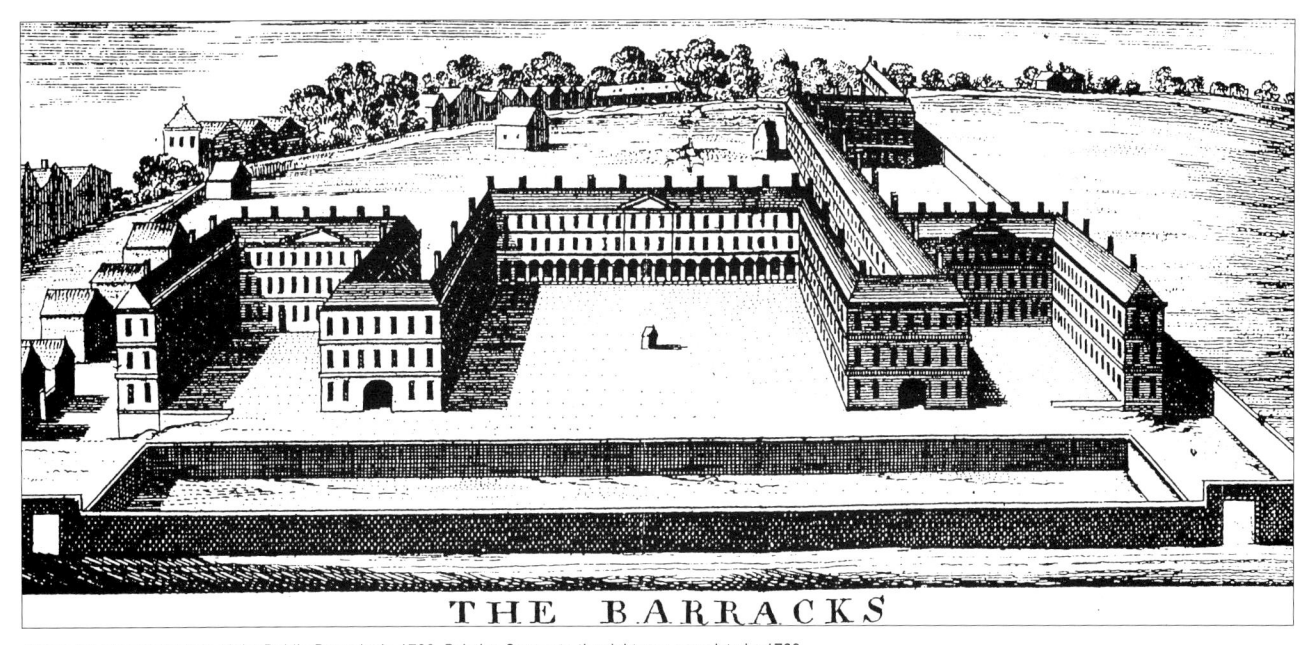

Figure 28 Brooking's view of the Dublin Barracks in 1728. Palatine Square to the right was completed c.1760.

Figure 29 Dublin Barracks. The barrack rooms were originally accessed by passages along the front, above a ground-level colonnade. This now only remains in Palatine Square.

generally preferred to live more comfortably outside the barracks) comprised the colonel of the regiment, the lieutenant colonel, a major, a chaplain and a surgeon.[7]

The earliest interior plan of the barracks, by James Bastide in 1722, indicates what were probably the officers' quarters in the front ends of the three squares and in the two sections facing to the east. This follows the practice of French engineers like Vauban, whose barracks had distinct end pavilions for the senior ranks. Each apartment consisted of a room with two small antechambers off, either side of a stair passage from the entrance. The stables in Horse Square were typical of eighteenth-century cavalry barracks in having ten stalls either side of a passage leading from front to back, each section corresponding to the troopers' rooms above. Nineteenth-century stables tended instead to have stalls backing onto an axial corridor running the length of the building. Bastide shows 150 stalls, equivalent to the three troops which Burgh expected to accommodate.

The completion of the main barracks in its eighteenth-century form was made by closing the fourth, east, side of Palatine Square, c.1767. This new range was deeper, and it seems that the other three sides of the square were rebuilt at the same time, also to a deeper plan. These later buildings

Figure 30 Dublin Barracks. The north side of Palatine Square from the east.

were taller, with a parapet, unlike the moulded eaves detail on Burgh's work. In the mid-nineteenth century, larger windows were inserted into the room over the main archway from the east for a visit by Queen Victoria.[8] After 1790, the road along the rear of the barracks was re-routed and the site squared off. A new stabling block was built, and the old stables in Horse Square were converted for living space or stores and renamed Cavalry Square.

Between 1728 and 1758, a riding school was added behind Royal Square. During the eighteenth century, the widest trussed roofs in Europe were built to span riding schools. In one exceptional instance at Darmstadt in Prussia, built in 1771, the school had trusses 147.6 feet (45 metres) wide, a span which remained the greatest in Europe until

[7] Kerrigan (1985), p.100.
[8] D.L. Swan, *History of the Development of Collins Barracks, 1702–1992*, Report for the Office of Public Works (Dublin 1994); F. McCann, 'Collins Barracks', unpublished diploma thesis, Institute of Professional Valuers and Auctioneers (Dublin 1991).

the roofs over the shipbuilding slips in the British royal dockyards were erected soon after 1814. The Dublin school is only about 59 feet (18 metres) across, and the trusses are not visible, but a span of this width would be an important example of eighteenth-century roof technology.[9] The late eighteenth-century riding school at the Libourne Cavalry Barracks in France had a notable roof with arched trusses built up from laminated timber. Laminated beams in a segmental barrel vault span the riding school at the Royal Pavilion, Brighton, built in 1832.

The Williamite network outside Dublin

The rest of the network of barracks was already under construction the year the Limerick defenders surrendered (see Map 1, page 15). A big garrison barracks was built at Athlone in 1697, and was followed by Cork the year after, Nenagh in 1699 and Limerick in 1701; Navan and Drogheda were finished in 1702.[10] The peacetime garrison consisted of up to 14 regiments of foot and six to eight regiments of horse, which were widely dispersed throughout the country.[11] In 1704, there were 30 barracks for the horse, most of them for a single troop, and 43 for one or two companies of foot soldiers. The largest barracks were at Kilkenny, Cork and Waterford in the south, at Galway, Athlone and Dublin in the middle of the country, and in Carrickfergus, north of Belfast, with those at Kilkenny, Dublin, Athlone, Carrickfergus and Portumna providing lodging for both the cavalry and infantry. In addition, there were 30 smaller stations, generally for a single company, which were classed as redoubts, or minor defensible works. Some of the larger infantry barracks were also defensible, having a perimeter curtain wall with projecting corner bastions to cover the sides with musket fire, but many were no more than residential buildings to make up for the lack of inns for billeting, and a far cry from the semi-fortified quarters being erected in Scotland against the Jacobites (see Figure 20, page 23).

Once the builders had finished, each barracks was fitted out and stocked, according to a standard schedule, with bedding, furnishing and utensils appropriate to a troop of horse or dragoons and a company of foot. To each barracks was appointed a barrack master, responsible for keeping it 'fit for the Reception, Dwelling, Quartering and Entertainment of such Officers and Soldiers as shall or may be order'd to Quarter or Reside therin'. Arriving at their new quarters, the officers might expect to find their small rooms furnished with a table and two chairs, a pillared bed with curtains, bed-cords and a mat, a mattress, chequered quilt, feathered bolster, rug and blanket, and a pair of sheets. Two soldiers shared a bed 6 feet (1.8 metres) long by 4 feet (1.2 metres) wide, with a bolster and mat, a pair of blankets and two pairs of sheets, and there was a table and two benches for every six of them. Other than the barrack master and his family, no one else was entitled to reside at the barracks, and the men had to look after their own living arrangements (how far this was obeyed varied with different commanders, the length of stay in an area, and the personal circumstances of the soldiers). Basic utensils were provided, including fire grates, fenders and a coal box, implements to boil and fry food, a few iron candlesticks, and shovels, buckets and wheelbarrows to keep the place clean and sanitary.[12]

The new barracks were built in the centres of towns rather than in open country, emphasizing the intention to dominate the indigenous population and protect the Protestant interest. However, local patronage was also a strong influence, because of the economic advantage brought by the garrison to a settlement.[13] This resulted in a dispersed distribution, one that became increasingly anachronistic as the internal threat of Catholic insurrection diminished. By 1727, the numerous redoubts were occupied by barely half a company each, and many of the smaller barracks had been vacated altogether as the Irish garrison became concentrated in the larger towns.

By the 1760s, with the Catholic population quiescent, the organization and discipline of the army in Ireland had degenerated further. This was despite a system of annual rotation which brought

---

[9] R.J.M. Sutherland, 'Shipbuilding and the Long-Span Roof', paper read to the Newcomen Society (12 April 1989), p.3.
[10] O'Donnell (1973), p.51.
[11] The following section is based on Kerrigan (1995), pp.130–43.
[12] NAM Military MS, vol.133, 21, *Articles of agreement ... between the Overseers of the Barracks ... and William Thomson ...*, 2 February 1715.
[13] Bartlett and Jeffery (1996), p.219.

regiments into one of the six main garrison towns every three years, providing the opportunity to assemble and practise manoeuvres in brigades. Phoenix Park, just beside the Royal Barracks in Dublin, was the British Army's largest exercise ground in the eighteenth century.[14] Nevertheless, even the barracks in sizeable towns like Limerick, Cork, Kinsale and Waterford were in a decayed state. Attempting to improve the situation, Lord Townshend, the Lord Lieutenant, included recommendations for repairing parts of the network in a report on the security of the island. He saw the value of barracks both in strategic terms, for 'the defence of the country and support of the magistrates [and] the suppression of smuggling in Co. Kerry and Co. Down', as well as in the operational benefits which they conferred: 'the convenience of subsistence and assembly of the army [and of] a chain of barracks for regiments sent to Ireland from the north, and their regular movement southwards'.[15]

The Overseers of Barracks continued as a committee to which everyone of military, legal or religious consequence in Dublin was appointed. By 1746, it included the lord lieutenant, two archbishops, all the general officers and all the judges. Predictably, such a body of notables was not very effective, and it failed to fulfil its maintenance duties. The structure was overhauled in 1759, when a revised body, the Barracks Board, was established in place of the old one, and three years later an Ordnance Department, on the lines of the English office, took control of fortifications.[16]

Responsibility for barracks design lay with the Barracks Board's architects: Henry Keene until 1767, and Christopher Myers until 1776. Myers' replacement, William Gibson, attempted to regularize the planning of Irish barracks with a set of standard plans, which the secretary to the Board approved in 1784. These rather idealized layouts were adaptable for up to four companies of infantry, and for one or two troops or a squadron of cavalry, but it is uncertain whether Gibson's plans were ever put into practice.[17]

'A Nest for a Standing Army'

Clearly, the advantages of barracks were understood by everyone, from William III and the administrative and military establishment in Dublin to the engineer officers of the Irish Board of Ordnance. These were based principally on the way in which warfare had been transformed, first in the Low Countries and Germany, by the 'military revolution' of the late-sixteenth and early-seventeenth century. Instead of huge squares of massed pikemen lumbering about battlefields, the new system of fighting was based on linear formations of uniform units firing musket salvoes at one another, with co-ordinated shock action by the cavalry. To achieve this, the soldiers needed to be much more highly trained and disciplined in order to respond automatically and uniformly to the various commands they might receive. Such troops had to spend months and even years learning, practising and perfecting these responses through drill training, and the opportunities for this were enormously enhanced if they were provided with permanent quarters and a convenient space in which to practise. In this respect, barracks life has been likened to 'industrial production, [whereby] greater concentration allowed a much higher degree of control and coordination, and an inbuilt bias toward technical improvements'.[18] Corps cohesion, mutual support and unit identification ('bonding' in modern English) could develop more quickly and strongly within a body of men who lived, ate and slept together as a community than one which only assembled occasionally for the formal muster in a field or village square.

Other operational benefits followed. Orders could be transmitted far more quickly and reliably to a unit assembled in a barrack square than by a messenger sent round the local billets; troops could be maintained where they were needed, according to the geographical circumstances of national security and civil order, and in the context of a garrison army like that in Ireland the soldiers were given a measure of protection which they lacked when billeted in the inns and private houses of the local population.

[14] Ibid., p.222.
[15] Kerrigan (1995), p.143.
[16] McParland (1995), pp.91–101.
[17] PRO WORK38/1–4, *Model plans for Barracks in Ireland*, 4 June 1784.

[18] Jones (1980), p.162.

Yet none of these advantages was thought sufficient for the idea of a system of barracks to be taken up in the rest of the British Isles. Almost a century elapsed after the construction of the Dublin barracks before a start was made on a network in England based on a strategic consideration of national defence or of military logistics. But the reasoning behind the different circumstances in the two islands was the same: 'The crowning argument against the erection of barracks in England was the use to which they were put in Ireland; and it was obvious that the reasons which told for their establishment in the sister isle were conclusive against their adoption here.'[19] Despite the active deployment of the army throughout Britain, its quartering arrangements, inland and away from those few settlements mentioned in Chapter 1, continued to depend on the regulated billeting system established at the Glorious Revolution. For much of the eighteenth century, the issue of military barracks on the British mainland made all members of the propertied classes acutely nervous, with the result that successive governments and the army, while appreciating their potential benefits, avoided it for fear of exciting opposition.

The army and civil order in England

The distribution and movement of the Hanoverian army around the country reflected its priorities as an instrument of foreign war, national defence and support for the civil power. Regular units of infantry and cavalry were constantly passing through the main ports of embarkation bound for Ireland, the Low Countries, France or northern Germany, for India or the American colonies, and for such territories as British arms or commerce picked up for the Crown. The garrison in Britain between 1702 and 1714 varied between 7,300 and 19,000, as troops returned from Flanders.[20] The Royal Artillery and Royal Engineers, supplemented predominantly by Invalid Companies made up of veterans,[21] occupied the coastal fortresses and batteries (though many were depleted or vacant between invasion scares). Both regular and auxiliary forces were marched between these coastal strongholds, chasing smugglers, enforcing the law, and suppressing riot and disturbance in support of the Crown.

The pattern of these movements around the country has been analysed by J.A. Houlding to show both the principal areas in which troops were regularly stationed and the main routes that were taken marching between them.[22] Ireland was effectively occupied as a garrison, with troops permanently stationed there until 1720, as were the Highlands of Scotland until 1750. We have seen that both were provided with permanent barracks, although to a much lesser extent for the anti-Jacobite soldiers in Scotland than for those inhibiting Catholic insurgency in Ireland. Regiments from England plodded north for Scotland from either the barracks in Berwick-upon-Tweed or from Chester Castle, and they sailed for Ireland from the west coast ports of Bristol, Chester, Liverpool or the Clyde. The major embarkation ports for service abroad were Plymouth, Portsmouth and Bristol, followed by London, the Medway towns, Liverpool and Newcastle upon Tyne. Soldiers who survived colonial or Continental tours of duty returned mostly to the first three, followed by Chester, Liverpool, the Clyde or London, depending upon where they were stationed after they got home.

Within England and Wales, 15 'duty areas' have been identified within which one or more regiments were customarily stationed. The length of time spent in each place was determined by the requirements of civil order, and a policy of preventing any over-familiarity developing between troops and local people such as too long a stay might engender. Cornwall and south Devon was one such duty area, with infantry (the terrain was too difficult for mounted troops) being used against smugglers and the unruly tinners. A second took in Bristol, the south Cotswolds and west Wiltshire.

Without a network of barracks on the Irish, French or Spanish models, marching regiments had to be split up into separate, small units which took different routes, hoping to reach their destination at roughly the same time (see Figure 31). Between the duty areas and the ports, the army used nine

---

[19] Bell (1880), p.17.
[20] Chandler and Becket (1994), p.75.
[21] For an account of the formation and use of veteran corps, see M. Mann, 'The Corps of Invalids', *JSAHR*, **66** (1988), pp.5–19.

[22] Houlding (1981), ch.2.

Drill and the barracks square

Victorian gunners drilling within the square at St John's Wood Artillery Barracks.

The square was central to British barracks from the construction of Cromwell's Scottish citadels onwards. The need for a regular, formal space within military quarters arose directly from the re-invention of close-order drill by Prince Maurice of Nassau in the late-sixteenth century. Other European armies, which rapidly copied the Dutch, likewise depended on the discipline and well-rehearsed manoeuvres which were learnt, practised and perfected on some suitable open field. Incorporating a square for drill within the layout of the first barracks was natural. We can assume that the 'piazza' described by contemporaries as forming the centre of Cromwell's seventeenth-century citadel at Leith (see page 7) was for the purpose of practising drill.

With the relative absence of barracks in mainland Britain during the eighteenth century, such formal spaces remained rarities, while drill patterns and manoeuvre practices varied from regiment to regiment and between different commanders. The unification of the British Army's methods coincided with the general construction of its first barracks. It came with the issue of the 1792 Regulations, based on David Dundas's book *Principles of Military Movements*. The complex infantry manoeuvres of the Napoleonic period required up to two years' intense drilling to master fully, and the opportunities for practice were greatly reduced if a unit had first to be assembled from diverse billets around the neighbourhood and brought together in some public place such as that illustrated in Figure 33. Having the soldiers living close by the square within range of a bugle's call made rehearsal much easier.

Drill took up a great deal of the private's day, and even more of that of the recruit's. In the 1850s, an 'awkward squad' made up of clumsy, confused and unfit newcomers was drilled continuously from 6 a.m. until breakfast at 7.45 a.m., from 10 a.m. until 12 noon, and again in the afternoon from 2 p.m. until 4 p.m. They finally fell into bed at tattoo.

As well as mastering the complexities of drill, European armies from the seventeenth century also needed to maintain a high level of corps discipline, solidarity and 'steadiness', to maintain their effectiveness under the stress and disorientation of battle. Another benefit of communal barracks life – conformity to the army's rules and obedience to its officers' instructions – was reinforced by a harsh and brutal punishment regime. Until 1829, a court martial could order a flogging of unlimited length: a form of corporal punishment which on occasion turned into a capital one. Thereafter, the maximum number of lashes was limited to 500 strokes, and by 1846 to 50, and offences punishable by flogging were confined to mutiny, desertion, insubordination, violence, disgraceful conduct and the theft of army property.

Flogging was a lesson for everyone, for the punishment was carried out in the formal theatre of the parade ground, within an inner square formed by the rest of the unit. Lesser punishments were also performed there. 'Drumming out' involved the ritual stripping of the offender's facings and buttons, being marched around the square while the band played the 'Rogue's March', before being kicked out of the barracks gate by the smallest drummer boy, into the arms of the civilian police.

principal marching route corridors: strings of towns and villages, a day's march apart, in which they were billeted while *en route*. Marching could be painfully slow. In 1732, it took nine days for a regiment to be moved in five stages between Bristol and Exeter. From Portsmouth to Carlisle took 52 days in 1752, in 25 stages, with a week's rest at both Newbury and Preston.[23] And at the end of each day's marching, somewhere had to be found for them to eat and pass the night (see Figure 32).

The billeting system

In 1689, in place of the detested and abused free quartering arrangements known as 'roistering', whereby soldiers were imposed directly onto householders, the parliamentary drafters of the first Mutiny Act set down the legal procedure by which they were to be housed and fed in England in future (billeting on private householders remained lawful in Scotland until 1858, and into the twentieth century in Ireland). Quartering and billeting the soldiers was to be the responsibility of local government officials, 'Constables, Tytheringmen, Headboroughs, and other Chief Officers and Magistrates of Cities, Towns and Villages, and other Places in the Kingdom of England, Dominion of Wales, and Town of Berwick upon Tweed, and no others'. Rooms for the officers and soldiers of Their Majesties' Service were to be found by them in 'Inns, Livery Stables, Ale-houses, Victualling-houses, and all Houses selling Brandy, Strong Waters, Sider, or Metheglin by Retail, to be drank in their Houses, and no other, and in no Private Houses whatsoever'. In other words, the granting of an innkeeper's licence carried the obligation to house and victual such soldiers as the local authorities deemed appropriate to the size of the house. The Act then required the local justices of the peace to set 'reasonable prices' for the innkeepers, 'within the compass of the Subsistence Money paid to the Soldiers'. The Act thereby set the civil and economic context in which the army and the country – at least the law-abiding part of it – interacted.

Billets were allocated by justices of the peace or parish constables in the countryside and by town

[23] Ibid., pp.29–36.

Figure 31 Soldiers on a march, an 1805 watercolour by Thomas Rowlandson.

councils or their billet masters in the towns. Publicans were obliged to accept their charges at the rates set for billeting in the 1690s: 4d per day for an infantryman, 6d for a cavalry trooper, and 6d for his horse. Surveys of inns were carried out, both of local areas and nationally, to establish the capacity of the public house network. For example, in 1776 a list of suitable pubs around Chatham was compiled for the billeting officer of the Marines Division. It identified 56 in the nearby villages of Strood, Rochester and Brompton, and grouped them into four classes by the number of men which each could take.

Needless to say, the billeting system worked well enough in peacetime, during periods when food prices were low, and in areas which sustained sufficient public houses for the troops quartered locally. However, in wartime, when there were many more soldiers, especially in the embarkation ports and garrisons, or later in the century when the auxiliary militia forces were called up, the inns became overcrowded. When food prices were high, the innkeepers could not afford to feed the soldiers on the money the law allowed. Following a march from Canterbury to Devizes in 1756, one lieutenant colonel wrote: 'We have ruined half the public houses upon the march, because they have quartered us in villages too poor to feed us without destruction to themselves.'[24] Innkeepers repeatedly pleaded in petitions to Parliament for relief from the ruinous expense of billeting during the Seven Years War, the American War, and most of all in the long struggle with France at the end of the eighteenth century. High prices during 1794–6 and again during 1799–1801 pushed the finances of the system into severe imbalance, and innkeepers either went under or gave up their licences. One of hundreds of petitions came in March 1800 from rural Market Harborough, and took the form of a circular letter from all the innkeepers in every market town in the kingdom. It claimed that prices were causing a loss

---

[24] Quoted in Houlding (1981), p.39.

Figure 32 The arrival of a company of militia at an inn, by Thomas Rowlandson, c.1790.

of a shilling a day per man billeted, and proposed a parish tax to help pay for the army's upkeep.[25]

Nor was the billeting system of great benefit to the soldiers or to the army itself. A life endlessly marching between a series of inns and camps eroded the cohesion of the unit and generated friction between soldiers and the citizenry who were forced to put up with them. Bills for extended stays were frequently left unpaid, leaving the justices of the peace to settle disputes with the aggrieved publicans. Rates of army pay remained low, and part-time jobs, businesses or illegal activities were widespread among the soldiers as a means of supplementing a meagre income. As a result, recruits were commonly drawn only from those with no alternative to destitution and starvation except to enlist. At the outbreak of war, a reservoir of unemployed veterans assisted the initial filling of the rolls, but thereafter, numerous semi-legal expedients verging on kidnapping were resorted to by the recruitment parties.

'No Standing Armies': constitutional objections to barracks

An obvious response to this developing framework of military dispersion and circulation, and the friction which it caused, would have been to construct a network of permanent barracks across Britain in which the troops could be properly housed, with all the consequent benefits for discipline, training and so on. Such a project had indeed been proposed in 1697, but apparently foundered for lack of money.[26] However, expenditure was not the main objection to such a scheme. As stated earlier, long after the Glorious Revolution, strong ideological and political anxieties remained about the permanent existence of a full-time, professional army. These harked back to Cromwell's New Model Army (the first standing

[25] PRO HO49/437, *Market Harborough: Notice of Petition*, 8 March 1800.
[26] Clode (1869), p.398.

Figure 33 This watercolour by Thomas Rowlandson, c.1790, of a review in the Market Place, Winchester, shows how, in the absence of barracks, soldiers could be drawn up for parade in public areas.

army in modern English experience), to James II's use of the army (quartering his soldiers on chapels and particular towns to intimidate non-conformists and unsympathetic corporations) and to that of James's exemplar, Louis XIV of France, and the barrack-building absolutists of Europe. Equally exceptional was the fact that in England, the creation of the standing army had not reinforced the power of the king, thereby leading to the triumph of absolutism, as in many Continental States. On the contrary, an absolutist-minded ruler in the person of Charles I had been displaced by Parliament and Oliver Cromwell. The writers of the new constitutional arrangements in 1688 had these unique experiences in mind when drawing up the circumstances under which the army was to be kept on a permanent basis whilst not threatening the sovereignty of Parliament. The result was compromise: a standing army, which was both economically and militarily essential, but no permanent quarters.

Eighteenth-century objections to the building of barracks in England were founded on two sets of arguments, one ideological and the other financial. There were fears that if the suspect standing army was to be allowed to live in separate quarters, it would become distant from the people, over-loyal to its commanders, and potentially an anti-constitutional force in the hands of an ambitious commander (the powerful Duke of Marlborough came to mind) or of rulers intent on overriding Parliament. It was argued that the very inconvenience of billeting meant that the people continued to be aware of the army, and that they would thus continually demand its diminution. In the debate on the annual Mutiny Bill in 1741, the former Whig Secretary of State at War, Lord Pulteney, admitted:

'a standing army in quarters will always be more troublesome to the people than a standing army in barracks; but for this very reason I shall always be for keeping our army in quarters, that the people may be sensible of the fetters which are preparing for them, before such a number can be forged as may be sufficient for shackling them close down to the ground ... If the soldiers were all kept in barracks, the people would be insensible of their numbers and might not, perhaps, think of reducing them by law till the army grows so numerous, and became so closely united, as to be able to support itself against the law.' [27]

In the same debate, General Wade, who built counter-insurgency barracks as well as roads in his pacification of the Highlands, and was as aware as any European officer of their military benefits, complained: 'the people of this kingdom have been taught to associate the idea of Barracks and Slavery so closely together that, like darkness and the Devil, though there be no manner of connection between them, they cannot separate them'.[28] An admirer of Hawksmoor's barracks in Berwick-upon-Tweed observed: 'it would be a vast ease to the Inhabitants in most great Towns if they had them [barracks] everywhere; but English Liberty will never consent to what will seem a Nest for a Standing Army'.[29]

This liberal view of barracks, as the physical manifestation of a potentially autonomous, anti-constitutional armed force, was formally stated by Sir William Blackstone in his influential *Commentaries on the Laws of England*:

'To prevent the executive power from being able to suppress ... armies should come from the people ... as was the case with Rome till Marcus new-modelled the legions by enlisting the rabble of Italy ... The military power ... should be composed of natural subjects ... they should live intermixed with the people; no separate camps, no barracks, no inland fortresses should be allowed.' [30]

Essentially a plea for a citizen militia, this reference to barracks, though only a passing one, was repeatedly quoted by Opposition politicians when the Government started to build them in earnest in the early 1790s.

Blackstone's anxiety was a reflection of political reality. Both the insecure Hanoverian dynasty and the Whig ministry of Walpole were kept in power by the extensive use of the army, a *de facto* police force, to suppress dissent and harass opponents.[31] The principal legal justification for employing soldiers against civilians was the Riot Act of 1715, which indemnified soldiers from prosecution for murder in the event of someone being killed once a magistrate had read the Riot Act to an unruly crowd of more than 12. Troops were regularly used to subdue the frequent riots provoked by unpopular trials, industrial disputes or high food prices, and were frequently in conflict with ordinary people through the enforcement of the Game Laws. For the non-enfranchised population, the main options for political involvement were petitions for the lettered and riots for the rest. Civil disturbance became so common that 'the student of urban society in the eighteenth century is tempted to believe that with almost any public event involving the collection of crowds, there was the strong likelihood of a riot'.[32] Corruption, gerrymandering and coercion were institutionalized by Walpole's regime. With the militia unreliable and more prone to side with rioters than were regular troops, the State continued to be reliant on the army until well after the 1745 Jacobite invasion.[33]

The second argument against building barracks for the home forces was simply the increased costs

---

[27] Parliamentary History, 11 (1739–41), Debate on the Quartering of Soldiers, p.1,447.
[28] Ibid., p.1,442. This is the most frequently quoted remark on English barracks, and is always taken out of context to imply that Wade was opposed to them, which was not the case.
[29] Quoted in M.H. Crake, 'An Account of the Barracks at Berwick-upon-Tweed and Other Ancient Buildings', *Borderers' Chronicle*, 29 (1955), p.421.
[30] W. Blackstone, *Commentaries on the Laws of England*, 4th edn (Dublin 1771), 1, pp.413–14. The comparison with Rome would have struck a chord with the elite of the expanding British Empire, who were coming to see themselves as the inheritors of the Roman Republic and had no wish to be occluded by a British Caesar.
[31] 'Police' was a term used for the army in its domestic role long before a separate police force was established, as in Vanbrugh's reference to the infantry barracks at Berwick-upon-Tweed as 'Hawksmoor's brave designs for the police'. See Hewlings (1993).
[32] T. Hayter, *The Crowd in Mid-Georgian England* (London 1978), p.40.
[33] For accounts of the violence employed by the State, see I. Gilmour, *Riot, Risings and Revolution* (London 1992), pp.135–46; and C. Emsley, 'The Military and Popular Disorder in England, 1790–1801', *JSAHR*, 61 (1983), pp.98–117.

involved. The Whigs' standing army was viewed as an onerous burden by the tax-paying Tory country gentry. The *Gentleman's Magazine* wrote of public attitudes toward the army in 1743: 'the landlord looks upon the soldier as an intruder forced into his house, and rioting in sloth at his expense; and the farmer and the manufacturer have learned to call the army the vermin of the land, the caterpillars of the nation, and the devourers of other men's industry, the enemies of liberty and the slaves of the continent'.[34]

The problem was, 'the state wanted the services and flexibility of a standing army but lacked the resources to pay for it'.[35] To keep the cost down, the servicing of the army was in effect subcontracted to the officers to run as a business as well as they could. The billeting system kept down part of the expense of keeping a standing army by passing it on to publicans and innkeepers (and thence to the drinking public), who were obliged to accept it as one of the overheads that came with having a licence. As much was acknowledged in 1794 by the Secretary at War, who referred to billeting as: 'an old abuse ... [whereby] the soldiers of the state were not provided at the expense of the state but at the cost of a particular class of inhabitant', namely the publicans.[36]

As memories of James II's use of the army faded, the predominant objection to barracks, therefore, became less and less a reverence for traditional English liberties and more a reluctance to sanction the level of capital spending that would have been entailed. For instance, from 1739, the army never numbered less than 18,000 men, excluding those in Ireland. This figure would have equated to about a dozen large complexes, each the size of the Royal Barracks in Dublin.

The view of the basic constitutional impropriety of barracks expressed by Walpole's opponents, revived by those of Pitt fifty years later and restated by nineteenth-century army historians like Clode, was probably felt very slightly, if at all, by those who actually had to put up, and put up with, the soldiers at first hand. Requests for barracks to be built, as well as appeals for financial relief, came from corporations and from associations of innkeepers alike, especially in towns like Chester and Carlisle which were regularly disrupted by ill-paid and disorderly troops, and whose innkeepers grieved over unpaid bills and loss of business. Those of Berwick-upon-Tweed were uniquely successful in this respect, since their requests were granted. There, the need to ease the free movement of troops in the most overcrowded military town in Britain provided the impetus to the decision to build after the shock of the 1715 Rising.[37] The citizens of Edinburgh, who made a similar appeal at the same time, were less fortunate.[38]

In the 1741 Mutiny Bill debate quoted above, General Wade went on to put what was by then an accepted military argument for barracks in England, while admitting that he was banging his head against a mossy wall of prejudice:

'As to the inconveniences and dangers we have been frightened with in this debate, they do not at all affect me, because I take them to be all chimerical ... I could never yet conceive how barracks can be thought inconsistent with the liberties of the people ... an army in quarters is much more inconvenient and troublesome to the people, and the soldiers not so easily kept to their duty, as when they are in barracks; and therefore not only as a friend to discipline in the army, but as a friend to the people, I should choose to have our troops always lodged in barracks, when there is no occasion for having them in a camp.' [39]

---

[34] *Gentleman's Magazine* (1743), p.34.
[35] Chandler and Becket (1994), p.62.
[36] Parliamentary History, *32* (1795–97), p.934.
[37] Even so, the fitting out was never properly completed, and the barracks was soon also overcrowded: see Tabraham and Grove (1995), p.57.
[38] Warrant Books, *52* (1719), p.34; *55* (1729), p.314.
[39] Parliamentary History, *32* (1795–7), p.1,442.

Chapter Three
1750–1792: 'Out of Reach of Revolutionary Contagion'

George III came to the throne in 1760, the third Hanoverian monarch, but the first to be born in Britain. Four sovereigns removed from the anxieties surrounding the Glorious Revolution, and with a settled constitutional position, the first half of his reign witnessed a slow evaporation of the hostility to barracks for the army, and an acceptance of the views of professional soldiers like General Wade (see Chapter Two) concerning their strategic and operational value.

Not that there was any explicit change of policy. An anonymous pamphleteer writing in 1756 who proposed a chain of barracks along the marching routes of England – to 'disencumber ... publicans, restore discipline to the Army, and a right understanding between soldiers and the people' – had to admit 'how much the weight of opinion is against me'.[1] Blackstone's estimation of the political dangers of 'barracks [and] inland fortresses' was not published until 1769. Billeting remained the normal means of accommodating soldiers, at least throughout England and Wales, until the next century. Nevertheless, in the 1750s money was provided for a huge strategic barracks in the Highlands and for the troops guarding the principal naval dockyards, and in the succeeding decades two of the smaller corps, the Royal Marines and the Royal Artillery, were put into barracks to prevent an erosion of their effectiveness. By the 1790s, political opinion had come to support the military perspective sufficiently for the Prime Minister to sanction the building of the first strategic barracks for maintaining order in England – for cavalry units in the industrial towns – and these formed the blueprint for the national programme of barracks which was to follow.

Fort George, Ardersier

The garrisons and fortifications built in the Highlands during the first decades of the eighteenth century had proved ineffective in inhibiting the formation of Prince Charles Edward Stewart's army, which, even with its feeble artillery train, had been able to capture the forts built by General Wade at Inverness Castle and at the head of Loch Ness.[2] After Culloden (1746), and with war continuing against France, the English determined on a much larger and more strongly held northern presence to prevent a repetition of the scare suffered by the King and Government in London the previous year.

The instrument of this policy was to be a huge new barracks right in the centre of the Highlands, protected by a massive, modern fortification. The new Fort George was designed by William Skinner, the Ordnance Board's Chief Engineer and subsequently the first governor of the fort. Although the first intention had been to rebuild the earlier fort at Inverness, Skinner decided on a larger work, to be situated to the north of the town on a short spit of land projecting into the Moray Firth (see Figures 34 and 35, page 96). The bastioned trace which protected the barracks formed a long, narrow triangle, with the defences concentrated on the narrow landward end, and protected on the other two sides by water. The huge earthworks and their masonry facing had largely been completed when the authorities, alarmed by a French invasion scare, hastily armed the fort in 1759.

What made Fort George remarkable in a British context was the size of the garrison and the barracks built to accommodate it. Fort Cumberland, near Portsmouth, which was completed in 1747, had

---

[1] BL 1568/2626. *Reasons for building barracks ...* (London 1756).
[2] MacIvor (1976), pp.410–13.

Figure 36 Fort George, stable interior.

barracks for barely a hundred men.[3] The largest contemporary British fort overseas was Fort Townshend, on the Newfoundland coast, which was completed in 1780 and accommodated a hundred gunners and a little less than 300 infantrymen.[4] The barracks and fortifications at Fort George were begun in 1753, with the intention of housing two whole infantry battalions of 1,600 men. Although other European powers, especially the French, had built larger forts on the Continent and overseas, the new Highlands barracks was by far the largest fortified works under British control.

The barracks for the garrison formed two large, U-shaped ranges enclosing a barrack square (see Figure 37). The officers were accommodated in the pedimented sections at the ends of each block and in the middle, thereby dividing the men's barracks into four. Each officer had a square room with a small antechamber off. The lower ranks occupied sections like separate terraced houses, apparently each unit for a company. Eight men shared a small, square room furnished with four double beds, with a door into the central corridor on one side, and with a single window on the other.

As was usual, the fort contained separate accommodation, apart from the barracks of the more transient infantry garrison, for the units of the gunners who manned the artillery defences. This stood to the west, in two ranges facing across the parade ground towards the entrance to the fort. The two piles had an arcaded walkway along the front, with the governor's house at one end and the lieutenant governor's house at the other. To the east, on the seaward side of the barracks, were two large ordnance stores for guns, carriages, buckets, ropes and the paraphernalia of artillery. Behind these stood the provisions store, with the fort's own bakehouse and brewhouse, and houses for the permanent staff, the barrack master, baker and brewer. Plans for workshops for the fort carpenter, smith and wheelwright were drawn up in 1762, and a small chapel was added in the easternmost end of the fort, surrounded by the sea.[5]

The construction of this huge fortress served to put an end to any thought of French-assisted insurgency in the Highlands, and emphasized, with its glowering range of barracks, the manpower commitment that the British Army was making to stamp out Jacobitism once and for all. This was underlined by the huge cost which the State incurred – £200,000, twice Skinner's original estimate. James Boswell, visiting with Dr Johnson in 1773, found the juxtaposition of the comfort and refined company he found at the Governor's House and the huge fort on its 'barren sandy point' dreamlike.[6] The quadrangular, claustral layout of the barracks – similar to the Royal Barracks in Dublin – can also be interpreted as an attempt to use the form of the communal quarters to reinforce the sense of collective identification, and help dispel the feeling of isolation of the alien English garrison on its cold and lonely peninsula.

---

[3] Magrath (1992), p.7.
[4] PRO WO55/2269/4, *Plan of Fort Townshend, St John's Newfoundland*. The fort included a long barracks with a typical Ordnance Board plan, including officers in the ends, a separate quarters for the company of artillerymen, and a house for the governor of the fort, as well as a guardhouse, bakehouse, ordnance store and a provisions store for 400 men for twelve months.
[5] MacIvor (1976), pp.478–80.
[6] Ibid., p.478.

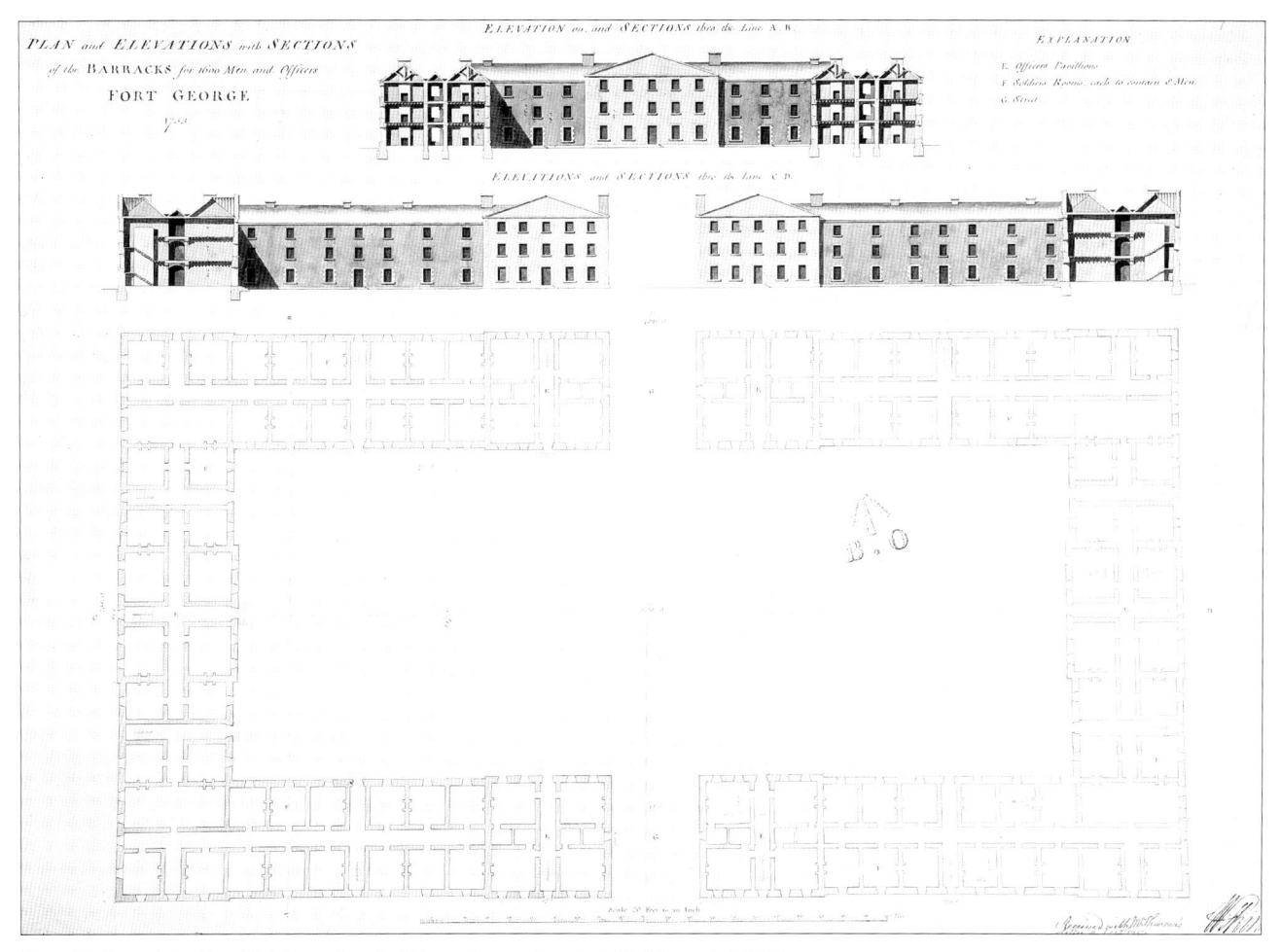

Figure 37 Plan and elevation of Fort George Barracks. This was drawn at the outset of building work, in 1753.

The impact of the Seven Years War on the dockyard towns

In the first four years of the Seven Years War, from 1756 to 1759, Ordnance Board engineers also designed large, new, permanent quarters for the garrisons protecting the royal naval dockyards. In the first strategic revision of the nation's defences since Marlborough, half a century earlier, so-called 'Lines' of regular, bastioned earthworks were built enclosing the dockyards and their surrounding ground, and new barracks were constructed within them. Lines provided protection to six defensible Squares close to Plymouth Dock (see Figure 38, page 97), the small settlement growing against the dockyard; for a new barracks at Hilsea, behind the entrance to Portsea Island (the Portsbridge Redoubt); and for a large, permanent barracks above the dockyard at Chatham.[7]

What were the reasons for this softening in Government policy towards barracks? The first was the pressure on the dockyard towns caused by the fluctuating tides of regulars, militiamen, seamen and marines, as well as the resident population of dockyard workers, competing for living room outside the walls of the dockyards. Space had also to be found in billets or in camps for periodic surges of population as troop ships returned or regiments marched in.

To add to the pressure on dockyard billets, in 1757

---

[7] PRO WO55/2281(2), *Index to the Board of Ordnance Drawings*.

the Prime Minister, William Pitt the Elder, reorganized the militia. This highly unpopular measure made supplying militiamen a county obligation: 32,000 men were sought between the ages of 18 and 45, to be selected by ballot and paid for out of the rates. They were required to go through one month's training each year, under the officership of the local gentry. In time of war, they could be called up, or 'embodied', which meant they became subject to military discipline. As a civil defence force, they could not be ordered overseas, but they could be used to defend the dockyards, thus freeing regulars for foreign service. In December 1759, during the second and more serious invasion scare of the Seven Years War, more than 18,000 militiamen were embodied. Plymouth was full of soldiers, with a garrison of 2,060 men in two battalions, and small incidents or misunderstandings regularly escalated into fighting. One involving the new barracks in Plymouth Dock occurred when two of the Squares were attacked by men of the Duke of Bedford's Militia, after one of their sergeants was arrested. Whilst demonstrating the strong corps loyalty natural within units of countrymen, the lack of military discipline also showed why the army was keen for the better regulation and management which life within barracks offered.[8]

In 1781, during the American War, the area was again groaning under the numbers of quartered troops, with over 8,000 men in arms around Plymouth and the dockyard. The Citadel was defended by 100 infantrymen and 300 Invalids. The recently completed barracks near the dockyard held 100 artillerymen, 350 infantry, and two militia regiments numbering over 1,100 men; three more militia regiments were encamped across the Hamoaze on Maker Heights, and an even larger militia camp with two brigades of 1,960 and 2,160 men each was on Roborough Down, the other traditional camping ground in the area.[9]

A further development adding to the congestion in the dockyard towns was the creation of permanent Marines corps. Until 1755, marine soldiers had been drawn from infantry regiments of the line; they served on ships under the split administration of the army and navy, and were disbanded or absorbed back into the army when they returned home. That year, the Royal Marines were established on a permanent basis in three Grand Divisions based, naturally, at the naval towns of Plymouth, Portsmouth and Chatham. The division quartered in Portsmouth consisted of 2,200 men, plus their officers. Although about two-thirds were expected to be at sea at any one time, this still left over 700 men billeted in the town. At Plymouth Dock, they took over one of the new Squares. In Chatham, they also had to borrow space from the Ordnance Board. The Commander of the Marine Division there wrote to the Master General in 1764 to ask that barracks space be made available for 500 men and their officers, 'so as to keep the Quarters of the Land and Marine forces separate and distinct'.[10]

Discipline was therefore a persistent problem in the dockyard towns for the military, naval and civil authorities. There were frequent cases of desertion, of misdemeanours committed by individual soldiers, particularly caused by drunkenness, of conflict between discharged sailors, Marine regiments and army units passing through, and between all three and workers in the dockyards. In an incident in Chatham in 1764, soldiers had to be called to sort out a fight between marines and dockyard workers over the bundles of offcuts which were the shipwrights' meagre perquisite, and which were coveted by the marines for warming their quarters.[11] In 1758, the son of General James Wolfe, himself a brigadier in the infantry, wrote evocatively to the Master General of the Ordnance describing the chaos in Portsmouth:

'The condition of the troops that compose this garrison (or rather vagabonds that stroll about in dirty red clothes from one gin-shop to another) exceeds all belief. There is not the least shadow of discipline, care or attention. Disorderly soldiers of different regiments are collected here: some from the ships, others from the hospital, some waiting to embark – dirty, drunken, insolent rascals, improved by the hellish nature of the place, where every kind of corruption, immorality, and looseness is carried to excess; it is a sink of the lowest and most abominable of vices.' [12]

---

[8] R. Whitworth, *Lord Ligonier and the British Army, 1702–1770* (Oxford 1958), p.301.
[9] P. Hatchett, *JSAHR*, **52** (1974), p.87.
[10] Quoted in Blumberg and Field (1935), p.205.

[11] Blumberg and Field (1935), p.208.
[12] B. Willson, *The Life and Times of James Wolfe* (London 1909), p.357, quoted in Lowe (1990), p.357.

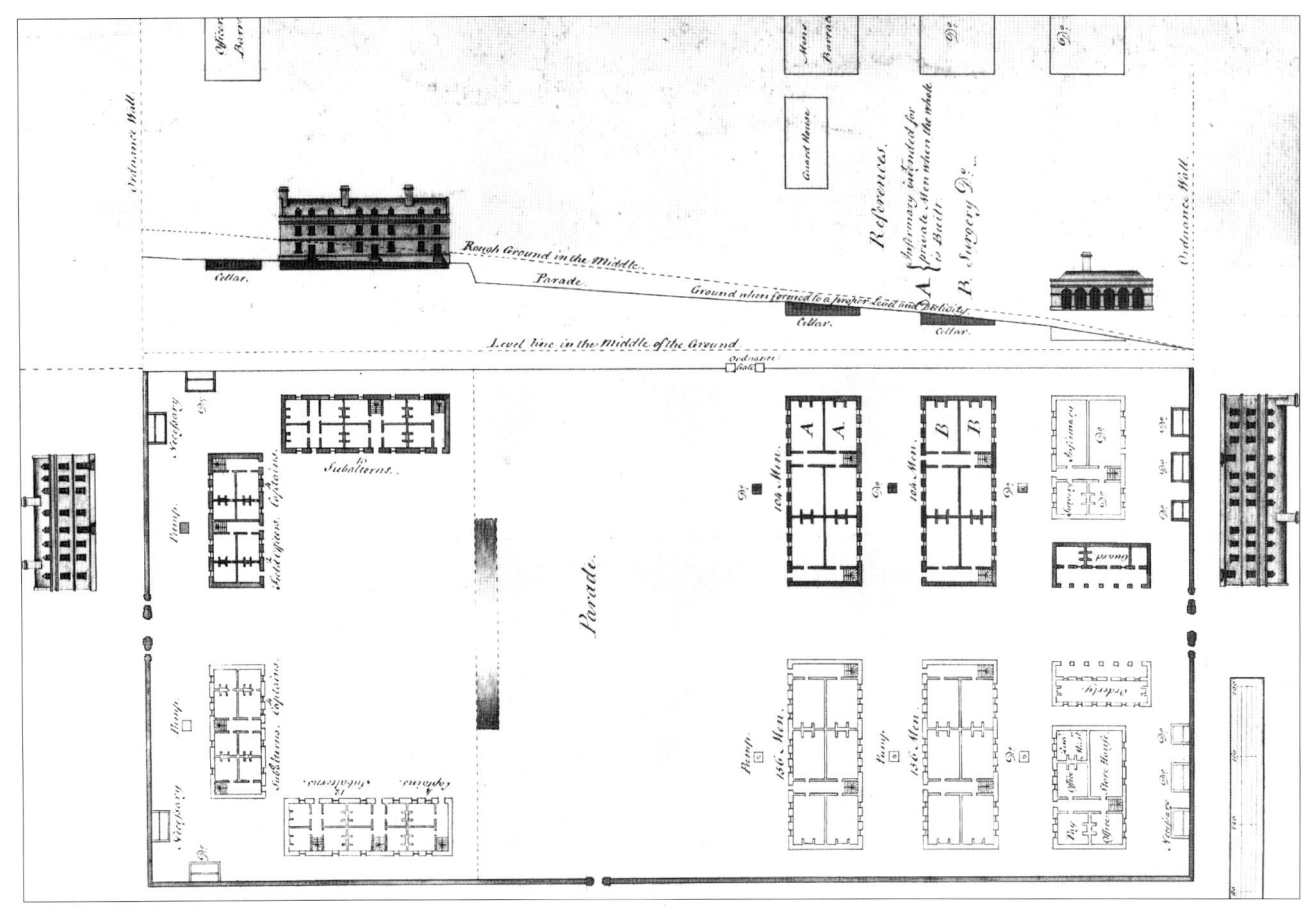

Figure 39 Chatham Infantry Barracks. The ramp between the upper and lower sections is shown across the centre. It and one of the guardhouses still remain.

The first dockyard barracks for the infantry

The Lines at Chatham needed to enclose the high ground to the east of the dockyard. In 1756, they were partly completed, and five regiments of foot – the 25th, 36th, 37th, 30th and 5th – were encamped within them on the heights at Brompton, overlooking the dockyard and the River Medway.[13] The Lines were planned by Captain Hugh Debbeig, and the work was supervised by Captain John Peter Desmaretz, the Architect of the Ordnance who probably drew up plans for the new barracks the following year.

The site chosen was at the base of a sharp slope across the road from the entrance to the naval dockyard. A rectangular compound was formed by a tall brick wall, parts of which still survive, and the ground was levelled to form the Lower Barracks, where the men's quarters were, and the Upper Barracks, containing the officers' accommodation. A double ramp provided access between the two (see Figure 39). The Board used a standard barracks unit similar to that at Berwick-upon-Tweed, in this instance for 84 men, which it massed in multiples of three. Externally, they resembled a contemporary terrace of houses, each one three storeys high and three windows wide, although without the overall unifying design employed at Berwick-upon-Tweed. Back-to-back eight-bed rooms opened off a through stair passage, 27 feet (8.2 metres) wide by 18 feet (5.5 metres) deep – roughly the same volumetric space as was allotted in the Ordnance's Scottish barracks of the 1720s. Standard room sizes were followed, appropriate to the rank of the occupant. Field officers were allowed four rooms, a garret for

[13] BL K Top 16-40, 1756. *Plan of the Intrenchment [sic] Including HM Dockyard and Ordnance Wharf at Chatham.*

their servant, and a cellar kitchen. Captains had two rooms and one for a servant, and subalterns a single chamber and a garret for a servant.[14]

Guardhouses, of a standard Ordnance design identical to those at Fort George, flanked the entrance, with the pay office and store to one side and the infirmary to the other. In the Upper Barracks were four separate blocks for two field officers, 12 captains and 37 subalterns. Externally, the officers' and other ranks' barracks were identical apart from more generous fenestration to the larger rooms of the higher ranks' section, of two storeys with a steep roof for the garrets; their internal planning was also very similar.

The Lower Barracks' capacity in 1794 was reported to be 864, 784 and 480 men in three terraces, at the usual density of 16 to a room in double beds, and a further eight men were lodged in each garret.[15] Fragments of the old buildings can also still be found within the inter-war rebuilding of what is now the Kitchener Barracks, with the steep roofs and central valley characteristic of the Ordnance Board's eighteenth-century housing.[16]

The new barracks built by the Board at Plymouth Dock were completely different in conception to those at Chatham. The Board laid out the Devonport Lines between 1758 and 1763 to protect the landward approach to the isolated dockyard. Inside them, it built six defensible barracks or 'Squares'. Each formed a quadrangle with bastions on opposite corners so that the sides could be covered by musket fire. The two larger ones at the north and south ends, Ligonier and Frederick Squares, were for four companies each and were built of stone. The four between, Marlborough, Granby, George and Cumberland, were more flimsily constructed of a timber frame filled with 'brick nog', and each held three companies. They were drawn up for the Ordnance Board by Major John Archer.[17] 'Officers and men shared each square, living up separate staircase entries in nearly identical, 25 feet [7.6 metres] by 16 feet [4.9 metres] rooms. The soldiers slept 14 to a room and two to a bed, while the officers apportioned a large share of rooms for themselves, their mess and their servants.'[18]

At Portsmouth, the main landward approach by which the dockyard could be threatened crossed a narrow causeway over Portsea Lake. In 1756, the Ordnance Divisional Engineer, William Dundas, drew up plans 'showing the situation of the Batteries and Line erected for the Defence of that Pass, also the Pavillions [sic] of Barracks to contain two battalions'.[19] These were long, wooden huts, an early instance of a type of semi-permanent barracks which was later very widely used for British military quarters. They were arranged in two groups of eight blocks along the south side of a square, with 16 paired blocks, presumably for the officers and stores, on the other three sides. By the 1850s, Hilsea was used by the Artillery, and one of the huts was still occupied. Apart from some small and antiquated quarters dating from the late seventeenth century known as Colewort Barracks, and the gunners' barracks on the Gunwharf which the Ordnance Board had built for the artillery in the 1720s, Portsmouth remained very poorly supplied with permanent military quarters until after the Napoleonic Wars.

Royal Marines barracks

The three new Royal Marines divisions created in 1755 initially had to make do with billets in the usual 'Inns, Livery Stables, Ale-houses, Victualling-houses and all Houses of Persons selling Brandy, Strong Waters, Cyder or Metheglin', the 1755 Marine Mutiny Act continuing to use the seventeenth-century designation for permitted quarters.[20]

The Marines, however, were soon to become the first complete British corps to be given their own barracks. These were provided in Portsmouth by 1765, in Chatham by 1780, and in Plymouth a year later. That the Marines should be so favoured

---

[14] NAM 8409-12. *Infantry barracks at Chatham*, 1757.
[15] RE Library, *Letter Books*, 30 October 1794.
[16] RE Library, 420/SE/2, *Chatham barracks*; RE Library 12303, *History of early military developments in the Medway Towns*.
[17] BL K Top 11-78-l, 1756; PRO WO55/2281. *Board of Ordnance plans of Plymouth barracks*.
[18] Breihan (1990b), p.34.
[19] BL K Top 14-19 and 20. *Plan of Portsea Lake showing the situation of the Batteries and Line erected of the Defence of that Pass ...*
[20] Lowe (1990), p.xv. The following section is based on this careful account of the establishment and routine at the Portsmouth Marines Barracks.

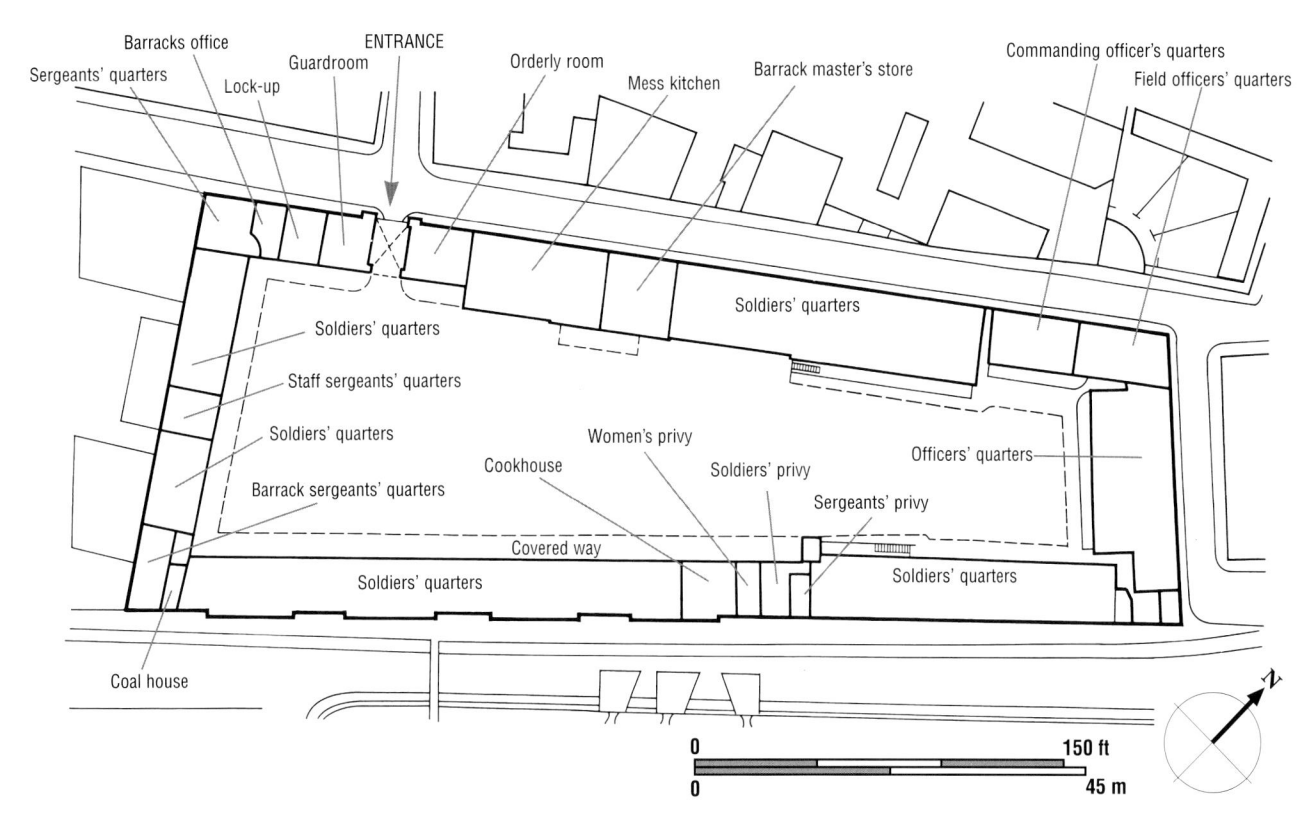

Figure 41 Plan of Portsmouth (later Clarence) Marines Barracks, redrawn from a plan by Colonel James RE, c.1861. Compare this with the watercolour of the barracks in fig. 40, page 98.

reflected in part the special difficulties which the Admiralty experienced keeping in good order a force billeted for long periods in the same town – less of a problem for the army, which could move its units regularly between their different duty areas.

The Marines at Portsmouth were marched into barracks in 1769. The thrifty Navy Board, responsible under the Admiralty for shoreside facilities until it was absorbed in 1832, converted the early seventeenth-century Kings Cooperage and brewery belonging to the Victualling Board, after it moved out and across to the Weevil Yard at Gosport (see Figures 40, page 98, and 41). The old brewery enclosed a long, narrow courtyard. The officers were allocated eight rooms between them; the men had 45 rooms, with 12 men in each sharing six wide beds. They were furnished with two dining tables and 12 stools, and had lockers for the men's kit. The Board added tiled, covered walkways along three sides for 'drawing up the men in wet weather' – the forerunners of the colonnades and verandas which became a feature of nineteenth-century barracks. The conversion work took almost eighteen months and cost, according to the estimate, about £5 10s per man.[21] The barracks was enlarged in 1828, probably at the same time its name was changed to Clarence Barracks. The Marines remained there until they moved across to the former Forton Naval Hospital at Gosport (later HMS *St Vincent*), in 1847.

All military supplies for the Marines, their uniforms, accoutrements, weapons, ammunition, as well as their food, were requested from the Admiralty, stored in the barracks, and issued as required by the quartermaster, who had a storeroom over the main archway into the barracks yard. The supervision of the barracks itself was the duty of the Barrack Master, a half-pay officer called Captain Horatio Spry, who was appointed in

---

[21] PRO ADM2/1162, 188.

Figure 42 This nineteenth-century engraving of Stonehouse Marines Barracks shows the narrow neck of land on which the barracks was sited, and the quay in the foreground from which the marines embarked.

January 1769. His duties were summarized in 1784 as:

'to take the said Barrack into your care and charge, together with the Beddings Furniture and Utensils therin ... to take care that the rooms ... be kept constantly supplied with Beds Bedding and such Furniture Utensils and Necessaries as are usually and customarily allowed ... to provide upon the cheapest and best Terms you can, Coals, Candles and such necessaries as are usually and customarily allowed ... and to supply the same in the usual proportions to the Marines quartered in the said Marine Barracks'. [22]

Perhaps because there were no suitable buildings which could be converted in the much younger settlement of Plymouth Dock (which grew later into Devonport), the Navy Board had to erect completely new barracks for the Plymouth Division: these were built between 1779 and 1783. The board selected a neck of land just south of Stonehouse Naval Hospital, backing on to an inlet midway between Dock and Plymouth from which the marines could board their ships (see Figure 42). This is the only surviving example of an English regimental barracks of this period, and is a complex of great interest.

There was no attempt by the Navy Board to do more than provide adequate rooms for the men in as efficient a manner as possible (see Figures 43 and 44). It consisted originally of a wide, three-sided quadrangle enclosing a parade ground, with railings and a guardhouse along the fourth, west side. As at Chatham, the officers lived in separate sections forming detached wings at either end of the square: the north wing, since rebuilt, held the commandant's and his deputy's houses at either end, with 24 single or 12 double quarters for officers in between. The south wing was the same, with houses at the ends for the field officers. The infirmary and surgeon's quarters were on Bunkers Hill to the north, with the divisional stables and the officers' canteen to the rear. The men lived in rooms with windows to the front and rear – an advance on contemporary Ordnance Board quarters with their dark, stuffy,

[22] PRO ADM2/1175, 247.

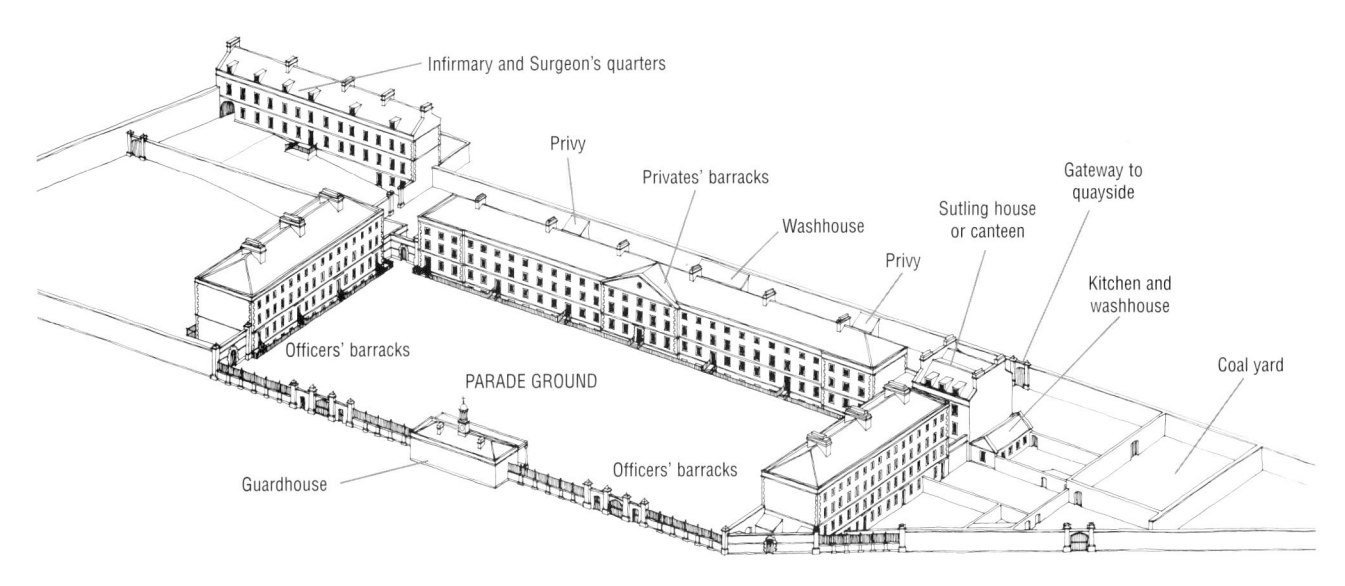

Figure 43 Reconstruction of Stonehouse Marines Barracks. The domestic character of the architecture is evident, with only the guardhouse to suggest that this is not part of a fashionable, palace-fronted terrace or square. The embarkation quay for the marines was to the rear of the principal barracks. The view of the barracks in fig. 42 was taken from the opposite direction. The plan in fig. 146, page 164, shows the barracks in the 1860s.

back-to-back rooms either side of a stair passage. The long marines' barracks was divided into seven sections, with a central pediment. Immediately behind was a long drill room with an open ground floor, and there was a school and tailor's shop above. To the east lay the quay and a shallow inlet, now silted up and built over, which was originally the point from which the marines left or returned from the sea.

The third Royal Marines Division, at Chatham, was also initially put out to billets. A corner of land was belatedly acquired in 1777 between St Mary's Parish Church and the dockyard, to the rear of the Ordnance Yard and across the road from the new infantry barracks. The Navy Board drew up plans for the barracks in April, the layout of the principal buildings being very similar to that devised for Stonehouse, with an open fourth side to the road with railings and a guardhouse, and a long barrack range with a central pediment (see Figure 45). The privates' accommodation was composed of modular sections of an identical plan to those built by the Ordnance Board, though it was proposed to put 16 men, rather than the Ordnance's standard of 18, in each room. The elevational treatment was architecturally more up to date, being treated as a single front with the windows evenly distributed, and a shallow roof behind a parapet which precluded the use of the garret rooms. There was a basement for the servants instead. The first intention was for three blocks, but the plans were increased to include six, and the total capacity of the barracks was raised to 600. The officers' quarters were likewise identical to those of the infantry. The division occupied the barracks for the first time in 1779, although only a small part of the total strength could be accommodated, and in 1782 the rest of the 5,700 Chatham marines not at sea were still billeted in local inns.[23]

In 1805, the spartan facilities for preparing food and washing were examined by Sir Samuel Bentham, then Inspector General of Naval Works, and his architect, Edward Holl. As part of his controversial remit to modernize and improve the naval yards, Bentham took in Marines' barracks. At Chatham, he designed a symmetrical range along the back perimeter wall of the barracks, with a central, open shed for cleaning clothes, cookhouses to each side, and a three-storey washhouse, stable and coachhouse at either end.[24]

[23] PRO ADM140/120, 1–7; NAM 8409-102.
[24] PRO ADM140/120, 11–24.

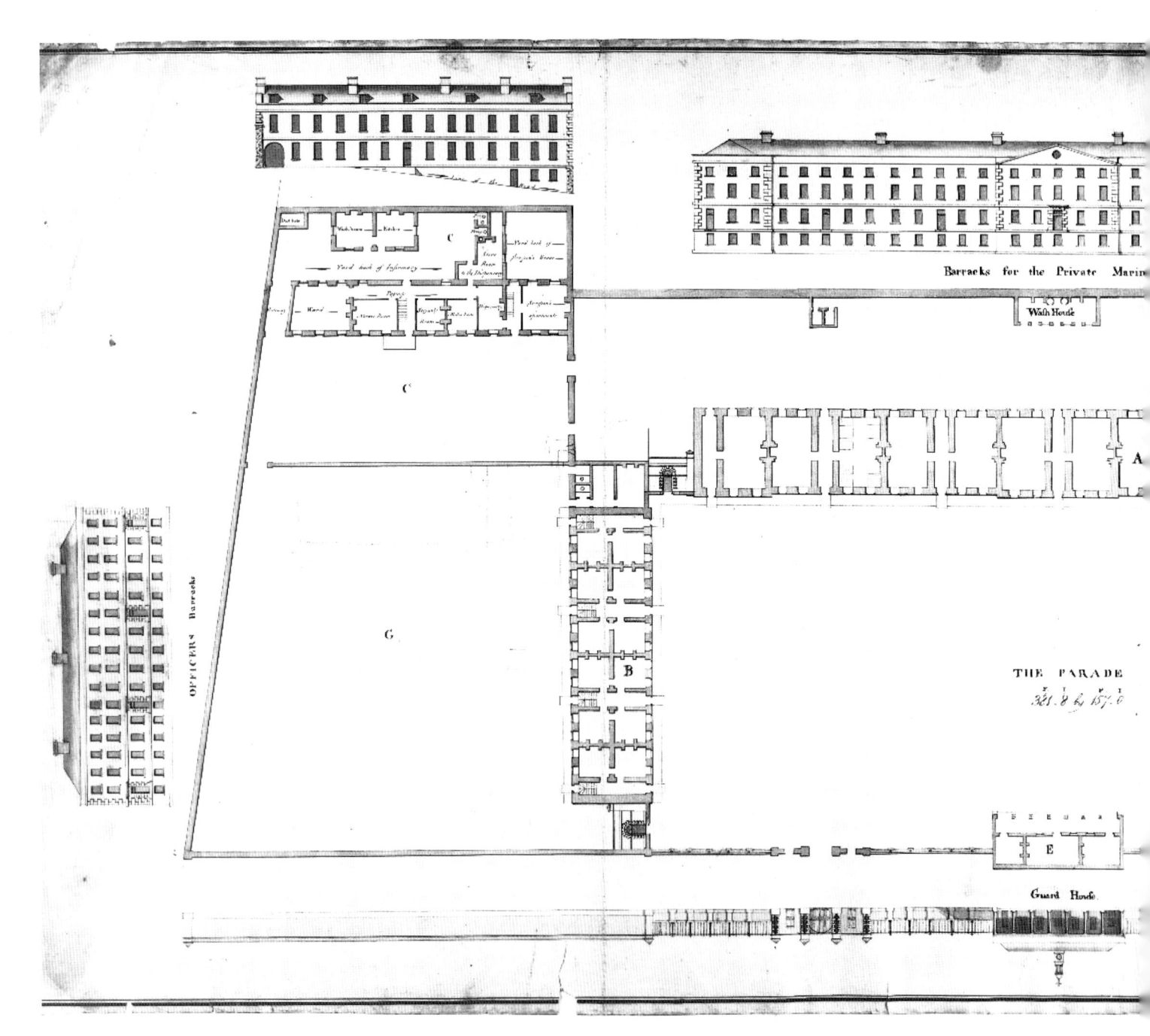

Figure 44 Stonehouse Marines Barracks: the original drawing on which the reconstruction in fig. 43 was based.

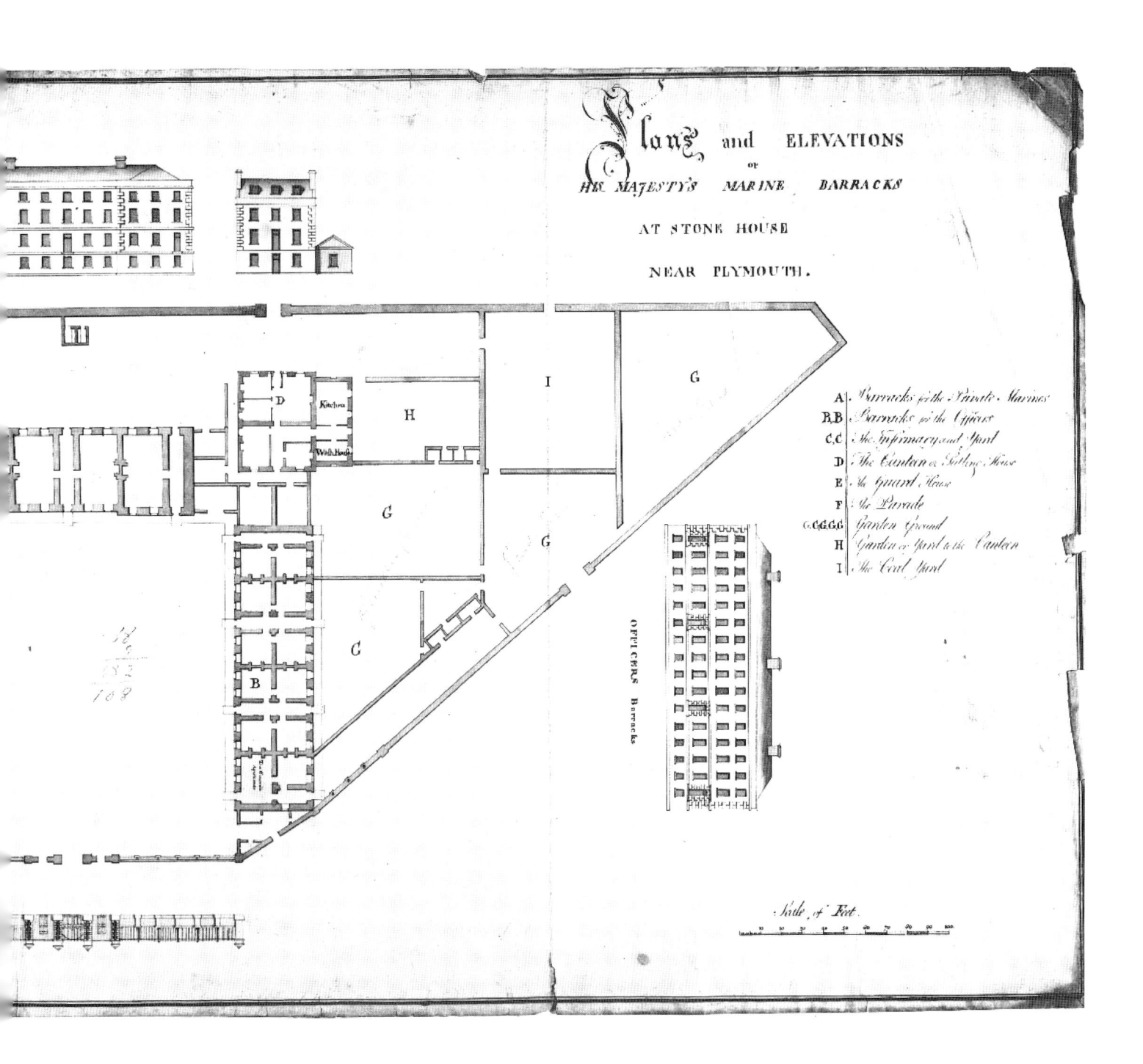

Plans and Elevations of His Majesty's Marine Barracks at Stone House near Plymouth.

A. Barracks for the Private Marines
B,B. Barracks for the Officers
C,C. The Infirmary and Yard
D. The Canteen or Tipling House
E. The Guard House
F. The Parade
G,G,G,G. Garden Ground
H. Garden or Yard to the Canteen
I. The Coal Yard

OFFICERS Barracks

Scale of Feet

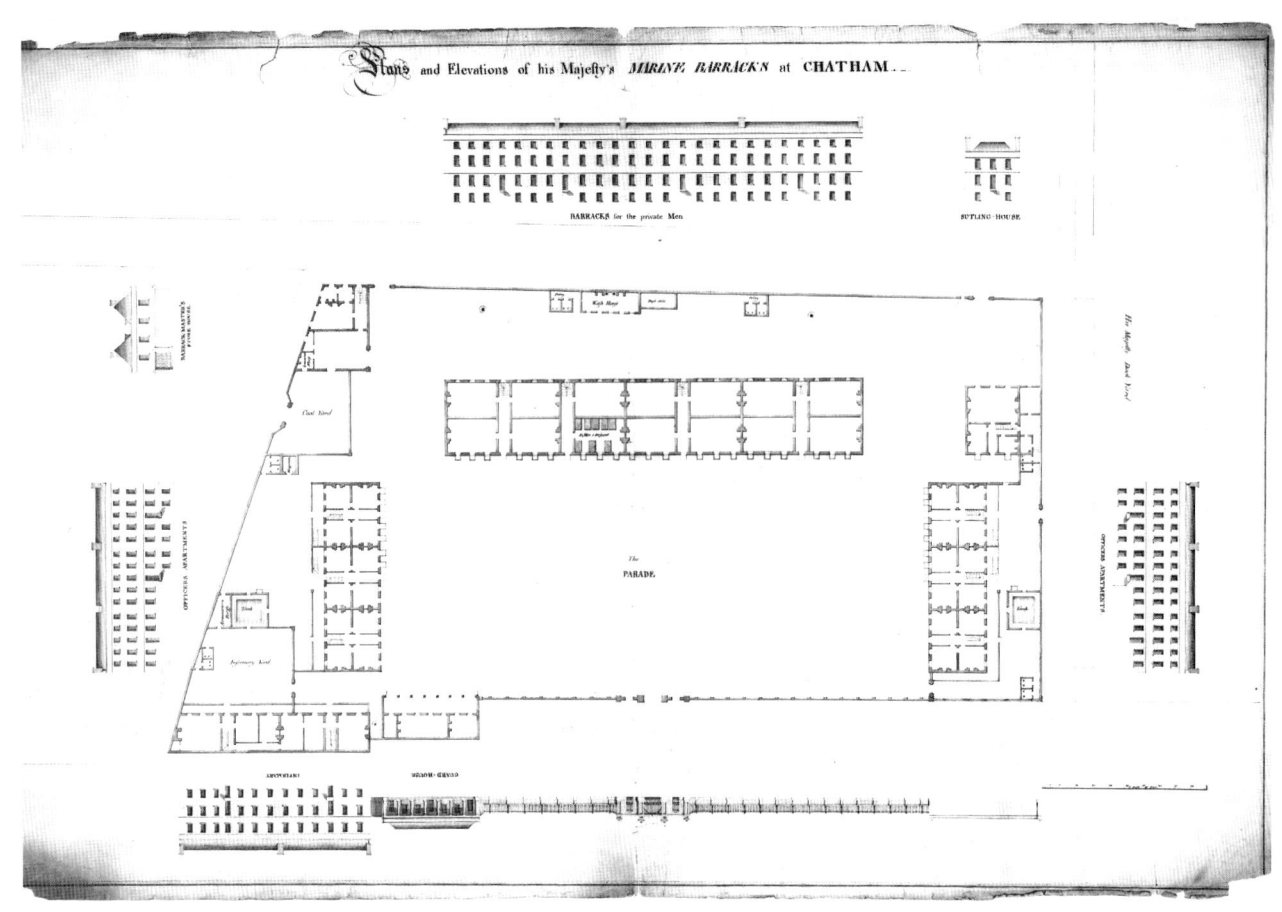

Figure 45 Chatham Marines Barracks. The planning of this barracks is clearly related to the Stonehouse Marines Barracks in Plymouth.

Bomb-proof barracks within fortifications

Despite these improvements to the quartering of troops around the naval yards, elsewhere billeting remained the only form of accommodation available to the army. Custom and economics continued to restrict new building to within the coastal forts and the capital.

Although the barracks at Fort George was by far the largest within a British fort, Skinner's great work followed the earlier practice, at Plymouth Citadel, Tilbury, and elsewhere, of building free-standing quarters within the fort (see fig. 11, page 16, and Figure 46). This could leave them exposed to bombardment, however. Skinner recognized this by including bomb-proof, vaulted casemates within the long sides which opened on to the main parade ground and could be occupied during a siege.

The problem became more serious as the range of artillery increased during the late eighteenth century. The Ordnance Board subsequently stopped erecting free-standing quarters within fortifications because they were too vulnerable to bombardment, and casemates (see Figure 47) came to be preferred for accommodation as well as for protecting the artillery. When Fort Cumberland, to the east of Portsmouth, was reconstructed after 1785, one of the 1740s gunners' barracks was retained, and is still there, but the new fort's 600-odd occupants were accommodated within shallow, brick casemates along the curtains which separated the five bastions. Twenty-six of the 56 casemates comprised heated barrack rooms in which some thirty men lived, and a further 16 each housed a gun.[25]

[25] Magrath (1992), p.15.

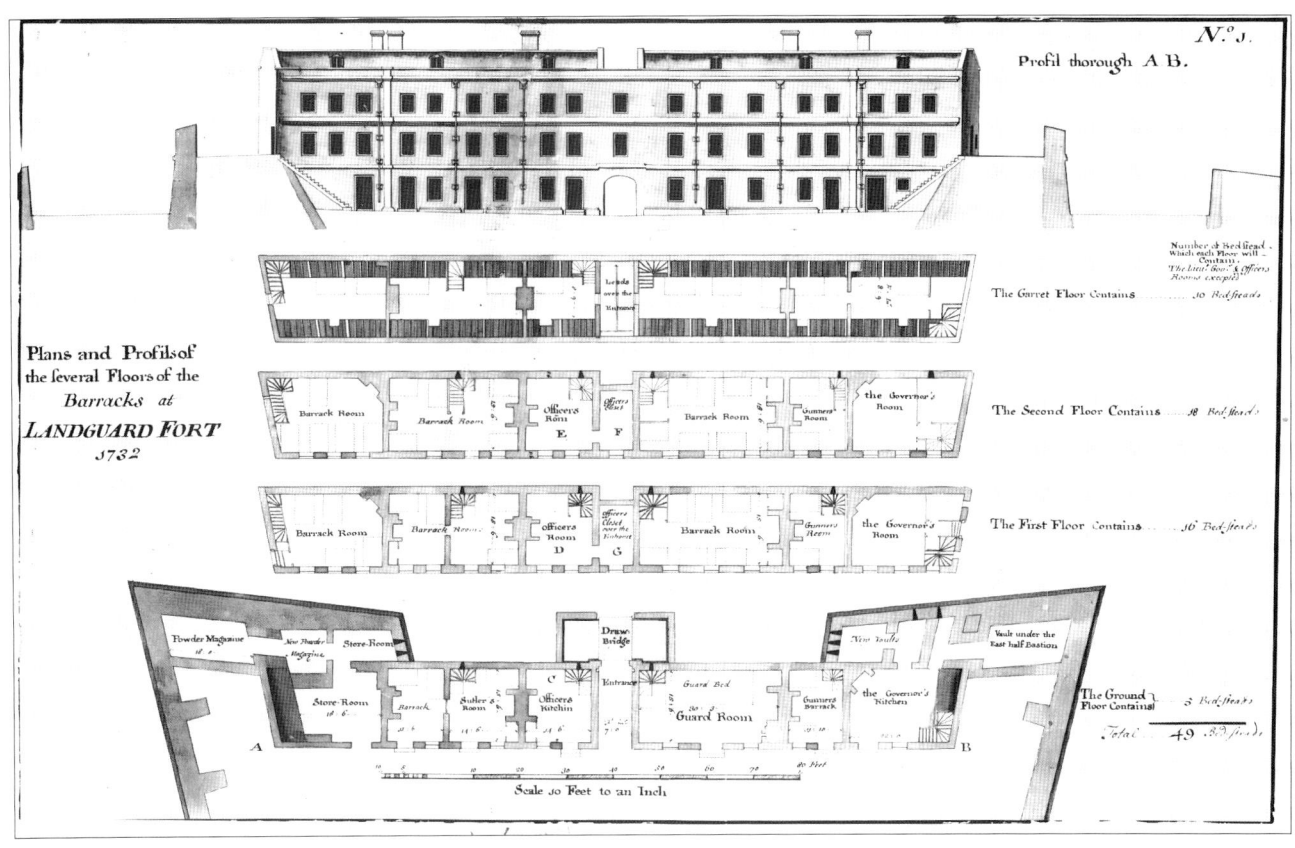

1750–1792: 'Out of Reach of Revolutionary Contagion'

Figure 46 This plan of 1732 for barracks at Landguard Fort in Suffolk, built in order to protect the port of Harwich, demonstrates the application of standardised Ordnance Board accommodation to the restrictions of a fort.

Figure 47 The vaulted casemates along the south flank of Plymouth Ciradel (see figure 11, page 16), begun in the 1670s and not completed until the 1750s, accommodated up to a thousand men. The interior photograph shows the cleats for holding small arms (below), sited between the soldiers' beds, and racking for accoutrements which date from 1846–8, when the barracks were remodelled.

Fort George in Guernsey was built between 1782 and 1812 at the centre of a group of artillery batteries as a 'keep of last resort', intended to be the strongest part and the final defence to which a garrison could retire. In such a work, casemates were considered necessary to protect the garrison. A similar defensible barracks was at first intended for what in 1783 became Fort Monkton, on the coast below Gosport. Instead, casemates were built for the guns, but rather vulnerable barracks were built for the garrison overhead.[26] A third new fort was erected during the 1780s at Fort Charlotte in Shetland, in response to the harassment of the north-west coast by American privateers. Here, the Chief Engineer in North Britain strengthened the existing earthworks of the old bastioned fort; casemates were not an option. The free-standing barracks built instead at Fort Charlotte were similar to previous Ordnance Board accommodation, with officers' rooms at either end and back-to-back rooms in between, off a central through corridor.

Accommodation for the Guards regiments in London

After the Restoration, London had been better provided with barracks accommodation than any other town in England. This continued to be the case throughout the eighteenth century, although political sensitivity and State finances prevented the construction of a large, central Guards barracks, in spite of the regular presentation of such plans. Units of the Horse and Life Guards were distributed among quarters close to royal residences, in the 1664 Horse Guards beside the Palace of Westminster, in St James's, at Somerset House and Kensington Palace, as well as in the old Savoy Palace, the Tower, and from 1689 out at Hampton Court (see Chapter One). For special occasions, or for policing duties when trouble was anticipated, extra troops were brought into the capital, and either billeted or put up in camps in one of the royal parks. In the summer of 1780, for instance, an extra 10,000 troops were camped for six weeks in St James's Park and Hyde Park, in an attempt to contain the protracted and violent demonstrations against the Catholic Relief Act known as the Gordon Riots (see Figure 48, page 98).

Obviously, for the ease of the soldiers, corps effectiveness and discipline, as well as to intimidate unruly crowds, the Government could have built a large, central barracks. Such a plan was indeed put to the Ordnance Board by the speculative architect Nicholas Dubois in 1718, at a time when the Board was already building barracks in Scotland and the dockyards; 1,335 feet (406.9 metres) long by 369 feet (112.5 metres) wide, this colossal projected pile would have consisted of three large quadrangles, a central Great Court with two Lesser Courts each side, with an infirmary, laundry and chapel, and it would have accommodated 5,264 Foot Guards, six to a room, and 128 officers. Like other such unbuilt projects for large barracks during the eighteenth century, it was to have been in Hyde Park, behind what is now Apsley House (see Figure 49).[27] Had it been built, the barracks would have been one of the largest single construction projects of the new Hanoverian regime – politically provocative as well as very expensive – but nothing came of it.[28]

By 1745, the Horse Guards was in such a decayed condition that the army requested it be replaced. The work was given to the Office of Works and its architect, William Kent, who produced a design that was approved in 1749, just after his death. The resulting building was completed within ten years, but it reveals little about Georgian barracks planning. Kent's Palladian principles obstructed any rational arrangement of the rooms, but he also realized – quite rightly – that its location at the heart of the British State, its central administrative function and its role as a backdrop to State military occasions required much more in the way of architectural display than the Ordnance Board would have provided. Its continuing active employment in all three roles is testament to the success of the design (see Figure 50). The central section over the main through archway contained the court-martial room, chapel and offices for the army. The Horse and Life Guards had rooms in the side ranges flanking the courtyard onto Whitehall, with stabling in the vaulted ground floor beneath.[29]

The only other barracks in London during the eighteenth century able to accommodate more than

---

[26] Saunders (1989), p.128.
[27] Colvin (1995), p.324.
[28] BL K Top 26-6-a. *Plan for the Barracks proposed to be built in Hyde-Park for His Majesties Foot Guards*. See also PRO WO55/2281.

[29] Colvin, *The History of the King's Works*, 5 (1976), p.436.

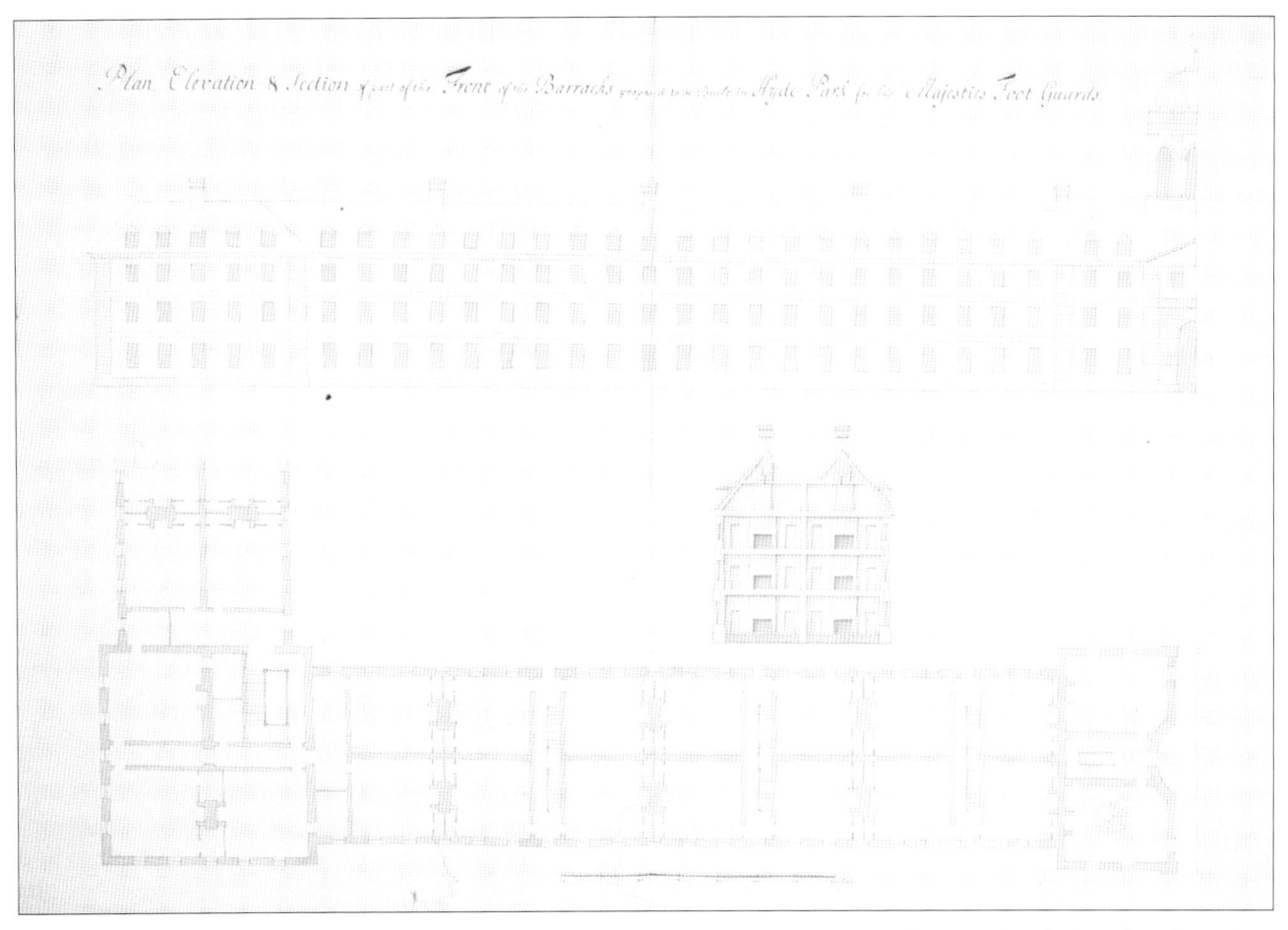

Figure 49 This proposed London barracks of 1718 was intended for the Foot Guards in Hyde Park. The drawing shows one half of the huge front elevation as far as the central dome. Double-depth rooms were separated by a stair passage, as was normal for Ordnance barracks of the time (see Figure 15, page 19).

two or three troops was in the old Savoy Palace, beside the Thames. Used as a depot for receiving new recruits and in a decayed condition, it burnt down in March 1776. Again the Office of Works was asked to prepare a replacement, and Sir William Chambers, in the throes of completing his monumental Government offices on the Strand at Somerset House, drew up designs for a large metropolitan barracks on the adjoining Savoy site.[30] It is not known what brief he had, but he may have felt that, with relatively few precedents, he was at liberty to start from scratch. The drawings show a palace for soldiers on a scale to match that for clerks next door. Cross-lit barrack rooms, connected by spiral stairs, formed the sides to a huge courtyard, with space for 3,000 officers and men of the Foot Guards. It had corner belvederes, twin domes to the

Figure 50 The Horse Guards has housed both the army administration and detachments of Guards regiments for over 200 years.

---

[30] J. Harris, *Sir William Chambers* (London 1970), pp.106–7.

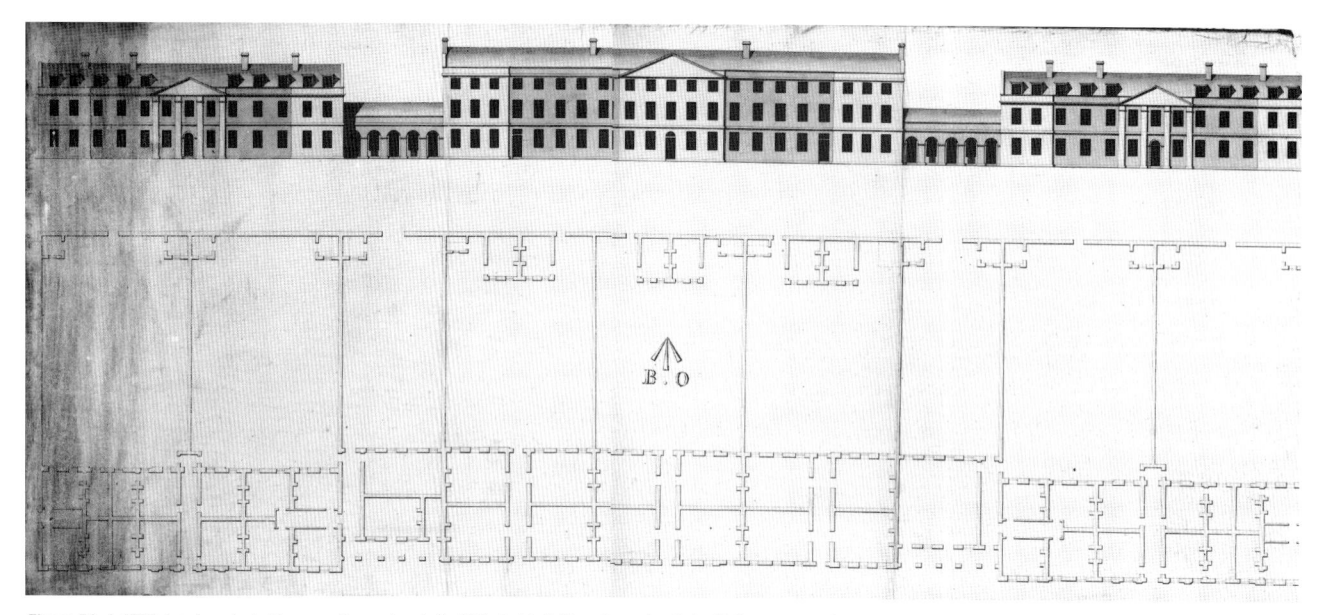

Figure 51 A 1774 drawing of what became the eastern half of Woolwich Artillery Barracks. As built, the outer sections were remodelled.

Strand, and a colonnade along the Thames. Sadly for us and for the Foot Guards, the plans were shelved. The elderly Chambers proffered them again after the start of war with France in 1795. By that time, however, with invasion threatening and tens of thousands of regulars and auxiliaries in arms, speed not splendour was the order of the day.[31]

The Royal Artillery Barracks at Woolwich

The only place in Georgian Britain which could rival the great military-industrial complexes of the royal naval dockyards at Chatham, Portsmouth and Plymouth was Woolwich, where a sizeable naval dockyard stood close by the expanding ordnance works of the Royal Arsenal. In 1741, an artillery training college was established at the Arsenal, the Royal Military Academy, for members of the Royal Regiment of Artillery. By 1761, the corps totalled 3,200 officers and men. A short terrace of quarters was provided within the Arsenal, but the need to accommodate such a large body of men impelled the Ordnance Board to look for a new site, and from the 1770s it set to work building a large, new, permanent barracks on Woolwich Common, overlooking both the dockyard and the Arsenal.

The order to commence building was given by Lieutenant Colonel Conway of the Ordnance Department in June 1774, and a plan and elevation from that year shows a long range of three buildings connected by short linking sections (see Figure 51). Minor changes were subsequently made, including the loss of the pediments to the outer buildings, and the addition of taller astylar ends. The short, recessed sections were in white stucco with a projecting colonnade, one to the front of the officers' richly decorated mess, another leading to the theatre. By August 1777, it was reported that work was complete.[32] Five years later, however, in April 1782, the Master General of the Ordnance, the Duke of Richmond, appointed the ascendant James Wyatt as Architect to the Board of Ordnance, because the barracks was still not finished.[33]

At some point thereafter, the three original buildings were doubled to six. The result was the prodigiously long façade for which the Royal Artillery Barracks at Woolwich is famous, as perhaps the longest residential building in Georgian Britain (see Figure 52). The process which led up to the finalization of the design and its doubling in size has unfortunately not emerged from the Ordnance Board's letter books, but it is generally assumed to

[31] Soane Museum, Drawer 4, Set 1. Despite the fire, troops continued to be lodged at the Savoy during the war with France.
[32] A.H. Burne, *The Royal Artillery Mess and its Surroundings* (London 1935), p.198.
[33] Ibid., p.355. Established in 1719, this post had been a sinecure held by the sons of the Surveyor General of the Ordnance since 1762.

Figure 52 English militarism? An 1855 engraving of the Royal Artillery's home. Superficially remarkable for its size, it is in fact made up of six modular sections.

has involved Wyatt in pulling the building together. He was producing drawings for buildings 'on Woolwich Warren' from June 1786, including officers' houses and a guardhouse in 1787, the riding house at the barracks in 1801, for the officers' mess room in 1802 (where what is probably his decorative scheme survives), and for the entrance, gateway and 'front of barracks' in November 1805.[34] At some point, the rather undersized triumphal arch was inserted at the centre, to try to focus the architectural effect and correct the squint caused by the two pedimented sections each side (see Figure 53).

Having massed all the accommodation at the front, gazing out across the common towards the new Royal Military Academy which Wyatt was building at the same time, all the ancillary buildings were organized to the rear. Soldiers' quarters, washhouses, cookhouses, stables, a hospital, magazine, three riding schools, granaries, stores and workshops were laid out to a grid like a Roman fort, which was entered, at least ceremonially, through the Roman arch at the centre. In 1808, when it was first occupied, the station was capable of housing 10 field officers, 77 captains and subalterns, 3,492 men and 1,718 horses. It was then the biggest single barracks in the country, and one of the largest in all of Europe.

It is common for architectural critics to slight this long façade by comparing it with the immense range of the Hermitage in St Petersburg.[35] They miss the point, however. This is not a poor Georgian terrace or a dull country house, it is an army barracks, and the biggest in the kingdom. All previous military accommodation in Britain – Fort George and the Royal Barracks in Dublin apart – pales into insignificance beside it. The Woolwich Barracks has the sort of forceful, overbearing presence that is associated in other countries with militarism, a feared word in a British context since it implies an independent-minded and assertive military point of view. It was surely appropriate to the Artillery's new quarters at Woolwich.

[34] Parliamentary Papers (House of Commons), 1810/11 (261), iv, CMI 15th Report, Ordnance Barracks and Fortifications, 23 July 1811, Appendix 5A, List of Drawings made for the Department of the Ordnance, p.355.

[35] See, for instance, E. Harwood and A. Saint, Exploring England's Heritage: London (London 1991), p.39.

Figure 53 The triumphal arch through the centre of Woolwich Artillery Barracks connects the two halves and leads to the main compound.

Civil unrest and the fear of sedition

None of these new English barracks seems to have generated any sort of political or popular opposition on the grounds that they threatened the constitution. Barracks in the dockyards were part of the defences necessary to safeguard the constitutionally correct protector of British independence, the Royal Navy, and even a large, inland barracks like Woolwich was permissible because the Royal Artillery operated the country's coastal defences and had no civil order role.

The long opposition to siting barracks within England was finally breached in early 1792. For a period after the French Revolution, before the excesses of the Terror and then war fatally stigmatized the example of France, there was a dramatic spread of radical ideas and popular political associations. Tom Paine's *Rights of Man* was published late in 1791. Political organization in the form of the Corresponding Societies spread among the artisan classes, which even went so far as to call for universal male suffrage. In 1792, Pitt's Government started to crack down on the radicals. On 21 May, the King issued a proclamation against seditious writings and meetings. Among those most exposed to such influences – and so far as the Government were concerned, most at risk were soldiers scattered in their billets among the pubs and inns, where such talk was likely to be especially fiery: 'ministers anticipated protest and sedition from those "accustomed to associate together" – from workers in manufacturing industries, or urban artisans, or miners, or colliers, or dockers. Men massed together in towns and large workplaces were widely believed to be potentially volatile.'[36] But despite the fears over the state of the industrial towns, it was in London, at Knightsbridge, just a quarter of a mile from Buckingham Palace, that the first moves were taken to put soldiers into barracks. Unfortunately, very little evidence of what lay behind this decision has emerged. A long, narrow strip of Crown land between Knightsbridge and Hyde Park was chosen for the construction of the first cavalry barracks on the British mainland, and the architect, James Johnson, was employed to design the buildings. It is not known if some previous work or personal connection recommended him for this task.[37] The plans were approved by the King in March 1792, and in December the following year the 1st and 2nd Troops of the Life Guard rode in and occupied the barracks for the first time.[38]

The layout is interesting, partly because it was one adopted only rarely for barracks in England. Two aspects stand out. The first is the planning of the troopers' quarters: a long, quadrangular range which formed the boundary wall on the Hyde Park side. Archways through the four sides led into the narrow, central courtyard, a sunless and damp parade ground, onto which the ground-floor stables opened directly. Access to the barrack rooms was by a passage along the inner side. Although claustral plans like this are rare in a British barracks, the enclosed character of the buildings was typical of the military quarters built in the unstable political climate of the 1790s. In 1805, it was rated for 384 NCOs and privates plus all their horses – a high concentration which must have severely taxed the sanitary arrangements – and by the mid-nineteenth century this had increased to 536.

The second aspect that makes Knightsbridge important is the officers' quarters, which was for the first time a separate and architecturally quite distinct entity from that of the lower ranks. Previously, officers had been lodged either in one part of the barracks, as at Berwick-upon-Tweed or

---

[36] Colley (1993), p.296.
[37] Colvin (1995), pp.547–8.
[38] *The Times*, 21 December 1793. Although normally known as 'Knightsbridge Cavalry Barracks', it was occasionally referred to as 'Hyde Park'.

1750–1792: 'Out of Reach of Revolutionary Contagion'

Map 2 Barracks in Britain before 1792

- ● Marines
- ■ Infantry Barracks
- ▶ Cavalry Barracks
- ◆ Artillery Barracks

England:
Berwick-upon-Tweed
Carlisle Castle
Chatham
Chester Castle
County Durham (Whitburn and Fulwell)
Devonport Squares, Plymouth
Dover Castle
Gosport
Guernsey and Jersey
Hull Citadel
Landguard Fort
Liverpool
London – Kensington Palace, Horse Guards, Knightsbridge cavalry
    and infantry, King Street St James's, The Savoy, Hampton Court,
    Tower of London
North and South Shields
Pendennis Castle
Portchester
Portsmouth – Hilsea, Fort Cumberland, Fort Monkton
Scarborough
Scilly Isles
Seaton Sluice
Sheerness
St Mawes
Stonar Castle
Tilbury Fort
Tynemouth Castle
Upnor Castle

Artillery:
Woolwich

Marines:
Chatham
Plymouth
Portsmouth

Scotland:
Bernera
Blackness Castle
Braemar
Castle Stuart
Dumbarton Castle
Edinburgh Castle
Fort Augustus
Fort Charlotte
Fort George
Fort William
Inversnaid
Stirling Castle

Ireland:
(These are the principal stations, and there were certainly other sites not shown which were empty when the returns were being made.)
Arklow
Athey
Athlone
Ballinrobe
Bere Island
Carlow
Carrick-on-Shannon
Cavan
Clare Castle
Clogheen
Cork Harbour and City
Drogheda
Dublin – Royal, Linen Hall
Dunmore
Enniskillen
Fermoy
Galway Castle and Shambles
Gort
Granard
Kildare
Kinsale
Leitrim
Limerick Castle
Longford
Managhan
Navan
Newbridge
New Ross
Oughteramle
Roscommon
Tullamore
Waterford
Westport

Sources: BL Windham Papers, MS 37891, f.11; CMI 2nd Report (1806), vi, 115, Appendix 41A, p.283.

in the Devonport Squares, or had occupied a terrace of houses which, while more generous in their room sizes, were not dissimilar to those of the soldiers, as at Tilbury Fort, or the Ordnance and Marines barracks in Chatham. At Knightsbridge, around thirty-five officers had rooms in a detached building in the centre of the site looking out to Hyde Park, of three storeys with a pediment.[39] Moreover, the ends of the infirmary stables and granary on either side were designed to look like pavilions, thereby enhancing and distinguishing the central building. This marks an important step in the progressive separation and distancing of the commissioned officers from the other ranks which took place during the eighteenth century. On the west side of the officers' quarters, in the narrower end of the site, were the riding school, stables for the officers' chargers, and the magazine.[40] The layout appears to have been determined by the narrowness of the site, and when it was rebuilt ninety years later, the plan was largely repeated (see the reconstruction of the second Knightsbridge barracks in fig. 127, page 149).

A separate Foot Guards' barracks was provided at the same time, or soon after, in rented buildings on the opposite side of Knightsbridge, in what would later become the Belgravia estate. Thomas Cubitt's map of the area in the 1830s shows a small, rectangular courtyard entered by an arch on one side, not unlike the cavalry barracks, and in 1805 it was rated for 500 men.[41] It was given up by the War Office some time before the Crimean War, though the buildings around Old Barracks Yard survived for much longer.

In the same month as the King issued his public proclamation, Pitt's Government took a more private decision, and sent a staff officer from the Horse Guards to carry out a covert investigation into the loyalty of troops billeted in the manufacturing towns. The officer chosen, who was to have a bigger impact on British barracks than any other single person, was the Deputy Adjutant General, Colonel Oliver DeLancey. He was a career soldier from an American loyalist service family, a cavalry officer, and a man as much soaked in the ethics and prejudices of the army as could have been chosen. His father had been an American loyalist general, and his brother was to enjoy a famous death at Waterloo. In the American War, DeLancey had been appointed to the Quartermaster General's staff by 1778, his experience there including running a network of spies out of New York. He returned to England after the war as the Lieutenant Colonel of the 3rd Dragoons.[42]

On 21 May 1792, DeLancey met with Pitt, Sir George Yonge (the Secretary of State for War), and Henry Dundas (the Secretary of State for the Home Department) at Dundas's house in Wimbledon. DeLancey was asked to ascertain 'the real state and disposition' of the troops quartered in the manufacturing areas, and the following day settled on a course of action.[43]

Riding north during May and June, he reported back to Dundas. His conclusions were that although most of the troops he questioned could be depended upon, some could not. On 13 June, he wrote: 'I therefore take the liberty to repeat my opinion that it is a dangerous measure to keep troops in the manufacturing towns in their present dispersed state, and unless barracks could be established for the men where they could be kept under the eyes of their officers, it would be prudent to quarter them in the towns and villages in the country, whence in case of emergency they would act with much more effect ...'.[44] Dundas accepted the advice and ordered him to proceed. During July and August, DeLancey made arrangements for cavalry barracks to be built for troopers quartered in Sheffield, Nottingham and Birmingham, each for three troops, and one double the size in the archetypal shock town of the Industrial Revolution, Manchester. At the end of August, George III, sea-bathing at Weymouth but abreast of the new development, wrote to Dundas: 'Colonel de Lancey seems to have [determined] the business of contracting for barracks at Manchester, Sheffield and Nottingham with every proper caution, local circumstances naturally occasioning some proving more expensive than others.'[45]

[39] Watson-Smyth et al. (1993), p.70.
[40] Parliamentary Papers (House of Commons), 1861, *xvi*, 1, *General Report of the Commission for Improving the Sanitary Condition of Barracks and Hospitals*, p.14; *Appendix to the Report*, 1863, pp.13–14.
[41] Parliamentary Papers (House of Commons), 1806 (115), *vi*, CMI 2nd Report, Appendix 41A, p.283; H. Hobhouse, *Thomas Cubitt, Master Builder* (London 1971), p.50.
[42] *Dictionary of National Biography*, **5** (London, 1908), pp.753–4.
[43] Parliamentary Papers (House of Commons) 1806 (46), *vi*, CMI 1st Report, *Barracks Accounts*, 21 March 1806, p.96; PRO HO42/20, *Letter from DeLancey to Dundas*, 22 May 1792.
[44] PRO HO42/20.
[45] This and the following section is drawn from PRO HO42/20, p.538.

The method by which DeLancey took the army into the building contracting business was based on the arrangements which he had been accustomed to making on campaign in America. Instead of sending a formal request to the Ordnance Board for it to take over the project, as would have been the proper but self-defeatingly bureaucratic course, he organized the construction of the first network of police barracks in England on his own initiative. All were for cavalry units, because mounted soldiers were quicker to reach a disturbance and more able to intimidate an excited crowd. Having settled on suitable sites outside the towns where the troops were considered at greatest risk from seditious influences, he contracted directly with landowners for a lease on behalf of Dundas, arranged an estimate with a local builder, provided a set of plans, and ordered the relevant officer of the local regiment to appoint a suitable architect or surveyor to supervise the work. On his measurements and valuations, the officer was instructed to make payments through the regimental agent, who controlled extraordinary regimental expenditures – those not detailed in the annual parliamentary army estimates.

The biggest barracks, for six troops of cavalry, was at Manchester (see Figure 54). By orders dated 7 August 1792, land was rented at Hulme, half a mile (0.8 kilometres) south of the town, 'the extent of the distance [being] absolutely necessary for the purposes of discipline'. A lease was taken for 'three lives', and Charles Nevin, architect, was appointed to oversee the work. A price of £7,900 was presumably accepted by the builder, who had until 31 December to complete the two barracks for the men, and until 1 March to complete the smaller officers' quarters, or suffer a £2,000 penalty. Plans and elevations of the simple two-storey buildings were provided by DeLancey.

These first four plans marked a sharp departure from earlier British barracks built by the Ordnance and Navy Boards. In a notably introspective layout, the officers were housed in a completely separate building at the head of the barrack square. This symbolically reinforced regimental hierarchy, and put the officers in a good position – both metaphorically and in practice – to keep an eye on the soldiers. These were to live two to a bed in heated, eight-man rooms above the stables, which were connected, like those at Knightsbridge, along the length of the building by a dark corridor. At Sheffield, a windowless rear elevation reinforced the inward-looking mentality which the barracks sought to develop, as well as rendering it more secure against a rabble. A high wall enclosed the barracks and the adjoining exercise ground, with a single gateway beside the guardhouse.

Two more towns, Coventry and Norwich, were also chosen and barracks were duly ordered for each during the summer of 1792. At Coventry, they were converted from an old coaching inn with stables and a yard at the back,[46] but new buildings were erected in Norwich (see Figure 55). A seventh was built at Hounslow – then a heath to the west of London used since the seventeenth century as an army camp, and clearly chosen in order to have loyal troops close to the capital in case of trouble. Hounslow is the only surviving example of this first generation of English police barracks. The two long, parallel ranges, facing one another across the wide parade ground, retain the small stores which contained the horses' fodder at either end. None of the drawings of these first inland barracks that have been uncovered are signed. However, James Johnson claimed in 1805 to have designed all of them, and his involvement with DeLancey during the Napoleonic Wars suggests that he may have been approached during 1792 on the strength of his experience at Knightsbridge.[47]

At the end of the year, the reversal in the State's attitude towards police barracks was formalized when Yonge appointed DeLancey Superintendent General of Barracks. His warrant from George III made no reference to the controversial nature of the assignment, stating blandly: 'the Barracks in this Kingdom being considerably increased, and the business relative there to having in consequence become very extensive, it is found necessary to appoint a person to have the superintendence of the same'. He was made responsible for the various

---

[46] Parliamentary Papers (House of Commons), 1847, *xxxvi. A Return from each Barrack in the United Kingdom*, p.169.

[47] Parliamentary Papers (House of Commons), 1806 (317), *vi*, CMI 2nd Report, *Barracks Establishment*, 18 July 1806, *vi*, Appendix 19.

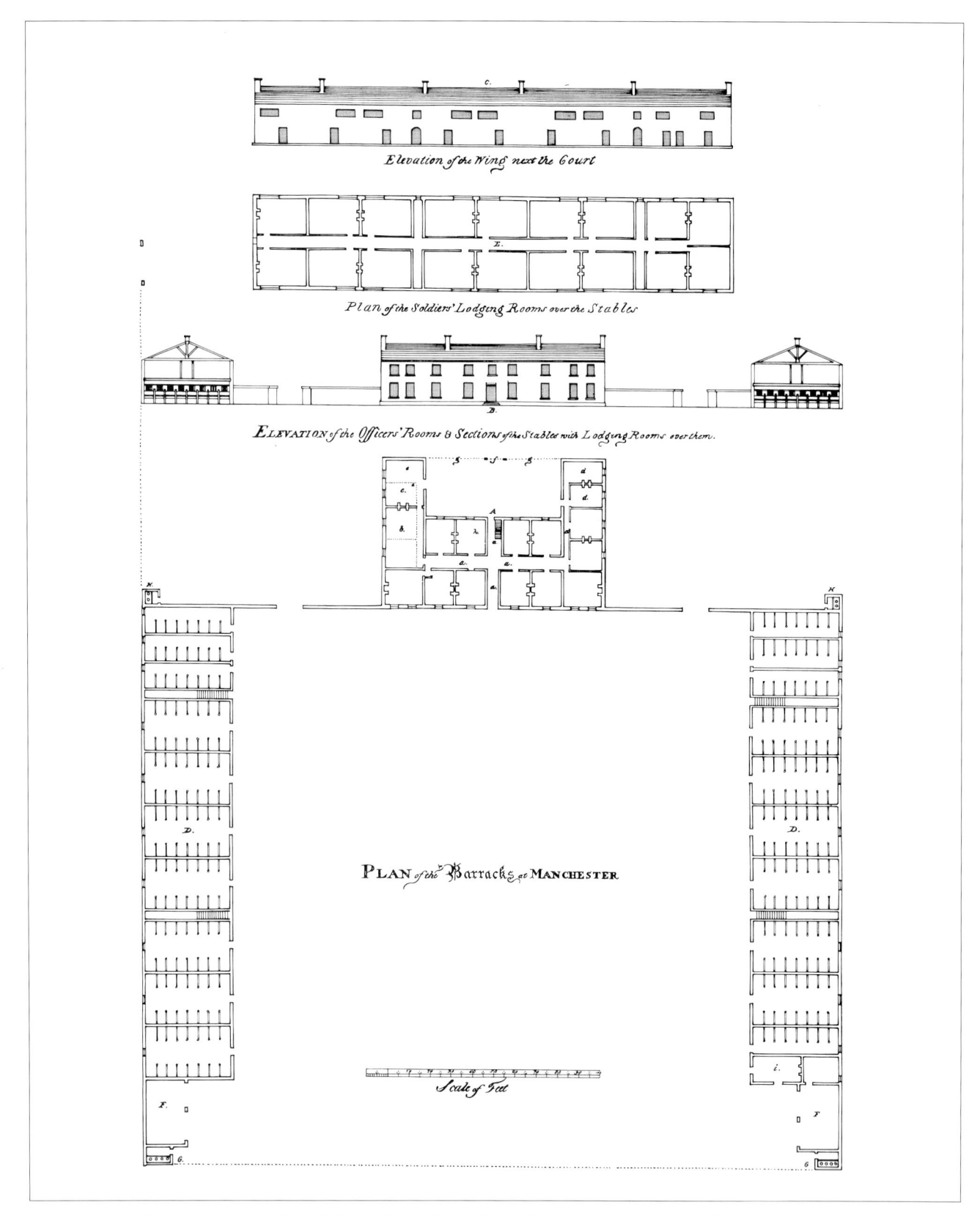

Figure 54 Hulme Barracks in Manchester, the largest of Colonel DeLancey's first police barracks for the cavalry. The officers' quarters head the square, with those of the troopers and their horses on each side. The enclosed plan (above right) is typical of DeLancey's approach.

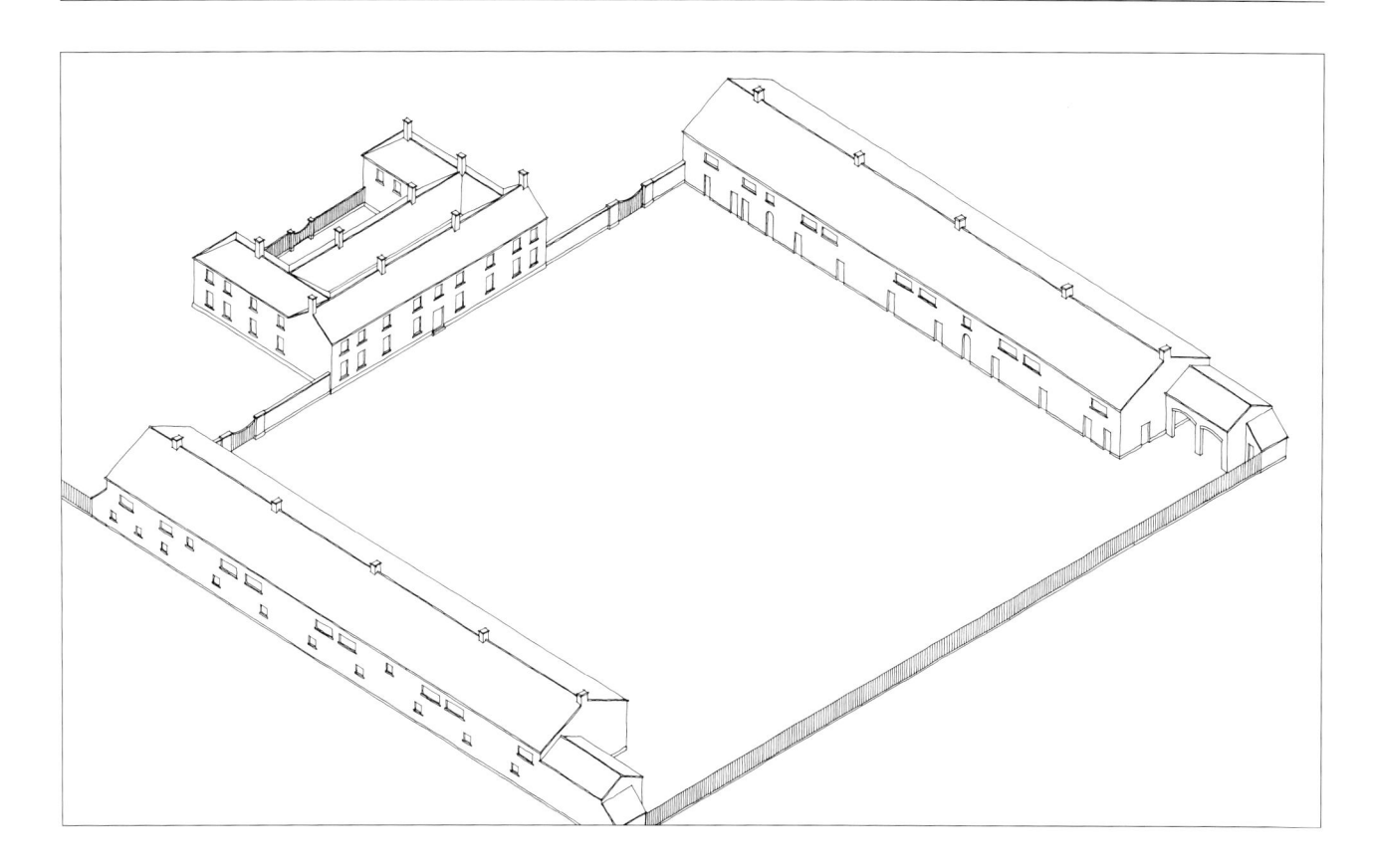

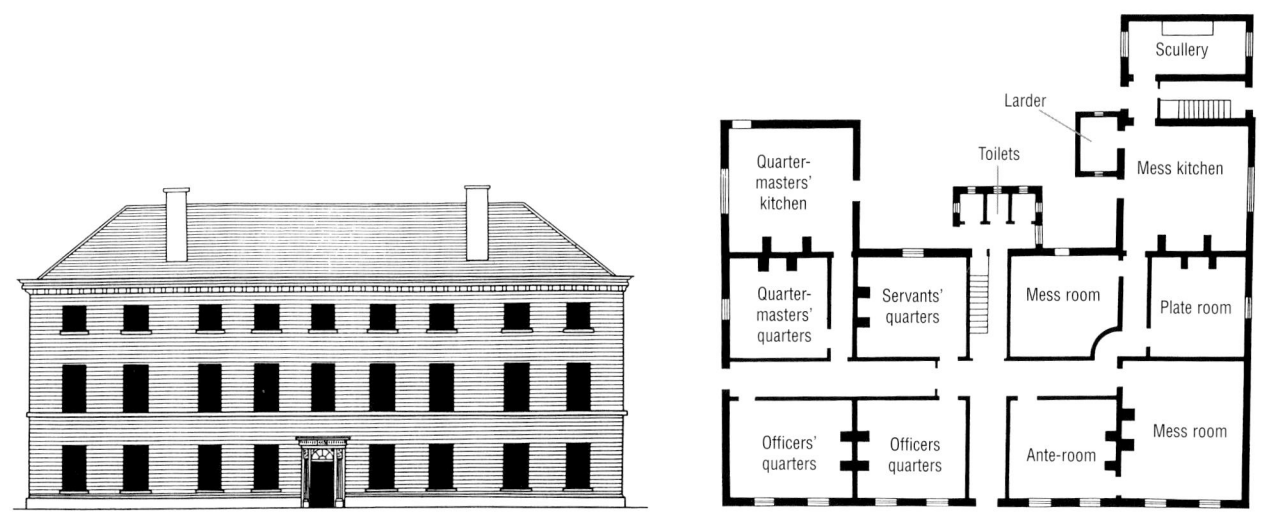

1750–1792: 'Out of Reach of Revolutionary Contagion'

Figure 55 The officers' quarters at Norwich Cavalry Barracks, redrawn from a plan of *c.*1800. The links to domestic architecture are still strong. The plan shows the officers' separate heated rooms; the top floor was for servants.

barrack masters, the regular supply of stores, fuel, candles and the soldiers' other entitlements, according to a new HM Warrant for the Regulations of Barracks. Half-yearly, or 'as often as it shall be thought expedient', accounts were requested (which would prove to be DeLancey's downfall), and he was allowed £1 a day plus expenses.[48] Therefore, to all intents and purposes, during peacetime and in the depths of the interior of the country, the long English prejudice against barracks had been broken.

---

[48] Parliamentary Papers (House of Commons), 1806 (46), *vi*, CMI 1st Report, *Letter of Service dated 1 January 1793, signed George Yonge, Secretary at War. Warrant for the Regulation of Barracks*, Appendices 1 and 2, p.31.

Chapter Four
1792–1815: 'No Barns, No Pigstyes'

In February 1793, war was declared against France. The fighting extended over twenty-three years, equivalent to the First World War grinding on until 1937. The size and duration of the conflict forced the British State to motivate and mobilize an unprecedented number of its citizens to rise to its defence. In order to maintain their enthusiasm for the fight, keep them reasonably healthy and, most importantly, where they were needed, close to the coast facing the French, it had to abandon its long disdain for barracks, and for the first time provide proper accommodation. Between 1789 and 1814, the army grew from 40,000 to 225,000 men, though for much of the time most of these were stationed abroad. More important in terms of the numbers involved in national defence was the militia, which was embodied in November 1793, and by 1797 could call on around 100,000 men. Tens of thousands volunteered as infantry, artillery and mounted yeomanry between 1794 and 1807. By 1804, half a million volunteers and militiamen were in arms, and the following year it was boasted that 810,000 men were serving in the United Kingdom: 'nearly one in four of the population was in arms ... greater than any other country on the globe'.[1]

Not only was the war conducted on a larger scale than previous Anglo–French conflicts, but the tactics which the mass armies were capable of adopting were new as well, especially those of the ideologically fired French. In former invasion scares, regiments of the army and the mobilized militia were marched to tented encampments along the coast during the summer months, until the deteriorating autumn weather reduced the risk of invasion. The regular army was then marched into the interior and billeted, and the militia sent home. This time, however, the British feared that the large and unconventionally led conscript army raised by the French *levée en masse* in April 1793 was capable of attempting an out-of-season winter crossing, so forces stationed in the maritime counties, watching the sea from likely landing beaches, had to be maintained at much higher levels than in the past.

For this, the existing barrack provision was both physically inadequate and strategically useless (see Table 2). There were only beds for about 40,000 men in the Ordnance Board's pre-1792 estate of old castles, forts and the dockyard barracks, and about a quarter of these were in the Northern, North-West and North British Military Districts instead of those facing France. The military response to this housing crisis, and the impact of the immense numbers on the areas where they were stationed, has only been studied in detail for three areas: Devon, Dorset and the North-East.[2] This means that what occurred in the crunch counties of Essex, Kent and Sussex is less well understood, but evidence submitted to a series of commissions of inquiry later in the war provides an abundance of material making the overall picture reasonably clear.

The predictable impact of the incoming army and militia regiments in the summer of 1793 was to swamp the billeting system. Risking their licences, publicans in Kent and Sussex removed their signs to avoid having to put up yet more soldiers. Associations of innkeepers petitioned for barracks, writing to their MPs, the War Office, Home Office and Treasury, even directly to the Ordnance Board. Professor Breihan has uncovered 21 of these petitions in local record offices. The Government responded cautiously. Regiments near the coast were empowered to rent serviceable agricultural buildings for when the camps broke up in the

---

[1] Hansard, 1st series, 3 (1805), *Lord Hawkesbury to the House of Lords*, March 1805, p.808, quoted in Colley (1993), pp.283–319.
[2] Breihan (1989), pp.9–14; Breihan (1990a), pp.165–8; Breihan (1990b), pp.133–58.

Table 2 Ordnance Board accommodation on the eve of the Revolutionary War, showing the official capacity of each region

Northern District	**1,574:**
North and South Shields	464
Tynemouth	470
Seaton Sluice	30
Carlisle	44
Durham: Whitburn and Fulwell	566
York	**3,047:**
Hull 'and dependencies' (rented and huts)	2,937
Scarborough	110
Eastern District	**5,790:**
Landguard Fort	400
Chatham	2,384
Upnor	96
Dover Castle	1,921
Sheerness	808
Stonar (cavalry)	176
Tilbury Fort	181
Southern District	**3,452:**
Hilsea huts	1,452
Portsmouth and Portsea	2,000
South-West District	**6,191:**
Plymouth	5,271 + 180 cavalry
Scilly	104
Pendennis Castle	744
St Mawes	72
North-West District	**803:**
Chester	56
Liverpool	170
London	**1,101:**
Tower	557
Knightsbridge	500
Hampton Court (cavalry)	130
Kensington	44
Guernsey & Jersey	**11,359:**
Guernsey & Alderney	5,015
Jersey	6,231 + 113 cavalry
North Britain	**7,261:**
Fort Charlotte	256
Fort Augustus	180
Fort William	430
Fort George	**1,760**
Dumbarton Castle	162
Stirling Castle	798
Blackness Castle	50
Edinburgh Castle	1,900
Berwick	624

Note: The figures above refer to infantry, unless otherwise stated.
Source: Parliamentary Papers (House of Commons), 1806 (6), *vi*, CMI 2nd Report, Appendix 41A, p.283; Parliamentary Papers (House of Commons), 1806–7 (99), *ii*, CMI 4th Report, *Barracks Construction*, Appendix 1, p.413.

autumn, but cart sheds and cow byres were even worse than overcrowded inns. Wet, cold and on a lower beer ration than units in billets, militiamen in Kent chanted: 'No Barns, no Pigstyes, small beer and good Quarters.'[3]

In June, the Government turned again to Colonel DeLancey. Yonge's successor as Secretary at War, William Windham, established him by a warrant from the King as Barrack Master General in charge of a new Barracks Department. The department was to be responsible for all military accommodation in Britain except that in fortified places, which, reasonably enough, remained with the Ordnance Board, since it continued to be responsible for manning and operating the country's artillery defences. Barracks or other forms of accommodation for the Horse and Field Artillery, for the gunners and any infantry garrisons inside coastal fortifications, for the Royal Engineers and all barracks in Ireland remained under the Master General of the Ordnance.

---

[3] Breihan (1989), p.10; Kent Record Office S5 U1590 03/14.

DeLancey took rooms in Spring Gardens, near the Horse Guards at the north end of Whitehall, and set about establishing an office and a regional staff. He appointed a deputy barrack master general, 13 assistant barrack master generals with responsibility for supplies, inspecting barracks and 'general duties', an accountant and two architects to look after design, estimates and the supervision of construction, and about thirty clerks and office servants.[4]

The Barracks Department began its work in a considered way, taking a strategic view of the needs of national defence, and building permanent barracks from durable materials (see Figure 56, page 99). As the pressure of events mounted with the real possibility of a French landing between 1793 and 1795, and calls came for new barracks from all around the overcrowded coast, DeLancey's more natural inclination to resolve problems by direct, personal action asserted itself, and decisions became more *ad hoc* and expedient, and the barracks of more temporary and lightweight construction. During 1803, when, for the second time, there was real fear of an imminent invasion, practically no masonry buildings were built at all, as the Department resorted to wooden huts and even to the traditional campaign expedient of sod-walled cabins.

During the war with France, forts as well as hospitals were taken over for barracks, and extensions and rented additions were made to the total barracks capacity too numerous for all to be noted here. Map 3 shows the existing permanent military quarters plus new barracks erected during the war by the Barracks Department and the Ordnance Board.

A coastal ring of cavalry barracks

DeLancey's first proposal, despite the need to accommodate the infantry militias, was for a coastal chain of cavalry barracks. It was to extend from Dumfries on the west coast of Scotland round to Dunbar on the east, but was concentrated along the southern and East Anglian counties of England.

Figure 57 Edinburgh Castle New Barracks. This massive range was completed in 1799, when the Great Hall, used as a barracks since the seventeenth century, became a military hospital.

Most of the barracks, 25 of them, were the minimum size for a viable cavalry station: a single troop of 58 men and their officers, with stabling, stores and basic facilities. At intervals, he planned larger regimental headquarters barracks. The largest was the massive New Barracks at Edinburgh, for six troops (see Figure 57), followed by four-troop stations at York and Winchester, three-troop stations at Lincoln, Leicester, Ipswich, Canterbury, Brighton, Dorchester, Exeter, Bristol, Gloucester, Shrewsbury, Perth and Hamilton, and two-troop stations in Northampton (see Figure 58, page 71).[5]

What DeLancey's precise purpose was in dispersing the cavalry in this way is unclear. The individual stations were too small to repel a landing, and they were too widely spread to concentrate a larger force in a short time. They may have been planned more for anti-smuggling operations, an interest of both DeLancey's and Pitt's since the 1780s, and their frequency along the Devon and Dorset coastline reflected Government anxiety over the vulnerability

---

[4] Parliamentary Papers (House of Commons), 1806 (317), *iv*, CMI 2nd Report, p.115.
[5] BL Windham Papers, Add. MS 37891, ff.11–12, *Report of Colonel DeLancey*, 20 July 1794.

British Barracks 1600–1914

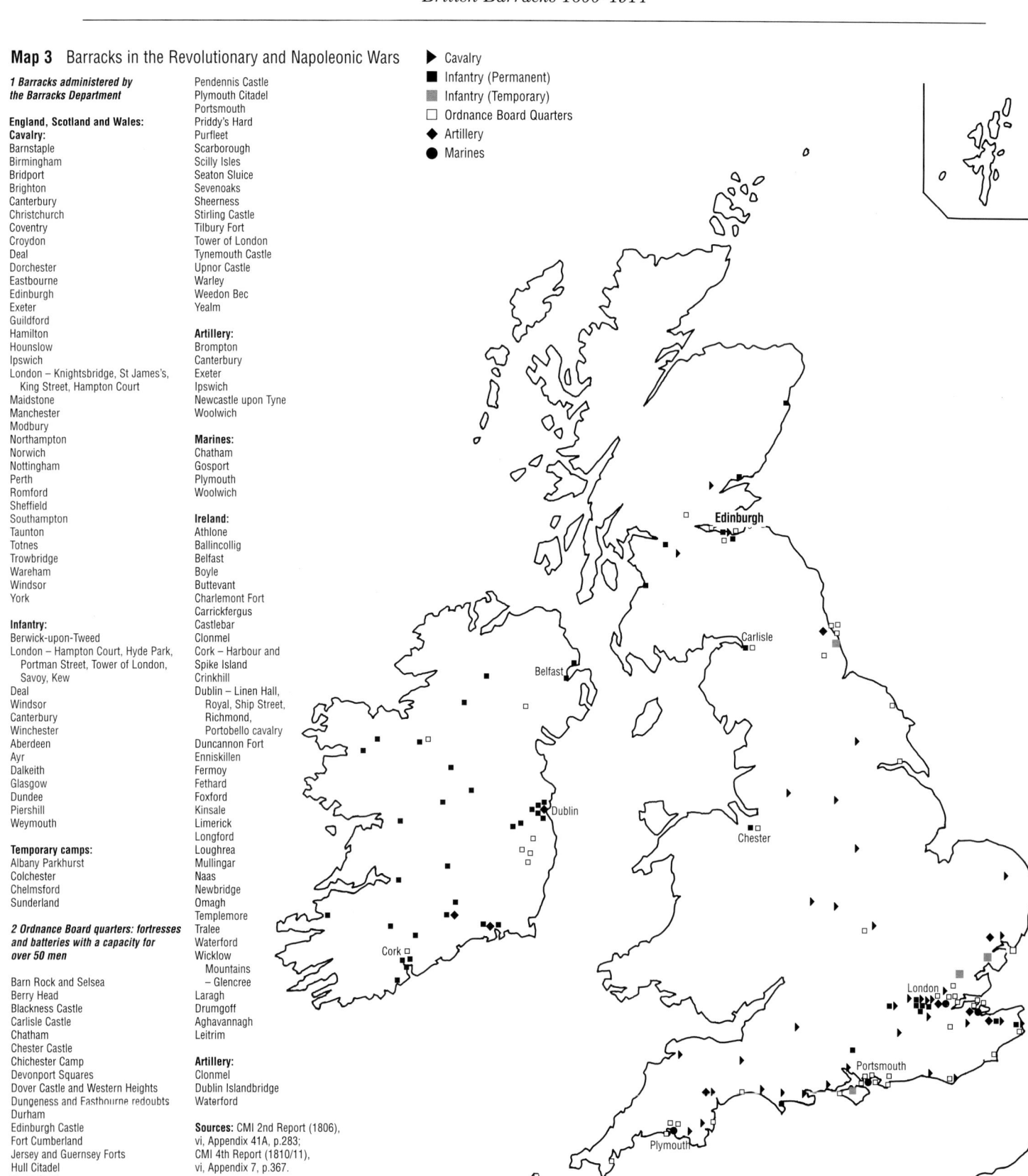

Map 3 Barracks in the Revolutionary and Napoleonic Wars

▶ Cavalry
■ Infantry (Permanent)
▪ Infantry (Temporary)
☐ Ordnance Board Quarters
◆ Artillery
● Marines

1 Barracks administered by the Barracks Department

England, Scotland and Wales:

Cavalry:
Barnstaple
Birmingham
Bridport
Brighton
Canterbury
Christchurch
Coventry
Croydon
Deal
Dorchester
Eastbourne
Edinburgh
Exeter
Guildford
Hamilton
Hounslow
Ipswich
London – Knightsbridge, St James's, King Street, Hampton Court
Maidstone
Manchester
Modbury
Northampton
Norwich
Nottingham
Perth
Romford
Sheffield
Southampton
Taunton
Totnes
Trowbridge
Wareham
Windsor
York

Infantry:
Berwick-upon-Tweed
London – Hampton Court, Hyde Park, Portman Street, Tower of London, Savoy, Kew
Deal
Windsor
Canterbury
Winchester
Aberdeen
Ayr
Dalkeith
Glasgow
Dundee
Piershill
Weymouth

Temporary camps:
Albany Parkhurst
Colchester
Chelmsford
Sunderland

2 Ordnance Board quarters: fortresses and batteries with a capacity for over 50 men

Barn Rock and Selsea
Berry Head
Blackness Castle
Carlisle Castle
Chatham
Chester Castle
Chichester Camp
Devonport Squares
Dover Castle and Western Heights
Dungeness and Easthourne redoubts
Durham
Edinburgh Castle
Fort Cumberland
Jersey and Guernsey Forts
Hull Citadel
Hurst Castle
Landguard Fort
Leith
Maker Heights
Monkton
North and South Shields
Northfleet
Pendennis Castle
Plymouth Citadel
Portsmouth
Priddy's Hard
Purfleet
Scarborough
Scilly Isles
Seaton Sluice
Sevenoaks
Sheerness
Stirling Castle
Tilbury Fort
Tower of London
Tynemouth Castle
Upnor Castle
Warley
Weedon Bec
Yealm

Artillery:
Brompton
Canterbury
Exeter
Ipswich
Newcastle upon Tyne
Woolwich

Marines:
Chatham
Gosport
Plymouth
Woolwich

Ireland:
Athlone
Ballincollig
Belfast
Boyle
Buttevant
Charlemont Fort
Carrickfergus
Castlebar
Clonmel
Cork – Harbour and Spike Island
Crinkhill
Dublin – Linen Hall, Royal, Ship Street, Richmond, Portobello cavalry
Duncannon Fort
Enniskillen
Fermoy
Fethard
Foxford
Kinsale
Limerick
Longford
Loughrea
Mullingar
Naas
Newbridge
Omagh
Templemore
Tralee
Waterford
Wicklow Mountains – Glencree
Laragh
Drumgoff
Aghavannagh
Leitrim

Artillery:
Clonmel
Dublin Islandbridge
Waterford

Sources: CMI 2nd Report (1806), vi, Appendix 41A, p.283; CMI 4th Report (1810/11), vi, Appendix 7, p.367.

Fort George, Charlotte, Augustus and William were not entered in these returns.

70

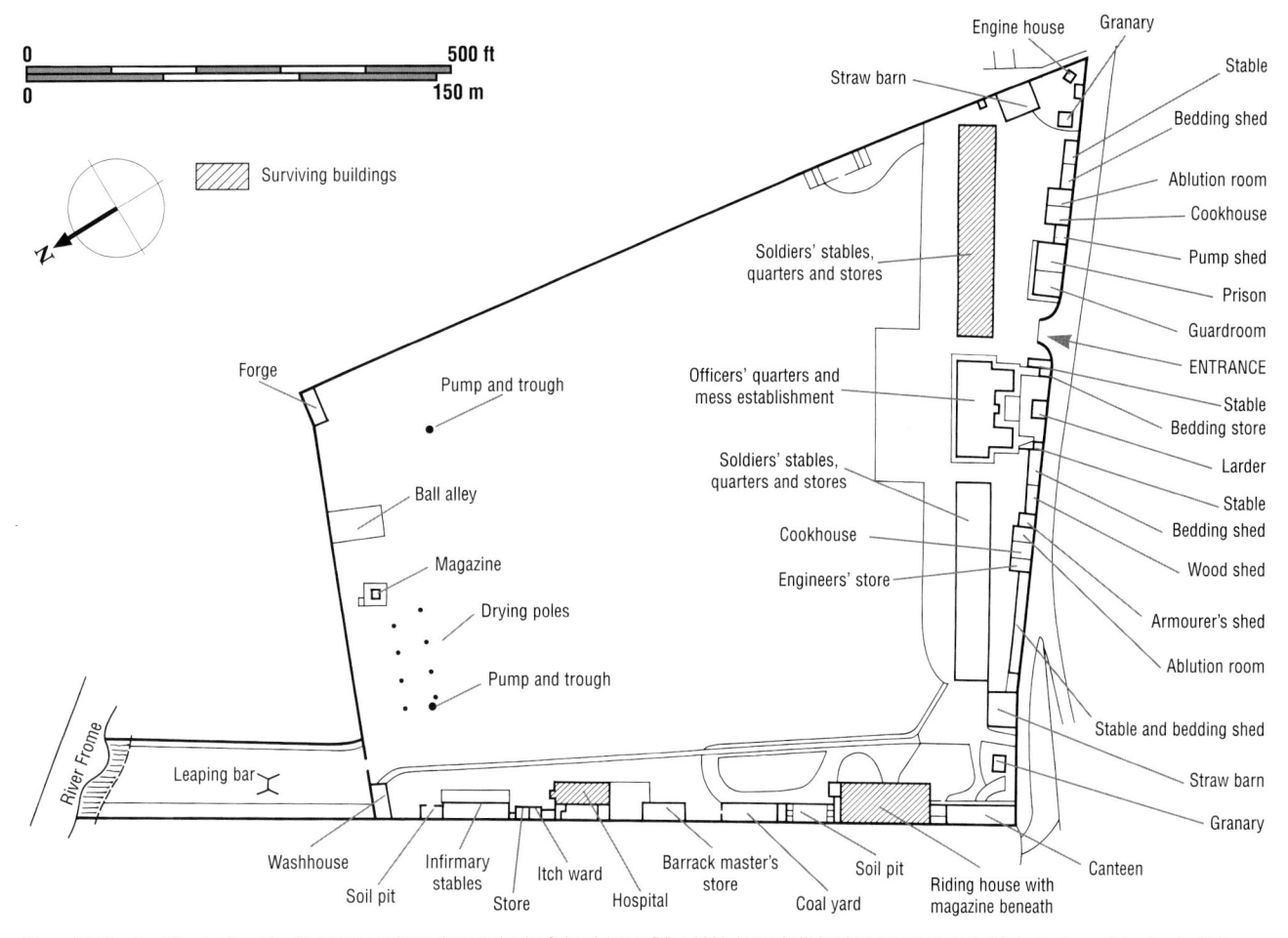

Figure 58 Marabout Cavalry Barracks, Dorchester, redrawn from a plan by Colonel James RE, c.1861. It was built for three troops as part of DeLancey's coastal network. All the ancillary functions were accommodated separately in their own buildings. Although there are ablution houses behind the barracks, the two pumps for washing are out in the field.

of its numerous small bays and beaches. The provision of barracks at Edinburgh, York and some of the inland towns appears to be a continuation of the pre-war policy of policing unrest and isolating the troops from seditious influences. In the event, only 13 of the small stations were built, including Barnstaple, Modbury, Totnes, Taunton, Bridport, Weymouth, Wareham, Trowbridge, Southampton and Deal, with the larger stations in Scotland, and from Exeter to Ipswich, Northampton and York. The single-troop barracks at Wells, and those planned along the east coast at Colchester, Saxmundham, Cromer, King's Lynn, Beverley and Scarborough, as well as the three-troop stations at Lincoln, Bristol, Gloucester and Shrewsbury, were all cancelled.[6]

The only permanent barracks built by the department for foot soldiers were in Scotland. The Department's office in Edinburgh under Colonel Baillie, the Assistant Barrack Master General, set about building permanent masonry barracks for the garrison at Glasgow for 1,200 men, at Aberdeen for 600 men, and at Ayr and Dundee for 400. Except for a Guards barracks at Windsor (see Figure 59) and one for infantry in Deal (see Figure 64, page 80), all the other new infantry barracks were either timber huts or converted premises.[7]

With part of his coastal chain under construction by July 1794, DeLancey seems thereafter to have responded to the urgency of the French invasion threat. The masonry barracks took time to erect and

---

[6] Parliamentary Papers (House of Commons), 1806/7 (99), ii, CMI 4th Report, Appendix 9A, p.227.
[7] BL Windham Papers, Add. MS 37891 ff.11–12.

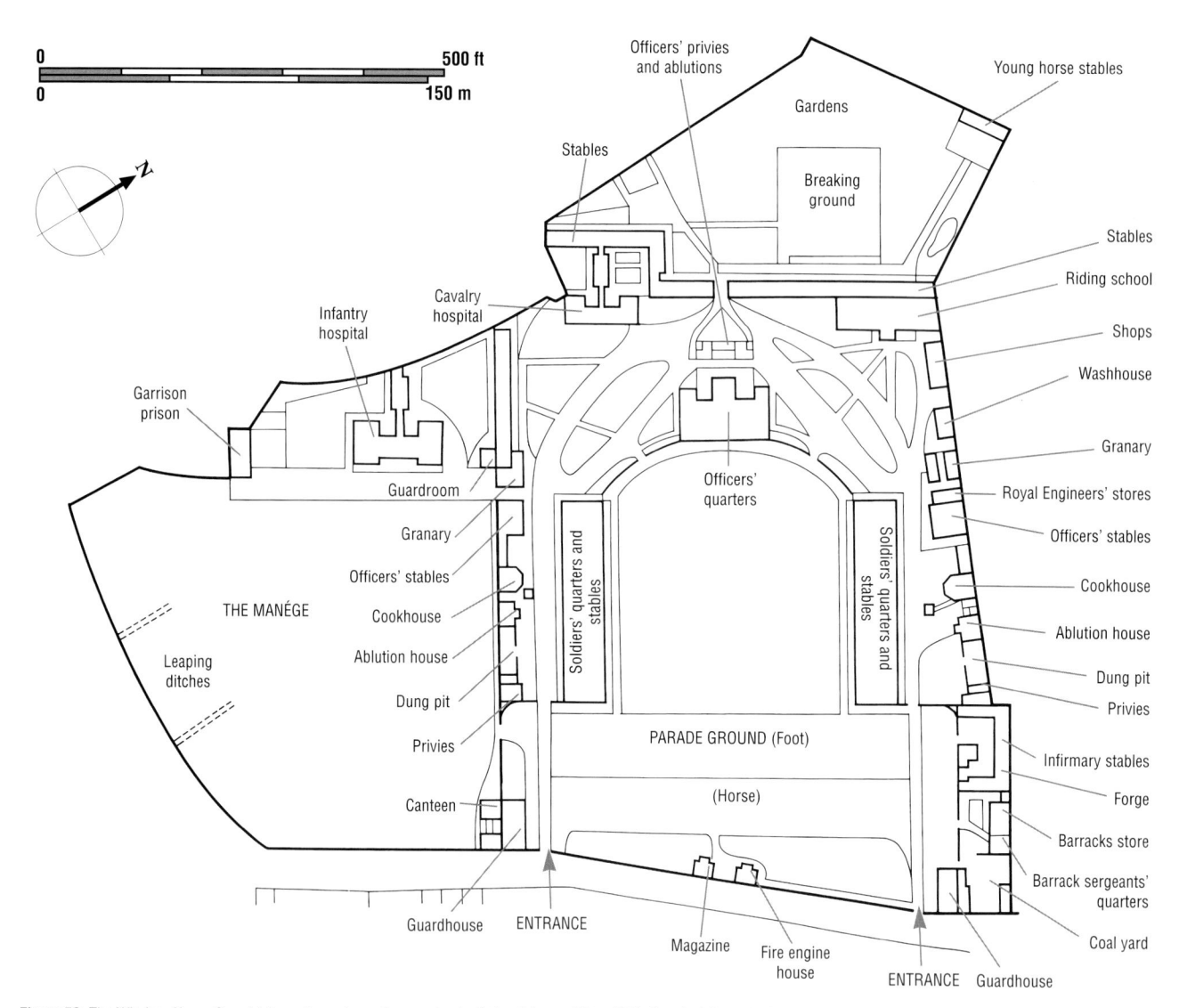

Figure 59 The Windsor Horse Guards' Barracks, redrawn from a plan by Colonel James RE, c.1861. A typical Barracks Department layout, with the main buildings symmetrical about the parade ground, and the stores and workshops along the perimeter wall, though the hospitals are later. The Manége was an area used for exercising horses.

for the walls to dry out: the Department's architects reckoned that stone barracks took twice as long to build and worked out 30 per cent more expensive than timber ones.[8] Dorchester was first occupied in June 1795, but Weymouth not until two winters later.[9] More rapid accommodation was needed, and housing the infantry was the priority. The first solution was to assemble temporary barracks from timber huts, and in 1794 the Commander-in-Chief, the Duke of York, himself ordered two large encampments of these at Colchester and Chelmsford, to be ready in time for the break-up of the camps in the autumn. They were to hold 2,700 and 1,700 men respectively.[10]

The second expedient adopted by the Department was to rent property and fit it up as quarters. In Revolutionary France, the State, as part of its attack on the Church, confiscated large numbers of religious buildings. Convents, monasteries, seminaries and churches were all requisitioned as barracks after 1792. No such easy quarry existed in

[8] Parliamentary Papers (House of Commons), 1806/7 (99), *ii*, CMI 4th Report, *Evidence of John Sanders*, Appendix 10, p.430.
[9] Breihan (1989), pp.10–11.
[10] Parliamentary Papers (House of Commons), 1806/7 (99), *ii*, CMI 4th Report, Appendix 9B, p.227.

England, where barns, stores, warehouses and malthouses, relatively open with adaptable floor areas, were rented instead, and hurriedly fitted out by contractors. Many more examples of these must survive than have so far been identified. The warehouses at what became the Cambridge Barracks in Portsmouth (now the Grammar School) may be a conversion by the Barracks Department. In Whitehaven, a new, iron-framed textile mill was taken over by the local militia, and thereafter was known as Barracks Mill.

During the winters of 1793 and 1794, DeLancey and his assistant barrack master generals hurried around the country entering into leases wherever space was needed. Extra accommodation for the cavalry was provided in Devonport, Canterbury, Guildford, Windsor, Brighton, Ipswich, Morpeth, Chester-le-Street and Newcastle upon Tyne, along with granaries, 'hay magazines' and forges (all vital for the cavalry), hospitals and stores. For the infantry, the Department rented and fitted out temporary quarters during 1794 and 1795 for 42,567 men, at a cost of £48,608.[11] Huge garrisons were assembled in Norwich and Poole, both with over 4,000 places. Poole was abruptly diverted from the Newfoundland cod trade and transformed into an embarkation port for the ill-fated West Indies expedition.[12] In Canterbury, strategically a key town between the Kent coast and London, the Department leased room for over 3,600 men at a cost of £8,750.

DeLancey could be imaginative in his choice of premises, and was far from blind to the opportunity for a deal. The long absence of barracks in Bristol, a large maritime town with a reputation for political unreliability, can only be explained by an abundance of pubs for billeting. Nevertheless, in February 1801, Windham passed to DeLancey a number of petitions received at the War Office from Bristol innkeepers appealing for relief. Although he priced the purchase of land and erection of a new barracks, he ended up taking a lease on Royal York Crescent, the immense terrace with which the first Clifton building boom had climaxed, but left empty when the speculators collapsed in 1793. DeLancey paid £8,300 for the carcass. Conveyancing was completed in August 1803, just as the Peace of Amiens appeared to have obviated the need for more barracks. It was auctioned off in 1809/10 and realized £11,373.[13]

Decisions about where new barracks should be built originated in a multiplicity of local and national circumstances. Orders stating the whereabouts and the required size of a new barracks came in the form of written and verbal orders from the Secretary of State at the War Office or from the Commander-in-Chief at the Horse Guards. They responded to requests from civilian representatives such as town corporations or innkeepers' groups, from officers anxious to find quarters for their men before the wet weather, as well as to orders from the Prime Minister and from the King. For instance, in August 1796, George III sent a message to his son requesting that he order DeLancey to prepare temporary barracks for 2,000 men at Ipswich, Canterbury, Horsham and Ashford, and for 4,000 at Chelmsford and Colchester. At the same time, the French prisoners of war were to be removed from the old King's Palace in Winchester, which was to be fitted out for infantrymen.[14]

The situation in north-east England in 1795 provides an illustration of the interaction between national and local conditions in precipitating the decision to erect a new barracks.[15] In February, local interests in Sunderland offered land on the nearby moor on which to build barracks because they were concerned about the likelihood of a French attack on the town's fleet of colliers, supplying the capital. Meanwhile, labour unrest in the mines, a mutiny by an Irish militia regiment in nearby Newcastle upon Tyne and complaints from local innkeepers as a result of having five regiments of infantry billeted in the town prompted the Mayor to renew the request two months later. This time, the Duke of York responded in person, giving DeLancey a direct order to build barracks in Sunderland for a thousand men. The Barracks Department's architects designed a plan for quickly assembled timber-framed barracks, which the contractor had ready and occupied by July.

---

[11] House of Commons Sessional Papers, 1796, a74 4583, pp.93–4.
[12] For an account of DeLancey's Poole station, see Breihan (1989), p.10.
[13] Parliamentary Returns, 1812, *ix*, 105.
[14] Parliamentary History (House of Commons), 1807, *ii*, CMI 4th Report, Appendix 9C and D.

[15] The following paragraph is based on Breihan (1990a), pp.168–9.

During 1795, the Ordnance Board passed several unneeded forts to the Barracks Department to be used for extra quarters, including Carlisle Castle, the casemates at Forts Cumberland and Monkton, Hurst Castle, Barn Rock and Selsea in Hampshire, as well as control of the London Guards barracks at Knightsbridge, Kew, Hampton Court and Kensington Palace. In 1796, DeLancey could report to Parliament that, including those started just before the war, the Department had built 42 permanent barracks with a capacity of 16,311; 32 were for the cavalry, including 13 single-troop barracks. Four permanent infantry barracks had been built, three in Scotland and one for the Guards to protect the Royal Family at Windsor, but the bulk of the infantry accommodation was in five huge hutment camps at Colchester, Chelmsford, Glasgow, Porchester and Sunderland, each for well over a thousand men. The camp at Colchester, for instance – a town used for many years before the war as an encampment between London and the Essex coast – was assembled following petitions from the innkeepers over the excessive cost of billeting. A hutment camp was erected for the infantry in 1794, and for cavalry in 1799. The Ordnance Board built huts for the artillery there in 1797. By 1803, there was capacity for 7,000 men, 450 horses and 200 officers, as well as 414 hospital beds. It was all demolished or sold off in 1816.[16]

In 1796, DeLancey was still intending to build five more small cavalry stations and a large hutment depot for receiving recruits at Parkhurst, on the Isle of Wight, to carry out the Winchester Palace refit, as well as erect an enormous 4,200-man barracks for seven Guards battalions in London. Only the Winchester conversion was carried out in the end, for a sixth of the cost of the London barracks, which joined the lengthening list of unbuilt schemes for a great London home for the Guards.[17] With more of the permanent barracks now complete and a relaxation in the threat of invasion, the War Office could reduce the level of troops in the Home Counties, and the pressure eased on the Barracks Department. During the next four years, and particularly after the Peace of Amiens in 1802, they gradually gave up leases on many of the rented properties, and the stated capacity of some crowded stations was reduced.

The resumption of the war in February the following year forced DeLancey to be at his most energetic again. With Napoleon and the *Grand Armée* camped across the Channel at Boulogne, in May the Quartermaster General, Major General Brownrigg, ordered DeLancey to prepare quarters for 47,405 infantry and 6,925 cavalry, to be ready by October when the camps broke up. A few days later, this was rounded up to 50,000 and 10,000 respectively by Lord Hobart.[18]

The choice of sites was left to the Barrack Master General and his assistants and architects, but the overwhelming need was in the south-east. Fifty-six hutment camps were either laid out and assembled from scratch or added to existing ones. John Sanders, one of the Department's architects, reckoned that during the summer of 1803, 20,000 artisans were employed on this enormous task throughout southern England.[19] In addition, the Department had to return to the rented sector to find sufficient room in Norwich, Great Yarmouth, Ipswich, Deal, Shoreham, Ashford, Worthing, Gosport, Hythe, Plymouth and Hull. The camps and temporary quarters provided by the Barracks Department in response to the invasion scare between 1803 and 1805 are shown in Map 4.

The hutment camps were mainly occupied by the militia. Apart from a small number guarding the Essex coast, the camps extended along the potential landing beaches south of the North Foreland all the way to Devon. About half were concentrated in Sussex, with five more in and around Plymouth, including two close to Devonport Dockyard. The additional huts for the cavalry were predominantly at existing camps such as Radipole (Weymouth), Exeter and Ipswich, but hamlets like Steyning in Sussex had their own brief experience of garrison life.[20] In 1795, 1799 and 1803, large camps were built in both Jersey and Guernsey to strengthen the island garrisons. Three more, each for a thousand

---

[16] Dietz (1986), p.12.
[17] House of Commons Sessional Papers of the Eighteenth Century, 1975, *160*, 4588, 4699 a-77, *List of Barracks intended to be built ... 1796*, p.91; BL K Top 26 7tt, uu, *Plan of a barracks for 2,000 men*.
[18] Parliamentary Papers (House of Commons), 1806/7 (99), *ii*, CMI 4th Report, p.118.

[19] Soane Museum, Drawer 20, J. Sanders, *A Letter to the Lords Commissioners of His Majesty's Treasury*, 1808.
[20] A.Watkinson, 'Steyning as a garrison town, 1804–14' (typed manuscript, undated, NAM).

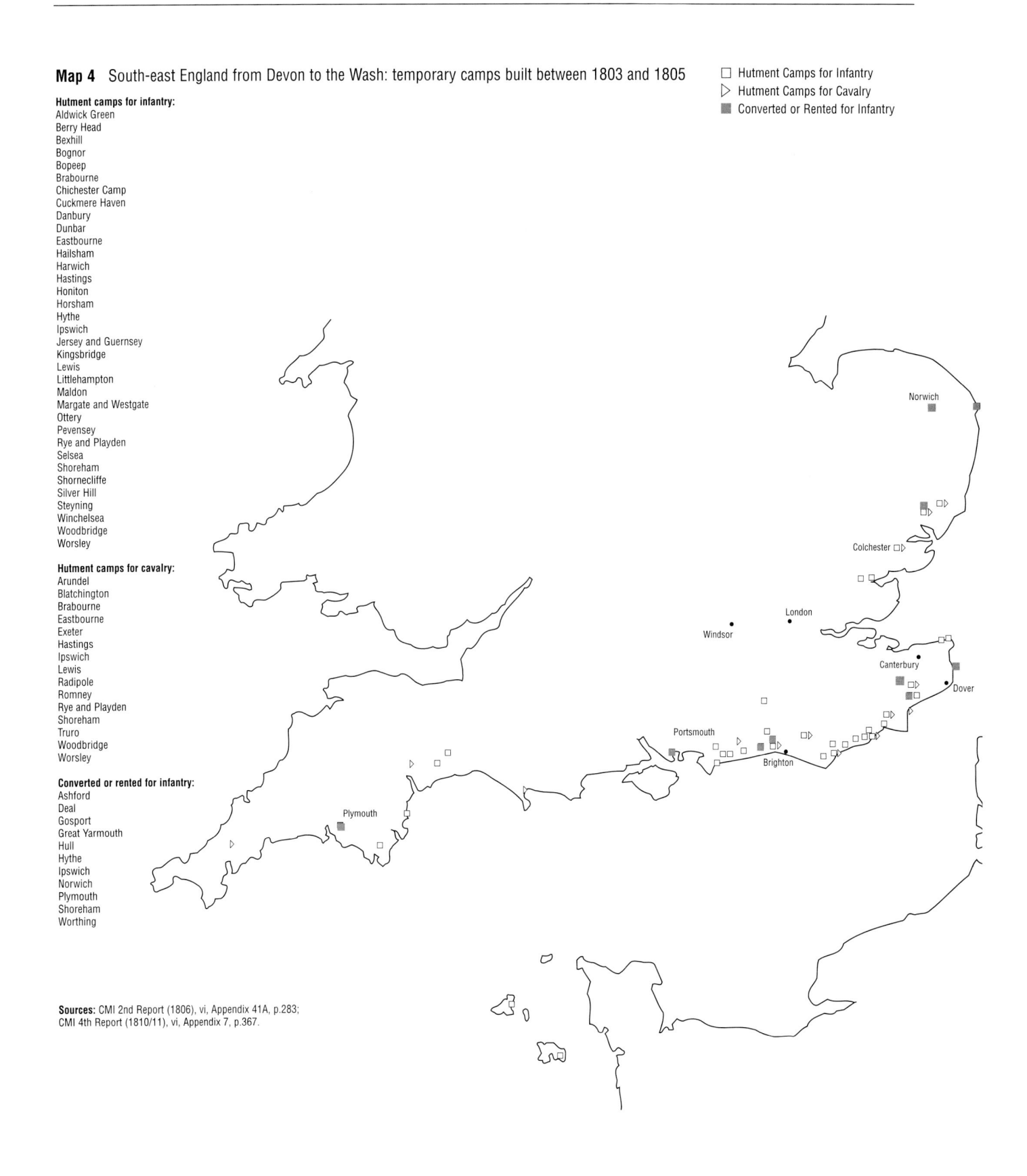

Map 4 South-east England from Devon to the Wash: temporary camps built between 1803 and 1805

☐ Hutment Camps for Infantry
▷ Hutment Camps for Cavalry
■ Converted or Rented for Infantry

Hutment camps for infantry:
Aldwick Green
Berry Head
Bexhill
Bognor
Bopeep
Brabourne
Chichester Camp
Cuckmere Haven
Danbury
Dunbar
Eastbourne
Hailsham
Harwich
Hastings
Honiton
Horsham
Hythe
Ipswich
Jersey and Guernsey
Kingsbridge
Lewis
Littlehampton
Maldon
Margate and Westgate
Ottery
Pevensey
Rye and Playden
Selsea
Shoreham
Shornecliffe
Silver Hill
Steyning
Winchelsea
Woodbridge
Worsley

Hutment camps for cavalry:
Arundel
Blatchington
Brabourne
Eastbourne
Exeter
Hastings
Ipswich
Lewis
Radipole
Romney
Rye and Playden
Shoreham
Truro
Woodbridge
Worsley

Converted or rented for infantry:
Ashford
Deal
Gosport
Great Yarmouth
Hull
Hythe
Ipswich
Norwich
Plymouth
Shoreham
Worthing

Sources: CMI 2nd Report (1806), vi, Appendix 41A, p.283;
CMI 4th Report (1810/11), vi, Appendix 7, p.367.

men, were approved in August 1803 at Musselburgh, Haddington and Dunbar in Scotland, the latter two also with room for 250 cavalry and a 12-gun artillery unit, all on land compulsorily purchased under the Defence Act.[21]

During 1804, some of these were still being completed, but after Napoleon marched his army off to obliterate the Austrians at Austerlitz, the pressure eased, and the Department's new work declined sharply. In 1805, it was engaged in building just two regimental hospitals, an additional ward at Parkhurst and stores in various places. Orders had been received for five new barracks, including one for 1,800 places at Pett, above the cliffs at Hastings, but it is believed that none were carried out. By then, the financial consequences of DeLancey's methods had caught up with him, and the Barracks Department was on the point of collapse.

The Barracks Department in action

The larger part of the work of DeLancey's organization concerned the management of its expanding estate, which it had to keep supplied, according to its warrant, and in reasonable condition despite the battering handed out by revolving units. DeLancey appointed half-pay officers as barrack masters to supervise each barracks, and although they were civil servants, he gave them a military rank so they would have some authority in dealing with visiting commanding officers. Through a commissary contractor, the Department purchased certain consumables necessary for barracks life – beer, coal, candles, fuel for the men and forage for the horses – and kept the barracks stocked according to strict allocations by rank and numbers of men. Furniture, sheets, blankets and towels, chamber pots, ironmongery and cooking utensils, coal buckets, bellows and candlesticks, and implements for cleaning the barracks and messing out the stables were all issued according to War Office schedules.[22]

The allocation of rooms was likewise strictly controlled by the Department's warrant, and less generously than in the pre-war Ordnance Board barracks. Within the officers' quarters, field officers were allowed two rooms, and two more were provided for a mess dining room and an ante-room. Captains down to infantry subalterns and dragoon sergeants had one room each. The regulation density for the rank and file of the cavalry was eight to a room, and the infantry, with fewer accoutrements, twelve. The function of each room was painted over the doorway. For the most part, men continued to sleep in pairs in wooden beds, or stacked in bunks. Sheets were changed every three months, and the roller towel once a week.[23] Theoretically, these Warrant Regulations should have formed the basis of the brief to which the Departments' architects worked, though in practice they can had been little adhered to. Several of the cavalry barracks had rooms of a uniform 16 feet 6 inches (5 metres) width, but their lengths varied widely. Most of the rooms at Knightsbridge Cavalry Barracks were a standard 12 feet by 8 feet (3.7 metres by 2.4 metres), a smaller number were 17 feet by 18 feet (5.2 metres by 5.5 metres), but in one part of the barracks the rooms were 41 feet (12.5 metres) wide and between 36 feet (11 metres) and 58 feet (17.7 metres) long.[24] Little consistency is apparent in room sizes.

In early 1794, DeLancey recruited James Johnson, the architect of Knightsbridge Cavalry Barracks, who, as we have seen (see fig. 56, page 99), may already have worked for him before the war.[25] Johnson was joined at Spring Gardens by John Sanders. He had been Sir John Soane's first pupil, and was a Royal Academy Gold Medal winner in 1788. His major works were the Royal Military Asylum in Chelsea (1801–3, now the Duke of York's School, and used as a barracks from 1823) and the Royal Military College at Sandhurst, which he took over and completed after first James Wyatt and then the barracks contractor Alexander Copland were removed from the long-delayed project.[26]

---

[21] Parliamentary Papers (House of Commons), 1806/7 (99), *ii*, CMI 4th Report, Appendix 14, p.460.
[22] Parliamentary Papers (House of Commons), 1806 (46), *iv*, CMI 1st Report, *Schedule of furniture and utensils*, Appendix 4, p.43.
[23] Parliamentary Papers (House of Commons), 1806 (46), *vi*, CMI 1st Report, *Warrant for the Regulation of Barracks No 4*, 24 March 1795, Appendix 1, p.38.

[24] Parliamentary Papers (House of Commons), 1847, *xxxvi*, *A Return from each Barracks in the United Kingdom*, p.327.
[25] Colvin (1995), pp.548–9. The same year, he was also appointed Surveyor to the Royal Mint and designed the new Mint in London.
[26] J. Selby, 'The Royal Military Academy, Sandhurst', *Country Life*, **145** (26 June 1969), p.1,662; Colvin (1995), p.844.

It must have been tedious, though not unremunerative, work. Sanders maintained that they never developed standard designs which could be used repeatedly because the situation of each barracks was different. In fact, the Department's output varied to a great and surprising extent, not only in room size but in planning and the overall layout of the barracks. No original drawings have been found of the architect's work, but much was built without drawings, just using specifications issued to the contractor.[27]

What standardization there was seems to have arisen more out of the contractors seeking cost savings than any drive by the Department to impose either efficiency or conformity of design. For example, four of the one-troop cavalry stations in the West Country were built by John Scobell. He received a plan, elevation and section of the stone barracks at Modbury from James Johnson, and repeated them in brick for those at Totnes, Barnstaple and Trowbridge.[28] The architects were paid 2.5 per cent of the building cost on top of their salary. Rather than looking for competitive tenders, which the Department claimed would have taken too long, the builders were paid as work progressed by the system of 'fair measure and value', on which Sanders and Johnson received a further percentage as the surveyors. By November 1804, Sanders had netted a gratifying £57,784, and Johnson £46,558.[29]

Likewise avoiding tenders, DeLancey chose to employ a number of large contractors known to him personally, and to whom he gave orders for several barracks at a time. This practice encouraged the formation of sizeable organizations, and some of DeLancey's favoured men – particularly those involved in building the hutment camps – have been cited as the predecessors to the large general contractors of the Regency, such as Thomas Cubitt.[30] One of the biggest was Thomas Neil, who was based off Sloane Square in London. DeLancey awarded him the contract for the timber barracks and the warehouse fitting out work around Sunderland in 1795, described above. When the war resumed in 1803, DeLancey also gave him a large slice of the hutment work, on 16 June ordering him to build temporary camps in Ipswich, Colchester, Thorrington, Maldon and Abberton in Essex, and Littlehampton, Steyning, Arundel, Rottingdean and Chichester in Sussex, to be ready by 29 September.[31]

Alexander Copland's was an even larger operation, with 'its own brickworks, sawpits and building tradesmen' based near Buckingham Palace.[32] He had the infantry hutments at Chelmsford ready for 2,400 men in five weeks during late 1796, and worked equally rapidly to get the large Radipole cavalry station outside Weymouth ready for troops to be received by the King in August 1798. In September 1798, he had over 700 men preparing huts in desperately wet and muddy conditions for the recruiting depot at Parkhurst, on the Isle of Wight.[33]

Planning and design: the permanent cavalry stations

Only four examples remain of the first and most numerous class of permanent barracks built by the Barracks Department: the single-troop cavalry barracks. These are at Weymouth, Barnstaple, (converted to a house after Waterloo), Christchurch and Deal. Deal was then an important military and naval town, with infantry and cavalry barracks, as well as large naval and military hospitals, which were also given over to barracks from the early 1800s. A typical example of the one-troop barracks was Christchurch (see Figure 60). At these small stations, the Department followed the traditional practice of combining the officers' and other ranks' quarters in a single building, merely articulating the superiors' section to distinguish it from the rest of the building. The ground-floor stables had a central gully and iron posts between stalls for 63 horses, and there was a wine cellar under the mess. The men's rooms opened off an axial corridor, and the attic was an open space for storage or extra accommodation, lit by dormers along the sides and in the hipped ends. The soldiers' only source of entertainment was the sutlery, which had a bar, taproom and beer store. The Department made about £25,000 a year nationally from the sutlers' franchise.

---

[27] Parliamentary Papers (House of Commons), 1806/7 (99), *ii*, CMI 4th Report, p.133.
[28] Breihan (1990b), pp.147–8.
[29] Parliamentary Papers (House of Commons), 1806 (317), *vi*, CMI 2nd Report, p.132.
[30] E.W. Cooney, 'The origins of the Victorian Master Builders', *Economic History Review*, 2nd series, **8** (1955).
[31] Parliamentary Papers (House of Commons), 1806/7 (99), *ii*, CMI 4th Report, p.145.
[32] Colvin (1995), p.270.
[33] Parliamentary Papers (House of Commons), 1806/7 (99), *ii*, CMI 4th Report, p.150.

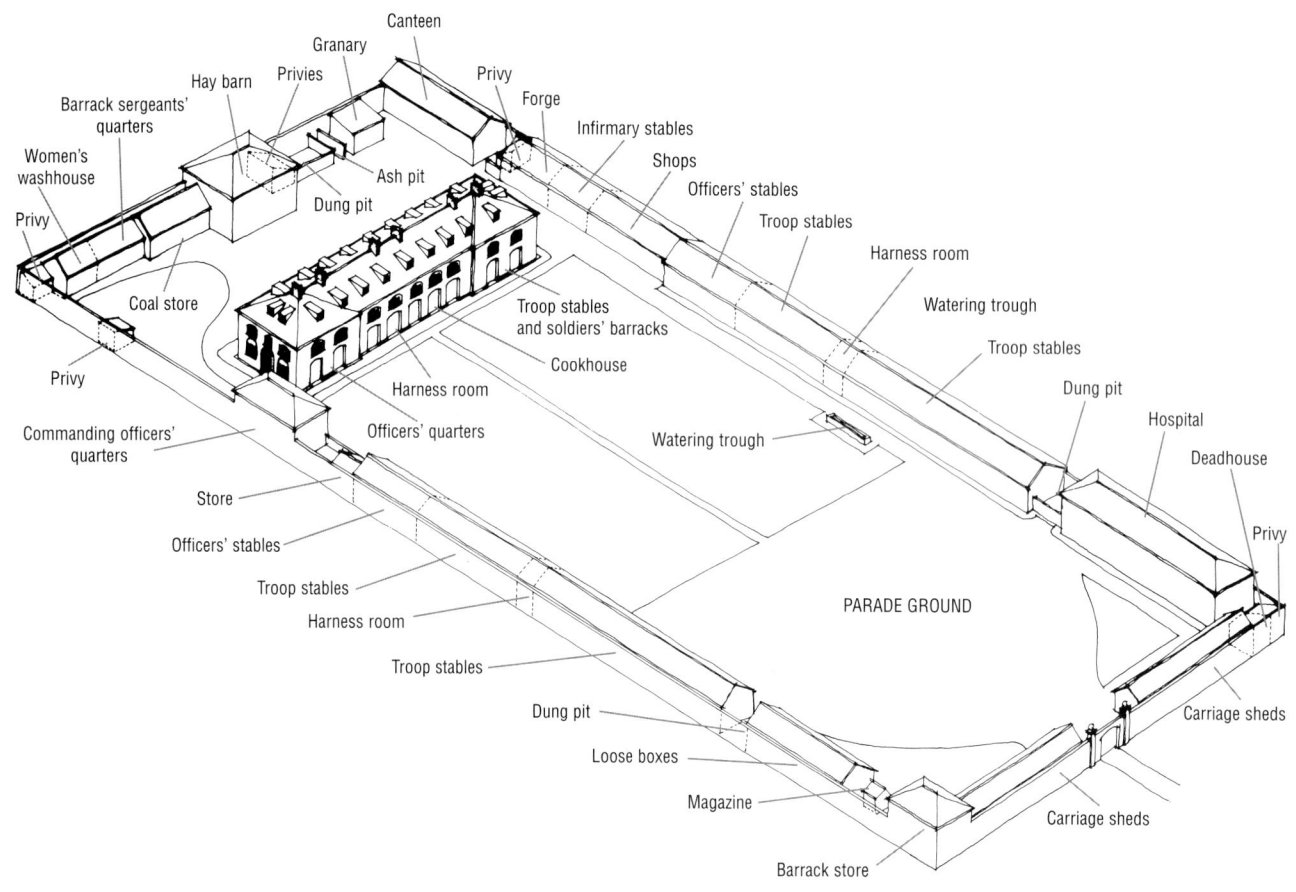

Figure 60 Reconstruction of the single-troop cavalry barracks at Christchurch, based on the surviving fabric and plan by Colonel James RE, c.1861. The officers occupied the left end, and the well-illuminated attic was used for storage or extra living space. The other surviving cavalry barracks at Deal and Exeter are similar, though not so much as to suggest that the builders followed the same drawings. Only the barracks itself still stands.

The lesser ancillary buildings only occasionally survive (see Figure 61). Privies and ablution houses (generally referred to as 'necessaries') were tucked away behind the barracks blocks, as were the washhouse and cookhouse. There were workshops for the farrier and armourer, and separate stables for the officers' chargers, the cream among the unit's horses. Forage barns and granaries formed an important part of any cavalry barracks. Contemporary illustrations show vernacular agricultural buildings raised on staddle-stones to keep out vermin. There were sheds for wood, bedding, straw, a yard for coal, and soil pits away from the living area.

Figure 61 One of the small forage barns or straw stores at Exeter has survived.

The barracks were stocked, maintained and supervised by the barrack master, who lived on site with his family. He bought stores, beer and fodder locally, and ordered fuel and candles, bedding and equipment from the Barracks Department commissaries, for which he had a store in the barracks. He was entitled to sell the horse dung swept from the stables to local farmers, if he could, to defray some of his expenditure.[34]

These small stations were intended for:

'one captain, two subaltern officers, one quartermaster, three sergeants, one trumpeter, one farrier and fifty-one rank and file, with sixty horses. Six large barrack rooms on the first floor each held eight soldiers. Each man had a bedstead with a mattress, bolster, pillow, a palliasse filled with eighteen pounds of straw, two blankets and a pair of sheets. There were pegs over his bed from which to hang his clothes, equipment and sabre. The room was furnished with a table, three forms, and a rack to take the soldiers carbines. A fireplace was fitted with an ordinary domestic grate; fire-irons and a coalbox were provided. The soldiers kitchen had a cooking range. There were dixie-type boilers for each room, and a full set of cooking utensils. Table ware provided included trenchers, beer cans and drinking cups. There were two smaller rooms; one for the three sergeants, the other for the four women who were allowed to live in the barracks with the troop. The women generally undertook the cooking and laundry, while the men cleaned the rooms and passages on their Thursday rest day.' [35]

The total cost of building the barracks was £9,616. Despite the supposed looseness of the Department's financial control, the single-troop barracks all cost a remarkably similar amount, about £130 per man, although they were far more expensive than the larger, permanent ones. The cavalry barracks at Hounslow and York cost around £100 per man, Manchester only £60 per man, and the wooden infantry barracks at Sunderland a mere £11 per man.[36] Perhaps it was cost, then, which curtailed the coastal cavalry chain.

Only fragments can be found today of the larger, permanent stations, most of which were demolished or sold off after the war. When the Barracks Department embarked on its enlarged construction programme, the symmetrical layout used at Manchester – a pair of barrack blocks facing each other across the square and a central officers' barrack on the third side, and ancillary buildings to the perimeter – was generally adopted (see Figure 54, page 64). The most complete surviving cavalry barracks from this period is the Higher (formerly Town) Barracks in Exeter, built in 1794 for around 180 men. It stands on a sloping site facing down towards the city. As a rule, the officers' quarters built by the Department consisted of a double-pile, E-shaped building, with service wings and rooms for the officers' servants at the back (see Figure 55, page 65). On the ground floor on either side of the front door were the dining room and ante-room, and the rest of the building was given over to bedrooms. It was the focus for what little architectural display the department allowed, often a pediment and conventional mid-Georgian doorcase and fanlight. Although it and one of the two men's barracks were rebuilt in the mid-nineteenth century, the west barrack block at Exeter remains substantially as it was built (see Figure 62), and is very similar to those at Deal and Christchurch.

Figure 62 Cavalrymen lived above their horses, as here at the Exeter Higher Barracks.

The larger barracks also had a hospital, run by the regimental surgeon and his staff. That at Exeter (see Figure 63), one of only two which survive from this period, 'was rated for twenty patients in 1805, it had six wards, a surgery, and a kitchen, with a privy and mortuary in the rear'.[37] There were also infirmary stables for sick or injured horses.

---

[34] J. Barker, *Christchurch Barracks*, Bournemouth (Bournemouth 1984).
[35] J. Rowe, 'The Cavalry Barracks at Barnstaple', *Devon and Cornwall Notes and Queries*, **36** (1988), pp.121–7.
[36] House of Commons Sessional Papers, 1795, 96.a78, 4583, *An Account of the Number and Names of all Barrack Masters ...*, p.99.
[37] Breihan (1990a), p.145.

Riding schools were provided for drill practice in all but the single-troop cavalry barracks. Although much smaller than the one at Dublin, they also had wide roofs with specialized trusses. Those at Exeter and Dorchester are the oldest military riding schools in England.

Figure 63 The small barracks hospital at the Exeter Higher Barracks.

Barracks for the infantry

The Barracks Department only built permanent infantry quarters at Glasgow, Aberdeen, Ayr, Dundee, Windsor and Deal, and of these, only the South Barracks at Deal is still standing (see Figure 64). It was erected in 1796 alongside that for the cavalry, close to the general military hospital (this later became the North Barracks, and the naval hospital the East Barracks). The large, central officers' quarters contained rooms for seven field officers, 22 captains and 56 subalterns and staff. It stood facing the parade ground, between the two barrack blocks for the privates and NCOs, which were each rated for over 900 men. To the back of each was a small, octagonal cookhouse, of which one still remains (see Figure 65). Although most food was cooked on the open-grate fires which heated the rooms, dedicated cooking facilities were sometimes built in the larger barracks. They were permanent versions of campaign cooking fires, which were also octagonal, with eight coal-filled trenches radiating from a central flue. These rudimentary kitchens

Figure 64 This range at Deal, with its central officers' quarters flanked by infantrymen's barracks, is the most complete and unaltered infantry barracks of the Revolutionary War. It was taken over by the Navy for a Marines depot and extended in the 1870s. The officer's quarters is the pedimented range in the centre.

Figure 65 The former cookhouse at Deal.

represented a preliminary step towards separate barracks kitchens, but there was little further progress in this direction for fifty years.

Timber-framed barracks

In the early part of the war, the Barracks Department's architects built six barracks which, despite being of timber rather than brick or stone, they referred to as being 'established', by which they meant permanent. The first were at Chelmsford and Colchester in Essex, in 1794, followed by Sunderland, Romford and Croydon a year later, and Maidstone in 1797.[38] The last three were all cavalry stations and relatively small, but the infantry barracks were substantial. Sunderland had a capacity of 1,528 men, probably in 'nineteen large barracks rooms housing thirty-six men each in double berths, and twenty sergeants' rooms each sleeping four men in two-level bunks'.[39]

The only evidence of their mode of construction is the surviving officers' quarters at Maidstone (see

Figure 66 The unique, surviving, timber-framed officers' quarters at Maidstone. Separate doorways led to the CO's rooms at the left end and the mess at the other, though this may be a later addition.

---

[38] Parliamentary Papers (House of Commons), 1806 (317), *vi*, CMI 2nd Report, Appendix 41A, p.283.
[39] Breihan (1990b), p.171.

Figure 66). This was an important cavalry station between Chatham and Brighton, and London and the Kent coast. Apart from the brick chimneys and slate roof, the building was entirely of wood, with a pine balloon frame clad in white weatherboarding. Flights of stairs divided it internally into three, and there were service wings to the rear. The officers had small, plain rooms with a fireplace in one corner and a built-in cupboard in the other, and they were issued with bedding, a table, bellows, fire irons and a chamber pot. It is noteworthy that the architectural conventions used to denote the importance of the officers – the pediment and details such as the fanlights – held good even for the hastily constructed timber barracks.[40]

Figure 67 The former timber huts at Weymouth are the only examples known to have survived from the many camps built for the infantry defences along the south coast.

Temporary hut encampments

By far the most numerous of the barracks built during the war years were temporary hutment camps. The dimensions of the huts, as one would expect from the Department, were left to the individual contractors, who each appear to have come up with their own solutions.[41] They were usually weatherboarded timber frames raised on brick footings. At the camp at Horsham in Sussex, which could house over a thousand men, they were surprisingly large: two storeys high, 112 feet (34.1 metres) long by 33 feet (10.1 metres) wide.

Internally, they were divided into eight-man rooms, with two-tier 'hutches' for the men to sleep in. As well as eight of these barrack huts, there was one for a hospital, an officers' mess and servants' accommodation, stores, a guardhouse, a canteen, three cookhouses and a magazine. The horses were stabled in a long, narrow shed, 270 feet (82.3 metres) long by 26 feet (7.9 metres) wide.[42]

The huts built in Devon were smaller, each sleeping about twenty-four men. They were arranged in three-sided quadrangles for either a troop of cavalry or a unit of infantry. The NCOs' huts were at the corners, and the officers lived in separate houses to one side. The temporary barracks at Chichester built by Thomas Neill in 1796 contained a cavalry section of eight 13-man huts, and a larger infantry encampment on the opposite side of the barrack field consisted of five open quadrangles, each with a central officers' hut, and a larger field officers' quarters and mess room (see Figure 68).[43]

Two big camps were even built of huts with walls raised from sods, though for obvious reasons they were not successful. One was at Bexhill, for 2,500 men, and another at Winchelsea, where there were 40 of these damp shelters, each supposedly for 32 men. They were in effect a revival of the original *barracas* – ephemeral havens which harked back to medieval campaigning.[44]

Within a couple of years of their hasty assembly, the hutment camps were being given up and the huts sold off, and only three fragmentary standing remains are known of today, all that is left of the big Radipole cavalry station, built on the hills above Weymouth. Now an undifferentiated expanse of inter-war houses, in 1804 it was the largest single cavalry station in the country. It was Radipole which Alexander Copland enlarged with such extraordinary rapidity in sixteen days in 1798. Initially for 404 men and 392 horses, Copland more than doubled the capacity in a few weeks to 912 men, 51 officers and 986 horses, in time for the arrival of the King at Weymouth.[45] On the west side of the former square stands a pair of delicate,

---

[40] RE Library, Chatham, *Plan of Maidstone barracks*. 420/71; *Queen's Own Gazette*, March 1933, p.53.
[41] Prefabricated huts were not generally available in Britain until the 1830s, so it is supposed that the hutment camps were built on site from prepared timber.
[42] A.Watkinson, 'Steyning as a garrison town, 1804–14' (typed manuscript, undated, NAM).
[43] Colonel James RE, *Plans of the Barracks of the Aldershot District* (London 1861); Breihan (1990a), pp.48–9.
[44] Parliamentary Papers (House of Commons), 1806/7 (99), *ii*, CMI 4th Report, Appendix 9Q, p.428.
[45] Breihan (1989), pp.11–13.

1792–1815: 'No Barns, No Pigstyes'

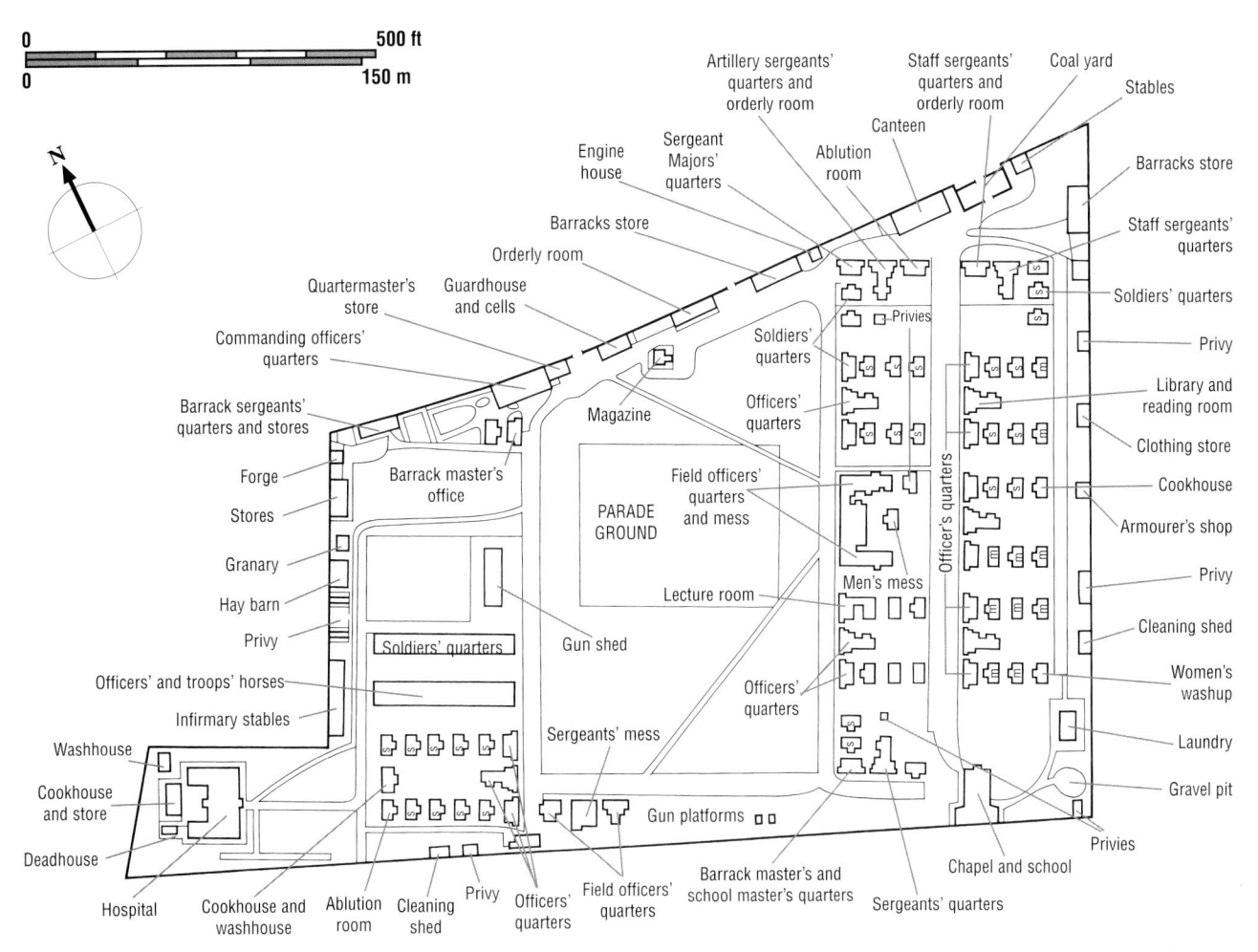

Figure 68 The camp at Chichester, redrawn from a plan by Colonel James RE, c.1861. The small cavalry section is at the south-west corner, with their barns and granary nearby; the larger infantry compound centred on the field officers' quarters and mess lies across the east end. Facilities like the sergeants' mess, library, chapel and the married quarters are later additions made in the 1840s and 1850s (s = soldiers' quarters; m = married soldiers' quarters).

wooden-framed cottages, enriched with later moulded and fretted boards, which may have been officers' houses. In the north-east corner is a row of seven plainer buildings which have been called 'stables', but were heated by corner fireplaces and are more likely to have been for troopers (see Figure 67).

Of all the other hutment camps, hastily thrown up under the threat of invasion and once home for thousands of men and their families, little trace remains. Their archaeological potential remains unexplored, but could well shed light on the material culture of a social group which has left few remains – in this case the nameless militiamen and volunteers who passed some incommodious months between 1803 and 1805 away from their homes. Today, often the only echo in the landscape of these vanished communities is the name 'Barrack Road' beside a lumpy field.

The barracks built by the Ordnance Board

The contribution of the Ordnance Board to this crisis in military accommodation was limited to housing the gunners and garrison troops in strongholds like Dover, and in coastal fortifications and batteries. It built several new barracks for the Royal Artillery, but its main building role was strengthening and manning the country's coastal defences.

Figure 69 The barracks at Maker Heights Redoubt No.2. This remains one of the most complete, and least altered, examples of a barracks from the Napoleonic period.

Building work came under the Chief Engineer of the Ordnance, General William Green. When he retired in April 1802, a separate Corps of Royal Engineers was established, and the title of the post changed to Inspector General of Fortifications. New construction work was instigated both by the Engineering Department under the Inspector General, Lieutenant General Robert Morse, and by the local engineers at particular stations. The Ordnance Board were also able to draw upon the design services of their architect, James Wyatt,[46] who claimed to have designed 'all the civil buildings of the Ordnance, and occasionally the Buildings for military purposes, when specifically applied to'.[47]

In the immediate post-war years, the first director of the School of Military Engineering at Chatham, Colonel C.W. Pasley, described how the Board usually worked:

'In the Ordnance Department, designs furnished by the architect are sometimes executed by the Engineering Department, as was the case with the Ordnance Barracks at Chatham, which were planned by Mr Wyatt, and executed under the charge of Lieutenant Colonel D'Arcy, then the Commanding Engineer at the station. But generally, it is more usual for the Engineer to design as well as superintend, unless the building should be much more decorated than the barracks mentioned.'[48]

The accommodation over which the Board had control was divided between that for artillery units manning coastal batteries, Martello towers and the main castles and forts and a much smaller number of barracks for field and horse artillery regiments. Coastal batteries were concentrated during the war along unprotected stretches of coastline from the Firth of Forth to Falmouth, and were dispersed in smaller numbers up the west coast as well. Some occupied older fortifications like the Henrician castles, which already contained accommodation (see Figures 2 and 22, pages 5 and 25), but timber huts were provided at others, such as the advanced batteries to the Thames forts at Tilbury and Gravesend.[49] More substantial quarters were

---

[46] See Colvin, *The History of the King's Works*, **6** (1973), pp.49–75. Wyatt's work with the Ordnance was investigated as part of the 15th Report of the Commission for Military Inquiry.

[47] Parliamentary Papers (House of Commons), 1810/11 (261), *iv*, CMI 15th Report, Appendix 5, p.314.

[48] C.W. Pasley, *Practical Architecture, a course for junior officers of the Royal Engineers*, 2nd edn (1862), p.261.

[49] Saunders (1989), pp.136–7.

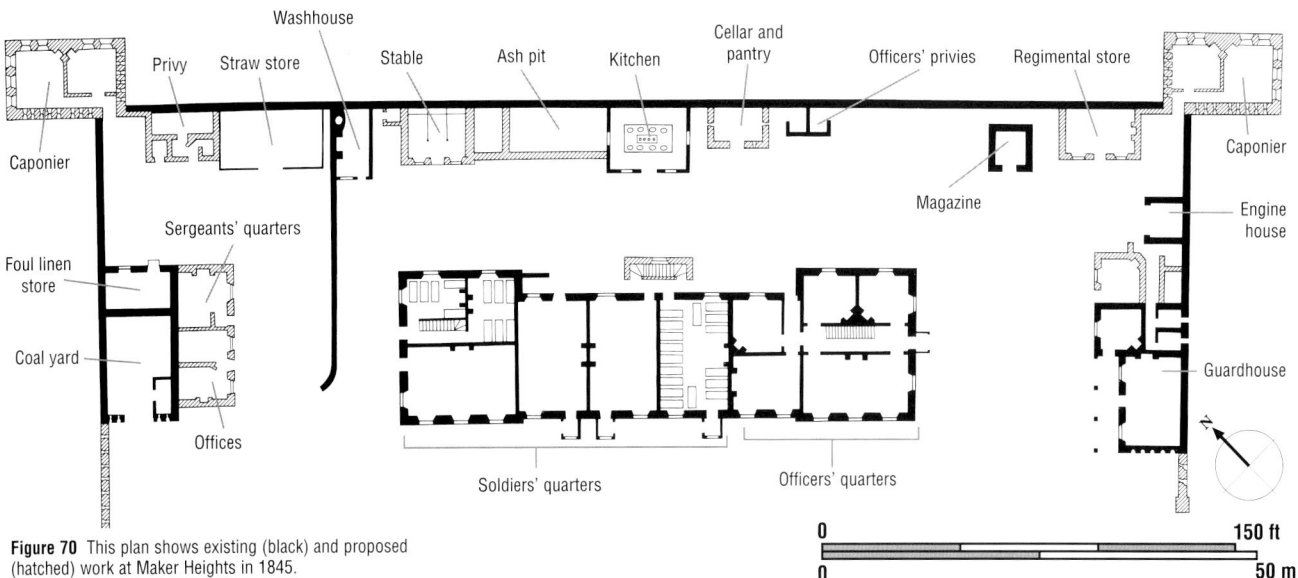

Figure 70 This plan shows existing (black) and proposed (hatched) work at Maker Heights in 1845.

sometimes erected, such as those for the garrison manning the redoubts on Maker Heights (see Figures 69 and 70). These were four advanced, detached artillery positions on the ground overlooking Devonport Dockyard from the west, each protected by sections of deep ditch which had been excavated in 1782. The Ordnance built a combined barracks range for about 200 men behind one of the redoubts in 1801. It was similar to the one-troop cavalry barracks, with the officers in a separate section at one end – the old arrangement, which obviously continued to be acceptable for small stations such as this. The upper floor was simply a weatherboarded timber frame, and was only rebuilt in masonry in 1859. The officers' stables, stores and a small magazine were set against the wall which closed the redoubt to the rear.[50]

Living space for the gunners had also to be included within the various different artillery batteries which the Board built during the war. In the Martello towers erected along the coastlines of Britain and Ireland from 1804 to 1812, the garrison of around twenty-four gunners and one officer lived on the first floor. This was divided unevenly into two rooms, each with a fireplace and a window, with a third small room for the quartermaster's store.[51] The English Martello line included three circular redoubts at Eastbourne, Dymchurch and Harwich, and in each of these more substantial works the garrison was accommodated in casemates which opened into the central space. In Ireland, however, large artillery batteries such as those guarding the crossings of the River Shannon had self-defensible barracks or blockhouses in which the artillerymen could shelter if attacked.[52] The biggest and most imposing work of this type was in England, at Fort Pitt, which protected the crossing of the River Medway south of Chatham. Fort Pitt was built over fourteen years from 1805, and included a tall brick keep and gun tower to the rear, containing casemated barracks for the defenders.[53]

In Chatham itself, the Ordnance built a barracks for the garrison defending the dockyards entirely made up of casemates, because of its particularly exposed situation within the ditch of the defensive Lines. The St Mary's Casemates formed a long, double-decker brick range of segmental-arched caverns with a nominal capacity for over 1,100 men. It was built between 1807 and 1812, but was soon given over to French prisoners of war. The problem with casemate barracks was that the long, vaulted chambers were poorly ventilated, with little natural light, and when filled with unwashed soldiers they rapidly became insalubrious and unhealthy. After the war, powder was stored in the casemates, but they were again occupied by infantrymen from 1844.

[50] A. Pye, 'Maker Barracks', *Exeter Archaeology Unit Report* (Exeter 1994).
[51] S. Sutcliffe, *Martello Towers* (Newton Abbot 1987), p.76.
[52] Kerrigan (1995), pp.204–46.
[53] V. Smith, 'The later nineteenth century land defences of Chatham', *Post-Medieval Archaeology*, 10 (1976), pp.104–7

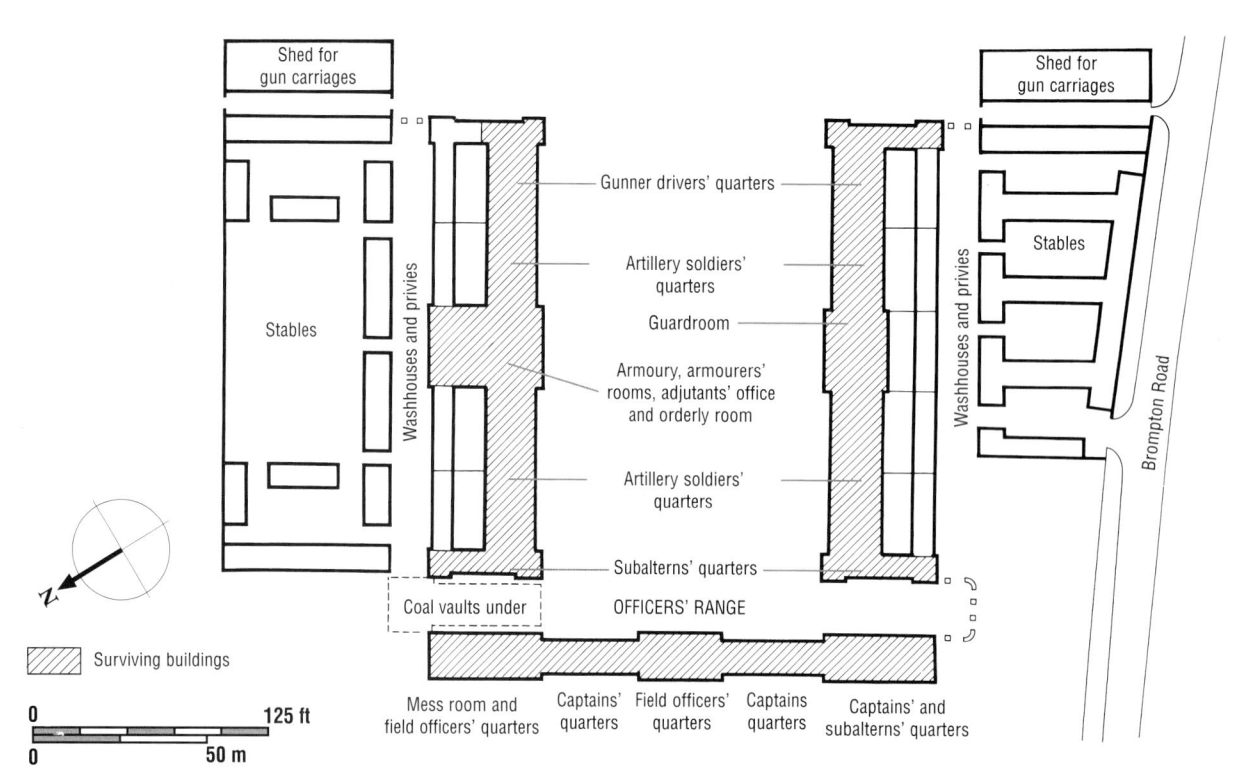

Figure 71 Brompton Artillery Barracks, Chatham, 1806, the largest built by the Ordnance Board during the war, redrawn from the original plan. A note warns, 'The drawings of the offices to the rear have not been received from Mr Wyatt,' but it is not clear how much responsibility he had overall.

Each one had a door and two windows in one end, and a fireplace in the other, 60 feet (18.3 metres) away. As each casemate was 16 feet (4.9 metres) wide but only 7 feet (2.1 metres) high, with a regulation occupancy of 24–30 men, each occupant had barely 250 cubic feet (7.1 cubic metres) of air.

Work on the completion of the Royal Artillery's prestigious home station on Woolwich Common continued until 1808. New barracks for artillery regiments were also put up at Jersey, Ipswich, Shornecliffe and Canterbury, and in Ireland at Castlebar, Conmel, Waterford, Longford and Athlone. Following the resumption of war in 1803, the Board built a prestigious new barracks at Chatham, two smaller ones in Exeter and Newcastle upon Tyne, and provided extra accommodation for an enlarged garrison on the Western Heights, complementing the crucial stronghold of Dover Castle.

For the new artillery barracks at Chatham, the Ordnance Board adopted the same expedient as had been so grandiloquently employed at Woolwich: assembling a more splendid whole out of stock components. The site chosen was land long used for camps on the hill above the dockyard. James Wyatt produced a drawing for the Ordnance in February 1804 (see Figure 71), and the barracks were completed in 1806.[54] Plans were signed by Lieutenant Colonel R. D'Arcy RE, the Commanding Engineer at Chatham, and the officer responsible for superintending their construction.

Wyatt and D'Arcy formed an impressive, three-sided quadrangle (see Figure 72). Each side was composed of a pair of two-storey 'modules' with three-storey Palladian pavilions at each end, similar to the lower sections at Woolwich, which were linked together by central colonnades of giant, stuccoed columns (see Figure 73). The two long, opposing ranges contained double-depth rooms housing a total of 338 gunner drivers and 956 artillery soldiers and their subalterns. On the north side was an armoury and

[54] PRO WO78/2649.

offices, with a large chapel in the middle, one of the earliest in a barracks and in the open, preaching-box plan adopted by the chapels in the naval dockyards. Behind were stabling for 200 horses and sheds for 30 gun carriages. Across the west end, commanding both the parade square and the view down to the River Medway, was the officers' quarters and mess. It was first occupied by the Foot Artillery, but the Royal Military Artificers (renamed the Royal Sappers and Miners in 1813) also had a company at Brompton from 1806, and in 1812 it became a Royal Engineers' establishment, as it remains today.[55]

The two smaller artillery barracks in Exeter and Newcastle upon Tyne are both reputed to have been designed by Wyatt, though neither appears in the list of his drawings for the Ordnance which he drew up in 1807, and the strong dissimilarities rather suggest that they were designed independently by their respective local engineers.

Figure 72 A view of Brompton Artillery Barracks looking toward the river, taken c.1870, with the officers' quarters and central mess in the centre.

Wyvern Barracks in Exeter, across the city from DeLancey's Higher Barracks, was built in 1804 (see Figure 74). Unlike the Barracks Department quarters, at Wyvern the officers of the Artillery shared the same barracks with their men, who occupied the lower wings to either side of the pedimented section. Their horses were kept in single-storey stables either side of the square, and on the opposite side were the quarters of the officers

Figure 73 Brompton Artillery Barracks. Each of the three sides was composed of two modular units, linked by a giant order of colonnades.

and men of the Royal Artillery Drivers, flanking the main entrance. The hospital, the magazine and all the gun sheds, the wheelers' shop, shoeing sheds and collar and harness-makers' shops – the workshops necessary to an artillery regiment – have all been demolished.

Within the tall pediment is a large coat of arms made of Coade stone (see Figure 75). Half a dozen of these, brightly painted sculptures in artificial stone, were ordered from Mrs Coade's catalogue by the War Department in the 1790s. One was for Fulford Barracks, the York cavalry station built by the Barracks Department in 1794, and was preserved when the barracks were demolished. The others were at Ipswich Artillery Barracks, the cavalry barracks at Northampton, Perth and Ayr, and the Scottish infantry barracks at Edinburgh, Hamilton and Glasgow. The only connection between this apparently disparate selection is their start date in late 1793 or early 1794.[56]

The Fenham Artillery Barracks in Newcastle upon Tyne was contemporaneous with Wyvern, but had a completely different plan, and was built from more expensive sandstone ashlar, rather than the brick that was otherwise universally used for barracks of this period (see Figure 76). The officers' quarters and mess (now student houses) were at right angles to one end of a long range for the gunners, who resided in rooms above the stables. Along Barrack Road, to the front, the perimeter wall was canted

[55] RE Library, 1960. *Historical record of Brompton barracks*, July, Annex 'A' to SME 21/2.
[56] A Kelly, Mrs Coade's Stone (Upton-on-Severn, 1990), p.275.

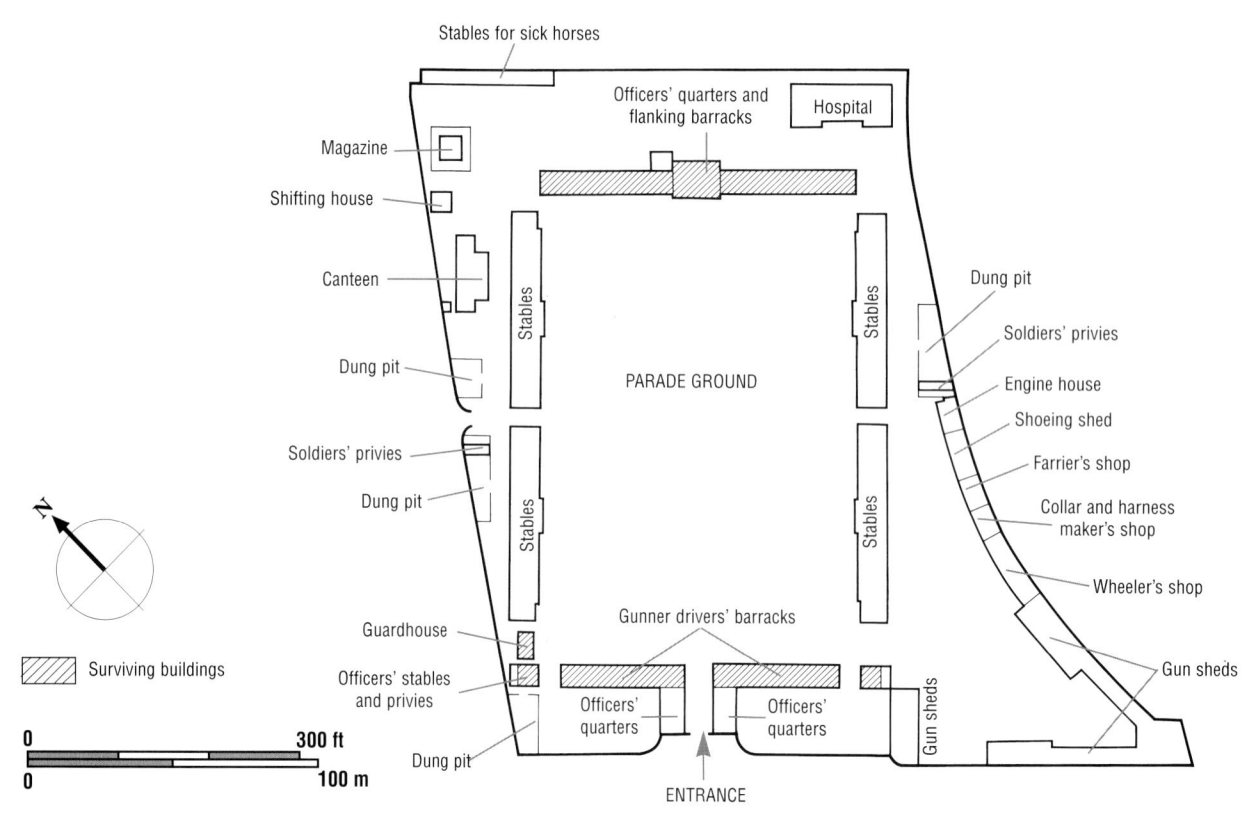

Figure 74 Wyvern Artillery Barracks, Exeter, redrawn from a plan of 1813. By this date, it was uncommon for officers and their men to share the same range of quarters. Unlike the cavalry, the horses of the Artillery were stabled in separate buildings.

Figure 75 Wyvern Artillery Barracks, with its Coade stone royal coat of arms attached to the central officers' quarters.

out, and the entrance, in the angle, was protected by two guardhouses (see Figure 77). Wyatt's hand may be discernable in the unusual oriel windows on moulded stone supports which gave the guard a field of fire up and down the road. Inside was the barrack master's office, and along the rear wall were the hospital for the men and the larger horse infirmary.[57]

Dover Western Heights and the Grand Shaft

The principal works which the Ordnance carried out in reaction to the invasion threat of 1803 were at the key strategic fortress of Dover. In July, the Commander-in-Chief asked that Dover be protected by extra troops to prevent a landing. Moving in its proper and considered way, the Ordnance, under the Commanding Engineer of the Southern District, Lieutenant Colonel William Twiss, prepared and had approved a plan to secure the Western Heights, the hill which overlooked the Castle to the south-west. The bone-shaped plan of fortifications which was adopted included an improved citadel at the far western end, connected by a deep, dry moat to a polygonal fort at the Castle end above the Drop, the steep valley above the town; the fort accordingly became known as the Drop Redoubt. There was to

[57] PRO WO55/2422.

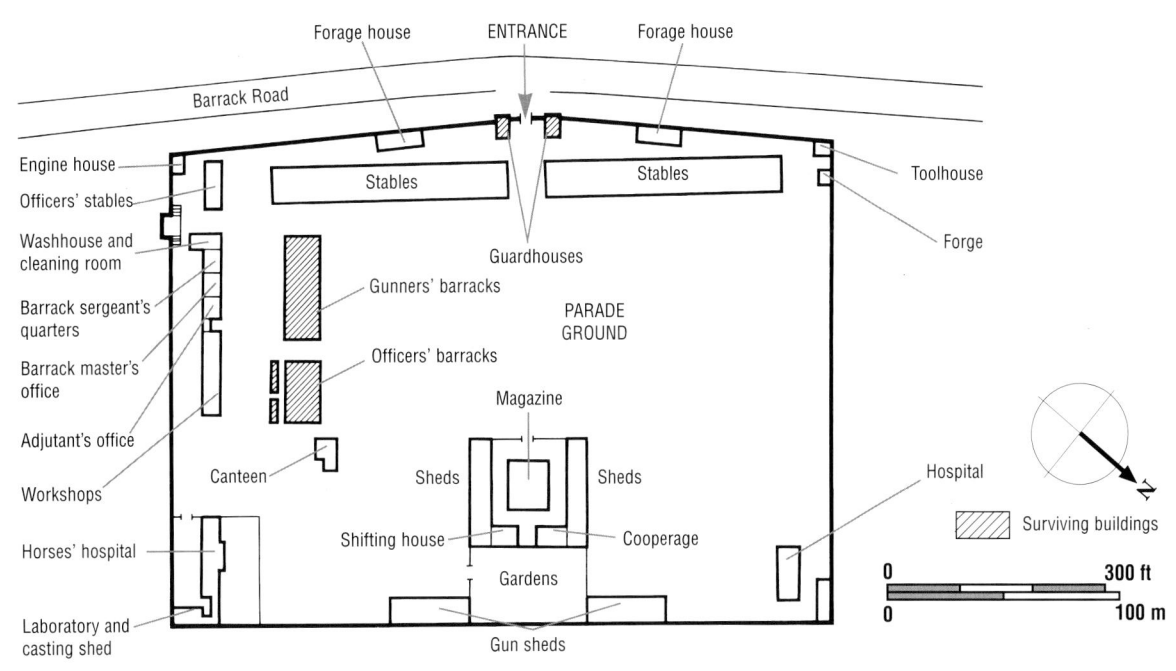

Figure 76 Fenham Artillery Barracks, Newcastle upon Tyne, redrawn from a plan of 1811. The buildings particular to the Artillery stand out – the large magazine enclosed by sheds with a shifting house (for filling cannon-balls) and cooperage, and the laboratory and casting shed in one corner.

be accommodation in the casemates of the Redoubt for 800 men, and more in the Citadel, so the Board decided the rest of the enlarged garrison only needed a single barracks for a further 700 men. In October 1804, the Barracks Department was ordered to build the new barracks on the Western Heights.[58]

On the slope between the Drop Redoubt and the cliff facing the sea, Twiss had a level platform cut back to make a parade ground. Above it were built three severe, three-storey terraces of barracks, stepping up the slope (see Figure 78, page 90). The front and the middle ranges were for the soldiers, who lived in deep, narrow rooms for 15 men, lit front and rear, each with its own stair. An NCO slept in the corner beside the stair door, and there was a single fireplace on one side. The officers' quarters and mess were to the right, where they and their servants had rather more commodious rooms, and the field officers' accommodation was at the back. The canteen, washhouses, cookhouses and privies, the armourer's and tailor's shops, and stores were in a line up the hillside to the left.[59]

What distinguished the barracks on the Western Heights was the unique method Twiss devised for getting the troops down from the hill to meet an invading force on the beach. Although the 'new barracks ... [were] little more than 300 yards [0.3 kilometres] horizontally from the sea,' he explained, '... on horseback the distance [was] nearly a mile and half [2.4 kilometres]'.[60] To avoid this slow, and in wet weather, hazardous route, Twiss constructed

Figure 77 Fenham Artillery Barracks. The architecture of the guardhouses suggests that a more inventive hand, such as Wyatt's, may have been involved.

---

[58] Coad and Lewis (1982), pp.160–5; Parliamentary Papers (House of Commons), 1806/7 (99), *ii*, CMI 4th Report, Appendix 9Q, p.445.
[59] EH Map Room, WD 2506, 2453.
[60] Quoted in Coad and Lewis (1982), p.163.

Figure 78 The Grand Shaft Barracks, with the Drop Redoubt behind and the Castle in the distance. The steps down to the shaft descend from the parade ground.

the Grand Shaft by which name the barracks is known. This was a 50 feet (15.2 metres) wide vertical excavation, dropping from in front of the square 90 feet (27.4 metres) to the level of the beach. Inside were three flights of concentric stairs, one above the other, winding around a central 12 feet (3.7 metres) wide light well. From the bottom, a wide tunnel sloped down to emerge at the cliff face, beside the guardhouse. It was completed by c.1807. Although the barracks was demolished in the 1960s, the Grand Shaft remains, a 'bold and imaginative solution to communication problems [and] a unique piece of military engineering' (see Figure 79).[61]

Barracks in Ireland during the Napoleonic Wars

The Royal Engineers in Ireland faced some of the same problems as their brother officers did in England: accommodating a reinforced and much more numerous wartime garrison. But these difficulties were compounded by the particular circumstances in Ireland of a local populace at best unenthusiastic to the cause of national defence, and at worst actively seeking to give every assistance and encouragement to the enemy. Because of the long-standing British policy of maintaining the Irish garrison in barracks, begun by Cromwell and put onto a national footing by William III, few settlements of any consequence lacked quarters of some sort. Many, however, were getting on for a hundred years old and inadequate by contemporary

Figure 79 The upper entrance to the Grand Shaft.

[61] Coad and Lewis (1982), p.163; EH Map Room, WD 2354.

standards, and much rebuilding had to be done. Additional works were carried out to improve the island's defences, both in places vulnerable to a French landing and in important internal strategic points, like the Shannon crossings. And in one instance, in the Wicklow mountains, a laborious programme of laying roads and erecting barracks had to be undertaken as a counter-insurgency measure against Irish nationalists.

Several large, new barracks were built by the Royal Irish Engineers before they were disbanded after the Union in 1801, and more were added thereafter by the Ordnance Board. In Dublin, the 1810 Portobello Barracks could accommodate almost a thousand men and over 700 horses, and the Richmond Infantry Barracks of the same year was even larger, for over 1,500 men. At Athlone – the headquarters of the Western Division and centre of the Shannon defensive line down the middle of the country – the new barracks built between 1783 and 1815 had quarters for 920 infantry, cavalry and artillery, and stables for over 200 horses. New barracks in Cork held 300 cavalry and some 3,000 men in 1811, and others were erected in Parsonstown, Mullingar, Limerick, Cahir, Naas, Tralee, Fermoy and elsewhere.

In planning terms, the Irish barracks of this period are quite distinct from those in mainland Britain. For instance, the two big Dublin barracks each consisted of a single, long range with a ceremonial archway through the centre, and officers' quarters at right angles to each side. This layout was also used at Naas and Parsonstown (see Figure 80, page 92). At Athlone, in contrast, the accommodation was placed within a series of closed or partially closed courtyards for the different branches of the army accommodated there.[62] Neither of these layouts is found in mainland Britain.

Much more numerous than the large garrison complexes, and more expressive of the military situation in the island, were small, defensible barracks (see Figure 81). The concept of secure quarters dated back to the Williamite works of the late seventeenth century, and they are much less common elsewhere in Britain. Unlike the self-defensible blockhouses erected within fortifications that are referred to above, defensible barracks were conventional in their planning and construction, but protected by a tall enclosing wall with salient corners or bastions with musket loops to provide fields of fire across the sides or entrance. As such, they were intended to safeguard the occupying troops against a hostile local force armed only with hand weapons, not artillery.

A sequence of five such defensible barracks was employed from 1800 to subdue insurgents who had been holding out in the boggy highlands of the Wicklow Mountains, south of Dublin, since 1798. As General Wade had done against the Jacobites in the Scottish Highlands, and numerous other regular armies have also done when dealing with elusive guerrilla forces, the British decided to lay a road through the mountains and to station troops in secure barracks erected at intervals along it. Each one consisted of a tall wall with bastions on two opposite corners enclosing an open 'square', and a barracks with ground-floor stables and quarters above for a captain and around a hundred men. Work on the barracks continued after the insurgents had surrendered late in 1803, but by then they had already been rendered redundant, and they were abandoned as military posts not long after the end of the war.[63]

The political and financial consequences for the Barracks Department

As soon as DeLancey's police barracks had been completed in early 1793, the old constitutional objections were again being raised. But with the governing and property-owning classes feeling threatened by both sedition and invasion, the concerns raised by the Whig Opposition in the House of Commons about the dangers of allowing the army to live in barracks sound ritualistic.[64] A motion was moved in February 1793 by an MP who had noticed the new barracks going up at Sheffield, near his home, and he invoked Blackstone's warning: 'no barracks or inland fortresses'. Charles James Fox, the Whig leader, duly asserted the

---

[62] Colonel James RE, *Plans of the Barracks of Ireland* (London 1858), p.2.
[63] Kerrigan (1995), pp.179–82.
[64] Colley (1993), p.289; R. Wells, *Insurrection: The British Experience 1795–1803* (Gloucester 1983).

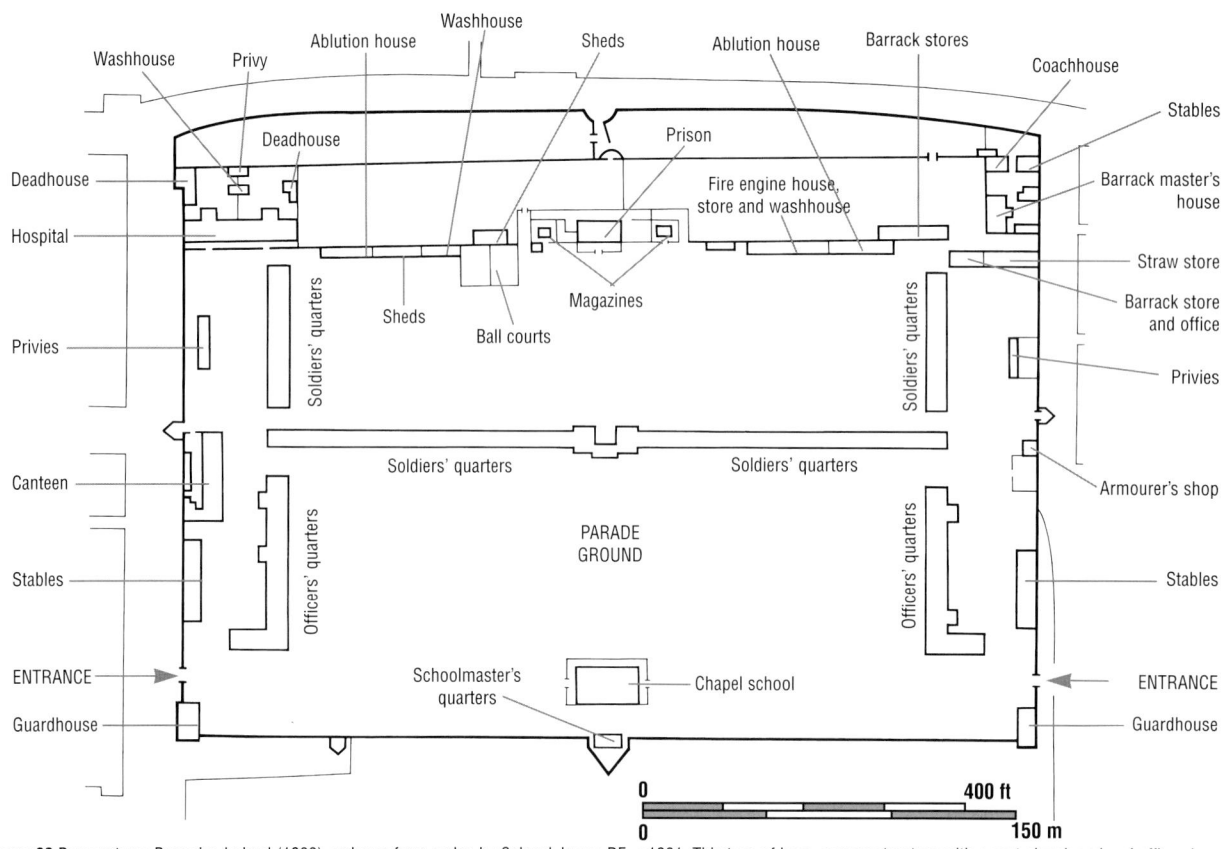

Figure 80 Parsonstown Barracks, Ireland (1809), redrawn from a plan by Colonel James RE, c.1861. This type of long, narrow structure with a central arch and end officers' lodgings was built at several Irish barracks, but not in mainland Britain. The chapel school is a later addition.

conventional view that 'the mixing of the soldiers with the people ... was the best security of the constitution against the danger of a standing army'. But the Government's majority was not seriously threatened. Pitt stressed the danger of the situation, both internally and from abroad, which made necessary the new barracks, saying: 'the circumstances of the country coupled with the general state of affairs, rendered it advisable to provide barracks in other parts of the country [to where they were already, in London, Scotland and the dockyards, etc.] ... A spirit had appeared in the country in some of the manufacturing towns which made it necessary that troops should be kept near them.' [65]

That same month, David Erskine published a polemical pamphlet on the recent 'unconstitutional and illegal Measure of Barracks' in the Manchester papers. He foresaw it as a 'harbinger of some more important mischief' and urged people to petition Parliament against 'this daring attempt on your

Figure 81 Defensible barracks at Drumgoff. The wild Wicklow mountains were brought under control by the construction of five such barracks linked by a military road. Like Ruthven and the other barracks built after the 1715 Rising in Scotland (see figs 19 and 20, pages 22 and 23), they were protected from musketry and hand arms by corner bastions, but did not anticipate artillery attack.

[65] Parliamentary History, 30 (1793), p.473.
[66] Albanicus (Hon. David Erskine), *Letters on the impolicy of a standing army* (London 1793).

Liberties'.[66] No such appeals appear to have been made, however, and by July, DeLancey was setting up the Barracks Department under the King's Warrant.

The Prime Minister himself appears to have been convinced of the value of barracks, both for controlling sedition and internal disorder, and for maintaining the loyalty and effectiveness of the troops during the war. He had been personally involved in sending DeLancey on his original mission, as we have seen, and remained committed to the decision to transfer the army into barracks, and to the means adopted by the Barrack Master General. In 1798, for instance, he wrote to the Commander-in-Chief, the Duke of York, with respect to three new hutment camps at Silverhill, Bexhill and Battle: 'I understand them to have been strongly recommended on military grounds, and I do not think the amount of the expense should prevent their immediate execution, and I will give instructions for providing the amount from the Treasury as soon as Colonel Delancey has stated to the Treasury what issue will be requisite in the first instance.'[67] Seven years later, in August 1805, he was still pressing the Quartermaster General: 'it is of the utmost importance to the health of the Troops, as well as in every other respect (when the season of the year is considered) that the barracks should be commenced without delay'.[68]

By this time, however, the rights and wrongs of barracks were less of an issue than the amount of money that the Barrack Master General and his swollen Department were costing the country. The second Commons debate on the subject, in 1796, opened with the claim that £1 million had already been spent on barracks without any parliamentary sanction. The Secretary of War, Windham, rehearsed the now accepted advantages of barracks. The existing ones were only for infantry, and in the wrong places. Billeting was unfair to the innkeepers who bore its cost. Suitable inns were not situated on the main marching routes, and the expense of barracks would anyway be less than billeting.

Moreover, they would protect the soldier from the 'poisonous infusion' of sedition, be good for discipline, and keep him out of the pubs. But the Opposition were now more interested in the way the Government had set up the Department without informing Parliament, and that it was apparently exceeding the army estimates in the Mutiny Act and spending large sums of money without Parliament's approval.[69]

However decisive DeLancey may have been in resolving the army's accommodation shortage, he had neither the training nor temperament for running a Department of State spending public money. Nor was he averse to enriching himself in the process. Over the ten years during which he ran the Barracks Department, no proper accounts were ever produced. When the Auditor General demanded them in 1796, DeLancey sent a copy of his warrant from the King, claiming Parliament had no authority to so order him.[70] The argument continued between the Department, the War Office and the Treasury until DeLancey was finally forced to resign in November 1804. His salary by this time had gone up from £1 per day to £8, over and above his army pay, and he had acquired Effingham Manor, a handsome estate near Guildford, bought out of departmental expenses.

The unaccounted expenditure of the Barracks Department and the arrears in its accounts were the main reasons for the concession by Pitt, under heavy pressure from the Opposition, of a Royal Commission in July 1805 to investigate administrative corruption, and the Department was the first to be examined.[71] The figures dragged from DeLancey and published in the 1st Report nine months later showed a total spend of about £10 million. Proper accounts were never settled, and only one person was prosecuted, DeLancey's Head Commissary, one of his personal appointees. DeLancey himself, by now a full general, retired to his regiment.[72] The Department was put under direct Treasury control through three civilian commissioners.

---

[67] Parliamentary Papers (House of Commons), 1806/7 (99), *ii*, CMI 4th Report, Appendix 9E, p.427.
[68] Ibid., Appendix 10, p.436.
[69] Parliamentary History, 32 (1796), pp.929–40.
[70] Clode (1869), p.253.

[71] For the political background to Pitt's concession of the Commissions see W.H. Greenleaf, 'The Commissions of Military Inquiry', *JSAHR*, 41 (1963), pp.171–81.
[72] Parliamentary Papers (House of Commons), 1806 (46), *vi*–1806/7 (99), *ii*, CMI 1st, 2nd and 4th Reports. For a summary of the Department's affairs, see Clode (1869), **1**, ch.12.

Nineteenth-century army historians such as Clode and Fortesque took a strongly censorious view of DeLancey, and of the politicians, Pitt and Windham, who set him up and protected him.[73] Nevertheless, it is hard not to see DeLancey's work in the circumstances as a pragmatic triumph and a major achievement. His, and presumably his political masters', perspective on the gravity of the national situation cannot be better conveyed than in DeLancey's own words, defending himself against the commissioners' criticisms of his administration:

'This numerous concern [the Barracks Department] was formed by me under circumstances of foreign war, of most serious and alarming domestic troubles, and when, all Europe being in a state of anarchy and confusion, it became necessary, without delay, to place the great army of this country out of reach of revolutionary contagion ...' [74]

He made no secret of his disdain for civilian procedures, twice telling the commissioners that he had only accepted the Superintendent General's post on the condition that he did not become 'a public accountant'. In his last communication with them, he complained frustratedly about the 'useless forms and rules which have tended to impede and embarrass the process of a material branch of the public service'.[75] The Office of Works under James Wyatt was equally chaotic in its financial controls, whilst the Barracks Department at least got things built. Had it been left with the Ordnance Board, more bureaucratic and tightly controlled by the Treasury, such a rapid transformation of the nation's military accommodation would have been unimaginable.[76] Even the Commissioners of Inquiry recognized this: 'In justice to the late Barrack Master General,' they wrote, 'it must be observed that in all the sudden and unexpected orders he received for providing barracks for large bodies of troops ... we find no instances in which he did not obtain the necessary accommodation, and within the time prescribed.'[77] The Barracks Department can be seen today as a mild and thankfully temporary instance of the phenomenon of 'military/bureaucratic absolutism', arising as a result of the overriding of constitutional principle by military exigency during a period of extreme national peril.[78]

It is impossible to conjecture what the consequences would have been for the health, discipline, training and morale of the troops, as well that of the populace among whom they were stationed, had such a vigorous building programme not been embarked upon. Continental powers, not least the French, had found it necessary to keep a large proportion of their army in barracks since the early eighteenth century; by 1770, 200,000 French soldiers of the *ancien régime* were housed in barracks.[79] Pitt's decision in 1792 can be seen as a belated recognition by the political class in Britain that the country could no longer indulge the constitutional principle of 'no barracks', and that the old billeting system was too great a disadvantage to a modern army involved in a Continental war. DeLancey's urgent campaign over the ensuing decade thus represented a process of catching up with the best European practice. If he had not been so single-minded, perhaps the Battle of Waterloo would have been even more of a close-run thing.

Later critics complained that DeLancey's barracks had been 'hastily planned, and all repeated with but little variation the errors of one defective model'.[80] In the circumstances, how could they be otherwise? Moreover, they represented an advance in the standard of military accommodation, as well as a change in the country's attitude toward its soldiers, such as the previous century had been unable to contemplate, and provided the basis for housing the bulk of the home forces until the Cardwell reforms of the 1870s.

---

[73] See, for instance, Fortesque (1905), **viv**, pp.903–5.
[74] BL 527 (2), 1808. *Observations of Lt Gen DeLancey ... upon the 4th Report and supplement to the 1st Report of the Commissioners of Military Inquiry*, p.46.
[75] Parliamentary Papers (House of Commons), 1806 (317), *vi*, CMI 2nd Report, Appendix 24.
[76] Clode (1869), **1**, p.254.
[77] Parliamentary Papers (House of Commons), 1806/7 (99), *ii*, CMI 4th Report, p.164.
[78] B.M. Downing, 'Constitutionalism, Warfare, and Political Change in Early-Modern Europe', *Theory and Society*, **17** (1988), p.8.
[79] Jones (1980), p.162.
[80] Bell (1880), p.1.

Colour Plates

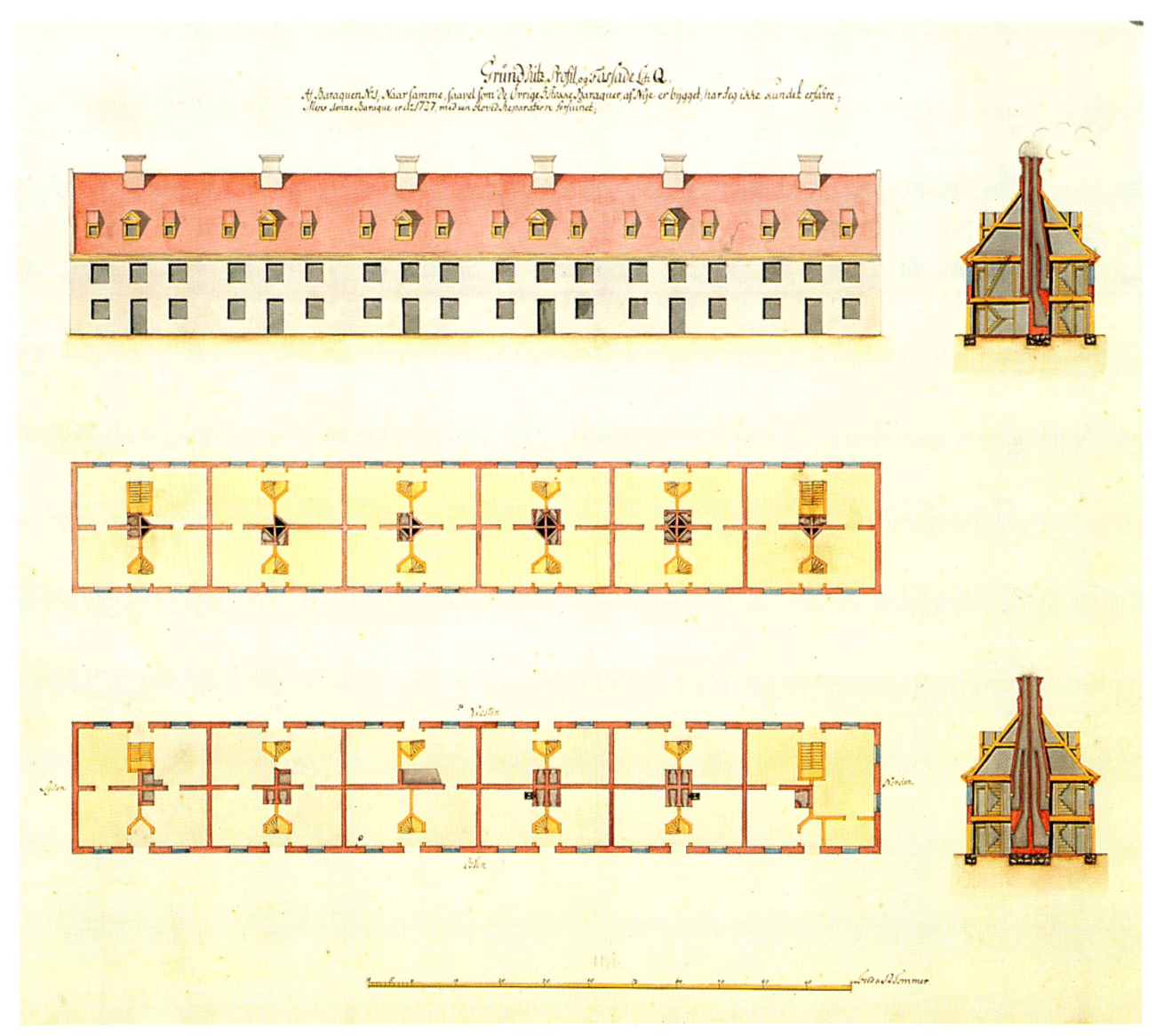

Figure 5 Kastellet Citadel, Copenhagen. Plan, cross-section and elevation of a barrack block designed by the Dutch engineer Hendrik Ruse, 1663–5.

Colour Plates

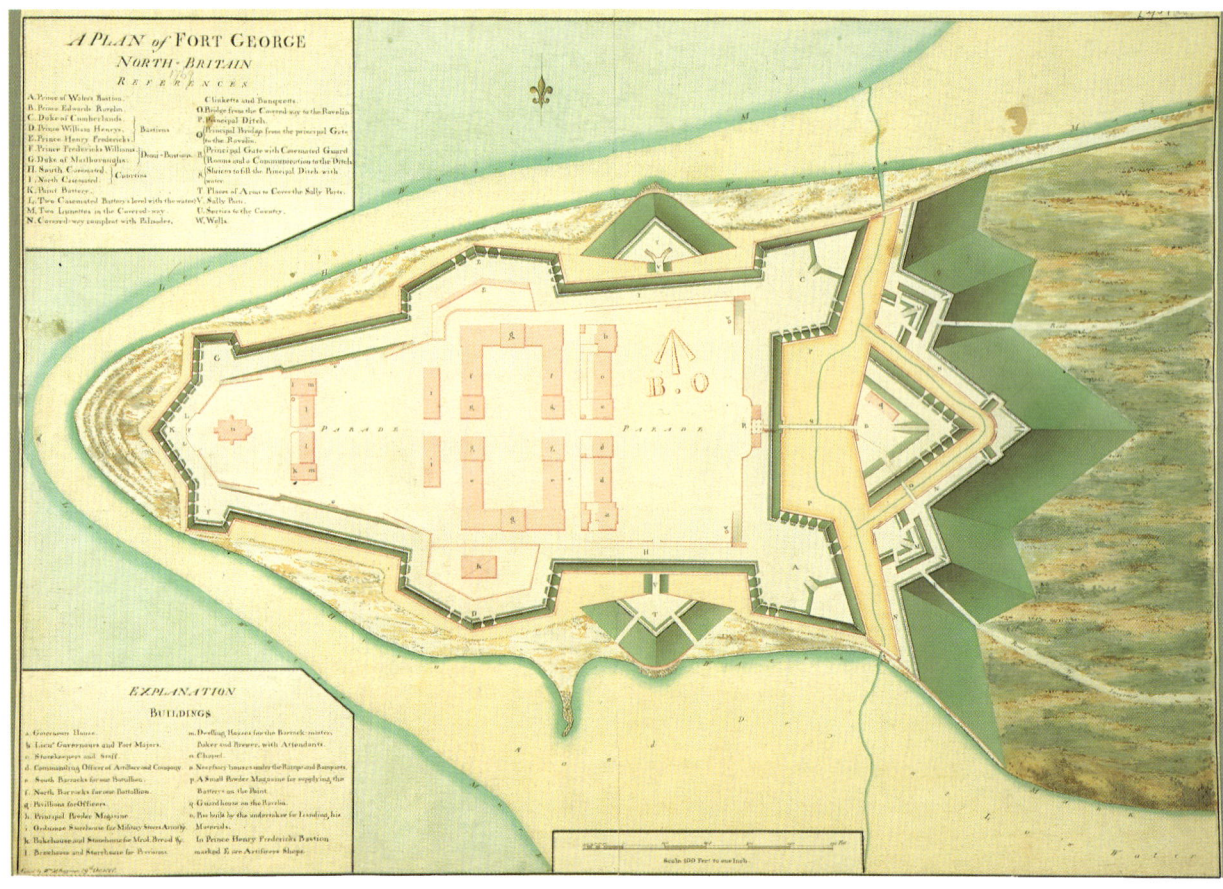

Figure 34 William Skinner's 1759 plan of Fort George, redrawn 1808. This shows the fort in its final form, including the chapel to the east.

Figure 35 Fort George from the air, from where the impressive layout of the defences and quarters can best be appreciated.

Colour Plates

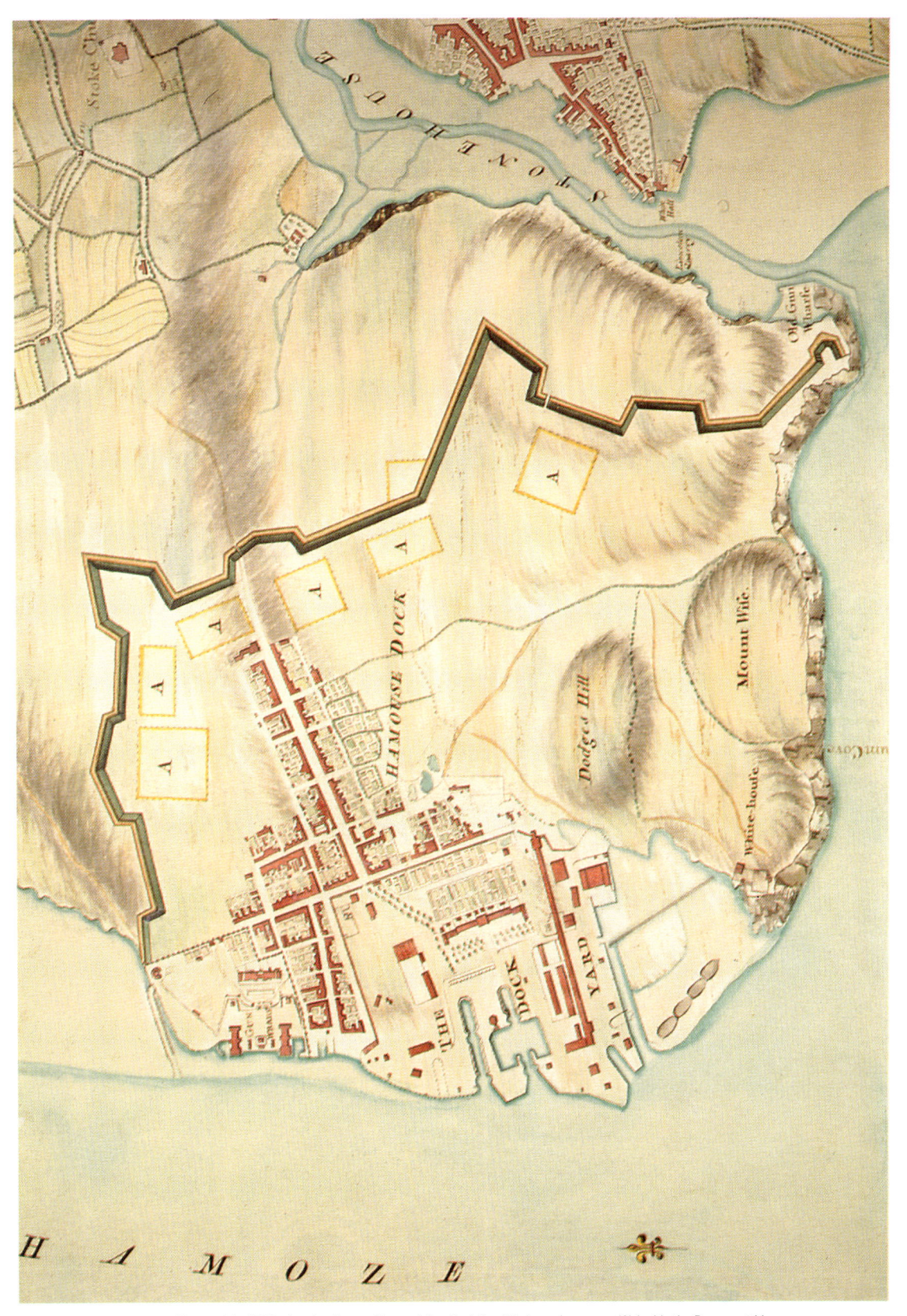

Figure 38 The dockyard at Plymouth in 1756, showing the positions of the six defensible barrack squares (A) inside the Devonport Lines.

Colour Plates

Figure 40 A late eighteenth-century watercolour of the Clarence Marines Barracks, Portsmouth. The first Marines barracks in Portsmouth, it occupied a converted cooperage and brewery.

Figure 48 Soldiers were camped in St James's Park, Westminster, in July 1780 because of anti-Catholic rioting in the capital.

Colour Plates

Figure 56 James Johnson produced drawings in 1796 for a new barracks in Hyde Park for 2,000 men. The end pavilions were for officers, and the men were to live in massive rooms stretching 60 feet (18.3 metres) from front to rear.

Figure 138 Aerial view of Fort Brockhurst, showing the keep in the foreground and casemates to the rear.

Colour Plates

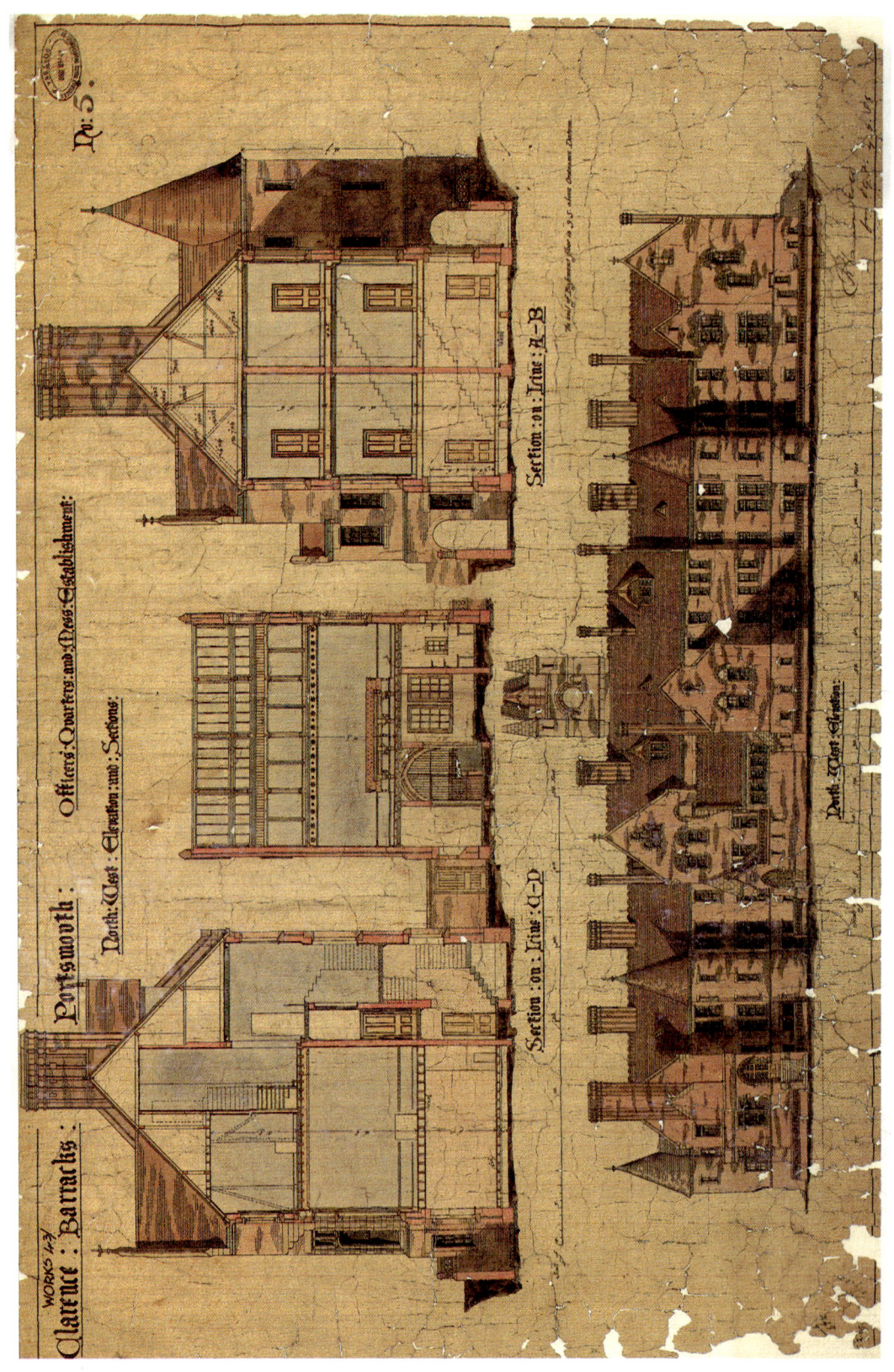

Figure 164 The officers' quarters, Clarence Barracks, Portsmouth. Note the billiard room in the middle.

Colour Plates

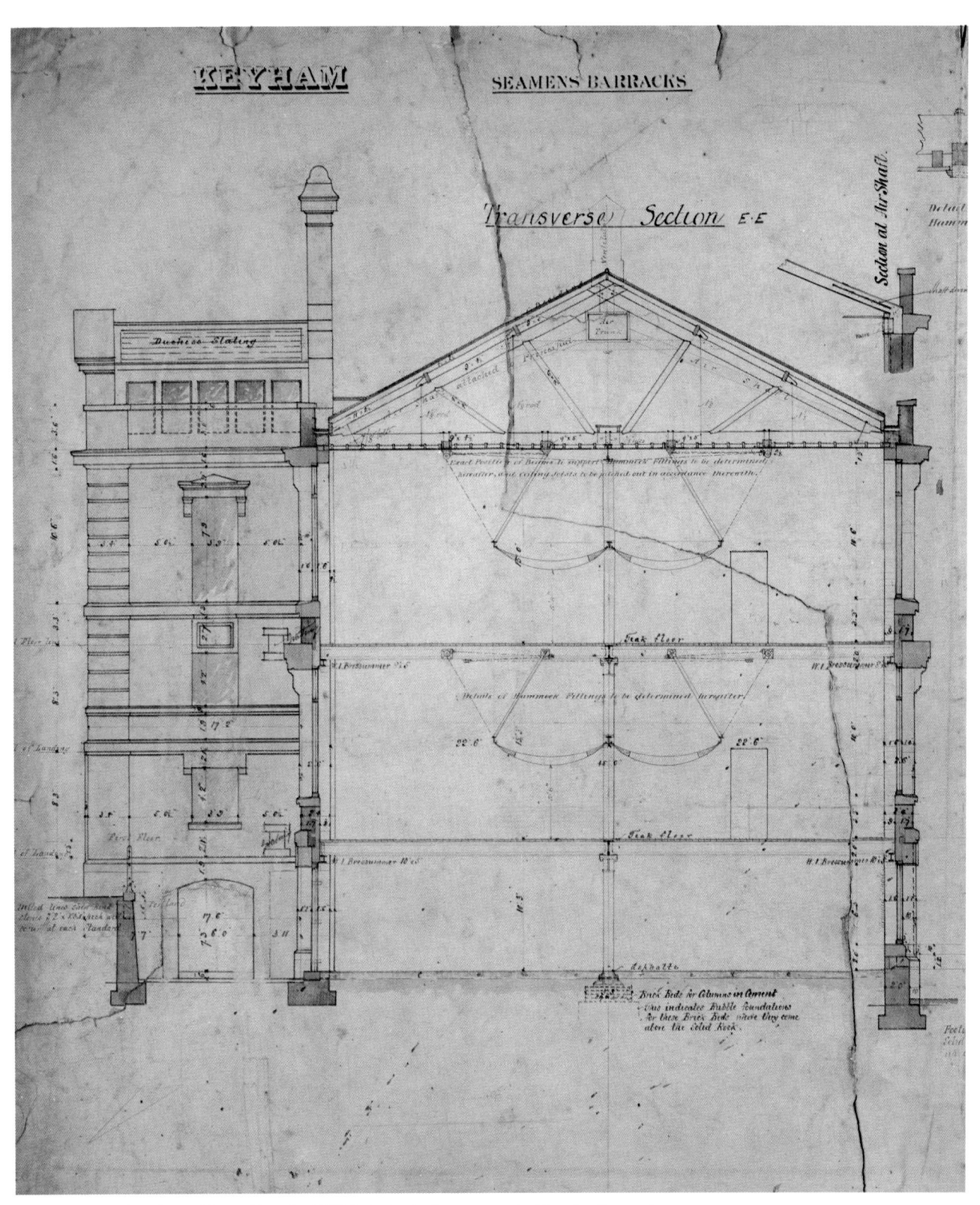

Figure 172 Section through one of the naval barracks at HMS *Drake* showing the arrangements of the ratings' hammocks.

Chapter Five
1815–1852: 'No Better Military School for Officers and Privates'

After Waterloo, the army at home suffered ten years of retrenchment and three more of stagnation. 'Modernization' and 'reform' were words rarely uttered in Wellington's army. Change was smothered by complacency within the ageing Horse Guards – flushed by their triumph against Napoleon – and the lack of interest at Westminster in doing more than forcing down the annual army estimates. Meanwhile, the rank and file endured deteriorating conditions in overcrowded and insanitary quarters, until the lantern of sanitary reform found them at the Crimean War.

In the country at large, the hardship brought on by post-war recession, exacerbated in industrial areas by the 1815 Corn Laws, brought a resumption of the radical political agitation of the pre-war years, and prompted equivalent responses by both the Government and the magistracy. The difficulties of policing large, excited meetings was laid bare in the Peterloo Massacre in 1819, when the Yeomanry – the local gentry, uniformed and on horseback – had to be rescued from the midst of the meeting by regular cavalry, and seven people, all of them women, were left dead. The civilian police force, established in London in 1829 but not widely distributed until 1856, was slow to relieve the army of its unpopular but commonplace civil order duties. Rather, new barracks constructed in the years either side of the Reform Act moved the military centre of gravity in England away from the counties of the French-facing coast towards the new industrial towns in the north, where civil authorities were struggling with social and political problems caused by slow political reform, rapid industrialization and uncontrollable urban growth.

Funding for the armed forces was cut by successive administrations of both parties, trying to control the swollen borrowing and the burdensome taxation bequeathed by a generation of near total war. Retrenchment was reinforced by a non-interventionist European policy and, of course, by peace. A determined policy of cutting military expenditure was a constant of Regency politics until the 1830s. Funding for the army had been reduced from £43.25 million in 1815, the year of Waterloo, to £10.7 million by 1820; in 1836, the low point, it was under £8 million.[1] This shrinking budget related directly to manpower, and with the post-war demobilization followed by annual cuts, the army establishment fell precipitously. The total number of men in service reduced by over half between 1815 and 1828, from 233,952 men to 102,539.[2] Of this, the home garrison settled at a figure of around 45,000 men, with a large proportion in barracks in Ireland. In 1819, for example, there were 23,061 men in England, 18,375 in Ireland, 2,321 in Scotland, and about 700 in both Jersey and Guernsey.[3] The dwindling budget for barracks was mainly expended on repairs, and there was very little left for new works.

After the final defeat of Napoleon, the geographical distribution of this much smaller military population was settled between the Horse Guards and the Treasury.[4] The location, size and type of barracks which were kept on reflects quite clearly what the army and the State perceived as the home forces' role, now that France – the traditional enemy and *raison d'être* for the standing army since the Glorious Revolution – was no longer seen as a threat. In 1816, Lord Palmerston, at the War Office, outlined the deployment and duties in England of the Guards and garrison, the traditional baseline of the army establishment for the protection of the sovereign and the realm. The Guards were based in

---

[1] Spiers (1980), p.74.
[2] Chandler and Becket (1994), p.164.
[3] Parliamentary Papers (House of Commons), 1819 (498), *xv, Return showing the distribution of troops stationed in Great Britain ...*, p.153.
[4] PRO WO55/1868, pp.339–405.

Figure 82 The first large military quarters to be built within Portsmouth was the Cambridge Barracks, where officers' accommodation was added to three Napoleonic converted warehouses for the privates in the 1820s. The urbane quality of the new range contrasts with the much more secure barracks being built in the north of England and in Ireland.

their various London quarters and at Windsor. Garrisons were maintained at Edinburgh and the Scottish forts and castles, at the long-standing coastal strong points of Berwick-upon-Tweed, Tynemouth, Hull Citadel, Plymouth Citadel, Pendennis Castle, Fort Cumberland and Landguard Fort, the castles at Carlisle, Chester and Dover, and in the dockyard towns of Plymouth, Portsmouth (see Figure 82), Chatham, Deptford, Woolwich, Milford Haven and Sheerness. The coastal garrisons were much reduced, with manpower being concentrated in barracks at Newcastle upon Tyne, Sunderland, Chelmsford, Colchester, Brighton, Liverpool and Bristol – the last all in billets. Detachments kept watch over the stores of guns held at the Ordnance depots, centred on the great midland warehouse complex on the Grand Union Canal at Weedon Bec (see Figure 83), as well as the smaller depots built during the Napoleonic Wars by the Ordnance Board at Great Yarmouth, Derby, Lincoln, Northampton and Brecon, and there were detachments guarding the magazines at Tipner, Marchwood and Hull. Although reductions in excise on goods such as silk had reduced the profitability of smuggling, stations to support the revenue in their operations were maintained on the Scilly Isles, at Trowbridge, at Harwich and on the Kent coast at Hythe, Folkestone, Deal and Margate. The new Coast Guard made use of the shoreline Martello towers.[5]

In Ireland, the new Royal Irish Constabulary took over several barracks after it was reorganized on a national basis in 1836, including Foxford, Arklow and Castlebar, but in mainland Britain, the cavalry continued to be preferred by the authorities for many civil order duties. In 1819, the cavalry regiments were distributed among the troubled towns where the Barracks Department had sited barracks in the early 1790s. Apart from the Horse and Life Guards in London and Windsor, regiments of dragoons, hussars and lancers were stationed in Birmingham, Manchester, Nottingham and York, and the larger south coast stations at Canterbury, Brighton and Exeter. Coventry and Ipswich were also kept on, though empty at the time. Maidstone, one of the 'temporary' wooden barracks, was used as the cavalry depot, for inducting new recruits. Six more cavalry regiments were based in Ireland at Dublin, Cork, Clonmel, Newbridge, Dundalk and Ballinrobe. The Artillery's home remained at Woolwich, with small detachments in Glasgow, Edinburgh and Dublin, and in forts in Jersey and Guernsey.[6]

The Treasury wanted to get rid of all the temporary barracks, so the Home Counties hutment camps were dismantled and abandoned, leases on buildings taken for temporary accommodation were not renewed, and lodgings built of timber were mostly disposed of, either converted or their materials reused. Radipole

Figure 83 The great arms depot at Weedon Bec, near Northampton. It was situated strategically on the Grand Union Canal between the Birmingham ordnance factories and London, with a place of refuge for the royal family. Later, the warehouses had fireplaces installed and were converted into barracks.

---

[5] Parliamentary Papers (House of Commons), 1816 (61), *xii*, *Return of the troops employed at the different military stations in Great Britain*, p.407.

[6] Parliamentary Papers (House of Commons), 1819, *xv*, p.153.

Barracks in Weymouth, for example, was dilapidated by 1822, and was sold off. Parts of it were evidently bought by a builder and were converted, since they have survived until the present day.[7] The barracks at Sunderland was retained, partly for its strategic significance in an area where many of the new barracks of the war years had been in rented conversions. Before 1828, the men's blocks were replaced with brick buildings, although the officers' wooden quarters remained for a while.[8] Albany Barracks, on the Isle of Wight, stood empty for twenty years until it was converted into a prison for juveniles awaiting transportation, in 1838.

One interesting aspect to the continued use of these wooden buildings was that some of them were hung with mathematical tiles. These specially shaped clay tiles are nailed to the frame and pointed with mortar to resemble brickwork, but whilst they are cheaper and quicker to build with than bricks, as a cladding they are a comparatively expensive technology, with complicated detailing of corners and openings. They were commonly used by speculative developers in order to pass off a flimsily built building as something more substantial. The Barracks Department architects suggested that some of the 'temporary' barracks like Sunderland which were kept on by the Treasury were subsequently protected by 'weather tiles', and it is possible that this is what they were referring to, though it is unclear why they would not simply have been hung with ordinary clay tiles or slates.

Two examples have been discovered, both on buildings believed to have been erected by Alexander Copland. The smaller is the surviving range of single-storey cavalry barracks at Radipole, in Weymouth, which has mathematical tiles on parts of the walls (see Figure 67, page 82). More impressive, especially since its recent restoration, is the one-time Prison Governor's House at Parkhurst Prison (see Figure 84). This formed part of the army depot hospital which moved to the island from Chatham c.1800. While this is a more important and self-conscious building, the use of mathematical tiles is still not easy to square with wartime requirements of speed and economy.

Figure 84 Parkhurst Depot on the Isle of Wight, a timber-framed building hung with mathematical tiles. The porch and cupola are later. The lead detailing to the windows and the stucco quoins give away the pretence of brickwork

Although they are only rarely mentioned in the periodic parliamentary returns of barracks, it seems that quite a number of smaller quarters were retained, or new leases taken, in locations which related to the changed strategic circumstances of the country. Some rented quarters, like the Portman Street Barracks, a closed courtyard behind Oxford Street for over 500 guardsmen, evidently also stayed in use after the peace.

Billeting continued to operate into the second half of the nineteenth century. In Scotland, it was still legal to billet soldiers on private householders up until 1858, and it continued to be so in Ireland when there was judged to be insufficient barracks space. However, whilst victuallers were bound by the terms of their licences to billet soldiers, the burden was lightened as the railway network spread from the 1840s and the traditional marching corridors were abandoned. A Commons Select Committee looked into the subject in 1858, and recommended that the power to billet should be retained for troops on the march and for emergencies, but it warned against the billeting of militia regiments except on marches, because of its bad effect on their training and discipline.[9]

Reshuffling the barracks administration

Having once been removed from the Ordnance Board, it was some time before responsibility for

---

[7] Breihan (1990a), p.13.
[8] Breihan (1990b), p.175.

[9] Parliamentary Papers (House of Commons), 1858 (65), x, *Select Committee on the Billeting System*.

barracks was returned to its natural home. After he resigned, General DeLancey was briefly replaced as Barrack Master General by Major General George Hewett, who struggled to supply the Commissioners for Military Inquiry with all the figures they wanted, before also resigning, to become Commander-in-Chief in India in 1807. The tainted post was then abolished, and the Barracks Department, with the rump of its civilian staff, was run by a Barracks Board with three Treasury-appointed commissioners. Having supervised the scaling down and vacation of surplus barracks after the war, it too was abolished in 1817; James Sanders went off to look for antiquities in Italy. The Board was then replaced by a caretaker Comptroller of Barracks.

In 1818, the Duke of Wellington returned from France, and a year later was appointed Master General of the Ordnance. One of the few army reforms which he allowed, consistent with his distrust of civilian interference, was to take responsibilty for barracks back from the Treasury and return it to a strengthened Ordnance Board in an overdue rationalization of defence lands and holdings. Colonel Sir John Burgoyne, later an influential Inspector General of Fortifications at the Ordnance from 1845 to 1855, advised the Master General on the change.[10] One of the main advantages was that 'having a Corps, which must be maintained on other accounts ... there was much advantage in breaking up a separate establishment [the Barracks Board], and in adding its duties to that of a military service that required similar qualifications'.[11]

Therefore, from May 1822, after thirty years of civilian design, the Royal Engineers resumed control. All barracks and military lands in the Empire were taken back by the British Ordnance Board, under the Inspector General of Fortifications, General Gother Mann, who was the senior engineer. The three military corps – the Royal Artillery, the Royal Engineers and the Royal Military Artificers (the Sappers and Miners) – came under him. Some small adjustments were made to the regulations governing barracks, the final abandonment of two-man wooden beds or bunks and their replacement by iron bedsteads being the most important so far as the soldier was concerned.

The Ordnance Board has the reputation of having been in a state of bureaucratic torpor during these years, with especially archaic accounting procedures. Repairs to overseas stations could take over a decade to be approved and effected, as in one instance of a barracks in the West Indies. This was largely resolved by Wellington's reorganization. The individual engineer officers responsible for design in the Ordnance were technically excellent, however, and the quality of training which they received at Woolwich and Brompton was in many respects better than that of their civilian counterparts.[12]

John Nash and the Metropolitan Improvements

The first new barracks to be built after the war were the result of initiatives by neither the Barracks Department nor the Ordnance Board, but arose out of the great development of Crown land carried out by the architect John Nash on behalf of the Prince Regent, later George IV, known as the Metropolitan Improvements. The Barracks Department had stopped new building work some ten years before the war with France finally ended, as we have seen. In 1812, however, plans were laid down for a new Guards barracks in London, and they were followed by three more in the capital over the next two decades. Although it has not been fully explained how they became involved, new quarters for the Guards regiments formed a significant component in London's largest single planned development, one of the most important examples of neo-Classical town planning in Europe.

The only barracks with which Nash himself had a proven connection was the first, built within the new Regent's Park itself. On his earliest plan, the barracks is shown on the north side of the park, flanking the canal (see Figure 85). On the second plan, published in 1812, both had been moved to the east to create more open space in the park itself, and the barracks was built between the back of Cumberland Terrace and the Cumberland Basin at

---

[10] PRO HO50/443, *Memorandum upon the Barracks Department of Great Britain*, 31 December 1823.
[11] Quoted in Watson (1954), p.149.

[12] G. Randzens, 'The British Ordnance Department 1815–1855', *JSAHR*, **57** (1979), pp.88–107; Weiler (1987), *passim*.

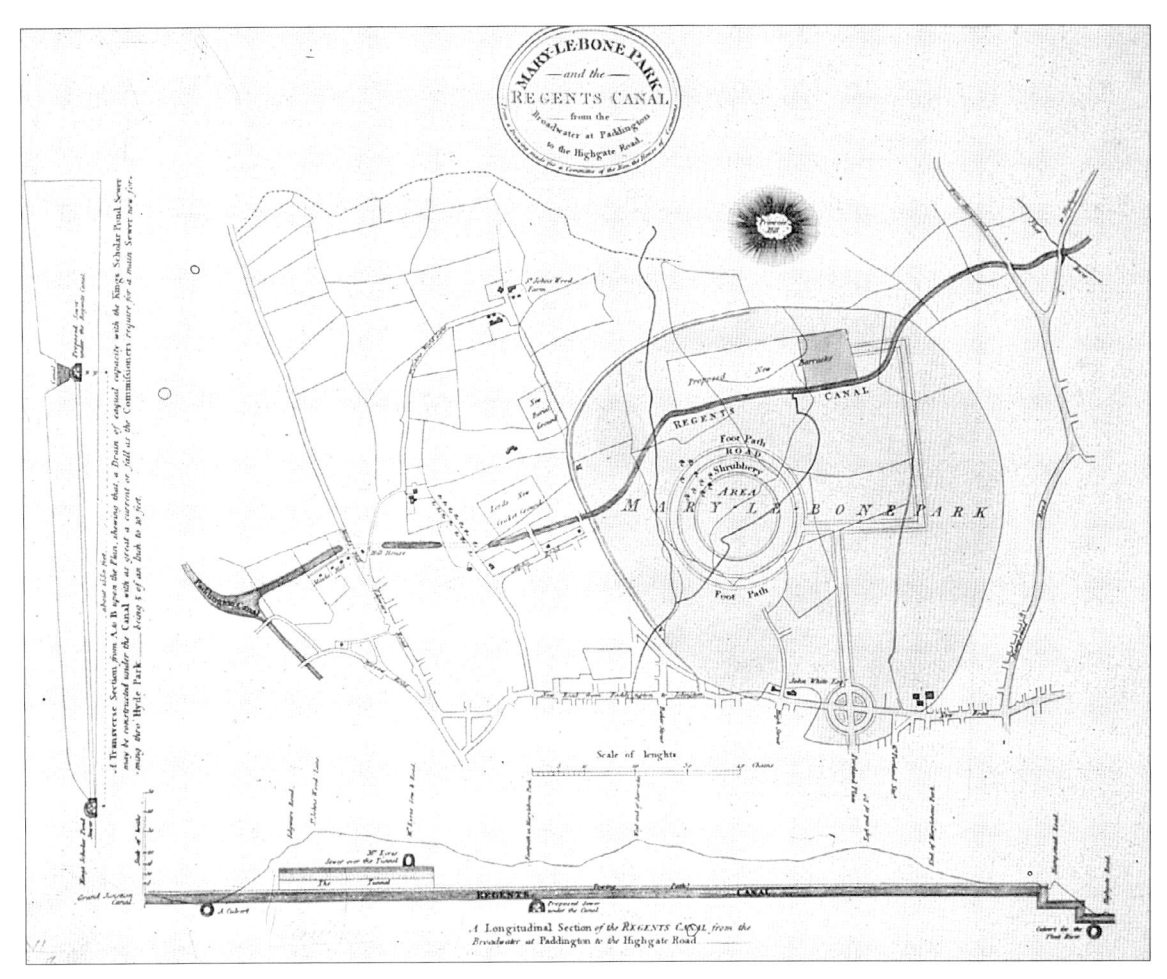

Figure 85 Nash's first plan of the new Regent's Park showing the barracks on the north side of Regent's Canal.

the end of the Regent's Canal. Obviously, Nash's brief for the Park included the provision of space for a barracks from the beginning. This request presumably came from the Treasury. The Regent's Park Barracks was built in 1820–21, just before the Royal Engineers regained control of barracks administration.[13]

Nash's involvement in the design of the barracks was restricted to laying out the ground and the drains.[14] The scheme was different to the plain quadrangles of DeLancey's Barracks Department, although this may have been determined by the narrowness of the site. The barracks was occupied by a Guards cavalry regiment, which had access – as it does today – to the park for exercising its horses. The troopers lived in three parallel barrack blocks at one end of the small parade square, each for a hundred guardsmen housed in ten-man rooms off a central corridor, above the stables. The infirmary stables, straw and forage barn, and dung pits were along the south perimeter, with the farrier, saddlery, forge and tailor's shop at the north. The plain, two-storey range for the officers was to one side, the only part of the Regency buildings to survive the rebuilding of the barracks in the 1890s. Mess rooms were only added later, the Guards officers still preferring to spend their off-duty time in town.

The second of the four new barracks was built between 1822 and 1835, to the north of the park at St John's Wood,[15] where it had a less direct relationship with the Metropolitan Improvements.

---

[13] Nash's partner as architect to the Department of Woods and Forests was James Morgan, who in 1855 won the prize to design a new Guards barracks in Chelsea. It is possible, therefore, that he had a hand in the Regent's Park Barracks, and later won the prize in his old age on the strength of that experience.

[14] PRO WO78/954, 955, *Plan of Marylebone or Regent's Park, London, received from Mr Nash, showing the intended Barracks*.
[15] PRO WO78/1338.

Figure 86 Interior of the riding school at St John's Wood.

Although it had been adopted by the Royal Artillery by 1825, it was originally intended for cavalry. Consequently, one of the first buildings on the site was the riding school, among the largest in London, and still used for its original purpose today (see Figure 86).[16]

Much more closely related to Nash's great redevelopment of Central London was St George's Barracks. On his plan of 1826, the proposed buildings are shown occupying the whole of the area to the rear of the proposed 'National Gallery of Painting and Sculpture'.[17] The barracks was built in 1826, about six years before work began on William Wilkins's overstretched façade, and was used as the main recruiting depot in London. An infantry barracks for 540 men, only one of the proposed three

Figure 87 View of the Guards' Westminster (later Wellington) Barracks, from one of the Doric guardhouses.

ranges in Nash's plan was built, a long, three-storey building with rooms either side of cross stair passages — a reversion to the eighteenth-century Ordnance planning found at Berwick-upon-Tweed. It was demolished at the end of the nineteenth century to make room for the National Portrait Gallery, which now occupies the site.

The fourth and largest of the barracks associated with the Metropolitan Improvements occupies a much more significant position in relation to Nash's great axis down from Regent's Park. As late as 1829, there were still plans for a terrace and crescent to terminate the route from Piccadilly, on the south side of St James's Park across from the Duke of York's Column and Carlton Terrace.[18] It was never begun, however. The best that was achieved was that the Ordnance Board was finally allowed to build the imposing barracks for which plans had been produced since the Hanoverian succession. The new Westminster Guards Barracks (see Figure 87) was built close to Nash's re-cast royal home, Buckingham Palace, at the same time as his last work, Carlton Terrace, was going up on the other side of the park. When it opened in 1834, it was renamed after the former Master General, Wellington. Work continued until 1854.

Design and construction was the responsibility of Sir Frederick Smith, the Commanding Royal Engineer in the London District, but as a consequence of its important site, Philip Hardwick

---

[16] J. Wanklyn, *Guns at the Wood* (London 1972)
[17] Commissioners for Woods, Forests and Land Revenues, 5th Report, 1826, *Plan of the Proposed Improvements to Charing Cross*.

[18] Parliamentary Papers (House of Commons), 1829, *14*, Commissioners for Woods, Forests and Land Revenues, 6th Report, Appendix 16; plan 5/6/1829.

was employed to design the important elevation facing Green Park – a rare collaboration between the Engineers and a noteworthy civilian architect. Smith and Hardwick did their best to rise to the importance of the location. Behind a long, iron railing, they placed two small guardhouses with Greek Doric porticoes facing one another across the parade ground. The main barracks was a long, white, stuccoed neo-Classical design, with pedimented end pavilions separated by carriageways through to the working part of the barracks at the rear. In contrast to the formal planning of the front, the rest of this large complex was squeezed into an irregular triangle out of sight to the rear. Rated at over 1,400 men, by 1861 it had a higher density of population than even the packed courts and rookeries of East London, and a bad reputation for fever.[19]

This sudden improvement in the accommodation of the London garrison during the Metropolitan Improvements might be taken to indicate a sea change in the relationship between the army and society, brought on by the war, comparable to the militarization of cities in Prussia, most notably Berlin. However, the link between the building of these four barracks and the redevelopment of the Crown estate was probably pragmatism and expediency in taking advantage of available sites, rather than an overall strategy. The incorporation of a barracks from the inception of the Regent's Park scheme suggests that the Treasury Commissioners running the project were in communication with those winding up the Barracks Board. As for the other barracks, Nash's skill in finding developers or clients to take over sites created by his new roads and spaces is well known, and maybe this is what brought the Ordnance Board into the picture: the development behind the National Gallery was useful to Nash, and the one on Birdcage Walk was crucial, salvaging something at the St James's Park end of his great rebuilding.[20]

It would, therefore, be a mistake to see the erection of four new barracks within the Prince Regent's prestigious development as evidence of a change in national attitudes towards the army or its accommodation. Indeed, no similar developments took place in other British cities. Barracks were more likely to be an *obstacle* to new development, partly because of the drab quality of their architecture and generally ill-maintained aspect, but principally because private soldiers were not considered desirable neighbours (see Figure 88). Gin shops and brothels flourished in the vicinity of barracks, and soldiers were often involved in outbreaks of violence. For instance, in 1821 there was rioting between guardsmen from Knightsbridge Cavalry Barracks and a mob protesting at the shooting of two civilians at the funeral of Queen Charlotte. The two Guards' barracks near Hyde Park found themselves in neighbourhoods undergoing a rapid change in character during the Regency period, and were increasingly in conflict with the social aspirations of people buying the new houses nearby. In 1854, the great builder and developer Thomas Cubitt complained that 'the character of the population which invariably follows any large body of soldiers, and takes up its residence close to them' would have a depreciating effect on property values. Developing the Belgravia estate on the south side of Knightsbridge in the 1830s, Cubitt was obliged to build around the small Foot Guards' barracks, but he later objected that 'the immediate neighbourhood of a Barracks is looked on by Builders as a great evil'.[21]

The military response to Chartism

The ending of hostilities with France meant a reorientation of the United Kingdom's strategic geography, and a return to pre-war priorities of internal order and control. The response by the State to the popular political agitation which was renewed from the 1810s was to resist change, and to continue the policy begun by Pitt of maintaining soldiers, in barracks, in areas where the local magistrates felt threatened. Outside London, new quarters built during the period of the anti-Corn Law riots, the Reform Bill riots and the Chartist agitation reflected the geography of economic stress and political protest in Britain in the first half of the nineteenth century. Falling real wages, cyclical unemployment and bad harvests were exacerbated

---

[19] PRO WO43/144, 145.
[20] J.M. Crook, 'Metropolitan Improvements, John Nash and the Picturesque', in C. Fox (ed.) *London, World City* (London 1992), p.77.

[21] H. Hobhouse, *Thomas Cubitt, Master Builder* (London 1971, 2nd edn 1995), p.454.

Figure 88 Thomas Rowlandson, in this watercolour of life in a cavalry barracks, reflected strongly held public views of the licentiousness which prevailed behind closed barracks doors.

by local conditions. Particularly hard-hit groups were those communities of handworkers whose skills and livelihoods were rendered obsolete by mechanization in the textile industry. Handloom weavers and wool combers in areas like Carlisle, Burnley and Colne, and Bradford suffered grievously and featured strongly among the Chartists.[22]

Although some officers preferred the Yeomanry to be employed in quelling disturbances, their poor discipline and the tendency for protesters to view them as protagonists rather than arbiters in local disputes meant that magistrates preferred to deploy regular army units, when possible. The Yeomanry's credibility with the Government as a policing force was fatally impaired by Peterloo; moreover, though strong in country areas, it was almost non-existent in the northern industrial counties where troops were most needed. In 1839, there were only 171 yeomanry in the whole of Lancashire, and none at all in Durham.[23]

At the end of the war with France, the Treasury and Horse Guards had elected to retain the permanent cavalry barracks planned before invasion was threatened, where troops could be protected from the radical talk of their peers, and dispatched promptly at the request of the magistracy to wave their sabres and intimidate angry crowds of artisans threatening property. The only new barracks built in England outside the capital during the immediate post-war years reinforced this pattern, with new cavalry stations established in Burnley in 1819 and in Leeds a few years later. Piecemeal improvements were much more common than completely new works.

At Carlisle Castle, the Ordnance Board had to deal with the problems of maintaining a garrison of two

---

[22] F.C. Mather, *Public Order in the Age of the Chartists* (Manchester 1959), p.8.
[23] Ibid., p.6.

to four companies – up to 250 men – in a comparatively turbulent part of the country, within a castle which local people held in high regard on account of its historical value. Although the medieval Great Chamber was converted for officers' use in the 1820s, a new barracks had to be built within the outer ward in 1837, and other small improvements such as the addition of a hospital, library and washhouses were made in the following decades.[24]

In Ireland, popular unrest in the 1830s was directed at the collection of tithes and rents, and the army was drawn into the consequent disputes. A larger campaign of new building works was undertaken in Ireland in connection with the formation of a military-style national police force in 1822. Beggars Bush Barracks, built in 1827 and the first new barracks in Dublin since the war, was a semi-fortified complex (see Figure 89). An imposing, arched entrance led through a high perimeter wall, covered from the flanks of two large bastions on either corner, and into a front square flanked by officers' quarters and mess. The large soldiers' barracks were to the rear, close to one of the first chapels included within a British barracks. Barracks were erected at the same time in Mitchelstown, Londonderry, Castlebar, Roscommon, Westport, Roscrea, Comer, Sligo and Mallow.

At the beginning of the Chartist disturbances in 1837, the distribution of the home forces in England continued the post-war division of tasks: colonial service or garrison duty for the infantry, and policing for the cavalry. The Household troop were in Windsor, Regent's Park and Knightsbridge Barracks, and the Foot Guards at Windsor, the Tower, and in Wellington, St George's, and Portman Street Barracks. Twenty-nine regiments of foot were garrisoning or passing through Chatham, five were in Portsmouth and three in Devonport, while the rest were spread around the coastal fortifications and Ordnance depots. The dragoons, hussars and lancers were all accommodated in DeLancey's barracks in Manchester, Birmingham, York, Coventry, Nottingham, Hounslow, Ipswich, Brighton and Dorchester.[25]

Figure 89 Beggars Bush Barracks (1827), Dublin, was protected by a large wall with a defensible trace like a fortification.

The Napier Report

In 1840, Sir Vivian Hussey, who replaced Wellington as Master General of the Ordnance, commissioned a report on the barracks situation in the northern textile towns. Echoing DeLancey's commission, Major General Sir Charles Napier, the Commanding Officer in the Northern District, was asked to assess the security situation in his area. Napier, like Sir John Moore before him, was one of the small number of senior officers of Wellington's generation who were concerned about the well-being of their men. This radical attitude extended to sympathy with the grievances – if not the methods – of the Chartists.

Napier was a strong believer in the value of barracks to the army, commenting in his report to Hussey: 'there is no better military school for officers and privates than a large garrison, and in these times it is perhaps wise to keep the soldiers together as much as possible'.[26] His two principal concerns, expressed in the report, were to avoid dispersing his forces in small detachments where they would risk becoming isolated, and to be able to move men sufficiently rapidly to arrive at a disturbance in time to be of use.

The report reads like an analysis of a hostile territory under occupation. He divided it into two halves, either side of the 'Yorkshire hills'. Essentially, Napier wanted to rationalize the

---

[24] H. Summerson, 'The Paradoxical Fortunes of Carlisle Castle, 1745–1850', *Fortress*, **4** (February 1990), pp.34–7.
[25] 'Return showing the barracks in the United Kingdom', *United Services Journal*, 1837, part 3, p.569.

[26] PRO HO55/451, *Report of General Sir Charles Napier upon the barracks in the Northern District*.

distribution of his forces, and concentrate them in larger, strategically sited, defensible barracks. The report reveals the existence of a surprising number of small, temporary barracks, which had either not been given up after the end of the war, or had been taken up since then (see Figure 90). In the Northern District alone, these had the capacity to accommodate over 3,500 infantry and 250 cavalry, though most had room for only one or two companies or a single troop. Napier had personal experience of such small barracks in Ireland, in one of which a company was burnt by insurgents during the war. The reason such places were dangerous, he wrote, was not because 'they cannot *resist* but that they cannot *keep watch*'.[27] Accordingly, he recommended abandoning the small outposts in Haydock Lodge, Rochdale, Bolton, Wigan, Todmorden, Blackburn and Liverpool.

In May 1840, he described the problems of policing the area:

'The more I see the more I am convinced of the impossibility of moving troops even a few miles in time to prevent disturbance. The leaders of the disaffected are so secret in their proceedings [and] they have the power to collect mobs so suddenly, that much mischief may be done in an hour or two – the troops arrive to quell the riot but not in time to prevent damage to property.' [28]

Some smaller posts were therefore maintained between the permanent barracks, in Brighouse, Bradford, Halifax, Dewsbury, Barnsley, Mansfield and Loughborough, and in the outskirts of Manchester.

His central recommendation was that several large, new barracks be built because, like the Anglican Church, the army had failed to keep up with the growth of new settlements in the manufacturing areas. Sites were chosen with a strategic view of communications in the whole area of the Pennines, for the first time taking into account differences which the new railway lines made to the movement of troops – a factor which would be of increasing importance to the distribution of the Victorian army.

The new barracks were to be built near a railway line. The towns initially selected were Bury (see Figure 91), Ashton-under-Lyne and Blackburn, but the last was replaced by Preston, partly in response to local pressure. The barracks at Bury and Ashton were built between 1842 and 1845, each for two companies of infantry, 270 men, and a 48-man troop of horse. Fulwood Barracks in Preston was started in 1843 and finished in 1848, and held a regiment of infantry, two troops of cavalry and 46 artillerymen – over 1,200 men. Finally, the late eighteenth-century barracks in Sheffield, described as being in a bad condition by Napier's report, was rebuilt during 1847–54, for a battalion of infantry and four troops of cavalry (see Figure 178, page 197).

Three more barracks were built around the same time in reaction to civil disorder and political agitation. The first was in 1845 at Horfield, just north of Bristol. Bristol had experienced the country's worst Reform Bill violence in October 1831, when the 3rd Dragoon Guards, called from billets three miles away, were forced to withdraw from the city, and much of the city centre, including the Bishop's Palace, had been burnt.

The other two new barracks were built the same year in South Wales. The Rebecca Riots, which occurred at the same time as the Chartist disturbances, were the most concerted campaigns of rural dissent in Britain, in which the anger of the participants was focused on the Turnpike Trusts. Accordingly, one of the Ordnance depots built during the Napoleonic Wars at Brecon was expanded into a barracks. It was designed by the local Royal Engineer officer, Colonel Ord, and erected between 1842 and 1844. The second Welsh barracks was built on a hilltop overlooking Newport, which had suffered considerable Chartist unrest in 1839. This was a much more defensible work, similar to those in northern England, with a bastioned perimeter wall with rifle slits covering the entrance. The buildings had central pediments, rather more elegant than those at Brecon, although it is reported also to be the work of Colonel Ord. Between 1841 and 1845, £212,000 was provided for this building work.

---

[27] BL Add. MS 49129, ff.8–9; *Letter of 21 Oct 1839*, Napier MSS, quoted in Spiers (1980), p.2.
[28] PRO HO55/451.

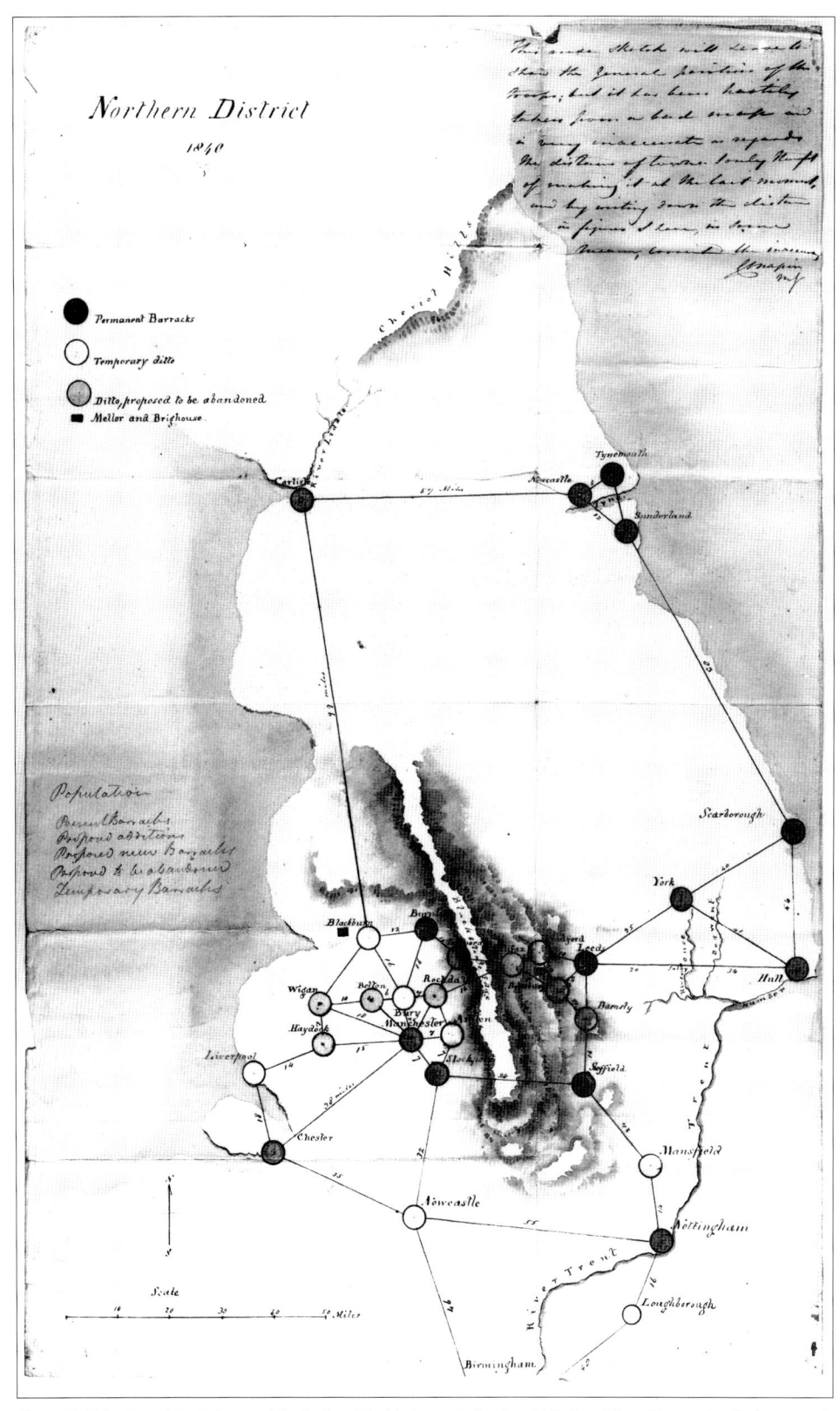

1815–1852: 'No Better Military School for Officers and Privates'

Figure 90 Major General Napier's map of the Northern District, demonstrating the distribution of the military stations in the area and the communication routes between them.

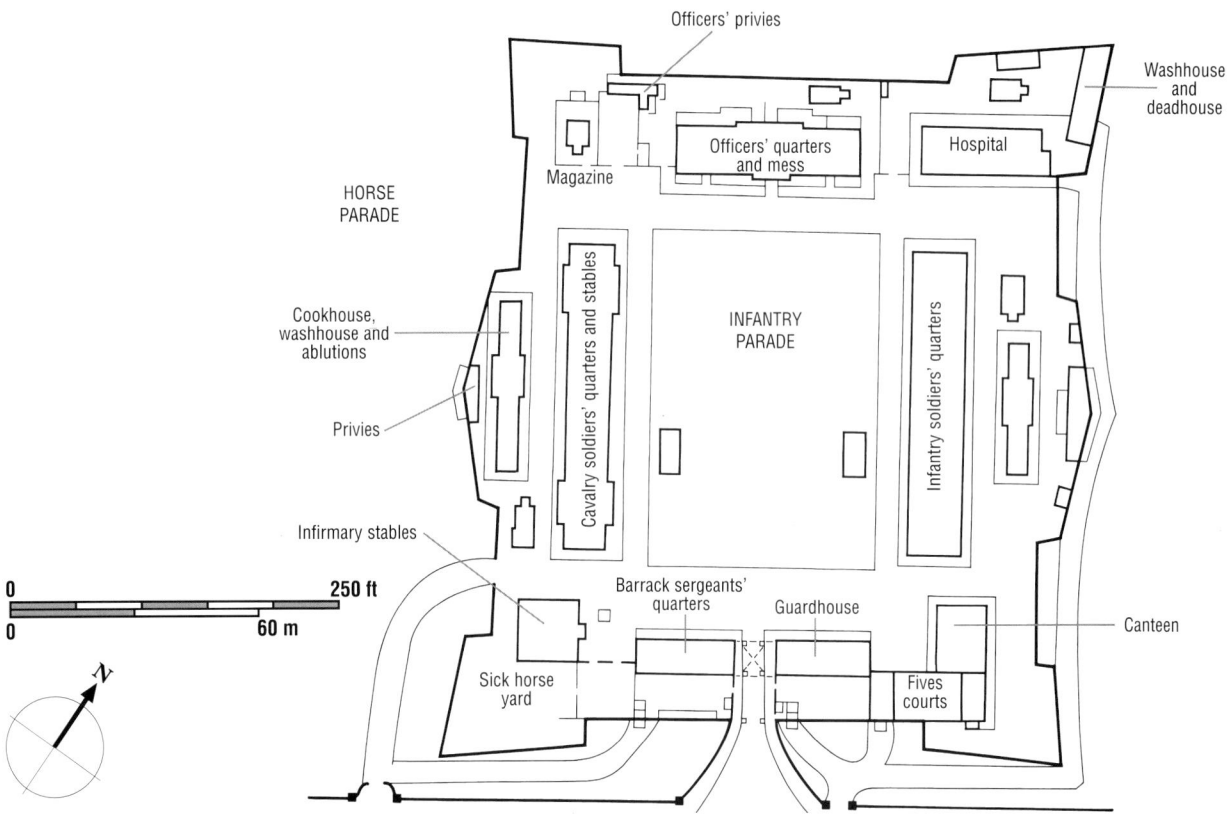

Figure 91 Napier's defensible barracks at Bury, Lancashire, now demolished, redrawn from a plan by Colonel James RE, c.1860. The layout of the accommodation and parade ground continues that established by the Barracks Department. The outline of the walls, derived from the late fifteenth-century *trace italienne*, was outdated for fortress design by the 1840s, but was sufficiently secure against a mob.

In comparison with the barracks of the Napoleonic Wars, the Royal Engineers now adopted a relatively consistent layout. For the first time in an English civil order context, the barracks were defensible, being surrounded by a wall with corner bastions from which the garrison could fire on an attacking force. In this they followed the pattern of defensive works around the Beggars Bush Barracks in Dublin, built in 1827. Napier was aware of how poorly armed the crowd were likely to be, with hand-made pikes, tools and few firearms, and the barracks were not designed to withstand artillery.

The layout of the Napier barracks centred on the parade ground, with the men's rooms each side in cross-lit rooms on each floor, separated by entrance passages with staircases (see Figure 92). The officers' quarters and mess were across one end, with an administrative range with a tall, central archway through from the entrance at the other (see Figure 93).

Fulwood is the only barracks built in response to Chartism that is still intact today – and still serving its original purpose, although no longer for civil order duties. It was designed by Major T. Foster RE, and built at a cost of £137,921. Unlike the other smaller barracks, Fulwood had two separate squares for infantry and cavalry, and the central officers' quarters divided the two and faced both directions (see Figure 94). The barracks hospital showed a distinct advance on Napoleonic models, the infantry and cavalry sections having separate sanitary blocks at the rear, attached by short passages, similar to the stemmed annexes that characterized the later pavilion-plan hospitals.

The argument over living conditions in the army: humanitarians versus traditionalists

Humanitarian officers like Napier might seek to improve the private soldier by ameliorating the worst aspects of military life, the brutal and

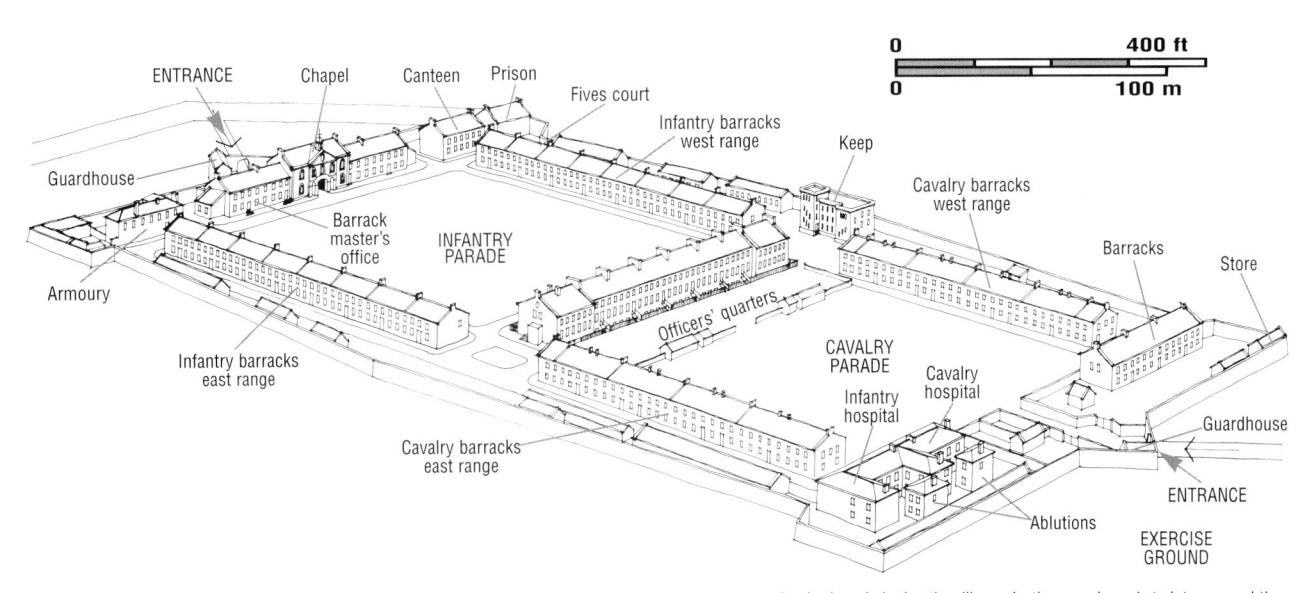

Figure 92 Reconstruction of Fulwood Barracks, Preston, as it stood c.1880. The entrances were protected at both ends by bastion-like projections, and musket slots covered the side walls against attack by disaffected Lancashire workers. The main entrance led through to the infantry square, separated by the central officers' range from that for the cavalry and artillery. The keep was added when Fulwood became a localization depot in the 1870s.

Figure 93 Fulwood Barracks. One of the innovations at these Napier complexes was the entrance range with its tall, central archway, which contained the chapel, the barrack master's quarters, offices and stores.

brutalizing punishment regime, tedious barracks routine, squalid conditions and dismal diet. The traditionalist view of the common soldiers, however, was that they were: 'incorrigibly idle, dissolute, vicious reprobates who required stern discipline to restrain their animal instincts. Any misguided attempts to improve their minds, morals or conditions of service would be utterly futile and would undermine discipline by fostering dissatisfaction and insubordination.'[29] Despite the example of Wellington's rationalization of barracks administration, the army hierarchy remained hostile to change – probably a natural consequence of military success and national ascendancy.

[29] P. Burroughs, in Chandler and Becket (1994), p.70.

Figure 94 Fulwood Barracks, showing the officers' quarters, with mess rooms to one end and servants' quarters in the basement.

Moreover, such attitudes were inevitable in an institution like the Horse Guards, 'authoritarian and largely self-contained ... [and] dominated by a closely-knit group of senior officers, who evinced an unyielding traditionalism and unquestioning adherence to Wellingtonian practices'.[30]

From 1836, there was some pressure from within the Government to change established procedures, through the young, reforming Secretary of State for War, Lord Howick. Individual officers with a paternalistic view of their men also took initiatives within their own regiments. At the same time, the erection of new barracks provided officers of the Royal Engineers with the opportunity to make some practical improvements to the living conditions of the rank and file.

What with the new quarters in the Northern District and Wales, and piecemeal improvements at existing ones, Ordnance Board spending on barracks rose by nearly 30 per cent between 1835 and 1850, from £27,000 in England and £22,000 in Ireland, to £35,000 and £27,000 respectively.[31] In 1849/50, the Board had to maintain 118 permanent barracks in England, Scotland and Wales, and 109 in Ireland, and there were a further 27 in the returns for 1849 which are referred to as 'temporary barracks', presumably rented quarters. There was capacity for 2,262 officers and 57,552 men in mainland Britain, and 1,638 officers and 33,504 men in Ireland (see Map 5).

Although some barracks, including those in Dublin, Woolwich and the dockyards, could hold several thousand men, and the Artillery in particular tended to be concentrated in fewer, larger stations, most were still quite small. The average barracks in Britain in 1849 held only 487 men and 22 officers, and in Ireland the average capacity was barely 300 men and 15 officers.[32] Despite the process of concentration effected by the move into barracks during the war with the French and continued as a general policy by the army since, the home forces in the mid-nineteenth century were still very dispersed in small posts, reflecting their civil role in the pre-railway era.

The wholesale reconstruction of the nation's ageing military accommodation was a priority for neither the Government nor the army, and living conditions changed little between the 1790s and 1850s. Analysis of the parliamentary returns for barracks in 1847 shows how bad the basic facilities in military accommodation were, and one can imagine how degrading barracks life must have been as a result. Sixty-three per cent of British barracks only had water pumped from a well, and at 19 of them, the only water for drinking, cooking and washing was that sent by Providence from the sky and which could be stored in cisterns like those fitted by de Gomme in the late seventeenth century. The men generally gathered around the well or a standpipe in the parade ground to wash, taking turns to work the pump. Sixty per cent of barracks had no covered building for washing in, and 74 per cent had nowhere to wash clothes either. The only barracks which received a regular supply were those in the few cities which had established a workable, piped network by that early date – Glasgow and Edinburgh, London, Leeds, Sunderland, Devonport, Exeter and Dublin. In Ireland, where the average age of the barracks was even greater than in England, over 90 per cent had no ablution house, and 87 per cent no washhouse for clothes. In the forts of the Channel Islands, the garrison was expected to wash in the sea.[33] WCs

---

[30] Ibid.
[31] Parliamentary Papers (House of Commons), 1849 (17), x, *1st and 2nd Reports from the Select Committee on the Army and Ordnance Expenditure*, p.2.
[32] Ibid., p.1.

[33] Parliamentary Papers (House of Commons), 1847, xxxvi, p.321, *A Return for each Barracks in the United Kingdom*.

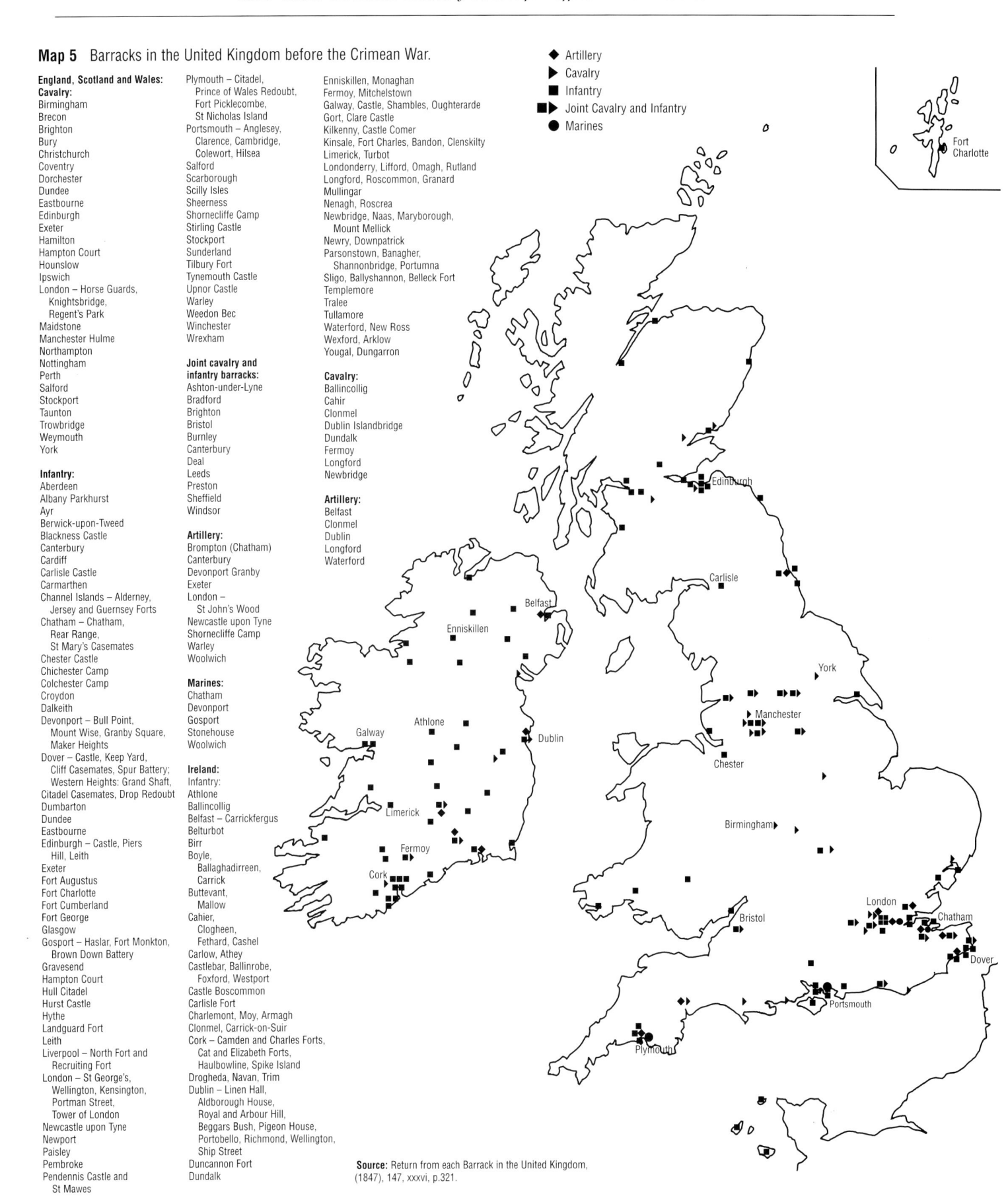

1815–1852: 'No Better Military School for Officers and Privates'

Map 5 Barracks in the United Kingdom before the Crimean War.

- ◆ Artillery
- ▶ Cavalry
- ■ Infantry
- ■▶ Joint Cavalry and Infantry
- ● Marines

England, Scotland and Wales:

Cavalry:
Birmingham
Brecon
Brighton
Bury
Christchurch
Coventry
Dorchester
Dundee
Eastbourne
Edinburgh
Exeter
Hamilton
Hampton Court
Hounslow
Ipswich
London – Horse Guards,
　Knightsbridge,
　Regent's Park
Maidstone
Manchester Hulme
Northampton
Nottingham
Perth
Salford
Stockport
Taunton
Trowbridge
Weymouth
York

Infantry:
Aberdeen
Albany Parkhurst
Ayr
Berwick-upon-Tweed
Blackness Castle
Canterbury
Cardiff
Carlisle Castle
Carmarthen
Channel Islands – Alderney,
　Jersey and Guernsey Forts
Chatham – Chatham,
　Rear Range,
　St Mary's Casemates
Chester Castle
Chichester Camp
Colchester Camp
Croydon
Dalkeith
Devonport – Bull Point,
　Mount Wise, Granby Square,
　Maker Heights
Dover – Castle, Keep Yard,
　Cliff Casemates, Spur Battery;
　Western Heights: Grand Shaft,
　Citadel Casemates, Drop Redoubt
Dumbarton
Dundee
Eastbourne
Edinburgh – Castle, Piers
　Hill, Leith
Exeter
Fort Augustus
Fort Charlotte
Fort Cumberland
Fort George
Glasgow
Gosport – Haslar, Fort Monkton,
　Brown Down Battery
Gravesend
Hampton Court
Hull Citadel
Hurst Castle
Hythe
Landguard Fort
Leith
Liverpool – North Fort and
　Recruiting Fort
London – St George's,
　Wellington, Kensington,
　Portman Street,
　Tower of London
Newcastle upon Tyne
Newport
Paisley
Pembroke
Pendennis Castle and
　St Mawes
Plymouth – Citadel,
　Prince of Wales Redoubt,
　Fort Picklecombe,
　St Nicholas Island
Portsmouth – Anglesey,
　Clarence, Cambridge,
　Colewort, Hilsea
Salford
Scarborough
Scilly Isles
Sheerness
Shorncliffe Camp
Stirling Castle
Stockport
Sunderland
Tilbury Fort
Tynemouth Castle
Upnor Castle
Warley
Weedon Bec
Winchester
Wrexham

Joint cavalry and infantry barracks:
Ashton-under-Lyne
Bradford
Brighton
Bristol
Burnley
Canterbury
Deal
Leeds
Preston
Sheffield
Windsor

Artillery:
Brompton (Chatham)
Canterbury
Devonport Granby
Exeter
London –
　St John's Wood
Newcastle upon Tyne
Shorncliffe Camp
Warley
Woolwich

Marines:
Chatham
Devonport
Gosport
Stonehouse
Woolwich

Ireland:

Infantry:
Athlone
Ballincollig
Belfast – Carrickfergus
Belturbot
Birr
Boyle,
　Ballaghadirreen,
　Carrick
Buttevant,
　Mallow
Cahier,
　Clogheen,
　Fethard, Cashel
Carlow, Athey
Castlebar, Ballinrobe,
　Foxford, Westport
Castle Boscommon
Carlisle Fort
Charlemont, Moy, Armagh
Clonmel, Carrick-on-Suir
Cork – Camden and Charles Forts,
　Cat and Elizabeth Forts,
　Haulbowline, Spike Island
Drogheda, Navan, Trim
Dublin – Linen Hall,
　Aldborough House,
　Royal and Arbour Hill,
　Beggars Bush, Pigeon House,
　Portobello, Richmond, Wellington,
　Ship Street
Duncannon Fort
Dundalk
Enniskillen, Monaghan
Fermoy, Mitchelstown
Galway, Castle, Shambles, Oughterarde
Gort, Clare Castle
Kilkenny, Castle Comer
Kinsale, Fort Charles, Bandon, Clenskilty
Limerick, Turbot
Londonderry, Lifford, Omagh, Rutland
Longford, Roscommon, Granard
Mullingar
Nenagh, Roscrea
Newbridge, Naas, Maryborough,
　Mount Mellick
Newry, Downpatrick
Parsonstown, Banagher,
　Shannonbridge, Portumna
Sligo, Ballyshannon, Belleck Fort
Templemore
Tralee
Tullamore
Waterford, New Ross
Wexford, Arklow
Yougal, Dungarron

Cavalry:
Ballincollig
Cahir
Clonmel
Dublin Islandbridge
Dundalk
Fermoy
Longford
Newbridge

Artillery:
Belfast
Clonmel
Dublin
Longford
Waterford

Source: Return from each Barrack in the United Kingdom, (1847), 147, xxxvi, p.321.

Figure 95 A barrack room in the Portman Street Barracks off Oxford Street. There appear to be closely spaced metal beds for at least thirty men. Food was heated in the large fireplace, and eaten at the tables down the middle of the room. The inhabitants' sparse possessions hang from wall racks.

were rare, even for officers' use. Private soldiers used communal lavatories undivided by partitions, sitting on ladder-like seats over rarely emptied cess pits. Open, wooden urine tubs stood in a corner of the barrack room for use at night, or by soldiers unwilling to go to the latrine; they were even used to carry cooking water.

Rooms were lit by oil lamps or candles, issued by the barrack masters according to the King's Warrant, though in bigger towns, where the provision of gas lighting by private companies was becoming more common, barracks like Regent's Park and St George's were at least partially lit by gas in the 1830s. At Chatham Infantry Barracks, gas was introduced between 1840 and 1856, and ablution rooms and flush lavatories between 1848 and 1868.

Heating in the winter was provided by open fireplaces, and coal was issued on a warrant by the barrack master. Some of the bigger barrack rooms might have had two fireplaces, but even these would have provided little more than localized heat in the winter (see Figure 95). The mid-eighteenth-century Keep Yard Barracks at Dover Castle had rooms 47 feet (14.3 metres) long and 30 feet (9.1 metres) wide. The literally cavernous casemates in the Drop Redoubt were 48 feet (14.6 metres) long, 18 feet (5.5 metres) wide and arched 16 feet (4.9 metres) over the beds, and one of the Cliff Casemates excavated from the chalk under the Castle was almost 60 feet (18.3 metres) long.[34] The fireplaces in the barrack rooms were also used for heating food. The only cooking apparatus possessed by most barrack cookhouses was the copper boiler in which the soldier's twice-daily diet of beef broth or boiled beef and coffee was made. Even the kitchens in the new cookhouses which the arch-reformer Bentham built for the Marines at Chatham were only fitted with boilers.[35] Despite the example of Fort George in the eighteenth century, which needed to be prepared in case it were ever besieged, and so was equipped with a bakery, the only barracks with ovens for baking bread or roasting meat was in Ireland, at Naas.

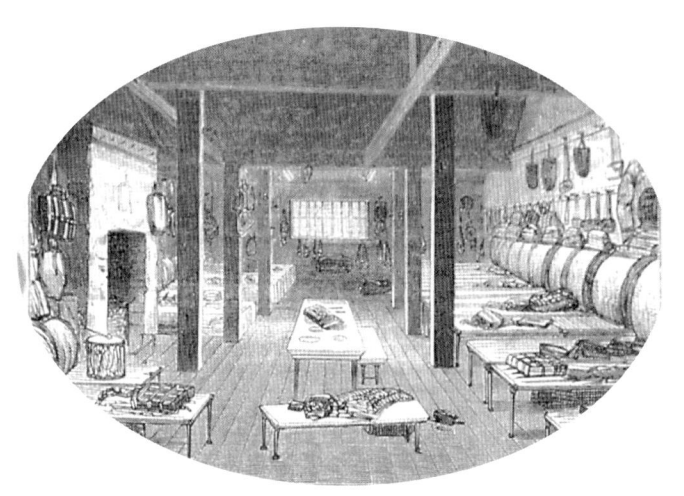

Figure 96 Another of the converted rooms at the Portman Street Barracks off Oxford Street.

Unable to dent the monolithic problem of the structural inadequacies of barracks, reform-minded officers sought to raise the character of the soldier by providing a better environment through improving sports and educational opportunities. Regimental libraries started as an innovation by individual colonels, who appropriated a suitable room within the barracks for their book collection. From the late 1830s, Lord Howick ordered the establishment of libraries at the larger barracks (see Figure 97), and in 1839, the Revd G.R. Gleig, chaplain of the Chelsea Hospital, drew up a list of authors suitable for inclusion for the War Office. It

[34] Ibid.
[35] PRO ADM140/120.

included Defoe, Fielding, Maria Edgeworth, Scott and Captain Marryat, as well as several theological volumes by Gleig himself.[36] All the Napier barracks except the two in Wales had libraries, and the principle was warily accepted by the Horse Guards in 1841.

The extent to which the ordinary rank and file benefited from this is doubtful, given the high level of illiteracy in the army: 60 per cent of private soldiers were still unable to read at the end of the nineteenth century. Regimental schools were established in 1846, and most larger barracks set aside a room for the schoolteacher. In St Mary's Barracks in Chatham, for instance, one of the long casemates was fitted up as a schoolroom for 58 infants, with the schoolmistress living in the heated, but lightless, far end.

As in civilian education, schooling was closely linked with the Church. Although Sunday Service was one of the fixed points of regimental life, only the large artillery barracks at Woolwich and Brompton had chapels. The posh Guards commissioned G.E. Street to rebuild their chapel at their London home in the Wellington Barracks in 1879, and later engaged William Butterfield to erect the pretty little chapel at their depot in Caterham. The East India Company chapel at the Warley depot in Essex was designed by Matthew Digby Wyatt and built in 1857. The large Napier barracks at Preston and Sheffield may have been the first to include a chapel from the beginning, whilst at some stations such as Hounslow, empty rooms or separate buildings were set aside for religious services. The role of the chaplain in education was reinforced by the construction of regimental chapels which included schoolrooms. These were built during the 1850s at barracks including Shoeburyness (see Figure 98), Chatham, the Lower Barracks in Winchester, and the Royal Barracks in Dublin. They were all simple Gothic buildings, although the vaulted Chatham chapel is distinguished from the rest by its unusual flying buttresses (see Figure 99).[37]

More common than either libraries or schools were fives courts. Providing better provision for exercise was another of Lord Howick's reforms, and money for 29 fives courts to be built within the larger garrisons was provided by the Treasury, which were erected during the 1840s.[38] At Preston, the fives court was efficiently incorporated into one of the

Figure 97 The crowded reading room in one of the St Mary's Casemates at Chatham.

[36] F.J. Huddeston, 'A Barrack Library of 1839', *JSAHR*, **2** (1923), p.37.
[37] It was in the 1854 regimental chapel of the Royal Barracks, Dublin, that Queen Victoria's son, the Duke of Cambridge, then commanding the Dublin District and later an ultra-conservative Commander-in-Chief, scandalized his mother by marrying Miss Louisa Fairbrother, 'an actress'.

[38] H. Strachan, *Wellington's Legacy: The Reform of the British Army, 1830–1854* (Manchester 1984), p.85.

Figure 98 The regimental chapel at the Horseshoe Barracks, Shoeburyness.

corner bastions. Like the regimental library, however, fives, with its public school origins, was unlikely to attract the private soldier.

The impact of the Royal Engineers' experience

In military as in civilian life, a major stimulus to improving living conditions in the early years of Victoria's reign was the systematic collection of medical statistics. These provided reformers with incontrovertible evidence of the link between the army's alarming level of natural wastage through illness and the soldiers' diet and housing conditions in barracks. Statistics were being collected by the War Office in the late 1830s, and were used by Howick to press for improvements. They subsequently avalanched onto the Horse Guards, threatening to smother the traditionalists, through the inquiries of the late 1850s into the conduct of the army in the Crimea. As early as 1806, however, Royal Engineers officers working in the West Indies, where mortality rates were especially high, had been carrying out improvements to local barracks in an effort to reduce the debilitating impact of the climate.[39] This experience spread through the Corps via the professional papers over the succeeding decades.

In 1824, Sir Charles Smith of the Royal Engineers submitted a plan to the Master General of the Ordnance for a standard barracks for use in the West Indies for 200 men (see Figure 100). Drawing on traditional building experience in the tropics, it was surrounded on four sides by a full-height veranda, 8 feet (2.4 metres) deep and paved with York stone. It combined masonry walls with iron internal members and fittings, including the stairs and windows. In rooms for 18–20 men, space, light and air were maximized 'within the bounds of economy', and the ventilation was controlled by sash windows, adjustable louvres and wire gauze screens. The efficacy of the screens in reducing illness in malarial areas had already been noticed, even though the part played by mosquitoes in transmitting the disease was unknown. It was thought the screens somehow 'diluted' the 'miasmata' – the noxious gases from the marshes which were thought to be the cause of the sickness.[40]

The casting of the ironwork was supervised by Captain Henry Brandreth. In 1837, the Admiralty went well beyond the reforms of the Ordnance undertaken by the Duke of Wellington and abolished the old Navy Board, replacing it with a new organization staffed by Royal Engineers officers. These were made responsible for designing and supervising the construction of all the navy's

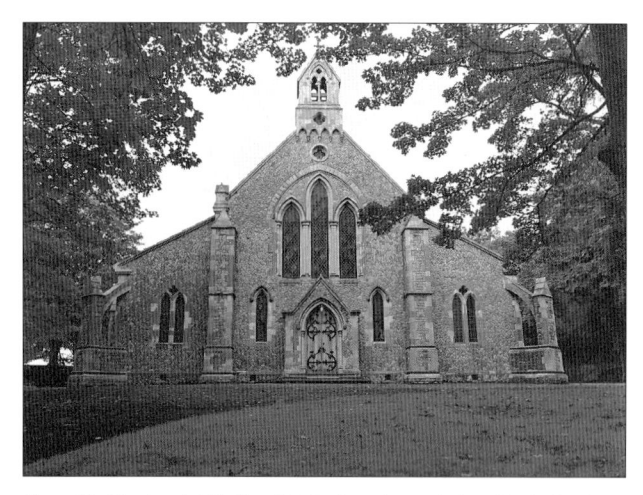

Figure 99 The chapel at Chatham Infantry Barracks was designed by the Royal Engineers and built in 1854. It was one of the largest of the first generation of religious buildings in barracks, and included a schoolroom at the rear.

---

[39] R.N. Buckley, 'The British Army in the West Indies 1793–1815', *JSAHR*, **56** (1978), p.87.
[40] H.R. Brandreth, 'Memorandum relative to a System of Barracks for the West Indies', *Professional Papers of the Royal Engineers*, **29** (1837).

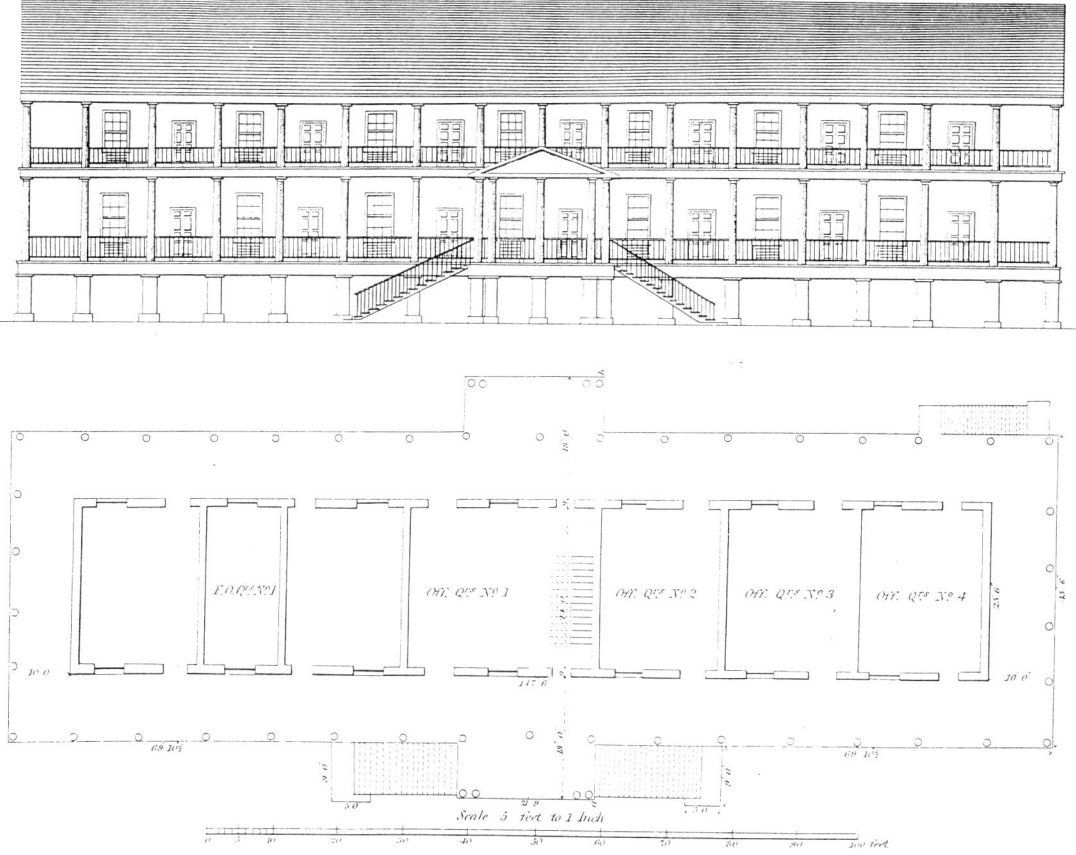

Figure 100 The officers' quarters at George Town, Demerara, in the West Indies.

buildings, in the dockyards and elsewhere. It was called the Admiralty Works Department, and Brandreth was appointed its first head. The group of Royal Engineers officers working in the royal dockyards under the Department have become better known in recent years, especially for the advances which they pioneered in the structural use of iron.[41] With Marines' barracks included within their brief, these officers were also active in the field of barracks planning. New Marines' barracks were built between 1848 and 1865 at Woolwich and Eastney, near Portsmouth, and large extensions were made to Gosport and Stonehouse. Their designers brought new and progressive ideas to the subject, many of which anticipated and implemented reforms to army practice of the immediate post-Crimean years.

First under Brandreth, and then from 1850 under

Colonel Geoffrey Greene, these officers included: Captain Sir Henry James, who adapted the Forton Military Hospital at Gosport as Forton (later St Vincent) Marines Barracks in 1847, and compiled his invaluable plans of British barracks for the Topographical Department (later the Ordnance Survey); Greene himself, who worked on Eastney and Stonehouse Marines Barracks; and Captain Francis Fowke, the architect of the Raglan Infantry Barracks, built at Devonport in 1854–6. Fowke became the most famous army architect of all for his work with Prince Albert, which included the Consort's Library at Aldershot, the Brompton Boilers, forerunner of the Victoria and Albert Museum, and the Albert Hall itself.

The new, 960-place quarters for the Marines Division at Woolwich (see Figure 101) was designed and started by Captain Sir William Denison,

[41] See Weiler (1987).

Figure 101 Woolwich Marines Barracks (later Cambridge Infantry Barracks) showing the full-length, double-height loggia.

Superintendent at Woolwich Dockyard from 1837 to 1845, and completed by Captain Beatson after Denison swapped posts with him at Portsmouth. The barracks were later transferred to the War Office and renamed after the Duke of Cambridge, the Commander-in-Chief. Now completely demolished except for the fine triumphal archway and flanking guardhouses, Denison's barracks marked a significant step forward in the consideration given to the physical well-being of the soldier. They also showed a new appreciation of the army's responsibility for the moral improvement of the soldier, one which was to become much more marked in the late Victorian army.

It was laid out much like the mid-eighteenth-century Marines' barracks (see Chapter 3), with a long privates' range, wings at each end for the field officers and the mess and the captains' quarters, and an open fourth side. This was divided into two by the large, Roman triumphal arch which opened into the parade ground. The raised corner pavilions of the long soldiers' range echoed those at Denison's home station at Brompton. However, its main architectural feature was the loggia, or veranda, extending all along the front for the full height of the building, which gave access into the barrack rooms, thereby avoiding the problem of corridors, and maximizing light and ventilation. This veranda was the first of its type to be built in Britain, but has obvious colonial precedents. As at the old Clarence Marines Barracks in Portsmouth, it could be used for drilling when the weather was poor, and was a precursor to the covered drill sheds of the later nineteenth century. The men lived in well-lit rooms facing both front and rear, each for one-fifth of a company, or 20 men. Another innovation was the allowance of separate rooms for the sergeants, off the stairway.

The barracks had a non-inflammable structure of brick jack arches on iron beams, and contained a pioneering central system of forced heating and ventilation. Air was warmed or cooled by an ingenious apparatus in the basement, designed by Denison, consisting of compartments containing 50 copper boxes, which were fed from a boiler with hot water in winter, or cold in summer. Air was pumped over the boxes and thence to the barrack rooms by a small steam engine. Stale air was drawn from the rooms by flues connected to the fires in the kitchens, which created a draught.

In the course of the work, Denison developed his thoughts on military accommodation, which he published in 1848. His paper is significant in being one of the earliest attempts to state a comprehensive design philosophy dealing with both the practical questions of what space should be allowed to the different ranks, and the attitudes and aims underlying these decisions. His approach was strongly motivated by religious conviction, and by a sympathetic attitude towards the soldier that was in marked contrast to that of the army traditionalists. He wrote:

'The soldier is usually taken from the least cultivated portion of the community; he brings with him the feelings and habits of his class, and those feelings are coarse and the habits gross. He is usually ill-educated, if at all, when he joins; he is then thrown into forced everyday companionship with great numbers of men equally uncultivated with himself; his temptations to idleness and vice are many and close at hand; the inducements to an opposite course of life few and remote; he is instructed in little else than mechanical duties, and is regarded in that respect rather as a thing than as a person; he is controlled more by fear than by hope or sympathy; and his virtues are and must be the result rather of accident than of acquirement. If human beings so circumstanced are, as a class, ignorant and vicious, where is the wonder?' [42]

Denison wanted better living conditions to raise the health of the soldier and reduce the gross wastage of men and money caused by disease, and a much greater effort to improve his 'moral tone' through education. Better heating and ventilation, baths, and modern, water-borne sanitation were needed. Much greater separation of the different ranks and classes of soldier should be made, in particular of married soldiers and their families, and of NCOs so that the distinction and authority of their rank should not be eroded by familiarity. The kitchens should be supplemented by bakeries, butcheries and washhouses, and a laundry and drying house should be made available for the use of the wives of married soldiers.

The private soldier needed to have much wider access to education, both for himself and his children. The subjects taught in the regimental school should include moral and religious knowledge, as well as the mechanical details of the soldiers' professions. Mindful of the need to 'make every effort to retain the soldier within the barrack square', Denison proposed separate reading rooms and libraries for NCOs and privates as well as for officers, fives courts, bowling greens, and space for cricket and 'foot-ball' (*sic*).[43]

So critical did the article seem that the editors of the Corps Papers added a postscript defending the 'improvements which have taken place since His Grace the Duke of Wellington became Master General of the Ordnance'. They cited as evidence the new Anglesey Infantry Barracks in Portsmouth, designed by Major General Cardew RE, which included many of the advances Denison advocated.[44] Nevertheless, the establishment view of the responsibility of the army, as expressed by the editors, remained a *laissez-faire* one: 'public example and opinion will do more to improve the condition of the soldier, than being prematurely forced, by the appointment of regimental chaplains and civil schoolmasters'.[45]

Senior officers in the Wellingtonian army remained sceptical or hostile to the possibility of raising the character of the soldier by providing a more amenable environment. The views of Denison and other humanitarian officers were to be vindicated within a few years, however, when the miserable living conditions of the rank and file became better known to the public as a result of the failures of the old guard in the Crimean War.

---

[42] Denison (1848), p.256.
[43] Ibid., p.255
[44] Ibid., p.256–8. Anglesey Barracks was later incorporated into the new naval barracks, HMS *Victory*, now known as HMS *Nelson*.
[45] Ibid., p.260.

The architecture of military education

The Royal Military College at Sandhurst

The most magnificent military buildings built in Britain in the war years had nothing to do with either barracks or forts. They were devoted to the schooling of young officers. Around 1800, the Ordnance Board's architect, James Wyatt, embarked on designs for two complexes of teaching rooms and lodgings: a new home for the Royal Military Academy at Woolwich, where cadets of the 'scientific corps' were taught, and a new school for young cavalry and infantry officers, the Royal Military College at Sandhurst.

Wyatt's proposals could not have been more different. At Woolwich, the new Academy consisted of a central school linked by arcades to outer ranges of barracks, with a complex of courts and gardens behind. The cadets lodged in rooms opening off a central corridor which continued through the arcades to the school, where stone stairs led up to the four main teaching rooms. This he modelled on the Tower of London, the Ordnance's original home. The style Wyatt chose was the Gothic of Fonthill; possibly intending to evoke ancient

The central school at Woolwich Academy

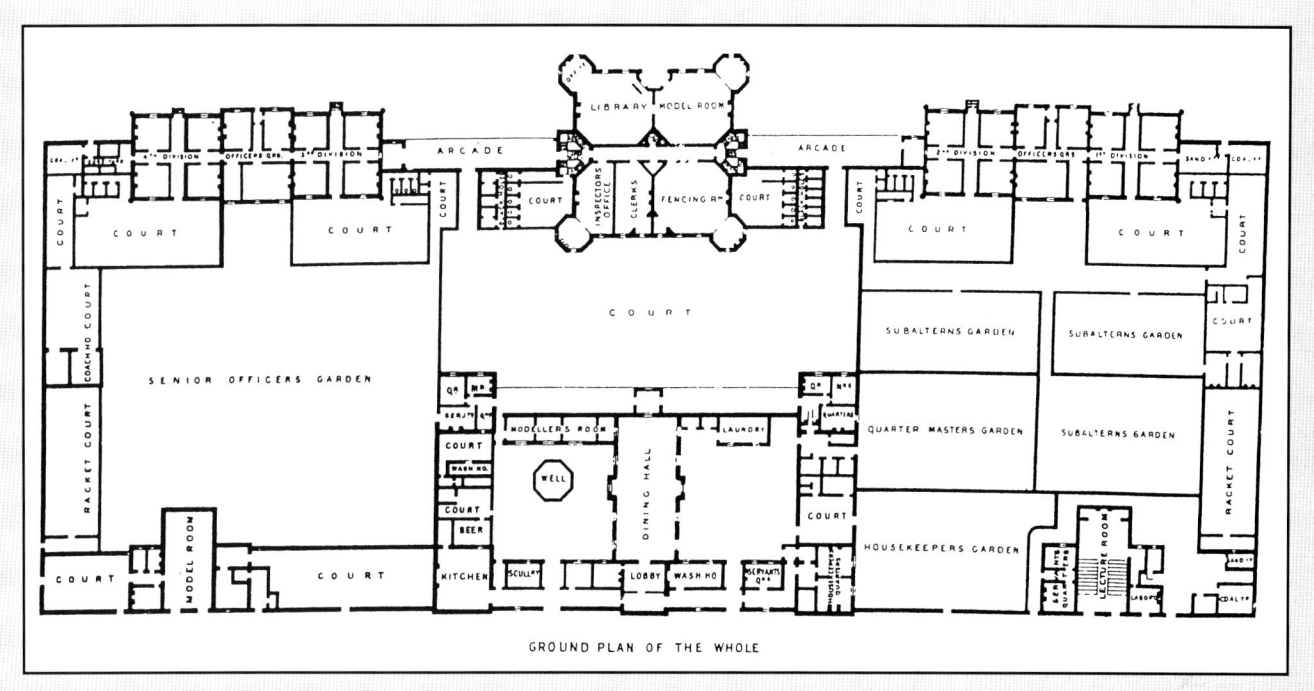

Wyatt's original plan for the Woolwich Academy

educational traditions, as was the intention of the Tudor Gothic extensions built at Rugby and Harrow a few years later. It was completed by 1806.

Sandhurst has some similarities of planning with Woolwich – a long spine passage linking separate sections with colonnades between – but stylistically it is quite different: a long, calm, Classical front broken only by a large, central portico. Solid stone was used here, and archaeologically correct Greek Doric. Wyatt had been relieved of the commission early on, and after a protracted fracas involving DeLancey's favourite contractor, Alexander Copland, his scheme was reworked and completed from 1811 by James Sanders, by then architect to the Treasury-run Barracks Department. Cadets first occupied the incomplete shell in 1812.

Despite the apparent prestige of their schools, officer training was little valued in the Wellingtonian army. By the Crimean War, Britain was spending only a fraction of the amount other Continental powers invested in educating their officer corps: in 1857, £1,300 per year, compared to £26,000 per year by the French, and £127,000 per year by the Austrians. Pressure for reform led to the formation that year of a Staff College at Sandhurst, for which the Government architect, Sir James Pennethorne, built a separate home in 1857. With the new School of Military Engineering (1872–4) at Chatham, an offshoot of the Royal Military Academy built by Sir Frederick Ommanney RE for the Royal Engineers, these two buildings embody the changes in military education since Wyatt's day. Whereas the Georgian schools appear to have been conceived partly as backdrops to parades and performances of drill, these were much deeper, more substantial structures which owed more to mid-Victorian office architecture. Even British officers were now expected to learn technical matters, as these serious-looking piles proclaim, and high birth and hunting skills were not enough. Staff officers, at least, needed to be more than the British Army's traditional 'congregation of sporting men and loungers' (Spiers, 1980, pp.151–7).

The School of Military Engineering at Chatham. A central lecture room was flanked by specialised teaching rooms. The facade is partly faced in fashionable Doulton terracotta tiles.

Chapter Six
1852–1872: 'Old, Gloomy and Bad'

It is a commonplace to describe the Crimean War as a watershed in the history of the British Army. With hindsight, the change seems foreshadowed by the death of the Duke of Wellington, standard-bearer of the reactionary Horse Guards, in 1852. A couple of years later, the organization he had sheltered from retrenchment and reform for nearly forty years suddenly had the chance to shine in an unexpected and, at first, popular foreign war. Within months of arriving in the Black Sea, however, almost every aspect of the Wellingtonian army was under attack.

The incompetence of the aristocratic officers leading the expedition emboldened radicals at home to demand the abolition of the purchase system of promotion, and a change to a more professional officer corps. The evident confusion between the military departments – the War Office, Home Office, Treasury, Horse Guards and Ordnance – and between civilian commissaries and military staff officers enabled the Government to rationalize the bureaucracy, abolishing the old Ordnance Board and asserting political authority through a new Secretary for War. Reports of the conditions of the sick and wounded in Balaclava and Constantinople propelled Florence Nightingale and her associates into a position to dictate a more humane approach to soldiers' welfare, and sympathy for the suffering of the rank and file drew the attention of the public to the state of their barracks at home. The inquiries following the war revealed, with their characteristic accumulations of statistical evidence, that the army's barracks were built to even meaner standards than accommodation for criminals or the workhouse poor, and soldiers in barracks had a life expectancy half that of their contemporaries in the slums outside.

From the first critical editorials in *The Times* in 1854, the army command endured a torrid year. Palmerston, who became Prime Minister in January 1855, repeated Pitt's tactic of conceding inquiries to defuse criticism, and by the summer, with peace reluctantly accepted, the reformers' tide began to ebb. With the comparative success of the army in the Indian Mutiny, which lasted from May 1857 to July 1858, the Horse Guards reasserted control over the pace of reform, and although the sanitary campaigners were more successful than the purchase abolitionists, even they lost influence after the death of Sydney Herbert in 1861. Although probably not the 'turning point in the history of the British soldier'[1], as believed by the War Office architect Ingress Bell at the end of the century, the 1850s did see the army forced to submit to influences already strong in civilian life, in artisan housing, urban planning, prison reform and hospital treatment.

Whilst statistics underlined the need to improve conditions, this could not happen without a decisive shift in priorities. At the time of the Crimean War, there were some 162 barracks, castles and forts being used for barracks in the whole of Great Britain, containing over 5,300 sleeping rooms with a capacity for 75,801 men.[2] What was needed was the equivalent to a slum clearance programme. All that was achieved was two model barracks for the Guards in London.

New plan forms, layouts and standard designs

Professional consideration of planning and design reached a more formal level within the Royal Engineers during the mid-1850s. When the Ordnance Board was abolished in May 1855, the

---

[1] Bell (1880), p.5.
[2] Parliamentary Papers (House of Commons), 1861, *xvi*, *General Report of the Commission for improving the Sanitary Conditions of Barracks and Hospitals*, Appendix, p.212.

Figure 102 Waterloo Barracks at the Tower of London (1854), with the White Tower to the left. This was an early example of contextual design within a historic site.

Corps retained responsibility for barracks under the Inspector General of Fortifications, General Sir John Burgoyne, as before, but his department was transferred to the War Office.[3] Under governmental direction, Burgoyne was instructed by the incoming Secretary of State for War, Lord Panmure, to 'superintend, plan, and construct all fortifications and barracks, at home and abroad', as well as 'the maintenance, lighting, and cleansing of all such buildings'.[4] At the same time, Panmure received a report on barracks, commissioned by Lord Raglan, the Master General of the Ordnance, before he left for the Crimea, which prompted Burgoyne to order the codification of the old Ordnance Board's practice into a standard synopsis for the guidance of officers with responsibility for new works.

The *Barracks Accommodation Report*, published in July 1855, highlighted three particular areas for improvement. It suggested that the kitchens should include a dining area so that the soldiers were not obliged to spend their entire day, including mealtimes, in their sleeping rooms; that the 'objectionable' practice of married soldiers living with their families alongside single men be stopped and separate quarters provided, and that the canteen – a franchised bar so overpriced that the soldiers preferred unregulated gin shops – be replaced by more attractive bars run by pensioned NCOs. More importantly, the report showed that, within the War Office at least, it was now accepted that part of the purpose of barracks was to effect a behavioural change on the soldier – or in the language of the 1850s, 'the creation of a higher tone of social habits' – by providing healthy living conditions, proper sanitation, decent food, and moral and physical education. In this way, the army could play its part in raising the 'sanitary and moral character' of 'the class of society from which the privates of the army are generally recruited'.[5]

The main part of the report was an analysis of the accommodation required for a regiment of infantry and of cavalry. This part was taken up by General Burgoyne, and the following year he sent the Horse Guards a proposal for a standard checklist, 'for the

[3] Watson (1954), p.152.
[4] PRO WO33/I.29.
[5] Parliamentary Papers (House of Commons), 1855, *xvi*, *Report of the Committee on the Barrack Accommodation for the Army*, p.iii.

Figure 103 A large, new barracks was built at Dover Castle in the 1850s, including officers' quarters and mess to the designs of the architect Anthony Salvin. The relative sophistication of the architecture and the quality of the internal fittings were appropriate to the importance of the castle garrison.

guidance of officers whose duty it may be to design a barracks or portions of a barracks', and instructed the officer working on the new barracks at Aldershot to follow its recommendations. The report and Burgoyne's synopsis both considered that there should be a greater segregation of the different ranks into detached accommodation. This is a process which can be traced from the early eighteenth century (when officers' quarters such as those at Berwick-upon-Tweed were merely distinguished by their architecture) to the more complete physical separation of officers from the other ranks around the middle of the century. By the 1850s, the process had continued to the point where it was considered proper that the staff sergeants – the sergeant major and quartermaster sergeant, the schoolmaster, paymaster, hospital and armourer sergeants, and the drum major – should also have separate rooms and messes from the common soldiers.[6]

What these moves towards codifying and standardizing barracks lacked was some fundamental guiding principal upon which to establish a model layout. Unlike hospitals, asylums or prisons, for which reformers, architects and other interested parties had been producing model or ideal block plans since the mid-eighteenth century, there appears to have been no interest in this aspect of barracks. There was nothing comparable to the pavilion principle underlying hospital planning, or the panopticon for prisons. The 'social planning' of barracks seems to have taken second place to strategic, operational and even aesthetic needs, and engineer designers were left to their own devices and instincts in order to express regimental hierarchy, military order, internal unity or insularity (see Figures 102 and 103): these were considered to be self-evident restrictions which could be guided by neo-Classical concepts of symmetry and formal space.

This lack of an accepted principle is apparent in the most important new type of barracks introduced during the 1850s: the large, permanent training camp, of which Aldershot was the first. These were not subject to the security considerations which were a notable feature of the Napier barracks, occupying instead large, green-field sites, and could apply some of the ideas of the sanitary reformers about light and fresh air. This facilitated a degree of experimentation in search of the best camp layout and, with the exception of the Irish camp at the Curragh, a rejection of the traditional, square-centred plan.

Aldershot and the permanent camps

One of the early initiatives of Wellington's successor as Commander-in-Chief, Lord Hardinge, was to

---

[6] Parliamentary Papers (House of Commons), 1857/58, *xxxvi*, *Synopsis of proposed normal sized, fitments &c. for all parts of barracks*, Lieutenant E.F. Du Cane RE, p.137.

Figure 104 Assembling several battalions for large-scale training exercises was the intention behind the new encampment on the open heath at Aldershot.

examine the distribution of the country's barracks. He recognized that the existing dispersed 'regimental system' was useful in so far as barracks acted as recruiting depots, but he saw that their 'distribution was determined by the popularity and economy of using [the army] as a police force in the large manufacturing towns and districts'.[7] As a consequence, regiments were scattered in units too small to allow brigade-scale exercises or practising complex manoeuvres. So dispersed was the home army that Hardinge found 'only seven barracks in Great Britain which can hold a thousand men, with the exception of London and the great naval arsenals'.[8]

During the summer of 1852, the army organized a successful training camp at Chobham, in Surrey. The following spring, Hardinge visited the barren, sandy commons of Aldershot Heath, and proposed to his Cabinet colleagues that the Government buy 8,000 acres of this inexpensive land. Here, '10,000 troops could be trained for five months of the year, giving to each division five or six weeks training'. Ten or twelve battalions of militia could be exercised at a time, in four reliefs over the summer, with the great benefit of mixing for 28 days with more experienced officers of the line regiments (see Figure 104). He pointed out the strategic value which the new railways conferred on the site, placed as it was with easy access to London, Dover and the main naval arsenals at Chatham, Portsmouth and Plymouth.[9]

Such camps were already a feature of some Continental armies. The Belgians had developed a large training ground from the 1830s, and the Prussians used Potsdam, near Berlin, in a similar way; the French were to develop the first *grands camps* a few years later. Prince Albert encouraged Hardinge to exploit the fleeting public enthusiasm for the war to obtain money from Parliament for a permanent barracks.[10] Work on the new camp was started in February 1854, and by 1856, two regular dispositions of wooden huts had been erected, the North and South Camps (later the Stanhope and Marlborough Lines), for 20,000 men, predominantly of the militia.[11] By 1859, there were 1,600 huts, divided into blocks of 22 for 528 men, and each one identified by a letter (see Figures 104 and 105). Laid out to a strict grid pattern, the barrack huts were in two parallel rows, with the cookhouse and quartermaster's stores in the middle. Each hut could hold 22 men, the squad division into which

---

[7] PRO WO33, *Memo on the advantages of Aldershot for a proposed permanent encampment*, 26 September 1853.
[8] Ibid. He could have been thinking of Alderney, Parkhurst, Dover, Preston, Winchester, Fort George, Dublin, Cork, Limerick, Newbridge, Parsonstown, Templemore or Fermoy, all of which could hold a regiment at full establishment; Parliamentary Papers (House of Commons), 1857–8, *x*, *Report into the Billeting System, List of barrack stations in Great Britain*, 1 April 1856, Appendix 8.
[9] Ibid.
[10] T. Martin, *Life of the Prince Consort*, **3** (London 1877) p.187.
[11] A full description of the establishment and early days of Aldershot Camp is given in Cole (1980), pp.25–36.

Key

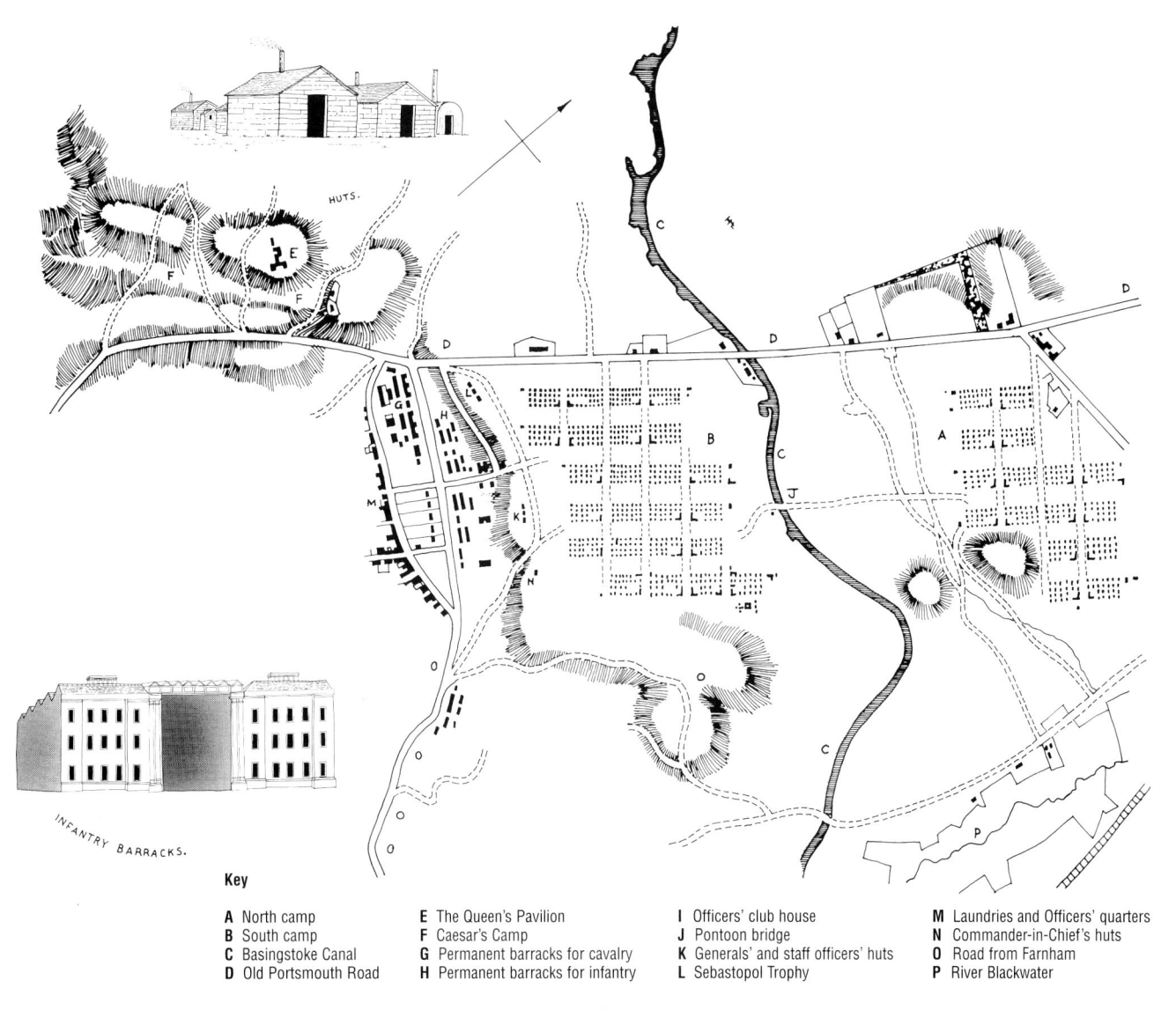

A North camp	**E** The Queen's Pavilion	**I** Officers' club house	**M** Laundries and Officers' quarters
B South camp	**F** Caesar's Camp	**J** Pontoon bridge	**N** Commander-in-Chief's huts
C Basingstoke Canal	**G** Permanent barracks for cavalry	**K** Generals' and staff officers' huts	**O** Road from Farnham
D Old Portsmouth Road	**H** Permanent barracks for infantry	**L** Sebastopol Trophy	**P** River Blackwater

Figure 105 An early impression of Aldershot Camp, with sketches of the North and South Camp timber huts, and of the innovative infantry barracks, with the glazed-roof exercise areas. The plan shows the permanent barracks as they were built.

the men were divided on parade. A parallel pair of rows included four officers' huts and most of the ancillary buildings – officers' mess, privies and washhouse, workshops, school, stables and armoury.

The permanent barracks, unimaginatively named the Wellington Lines, were built between September 1854 and 1859 (see Figure 106). The ground was plotted and construction was overseen by Colonel Sir Frederick Smith RE, and the buildings were designed by Captain R.M. Laffan, the Deputy Inspector General of Fortifications. The layout was completely different to earlier British barracks, with their consistently formal, quadrilateral arrangement centred on the parade square. For the first time there was no high wall around the camp to secure the barracks and maintain its separateness; the army so dominated Aldershot that this was unnecessary from a security standpoint, but it emphasized the difference between Aldershot and

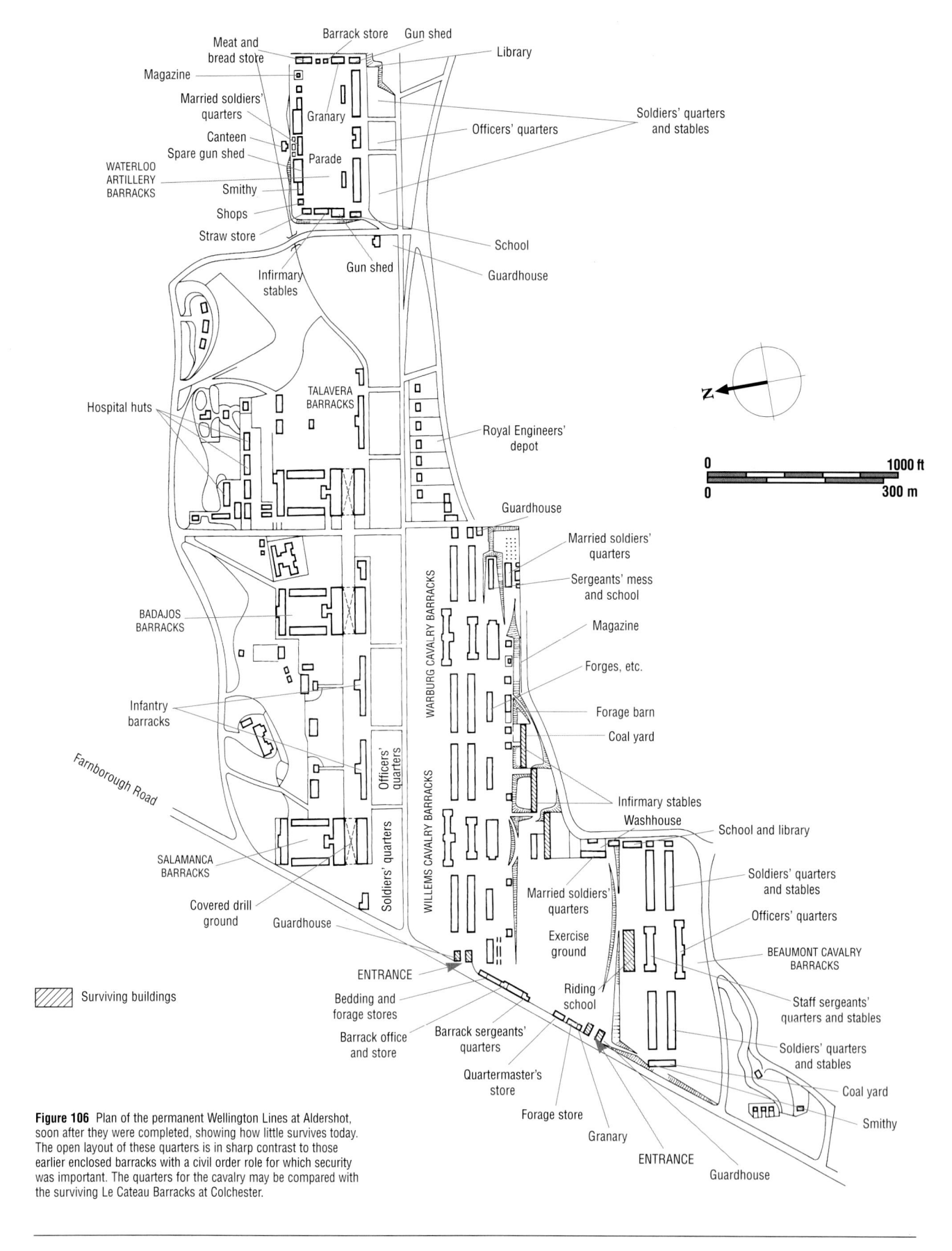

British Barracks 1600–1914

Figure 106 Plan of the permanent Wellington Lines at Aldershot, soon after they were completed, showing how little survives today. The open layout of these quarters is in sharp contrast to those earlier enclosed barracks with a civil order role for which security was important. The quarters for the cavalry may be compared with the surviving Le Cateau Barracks at Colchester.

Figure 107 The officers' mess at Warburg, photographed prior to demolition in the 1960s.

Figure 108 The old riding school of the Beaumont Cavalry Barracks.

previous barracks, with their intrinsic civil policing role. This was an entirely novel concept.

The three cavalry barracks, later named Beaumont, Willems and Warburg, were for 1,872 cavalrymen and 1,584 horses. The central ranges for the officers were among the most elegant ever built by the army. Their long, Italianate fronts could have been taken from contemporary domestic terrace architecture, with round-arched windows in a heavily rusticated ground floor, and pedimented end and central sections stepped forward, the latter with pilasters and a royal coat of arms (see Figure 107). The troopers' lodgings were in four parallel, three-storey blocks in pairs either side of the officers' quarters. Opposite the mess buildings was a large riding school, with more rusticated brickwork and an arched arcade all round. The barracks were traditional in plan, with central stairs to ten sleeping rooms, and ground-floor stables.

The three infantry barracks, Badajos, Salamanca and Talavera, for 4,173 infantrymen, followed a similar block plan, but the quarters for the rank and file were of a new design, with well-ventilated, cross-lit sleeping rooms, accessed by a full-height, cast-iron veranda or walkway which extended along the front. Pairs of tall barracks were linked by glazed iron roofs which provided a sheltered area for covered drill, although these were taken down before the First World War because people kept falling through them.[12] To the east was a barracks for 339 artillerymen with 214 horses, and their officers. All were demolished during the great rebuilding during the 1960s, so that all that is now left of this huge and innovative complex is a pair of entrances with their guardhouses, and the riding school of the old South (later Beaumont) Cavalry Barracks (see Figure 108).

Figure 109 The Consort's Library, Aldershot, designed by Francis Fowke, and stocked by Prince Albert's gift.

[12] Ibid., p.59.

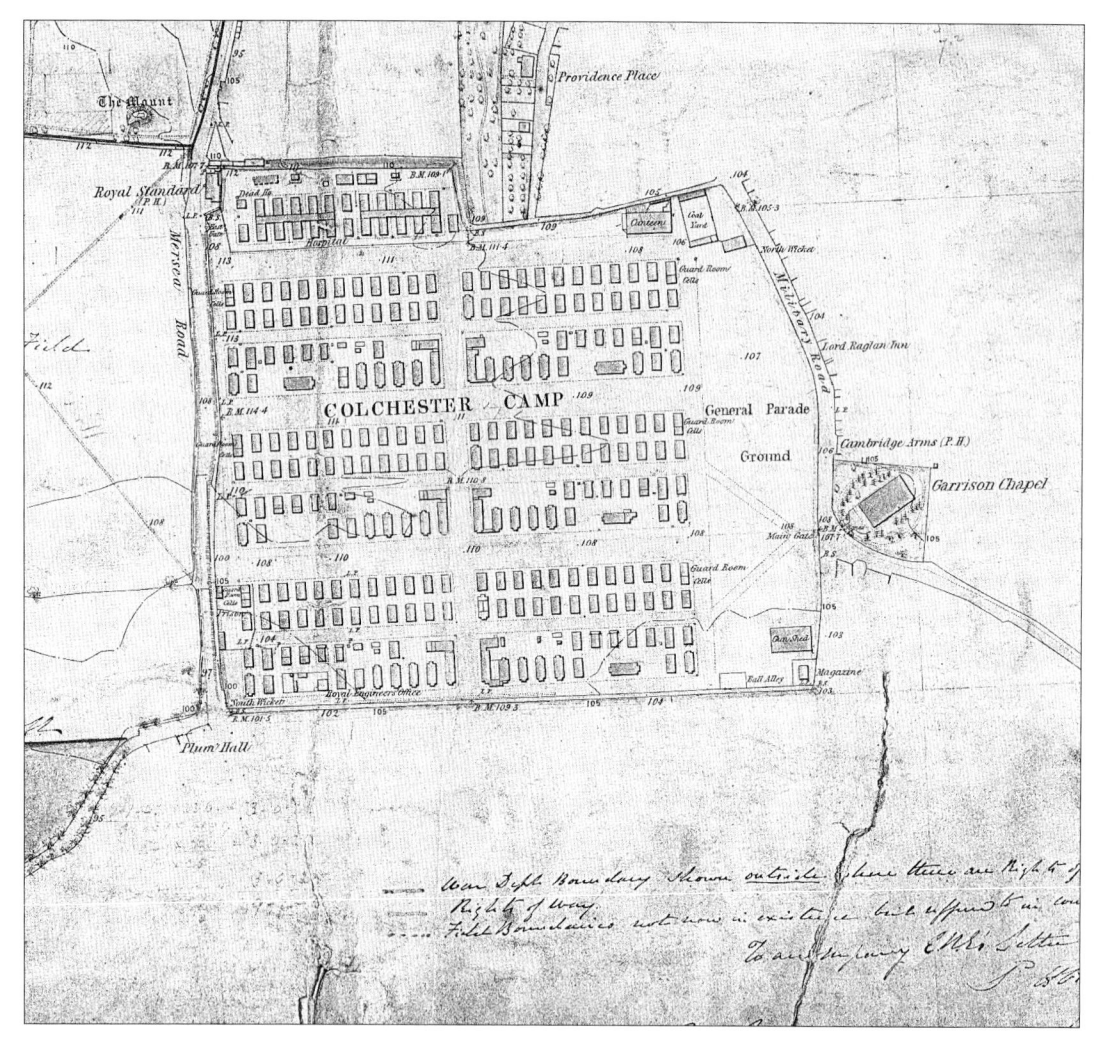

Figure 110 Plan of Colchester Camp, c.1860. The huts follow the company plan used at Aldershot. At the top is a hutment hospital similar to those designed by Isambard Kingdom Brunel. The timber garrison chapel is still used for its original purpose. The Lord Raglan Arms and the Cambridge Arms indicate the mutual dependence of the army and the licensed victualler.

Prince Albert, unofficial patron of the camp, provided a library for the officers which was designed by Captain Frances Fowke and stocked with a collection of a thousand books donated by the Prince (see Figure 109). It opened in June 1860. The oldest surviving barracks library, much of the original furniture and fittings as well as the Prince's book collection are still in place.

Land for two more camps was bought in 1855–6, both old Napoleonic War sites, at Colchester for three battalions, and at Shorncliffe for five. A third was laid out near the naval dockyard at Pembroke.[13]

The camp at Colchester (see Figure 110) was originally assembled in 1855, and first occupied in January 1856.[14] There were six blocks of huts on the Aldershot model, with a camp canteen, and a fives court for the officers. The camp hospital also consisted of huts, with ten wards opening off a central passage. This was very similar to the emergency hospitals which Isambard Kingdom Brunel provided at the Government's request and which were shipped out to the Crimea during the winter of 1855, thereby dramatically improving mortality figures (see Figure 111).[15]

The old Barracks Department camp at Shorncliffe,

[13] Parliamentary Papers (House of Commons), 1861, *xxxvi, Purchase of land etc. for barracks*, pp.291–309.
[14] A. Robertson, 'The Army in Colchester: Its Influence on the Town, 1854–1914', unpublished MA thesis, Essex University (1992); Dietz (1986), p.15.
[15] D. Toppin, 'The British Hospital at Renikoi, 1855', *The Arup Journal* (July 1981).

Figure 111 The army's camp at Balaclava included some timber huts which were made in Britain and assembled in the Crimea.

The last of the new, large training camps was built in Ireland. The place selected was in a rich horse-breeding ground south-west of Dublin, called the just south of Folkestone, had been vacated, like that at Colchester, after Waterloo, although the Artillery stayed on in the brick barracks built by the Ordnance Board. The new camp was quickly assembled during 1855–6. The same plan of huts for a half-battalion was followed, ten of them in pairs surrounding open ground on a windy plateau by the sea. There were five separate regimental mess buildings, four expense magazines, a holding establishment for a hundred prisoners, and a hospital for 300 men.[16]

The size and relative isolation of the camps meant that churches were included from the start (see Figure 112). At Aldershot, an early corrugated-iron church was soon followed by three wooden churches, two of them for Roman Catholics. A large, new, brick church was built for the camp in 1863 to a design by Philip Hardwick, who had obviously made contacts within the army through his work for Wellington (see page 108). At Colchester, a large, timber church was built in 1854 which continues to be used by the garrison today. The simplicity of its construction – a rectangular, timber box reinforced by curved, cast-iron braces – reflected the need for ample, cheap space into which substantial bodies of men could be marched on Sunday mornings. A prefabricated church of the same age of more Gothic style, clad in corrugated iron with pointed windows, can be found at Deepcut, near Bisley in Hampshire.

Figure 112 Prefabricated timber churches were erected by the army for the camps in the 1850s. Two examples survive at Colchester (top) and Deepcut (bottom).

[16] Parliamentary Papers (House of Commons), 1861, *xxxvi*, *Return Showing the Cost of Land etc purchased for Barracks*, p.305.

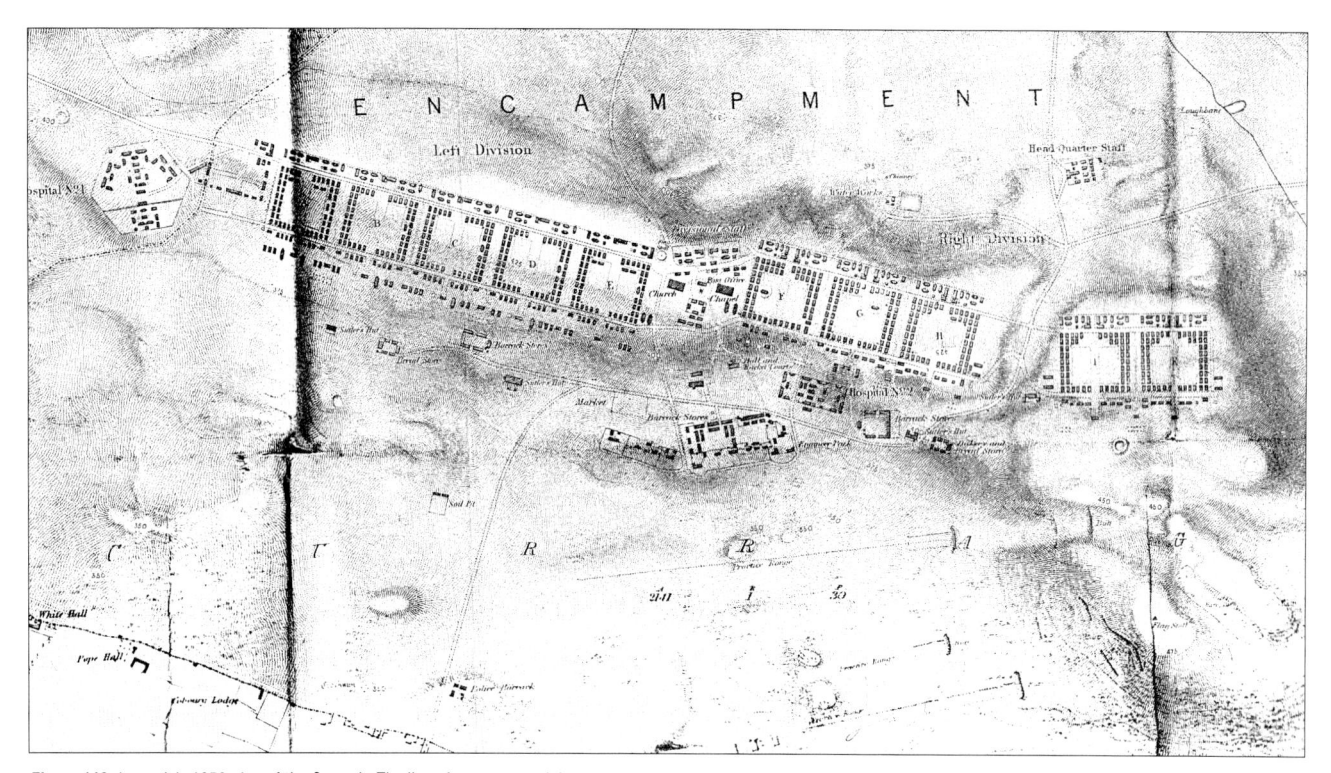

Figure 113 Lugarde's 1858 plan of the Curragh. The line of squares, reminiscent of infantry formations, was divided into two by a clock tower, flanked by wooden churches for Protestant and Catholic soldiers. Other interesting details are the octagonal hospital compound and the widely spaced facilities such as the sutleries.

Curragh of Kildare (see Figure 113). It had been used for military assemblies since the seventeenth century, and like Colchester and Shorncliffe, held a large encampment during the Napoleonic Wars. At the beginning of 1855, the Inspector General of Fortifications ordered a camp to be prepared there for 10,000 men, the same size as Aldershot. It was laid it out along a ridge by Lieutenant Colonel Lugarde RE, in ten separate, square encampments, each for a thousand men, a formation derived from the fundamental regimental divisions and loyalties of the British Army. Lugarde intended that each square should provide for the 'separation of the regiments in their discipline, recruitment, and punishment drills, good regimental police arrangements, facilities for the assembly of troops on ordinary occasions, and general parade, and the avoidance, as much as possible, of the risk of ... fire'.[17] It cost £192,821: four-fifths of this amount for the huts, and the rest for permanent accommodation, schools, Catholic and Protestant churches, water supply, drains, roads and a rifle range.[18]

Colchester Camp grew rapidly, and was doubled in size during the 1860s to include two permanent cavalry barracks. Drawings of the earlier of the two, called simply 'Cavalry barracks', were signed off by Burgoyne in 1861.[19] The troopers' barracks had a veranda to one side for access, and stables beneath, in parallel rows with the officers' stables. More interesting from an architectural perspective was the officers' quarters, which formed an enclosed courtyard, with a double-height mess room in the centre of the long side.[20]

The Le Cateau Cavalry Barracks was added shortly after, following much more exactly the layout of the first permanent cavalry quarters at Aldershot, having a central officers' range and parallel rows of barracks behind (see Figure 114). The design of the men's blocks was also innovative (see Figure 115). The horses' stalls ran the length of the ground floor off a central, gullied passage, and stock and forage stores were built into the corners. The men's living quarters were still placed above their horses', but the floors

---

[17] NAM 355,716(418.5). H.W. Lugarde, *Narrative of operations at the Curragh, Kildare* (Dublin 1858).
[18] D. Swan, 'The Curragh of Kildare', *An Cosantoir*, **32** (1972), p.39.

[19] Royal Commission for Historical Monuments in England, Swindon, *PSA Drawings Collection*, CTR 238, 239, 155.
[20] PRO WORK43/438; H. James, *Plans of the Barracks of the Eastern District*, Ordnance Survey (London 1867).

1852–1872: 'Old, Gloomy and Bad'

Figure 114 Le Cateau Barracks, the officers' quarters.

were of concrete supported by iron columns and beams, and the stables were well ventilated, to render them more hygienic. In the central stair section dividing the two dormitories, there were separate rooms for the NCOs, and night urinals, indicating the abolition of the noxious urine tub. The wider ground-floor stables formed a flat-roofed terrace along one side of the barrack rooms. These were among the earliest of the larger dormitories which became the norm for Victorian barracks, each generally accommodating a quarter of a hundred-man company, in contrast to the smaller 14- or 16-man rooms of the Georgian army. Le Cateau thus represented a considerable improvement on earlier cavalry barracks.

Le Cateau included a separate sergeants' mess, a schoolroom and a riding school. This was based on a model prepared in the Inspector General's office in 1862 which specified that riding schools needed to be three times as long as they were broad, and high enough so that the lance could be carried, with a spectators' gallery for superior officers.[21] With the clearance of the nineteenth-century barracks at Aldershot, the Le Cateau and Cavalry Barracks at Colchester are now the only remaining examples of the new barracks planning which came out of the training camp concept and which, while still ordered and symmetrical, abandoned the enclosed, hierarchical, parade-centred layout in favour of a more open configuration.

The Horseshoe Barracks, Shoeburyness

Any discussion of experimental new layouts of military accommodation in the 1850s should mention the British School of Gunnery, which was established beside the Essex marshes at Shoeburyness from 1849. Technically an artillery training school rather

Figure 115 The troopers' barracks at Le Cateau, one of the first strongly influenced by the Sanitary Movement, represented a move away from the massive blocks of the Georgian army to smaller buildings with natural light and ventilation. The stable interiors (below), with their cast-iron columns and jack-arched ceilings, are amongst the most advanced of their type.

than a barracks, it included accommodation for the cadets which reflected the more active development of alternative plan forms and layouts by the Royal Engineers which was under way by this time. It became necessary to move gunnery practice away from Plumstead Marshes near the Woolwich Arsenal because it was impeding traffic on the Thames. Land at Shoeburyness was bought, and a range opened there for an 'experimental school of gunnery'. It was a sign of the early appreciation of the transformation

---

[21] C.B. Ewart, 'Military riding schools', *Professional Papers of the Royal Engineers* (1862), paper 11, p.181.

Figure 116 The entrance to the Horseshoe Barracks at the British School of Gunnery. Archways and clock towers were a prerequisite of barracks in the 1850s.

of artillery, which was to pose great challenges to the armies and navies of Europe during the coming decades.[22]

After seven years, a more permanent establishment was laid out under Captain T. Inglis RE, the Inspector of Works at Woolwich Arsenal, who is believed to be the author of the gunnery cadets' Horseshoe Barracks (see Figure 116). This consisted of eight blocks, each of four rooms for 12 men, placed around the perimeter of a circular parade ground. A pair of washhouses stood to the rear, and a separate cookhouse connected by a covered way. Two further blocks stood along the road front, so that the plan of the complex resembled the Greek letter omega, or less exactly, a horseshoe – hence its name. The neck was closed by an archway beneath a clock tower, with a guardhouse either side. There were a small hospital, a canteen, recreation rooms, a library and various sports facilities at this isolated base.[23]

Circular plans are sufficiently rare in architecture for one to be tempted to look for a symbolic or sociological explanation in the plan at Shoeburyness. The scheme was so completely at variance with the strong, quadrilateral and hierarchical British tradition of barracks planning that it might represent a small experiment by Captain Inglis in engineering the social behaviour of the inhabitants. For instance, John Nash laid out the *cottage ornée* of Blaise Hamlet in a circle – admittedly a much more uneven one because it aimed at a Picturesque effect – partly to try to imitate the social context of a village green with a mutually dependent community living around it. Perhaps, in his more military manner, Inglis was

---

[22] Parliamentary Papers (House of Commons), 1861, *xxxvi, Return showing the Cost of Land etc purchased for Barracks*, p.305.
[23] Essex County Record Office T/P 83 1–5, *Survey of the Hundred of Rochford 1867–8*; D. Glennie, *Gunners Town*, (1948, no location).

attempting the same, but sadly, there is no evidence to support such a hypothesis. The Horseshoe Barracks remained a one-off phenomenon.

'Old, gloomy and bad': the Sanitary Commission Report

Despite the much higher standards which were coming to be applied to the design of new barracks, levels of sickness and mortality remained depressingly high. The sanitary reformers, driven by Florence Nightingale and encouraged from within the Government by Sydney Herbert, continued to campaign for improvements after the end of the Crimean War, and in early 1857 Palmerston conceded a Royal Commission to look more closely into the question. Chaired by Herbert and including several prominent reformers, the report produced a stunning revelation of the prevailing squalor in British barracks. Comparing military and civilian conditions, it produced the damning evidence that the mortality rate among the male civil population aged 20–40 was 9.8 per thousand, while that of soldiers within the barracks was almost twice as high, at 17.11 per thousand. Given that soldiers had food, shelter and regular exercise, and that even the far from rigorous selection process of recruitment filtered out the patently incapacitated, this presented crystal-clear proof of the debilitating effect of barracks life.

The squalid living conditions exposed by the Commission shocked the press and the public.[24] Soldiers were discovered squeezed together in damp, draughty rooms, inadequately warmed by open fires that were also used to heat their food, and with limited or blocked ventilation. Many barrack rooms had windows in only one wall. Only a tiny number had gas lights; most were gloomily illuminated by candle. Apart from their regular parade and drill, men often passed much of the day cooped up in the same crowded room, where they ate, cleaned their equipment, drank, argued, whiled away the time and slept. Out of 250 British barracks, only 23 included separate married quarters. In all the rest, married soldiers, their wives and children all shared the barrack rooms with minimal privacy, cheek by jowl with the private soldiers, in a manner that was particularly shocking to Victorian sensibilities. Lavatories over cess pits were often close by the barrack rooms, pervading them with the smell of excrement. Many barracks, like the Shambles in Galway or Four House Barracks in Portsmouth, occupied old buildings packed round gloomy courts. Not surprisingly, consumption and dysentery were endemic. Most had been hastily erected by the Barracks Department sixty years before, and were found to be poorly built and with many design faults, lacking ventilation and inadequately lit and heated, poorly sited and drained, with defective or absent sanitary arrangements.

The Commission's proposals to reform barracks accommodation involved 'establishing a watchdog agency, formulating an improvement programme, and allocating more money for construction, rehabilitation and repair'.[25] Faced with public condemnation, conservative senior officers protested that the squalor was exaggerated. In March 1858, the Commander-in-Chief, the Duke of Cambridge, assured the Lords: 'the soldier had not been neglected in the past, he was simply more appreciated at the present'.[26] Despite the Horse Guards, however, Panmure was forced to accept Herbert's central recommendation to form four sub-commissions, of which the principal one was to investigate the sanitation of barracks and hospitals. A new Commission for Improving Barracks and Hospitals was set up, chaired by Herbert, and as a gesture granted £100 per barrack for urgent improvements, though the commissioners must have known this to be drop in the ocean, given that they thought there was not a barracks in the country which 'could be considered in no other light than never having been completed'.

The Commission, which subsequently became the standing Army Sanitary Commission, was chaired by Sir John Sutherland, an army physician and sanitary expert, and included Captain Douglas Galton RE, the Assistant Inspector General of Fortifications, and one of the key proponents of the pavilion principle in hospital design. Both were close associates of Florence Nightingale. The Commission's methodology and its subsequent

---

[24] See, for instance, *The Builder* **787** (1859), p.690.
[25] Weiler (1987), p.230.
[26] Spiers (1980), p.159.

recommendations were informed by their understanding of the way in which disease was transmitted. The water-borne nature of cholera transmission had been demonstrated in the mid-nineteenth century by careful analysis of the geography of cholera deaths. Bronchial illnesses were less well understood, however, and were thought to be communicated by 'noxious emanations' present in the air, in stagnant water and poorly drained ground, and adhering to the walls. This 'miasmic' theory influenced the direction of both hospital and barrack design till the end of the century. It prompted the Army Sanitary Commission to search out and condemn barracks which had rooms, corners of buildings, or courtyards in which the stagnant air might accumulate. The Royal Barracks in Dublin, for instance, had 'narrow dark lanes between lofty three and four storey buildings, without any outlet sufficient to prevent stagnation of air'.[27] This, rather than poor sanitation, was thought to be at the root of the nineteenth-century barracks' reputation for high rates of fever and death.

The Commission inspected 162 barracks in England, Scotland, Wales and Ireland between 1858 and 1861, and calculated the volume of space available in each room. The regulations claimed that there was space for 75,801 men. The Commission calculated that if 600 cubic feet (17 cubic metres) were allowed each soldier, as the Royal Commission had recommended, there was only space for 53,806 – in other words, by a standard comparable to that applied in civil prisons, the country's barracks were overcrowded by more than one-third.

Particular sites were grossly congested. The enormous Chatham Infantry Barracks by the dockyard, built over a hundred years earlier, had twice as many men as it should have, with less than 300 cubic feet (8.5 cubic metres) for each; the nearby St Mary's Casemates were almost as bad. Some of the older fortifications were severely overcrowded, particularly the seventeenth-century Plymouth Citadel (see Figure 117), but the newer barracks built by the Ordnance were also among the worst. Brompton Barracks (the Royal Engineers' own home station) and that of the Royal Artillery at Woolwich were both among the five most overcrowded in England.

The worst conditions were in lodgings adapted from existing buildings (see Figure 118). The old Clarence Barracks of the Portsmouth Marines Division – a late seventeenth-century brewery converted to barracks a hundred years earlier, and surrounded by closely packed houses – was 'quite unfit for habitation'.[28] Others condemned included two in Dublin (Thomas Burgh's Linen Hall, which was used as a barracks for over a thousand men, and the former Arbour Hill Prison behind the Royal Barracks), Stirling Castle (which had been crudely adapted for barracks after the 1715 Rising), the converted Portman Street Barracks in Central London (see Figures 95 and 96, page 118), and former mills or factories in Belfast, Coventry and Perth, in which beds had been placed by the Barracks Department, but no other effort had been made to render them inhabitable.[29]

Cavalry barracks with rooms over stables were condemned for the first time: 'Every barracks we have seen constructed on this plan is saturated throughout with ammonia and organic matter; and in cases where the barrack rooms have been shut up and unoccupied for some time, the putrescent odour experienced on entering is indescribably offensive.'[30] Indeed, the Commissioners found barely one barracks in which they felt there was enough fresh air. The rooms at Berwick-upon-Tweed were described as 'back to back, low, dark and bad'. They consistently referred to the awful smells which pervaded the places they visited. This was often caused by thoughtless or inadequate planning. At the Clarence Barracks, 'the privies are close to one of the cook-houses, and the smell pervaded the kitchen most offensively'.[31]

Poor ventilation was compounded by the long-standing practice of building 'double' barracks with back-to-back rooms, or having a corridor closing one side from the outside air: 'cross-lit' rooms were held as a fundamental rule of good sanitary practice. Even new barracks were found inadequate. The Wellington Lines at Aldershot had rooms so deep

---

[27] Parliamentary Papers (House of Commons), 1861, *xvi*, *General Report of the Committee appointed for Improving the Sanitary Condition of the Barracks and Hospitals*, p.15.
[28] Ibid., p.16.

[29] Ibid., p.21.
[30] Ibid., p.19.
[31] Ibid., p.16.

Figure 117 Plymouth Citadel. The late seventeenth-century storehouse was converted into barracks in the 1840s, when the outer doors were inserted.

Figure 118 The eighteenth-century Keep Barracks within Dover Castle were rated for 241 men. They were condemned as 'old, gloomy and bad'

that they were 'deficient in light and means of natural ventilation'. The large, new Raglan Barracks in Devonport was praised for its improved sanitary arrangements and for avoiding back-to-back rooms, but criticized for the excessive size and darkness of the rooms. At Woolwich and the new St George's Barracks at Gosport, men lived in dank semi-basements.

Casemates, which generally only provided accommodation within defensible works, were ruled only fit for temporary occupation, or during a seige. The mid-eighteenth-century Cliff Casemates under Dover Castle were up to 227 feet (69.2 metres) long, hollowed out of the chalk and lit at only one end. Those at Fort George had damp floors of earth. St Mary's Casemates had an official occupancy of over 1,100 men, and when the commissioners visited, it was full of invalids brought back from Russia. The report noted: 'from returns for the twenty-two months preceding 31st October 1857 ... the admissions [to hospital] were four and a half times the strength, and the deaths were in the enormous ratio of 103 per 1000 per annum! Of these deaths, 40 per cent were from consumption.' [32]

Not only were they poorly planned, many of the barracks visited were barely kept clean, and cavalry stations like Hulme Barracks in Manchester also had mountains of dung to contend with:

'In the narrow lane left between the barracks and the boundary wall are placed not only the latrines and ashpits, but litter heaps, dungpits, ablution houses, cook-houses, &c., and if, as often happens the pavement is in a bad state, this narrow lane resembles nothing so much as one of the filthiest and most neglected alleys in the filthiest part of our towns.' [33]

The way forward

The Royal Commission made a series of recommendations which were subsequently accepted by Parliament. These projected a new minimum allocation of 600 cubic feet (17 cubic metres) and 60 square feet (5.6 square metres) per man, and the provision of day rooms so that the barracks were only used for sleeping; the offensive urine tubs were to be removed from the rooms, and replaced by outside privies with water closets; separate bathhouses were to be provided for the men; proper heating was to be installed, linked to a ventilation system, in the way that Denison had introduced at Woolwich, and there were to be kitchens with modern stoves, laundries and workshops. As well as these modifications, the Commissioners insisted that barracks should all have separate married quarters, there should be libraries and reading rooms for the ranks as well as for officers, and that a more structured form of exercise should be provided through gymnasiums.

[32] Ibid., p.30.
[33] Ibid., p.16.

Military hospitals

Disease, infection and malnutrition carried off far greater numbers of British servicemen during the eighteenth century than combat. Fleets returning from routine cruises in warm waters deposited thousands of sick or scurvy-ridden seamen in the dockyard towns, and in wartime, large numbers of wounded soldiers were returned as well (Coade, 1989, pp.293–301). Both services contracted with private doctors to provide medical services, and rented space for hospital accommodation. This was a particularly costly arrangement for the Admiralty, which belatedly accepted that it would be cheaper to build its own hospitals in 1741.

Although the better civilian hospitals, such as James Gibbs's St Bartholomew's (1729–68), provided some guidance, military hospitals had different requirements. There was no need for separate women's wards, for instance, but a wider range of conditions was treated by the services than the voluntary hospitals would accept – a higher proportion of surgical cases, especially during wartime, as well as madness, dysentery, scabies, tuberculosis, venereal disease and other infectious diseases.

Relatively isolated sites were chosen near the Portsmouth and Plymouth dockyards, close to the shore for ease of landing the patients and surrounded by tall walls in order to prevent recuperating seamen from skipping off when they felt better. The first was started in 1746 at Haslar, south of Gosport. The influence of the three great Royal Hospitals at Kilmainham, Chelsea (see Figures 25 and 26, page 30) and Greenwich, though for retired rather than sick or injured servicemen, can be seen in the huge closed courtyard at Haslar, with its internal cloister. But Jacobson split the sides (only three were completed) into parallel ranges with a narrow well between, pointing to an awareness of the value of light and ventilation in recuperation. The second naval hospital, Stonehouse, on a creek midway between Plymouth town and the dockyard, was begun in 1758. Important changes were made to the layout at Stonehouse, where smaller wards in 11 separate pavilions were connected by a single-storey arcade for transporting patients. This disaggregated layout earned praise, at home and in France, for limiting the spread of contagion, and it was followed by the army for the first large military hospitals which were erected in the 1790s, one across the water from Stonehouse, and the others at Deal and Gosport, though the pavilions were placed in a single line rather than round a courtyard.

Despite the evidence of lower wartime mortality at Stonehouse, during the Napoleonic Wars the closed cloister again provided the model for the new naval hospital at Great Yarmouth, whilst that built at Deal was a straight pile not unlike the contemporary army barracks nearby.

In contrast to the Navy's approach, army medical treatment was parochial in scale right up to the Crimean War, organized in separate regimental establishments even within supposedly general hospitals like Deal. The level of casualties from the war forced the abandonment of this inefficient system and the small and poorly planned buildings it generated. The subsequent construction of a series of large military hospitals in the post-war period benefited from official acceptance of the pavilion principle used at Stonehouse but more enthusiastically adopted by French than British planners, who had not displayed any awareness of its advantage in hospital or barracks planning. This took a grip on the architecture of health as firm as that of the cruciform plan on churches, despite being based in part on a faulty idea of contagion, the 'miasmic' theory.

1852–1872: 'Old, Gloomy and Bad'

An aerial view of the naval hospital at Stonehouse.

Providing evidence for the potential of the pavilion plan was the prefabricated tin hospital designed by Isambard Kingdom Brunel, which was shipped out to the Crimea in 1855. Separate, cross-lit fifty-bed wards were connected by a spine walkway, and provided with mechanical heating, ventilation and water-borne sanitation. When the official army hospitals were suffering mortality rates of up to 40 per cent, they were as low as 3 per cent at Renikoi.

In England, the first exposition of the plan in its pure form, the Royal Herbert Hospital at Woolwich, was erected between 1861 and 1865 by Captain Douglas Galton RE, one of Florence Nightingale's acolytes and a key member of the Barracks and Hospital Improvement Commission. Further examples followed, with some variation in detail, and the pavilion principle held sway over a period of great expansion, in both military and civil hospital provisions for almost half a century.

A model version suitable for a barracks was circulated by Galton in 1861, with single-storey in-line wards, one of which was built at Hounslow (see Figure 120, page 145), where it can be contrasted with the original DeLancey infirmary of c.1792. A standard two-storey pavilion hospital was built at the localization depots in the 1870s, with the administrators' and orderlies' rooms at one end, and the corner lavatory tower forming a distinctive feature at the other.

The pavilion idea of large dormitories with separate but integral sanitary facilities was used for military accommodation from the 1860s until the end of the century. The barracks built by the navy, such as at HMS *Drake* (see Figure 171, page 191), bear a close resemblance to pavilion wards, though on a larger scale. No complete barracks were laid out on the pavilion plan, though the massive New College accommodation block at Sandhurst, built in the decade before the First World War, comes closest to the idea of separate ranges arranged into a single, interconnected pile.

The Edwardian general hospitals were, like their barracks equivalents, the last monolithic institutional military buildings built in this country. By the First World War, both were being constructed more cheaply as hutted complexes, which have proved as ephemeral as their predecessors have been enduring.

A model of the Royal Herbert Hospital, now successfully converted into housing. Here, Galton established the classic fish-skeleton layout of large, cross-lit wards off a spine corridor. The hospital was entered through a large archway in the imposing central administration block, which became the focus of architectural interest.

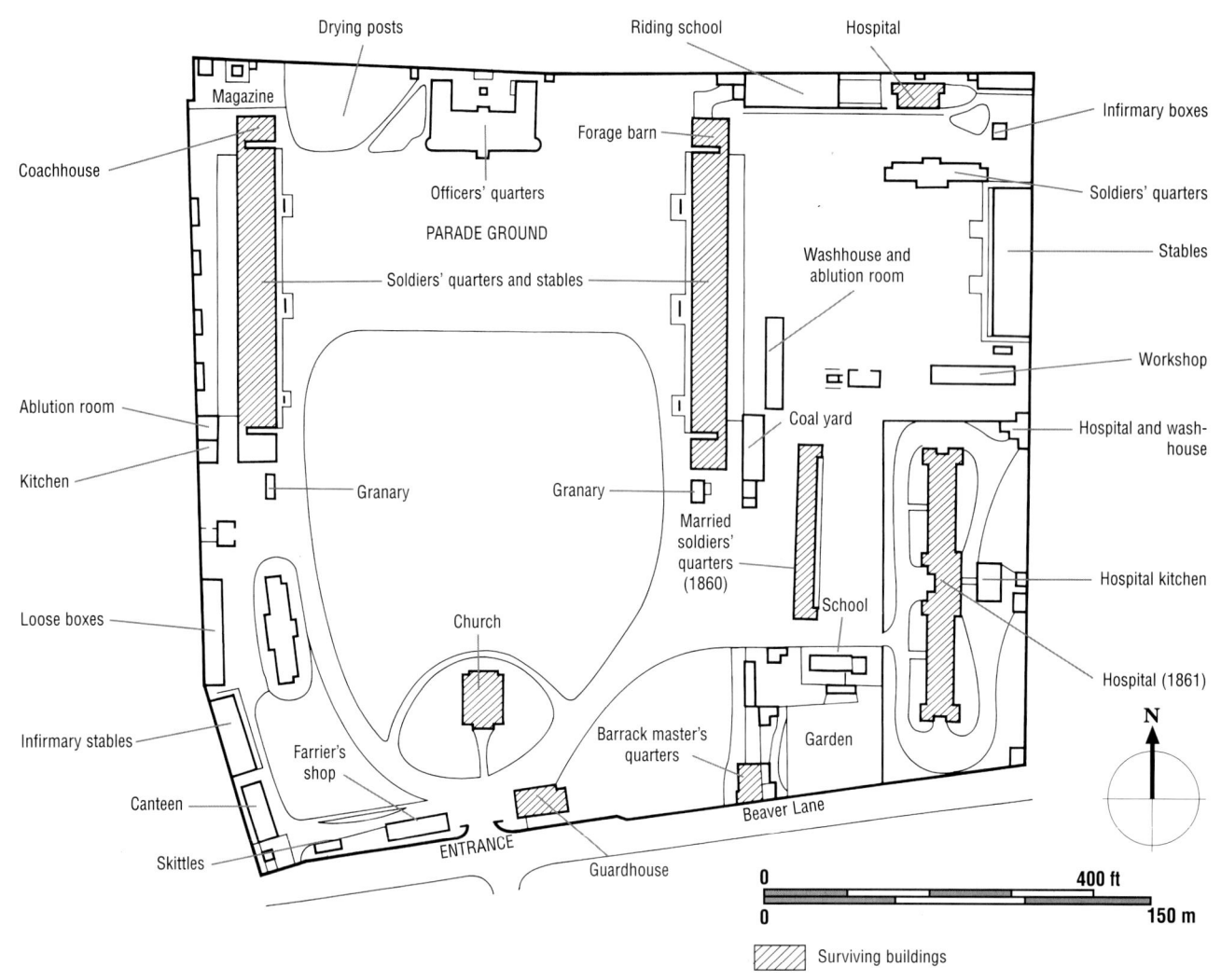

Figure 119 Hounslow Barracks, redrawn from a plan by Colonel James RE, c.1861. The symmetrical late eighteenth-century complex occupies the main part of the site, with the riding school and small hospital at the top. The recently added veranda access is shown on the front of the barrack ranges. The church was converted from an earlier building in the 1840s. The model married quarters (see fig. 121) and the two-ward pavilion hospital (see fig. 120) were added in 1861. Hounslow was again extended to the west ten years later, when it was made into a localization depot, and the officers' quarters were rebuilt.

When Herbert was appointed Secretary of State for War in 1859, funding for improvements rose sharply, from £144,000 before the war to £222,700 in 1856–57 and £726,841 in 1859–60.[34] The worst barracks were closed. The Army Sanitary Committee was made a statutory body in 1862, and continued to report on the progress made. In the Army Vote for that year, £30,000 was earmarked for 'sanitary works', which included the construction of a concrete 'gallery' along the front of the Hounslow Cavalry Barracks, so that the rooms could be opened from front to back (see Figure 119). Another £30,000 was allocated for new married quarters, with smaller sums for garrison chapels, soldiers' reading rooms and other improvements (see Figure 120).[35]

However, progress was both slow and uneven. The Commission reported that by 1861, less than 3,000 of the 5,300 barrack rooms visited had ventilation fitted, and only 346 NCOs' rooms, 86 guardrooms and 67 schools. A third of them had baths with piped water, and nearly half now had WCs installed.[36] Ventilation shafts to carry the foul air from the stables had been introduced at 13 out of some 80 cavalry stations. Galton's improved grate, which heated and circulated warm air more

---

[34] Parliamentary Papers (House of Commons), 1857/58, *xxxvii, Amount expended on Barracks in the United Kingdom*, p.123.

[35] PRO WO33/11 187, *Army vote*, 1862/3.

[36] Incredibly, even twenty years later a senior Royal Engineers officer was still putting forward the view that the dry conservancy method was right for barracks and hospitals, and condemning the water-borne system of waste removal, which throws into question the corps's reputation for progressiveness. M. Synge, 'Suggested improvements in sanitary arrangements for hospitals, barracks, camps and shipping etc.', *Royal United Services Institute*, **108** (1874), no.78.

effectively, can still be found in barrack rooms which were upgraded at this time.[37]

Herbert had hoped to help finance the expenditure on improvements by ploughing back money raised through selling the worst barracks, but the Chancellor, Gladstone, refused to allow it. Sydney Herbert died in 1861, and the momentum of improvement was not sustained. By 1864–5, expenditure on barracks had fallen back to £313,112. Meanwhile, standards and expectations had risen: in 1864, for instance, the Army Sanitary Commission finally decided that quartering men over horses was unacceptable, necessitating the construction of separate stables. Money was concentrated on constructing gymnasiums at the larger stations, and moving married soldiers and their families into separate quarters. If the localization programme in the 1870s had not initiated a new building campaign (see Chapter Eight) the undoubted improvements in the health of the home army which took place during the latter decades of the nineteenth century would have been much longer in coming.

Married soldiers' quarters

One of the central recommendations of the Royal Commission was the provision of separate apartments for married soldiers, and it was pursued with enthusiasm by Dr Sutherland. In June 1860, the Inspector General for Fortifications' office sent out a plan for a model married quarters which was to be erected at Hounslow (see Figures 121 and 122). This tall range, which stills stands, is of three storeys with a single, central stair which opened on to full-width walkways, the equivalent of the covered veranda then considered suitable for single men's barracks. There was space for 42 families, each with a one-room apartment containing a bed, a child's crib and two cupboards, with a fireplace for cooking. Lavatories were provided at either end of the veranda.[38] In the localization depots of the 1870s, more commodious quarters were allocated to married soldiers, with a separate bedroom and sitting room as well as a rear scullery/kitchen. A

Figure 120 Douglas Galton circulated plans for a model small, pavilion-plan hospital to the Royal Engineers, and the first was built at Hounslow.

schoolroom with the schoolteacher's apartment above was provided at one end of the building, with a laundry and washhouse at the other.

Army gymnasiums

As a result of another of the Royal Commission recommendations, an order was made in 1862 for gymnasiums to be built at all barracks. The first army gyms were strongly influenced by the work of Archibald MacLaren, an exercise enthusiast whose Oxford gym (now an office) was the prototype on which the army based its own early designs. It was a rectangular, two-storey hall, open inside, with a large, octagonal lantern carried on tall, iron columns. After a visit to inspect MacLaren's gymnasium, the Army Gymnastic Staff, newly formed in 1860 and based at Aldershot, began to develop physical training programmes for soldiers. The first army gym was at Aldershot (see Figure 123), a Classically styled building with pilasters and end pediments, and a small lantern. Six more were built in the next two years, and of these two survive: one at Sandhurst (see Figure 124) and the other at the Royal Engineers' base at Brompton Barracks (see Figure 125). MacLaren himself was a consultant for the large Brompton Gym, which had a T-shaped plan with a long hall for mock fighting called the School of Arms, and a gym across the end.

---

[37] Weiler (1987), pp.255–60.
[38] PRO WORK43/1408, *Proposed new married soldiers' quarters, Hounslow cavalry barracks.*

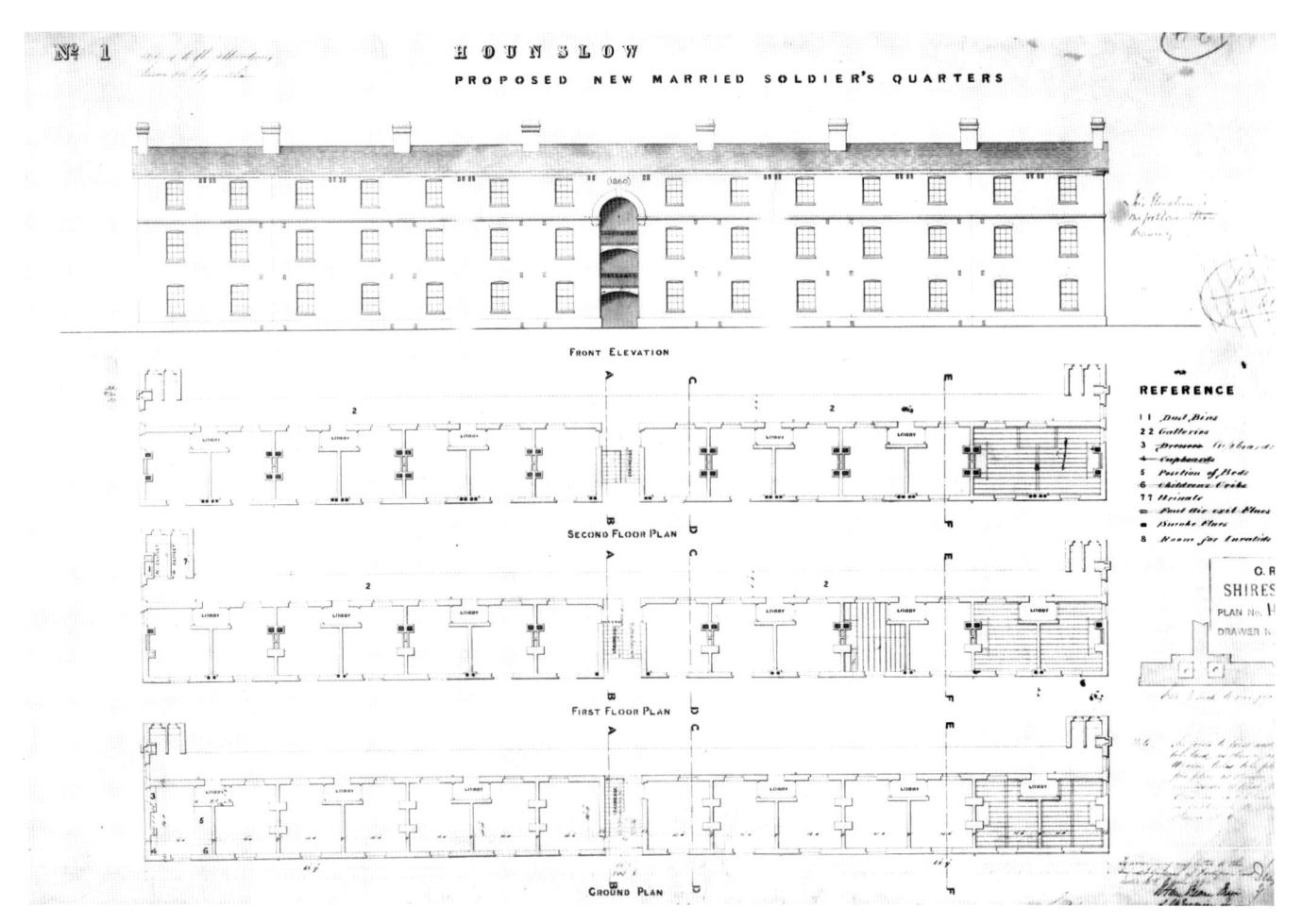

Figure 121 The model married quarters at Hounslow. The drawing shows the front elevation and tiny size of the one-room apartments.

Figure 122 The model married quarters at Hounslow, seen from the opposite side to fig. 121, showing the access decks and privy towers at the ends. They are similar to model artisan housing of the period.

Tall lanterns were highly visible features of the first generation of gymnasiums because of the emphasis placed on natural light and good ventilation. They were carried by strong queen-post roofs with trussed ties from which exercise apparatus could be suspended. At Brompton, some of the original wall racks remain, to which the 'escalading apparatus' was attached (see Figure 126).[39]

A second generation of larger gyms was built in the 1890s, reflecting both the increase in the amount of training given to recruits and changes in the syllabus away from simple strength exercises to gymnastics and sports like boxing. So popular were displays of gymnastics and sporting competition that public galleries were included. The first of these was the Fox Gymnasium at Aldershot, built in

[39] MacLaren (1865), pp.217–30.

Figure 123 The first army gymnasium was at Aldershot, with typical sports and exercises of the period.

1894, and others followed, culminating in the enormous, Baroque New Gymnasium at Sandhurst, part of the New College extensions of the early twentieth century. In 1900, the first army swimming pool was built near the Fox Gym, similar in construction but with an ornate, domed stair hall.

Model barracks from the architectural profession

One of the proposals of the 1855 War Office report had been to hold an architectural competition to attract designs for a model barracks, in order to involve the civilian architectural profession, stimulate new thinking and deepen the pool of ideas. New barracks for both infantry and cavalry guardsmen were to be built in London, for 1,000 men, and the recommendations in the report provided the competition brief. A large number of entries was received by the War Office, and during 1856 there was an exhibition of all the proposals at Burlington House. The prize for the cavalry barracks went to Matthew Digby Wyatt, and for the infantry barracks to George Morgan, Nash's old partner on the Metropolitan Improvements, now aged 82. However, despite the enthusiasm of the building and architectural profession,[40] the War Office procrastinated, and nothing was decided until the issue was given further impetus by the Royal Commission's report.

A much modified version of Morgan's design was finally built in 1863 (after his death) as the Chelsea Barracks, in Central London. Demolished in the year of its centenary, it formed an immensely long four-storey range, divided in the middle by a pair of campaniles, either side of the entrance. The buildings were described excitedly in the *Guards Magazine* in 1863 as: 'the most convenient, and in

[40] *The Builder* **688** (1856), p.201.

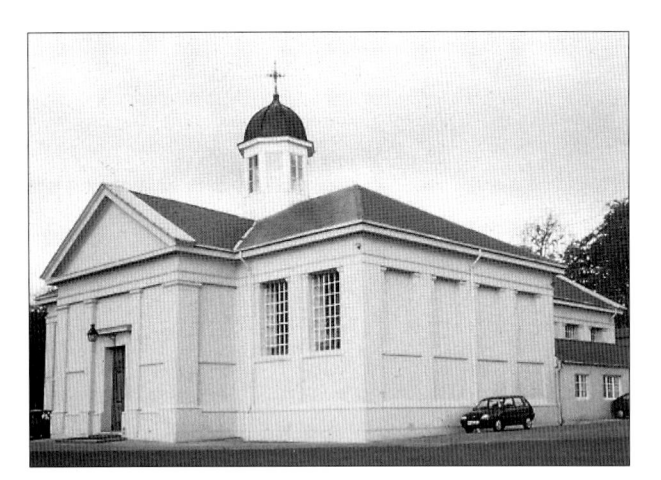

Figure 124 Sandhurst Gym (now the library) was another of the first generation.

Figure 125 Brompton Gym was designed for the army by the exercise pioneer Archibald MacLaren, and is still in use.

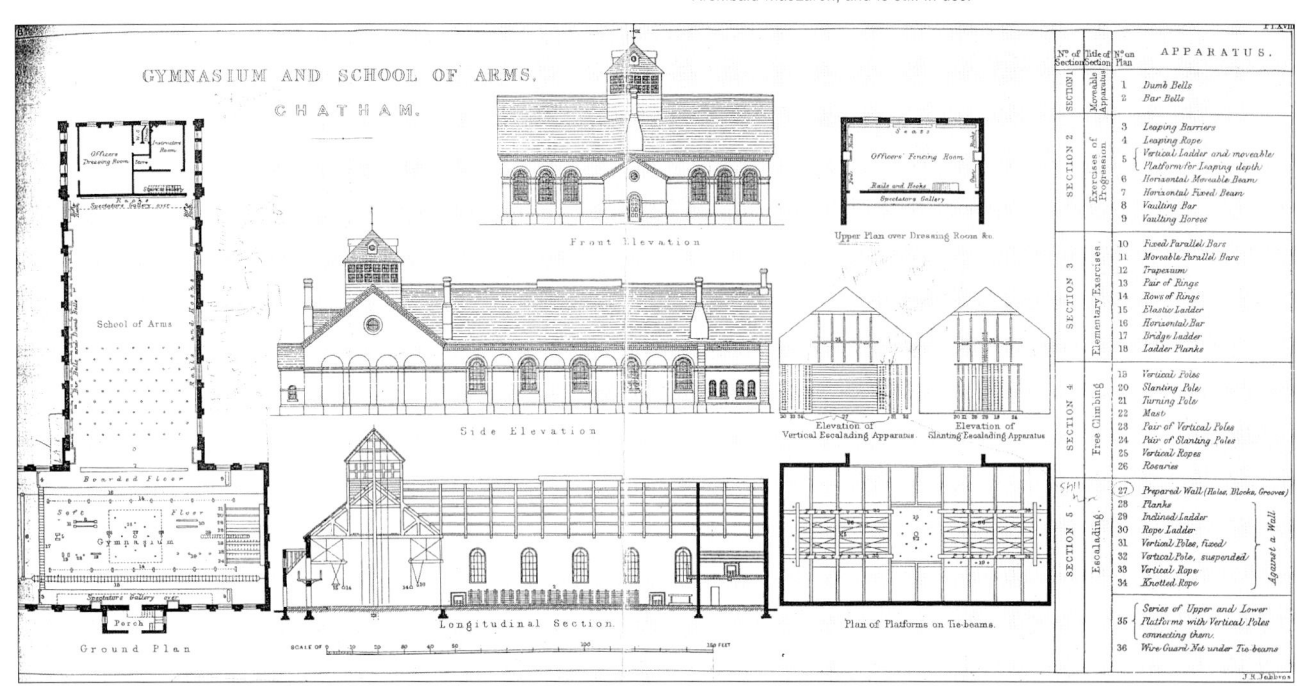

Figure 126 Plan of Brompton Gym showing the various exercise equipment.

all respects the most perfect for their size in the kingdom'.[41]

The prize for the cavalry barracks was to rebuild the much decayed quarters at Knightsbridge, supposedly designed by James Johnson and built in 1793. In the end, construction did not begin until 1878, the year after Wyatt's death, and the project was taken over by Major General Sir Elliot Wood RE. Constrained, as Johnson had originally been, by the long narrow site, the guiding principle pressed by Sutherland and Galton – subdivision of the separate parts – was not an option, and the quarters had to be stacked vertically instead (see Figure 127). In effect, Wood raised Wyatt's elevations on Johnson's plan. The previous quadrangular range had been singled out for strong criticism by Sutherland and his commissioners, but it was retained for the 352 troopers and NCOs occupying the new quarters, as was the use of the

[41] Quoted in Watson-Smyth et al. (1993), p.142.

1852–1872: 'Old, Gloomy and Bad'

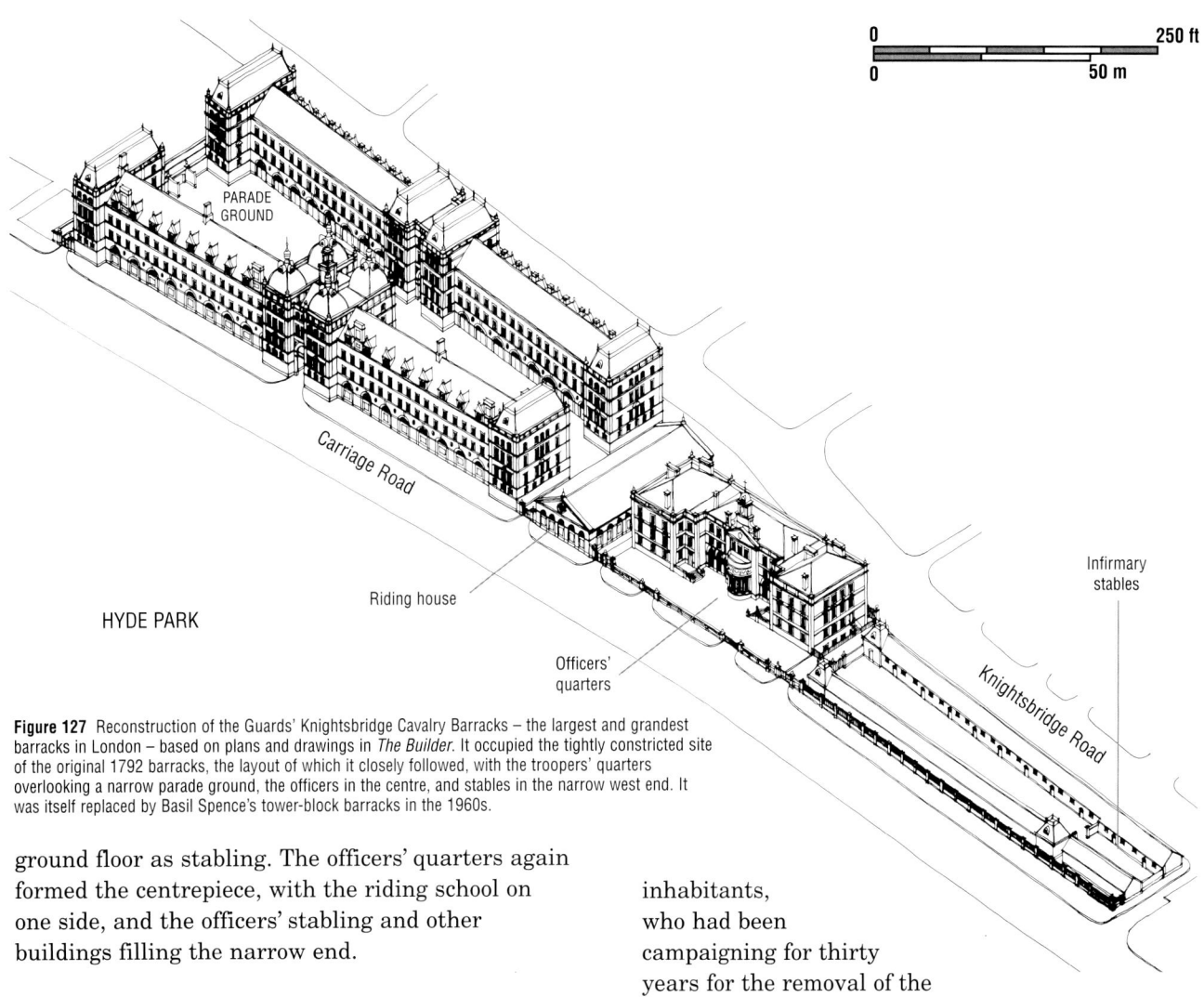

Figure 127 Reconstruction of the Guards' Knightsbridge Cavalry Barracks – the largest and grandest barracks in London – based on plans and drawings in *The Builder*. It occupied the tightly constricted site of the original 1792 barracks, the layout of which it closely followed, with the troopers' quarters overlooking a narrow parade ground, the officers in the centre, and stables in the narrow west end. It was itself replaced by Basil Spence's tower-block barracks in the 1960s.

ground floor as stabling. The officers' quarters again formed the centrepiece, with the riding school on one side, and the officers' stabling and other buildings filling the narrow end.

Although the new barracks ignored the basic prescriptions for layout of the sanitary reformers, it was apparently popular with its inhabitants, the 1st and 2nd Battalions of the Life Guard, who marched in during 1880. The *Household Brigade Magazine* claimed: 'for architectural features, sanitary arrangements, and commodiousness it is said to be the finest in Europe, and certainly in advance of anything of the kind attempted in any part of the United Kingdom'.[42] The rich architecture, an eclectic mix of Renaissance Italian and contemporary French styles, adorned with polychromy, modelling and sculpture, reflected the social status of the Life Guards. The War Office had also to take account of the complaints of the local inhabitants, who had been campaigning for thirty years for the removal of the old barracks because of the detrimental effect on an upwardly mobile neighbourhood. The restrictions of the site again presented obstacles when the barracks was rebuilt for the third time in the 1960s by Sir Basil Spence. He overcame them by going further upwards, and creating the first tower-block barracks. The pediment that now sits rather curiously over the entrance to the modern barracks was preserved from Wyatt's riding house.[43]

---

[42] Ibid.
[43] I am indebted to Harriet Richardson for showing me her account of the barracks for the Knightsbridge volume of the Survey of London, as yet unpublished.

Chapter Seven
1847–1869: 'The Three Panics'

As well as being a decade in which the army's insular self-confidence was ruptured, the 1850s saw the whole country's sense of security undermined by renewed anxiety over French intentions and Britain's capacity to defend itself. These fears were sarcastically dubbed 'the Three Panics' by Richard Cobden.[1] The first blew up in 1847, after a report by General Burgoyne, the Inspector General of Fortifications, had cast doubt on the security of the national defences, coinciding with apparent hostility from the regime in France. The Duke of Wellington recommended the immediate embodiment of the militia, but the scare swiftly dissipated when Louis-Philippe was deposed by the 1848 revolution and came to live in Kent.

The second panic in 1852 was driven by technology. It was talked up in Parliament by Lord Palmerston, whose proposition that 60,000 troops could cross the Channel overnight on a 'steam bridge' of modern warships from the new French naval arsenal of Cherbourg ignored the corresponding improvements which steam had brought to British naval defence. Again it was decided to reform the militia to defend the country, and this time an Act of Parliament was passed. It led directly to a national programme to embody and train 80,000 men, and to build each new local force a secure home and armoury.

Despite shortly joining forces with France to fight the Russians, these invasion fears persisted through the 1850s. The third panic was the most justifiable, and had the greatest consequences for national defence. This time, concern over French intentions was heightened by their brief technological lead in iron warship construction, caused by the launching of *La Gloire*. Palmerston appointed a Royal Commission to investigate and recommend improvements to the defences around the naval dockyards.[2] Its conclusions led to Britain's biggest ever fortress-building programme, with 19 new forts and 57 batteries under construction around the coast by 1867.[3] The creation of a national network of militia quarters and the transformation of the regular army's accommodation in the coastal fortifications can only be understood in the context of the country's defensive response during the 1850s and early 1860s to these perceived threats from France.

The amateur military tradition

Amateur auxiliary troops have been raised to supplement the regular army since the mid-sixteenth century, and a parallel 'amateur military tradition' to serving in the regular army can be traced from that time up to the present day.[4] Militia service was an obligation imposed on citizens by the State to spend some time each year in military training, and to be ready to defend the kingdom if called upon. It was based on the ownership of property until 1757, and on a compulsory, though widely flouted, ballot until the suspension of this system in 1831. Militia service was revived as a voluntary institution from 1852, being replaced by the establishment of the Territorials from 1908. A separate form of auxiliaries called 'volunteer forces' was raised locally, paid for by local subscription, and was intended for the defence of particular localities. Although independent of the regular army command structure, after 1778 their formation was governed by legislation. They were raised, or embodied, during the Civil War, to fight the Jacobites in 1715 and 1745, and during the American War of Independence. They were of most significance for their effect on barracks provision

---

[1] R. Cobden, *Political Writings*, 3rd edn (London 1868), **2**, p.243.

[2] PRO ZHC1/25577, *The Report of the Commissioners appointed to consider the Defences of the United Kingdom,* 22 August 1860.

[3] A. Saunders, 'Palmerston's Follies – a centenary', *Journal of the Royal Artillery*, **87**, 3 (1960), pp.138–44.

[4] See Becket (1991).

Figure 128 The militia storehouse at Cirencester was one of the more convincing mock castles of the reformed militia.

during the French Revolutionary and Napoleonic Wars (see Chapter Four), when large numbers of voluntary troops were raised as infantry and artillery, and as Yeoman cavalry. Volunteer units were again encouraged from 1852 until 1908.

In these various guises, auxiliary troops existed to supplement the regular forces in the event of invasion. Although they could and did serve in Ireland, and were used ineffectually against Bonnie Prince Charlie, they were legally forbidden from being sent overseas. In fact, most militia duties have been concerned with maintaining internal order. Regular troops were traditionally preferred by magistrates because of their greater discipline and reliability, but the Yeoman cavalry in particular – a voluntary local force from the horse- and property-owning class – were extensively called upon in the industrial and political disturbances of the years before the Reform Act. Their most notorious action remains the Peterloo Massacre of 1819.

Although a citizen army for national defence was seen as less of a potential political threat to the State than a permanent standing army (the militia is sometimes referred to as the 'Old Constitutional force'), auxiliaries were no better served for accommodation than regular troops before the end of the eighteenth century. An Act of 1802 encouraged the construction of local stores where their arms and equipment could be kept secure, but apart from the hutment camps of the Napoleonic Wars, there was only occasional, privately built, separate barracks provision for the auxiliaries before the 1850s.

The armouries of the reformed militia

By the Militia Act (1852), which followed the second panic, British volunteer forces regained their statutory existence for the first time in twenty years. The lord lieutenants of each county were expected to raise a total of 50,000 men in the first year and 30,000 the year after. Rather than re-impose a ballot to select who should take part – a method which had provoked extensive public disorder when introduced by Pitt the Younger in 1757 – men were encouraged to volunteer, although the threat of a ballot remained if the required numbers were not forthcoming. By a further Act the following August, the county lieutenants were ordered to find a militia 'storehouse', or to build one if no existing building was suitable. This was to act as a secure store for the militia's arms, accoutrements, clothing and other materials, with barrack accommodation for a sergeant major and a minimum of six NCOs to form a permanent guard. It had to include a parade ground for mustering and drilling the troops, where arms, clothing and equipment could be issued or collected. In 1854, Palmerston had the Board of Ordnance draw up a model plan which was circulated to the county authorities. But in most counties, the need to attract volunteers, combined with the requirement to build a secure home, fertilized the conception of a novel building type: the combined barracks-armoury.

The Militia Returns of 1855 show that two years after the Act, about a third of the county militia regiments were continuing to rent premises, the militia in Devon and Northampton were converting local gaols, while the rest of the counties had bought land or had already started building their new storehouses. Several counties which raised more than one regiment asked the county surveyor to prepare a model design. In Middlesex, for example, a county which supported seven militia regiments,

1847–1869: 'The Three Panics'

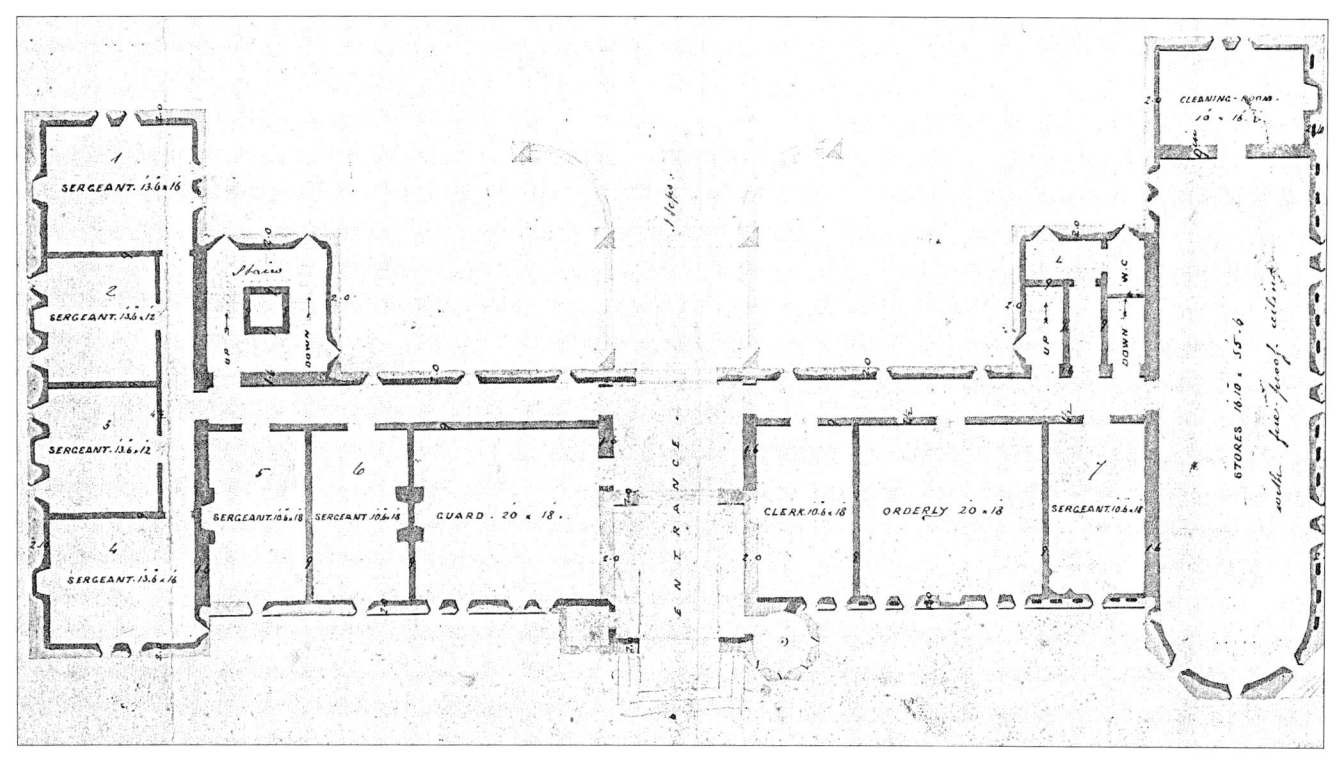

Figure 129 Plan of the ground floor of Cirencester Militia storehouse. The armoury and magazine occupied the tower-fronted wing to the right.

the new storehouses consisted of a house for the adjutant, a mess, guardroom and cells, a large armoury, quartermaster's stores and a magazine, and rooms for 20 NCOs. The parade ground included a covered way for wet-weather drilling. Similar buildings were erected at Barnet, Hounslow and Uxbridge, each costing £7,000–10,000. Large storehouses were built for the East and West Essex Militia at Colchester and Chelmsford. They included armouries for 900 stands of arms and accoutrements for 1,000 men, with accommodation at Chelmsford for 12 staff sergeants, each with a sitting room and bedroom. They were estimated to cost more than £4,500 each.

This construction programme also provided local elites with an opportunity to represent the ancient values of amateur soldiering in architectural terms, even if these tended to be the masonry equivalent of the Ruritanian frogging favoured for the militia's uniforms. Most of the stores displayed a desire, characteristic of the Picturesque movement, for an emblematic expression of their military role, and many took as their stylistic models the domesticated castles of the fifteenth century – buildings which alluded more to the status of castles than to their strength. The commonest architectural emblems applied to the militia's new homes were machicolations, crenellations, turrets and arrow slits. As a commentator on the new drill hall for the militia in Bloomsbury in London noted: 'Tudor was chosen, the English style having the semi-military character necessary to the building.'[5]

One of the most attractive extant examples was built at Cirencester for the Royal North Gloucestershire Regiment (see Figure 128), for which the plans, correspondence with the War Office, and minutes of the lieutenancy meetings survive.[6] The county's lieutenancy met in the Shire Hall in November 1853 in order to determine the best means of executing the terms of the recent Act. A site on Lord Bathurst's land was settled on in Cirencester, and one next to the prison in Gloucester was chosen for the South Gloucestershire Militia. Similar designs for the two barracks were

[5] *The Builder* **44** (1883), pp.749–51.
[6] Gloucestershire County Record Office, Minutes of Lieutenancy Meetings.

Figure 130 An early design for the storehouse of the North Gloucestershire Militia at Cirencester.

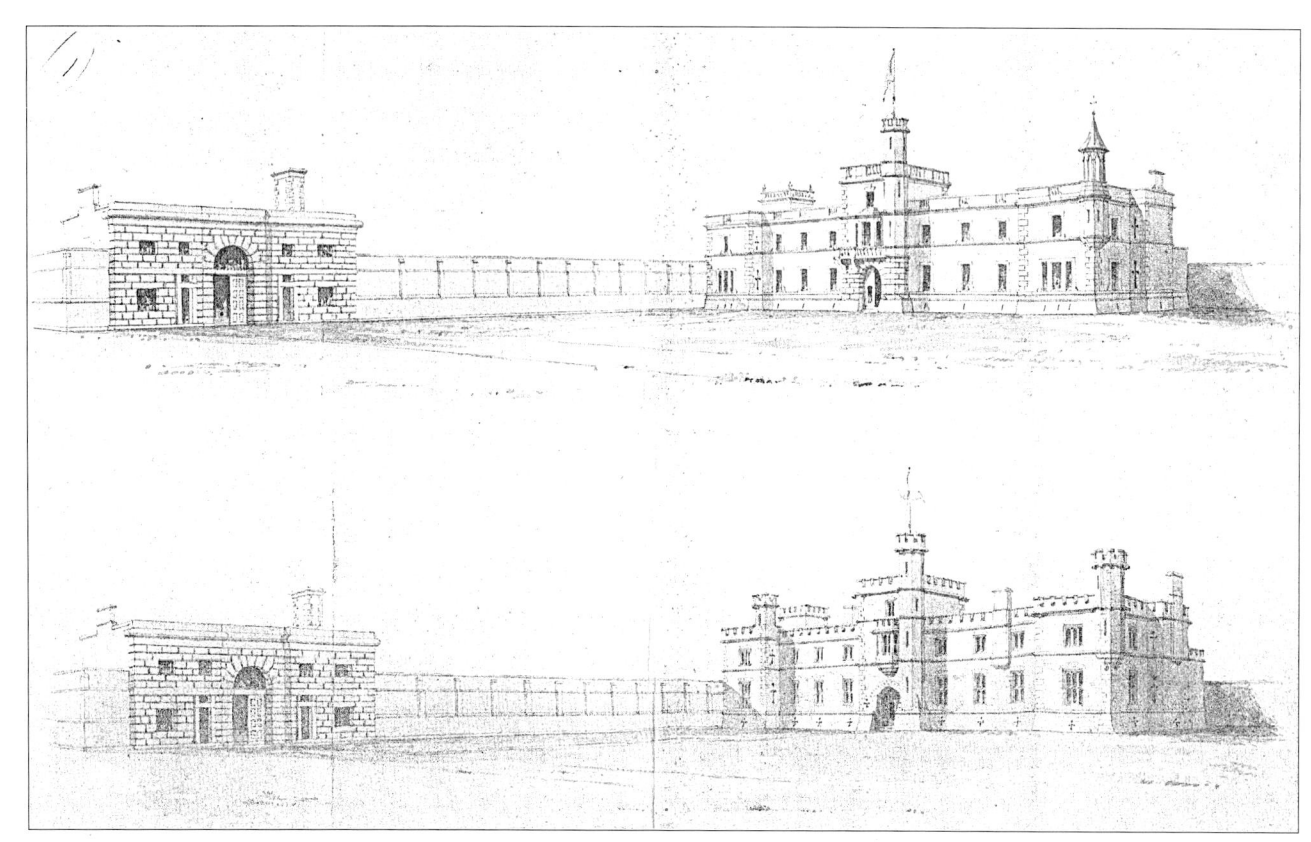

Figure 131 Alternative views of how the Gloucestershire Militia should present themselves.

Figure 132 The armoury and barracks of the Suffolk Militia at Ipswich, a typically Picturesque building, with chimney turrets and a drawbridge spanning the basement 'moat'.

produced in early 1854 by Thomas Fulljames, who had trained under Thomas Rickman in the 1820s before being appointed County Surveyor in 1829. The irregular, Picturesque façade of the Cirencester storehouse concealed a regular, E-shaped plan (see Figure 129). Built on falling ground, the rear doorway stood at the head of an elegant sweep of stairs down to the parade area. Inside were seven sergeants' rooms on the ground floor, and a large, fire-proof store occupied the south wing. On the first floor were six more NCOs' rooms, with four sitting rooms, a central suite for the sergeant major, and the armoury. The basement contained a kitchen and pantries, three detention cells and a magazine.

Various sketches and drawings show that the architect and members of the building committee looked for the most appropriate of the available contemporary styles with a suitable military flavour, Gothic or Italian Renaissance, to achieve the aesthetic associations they felt were appropriate for the new headquarters (see Figures 130 and 131). At Cirencester, they finally opted for a Gothic building, convincingly solid, with its battered basement, square entrance tower and stair turret, and with a heavy, round tower enclosing the armoury.

Other surviving militia barracks exhibit similar approaches to planning and architecture (see Figures 132–4). The Lincolnshire County Surveyor, Henry Goddard, produced plans for the militia storehouses in Grantham and Lincoln for the Royal South and North Lincolnshire Militia. They consisted of a severe, obviously defensible store for the arms and accoutrements, with a tall wall around the parade ground to the rear. The NCOs' quarters were in separate terraces nearby. At Newcastle under Lyme there was a more eclectic design, though it also had a central tower and archway, with towers at each corner of an inner courtyard for drawing up the men. The Royal London Militia Depot at Finsbury, designed by Joseph Jennings and used by the Honourable Artillery Company, was in the Elizabethan manner, with regular mullion and transom windows, corner turrets and rows of crenellated chimney shafts.[7]

At Macclesfield, a large parade ground was surrounded by offices and NCO quarters in a polychromatic French Gothic style, designed by a local architect, Frederick Pownall. The Duke of Cornwall's Militia at Bodmin built their headquarters like a minor Loire château (see fig. 154, page 173) –

Figure 133 Note the contrasting architectural styles adopted by the Militia storehouses at Newcastle under Lyme (top) and Grantham.

[7] *The Builder* **15** (1857) p.338.

Figure 134 Stockport Militia drill hall.

a most inappropriate architectural association, given that the ancillary force was revived because of fears of the arrival of the French.

Militiamen served for five years, and were expected to train for 21–56 days during the summer. To allow them to do so without hindrance from the weather, from the 1870s a number of militia regiments constructed large sheds under which to drill, including that of the South Gloucestershire. The earliest covered drill sheds were the high roofs which had been erected between the infantry barracks at Aldershot. Some spectacular examples were built during the second half of the nineteenth century by the militia, and by the time the navy built barracks from the 1880s, they were becoming an accepted part of modern barracks.

It is not easy to identify in these diverse buildings a common plan which could provide evidence of the model suggested by the War Office, and in any case,

Palmerston had allowed variation according to local circumstances.[8] Some, such as the Gloucester Barracks, were started before Palmerston sent the plan out to the counties in March 1854, and the preliminary thinking on these seems to have been based on the requirements for storehouses outlined in the 1802 Militia Act. The construction of the buildings and their external architecture reflected the need to make them secure against both foreign attack and insurrection – clear evidence that the militia was still an auxiliary force available to the civil authorities should they feel threatened, and that the Chartist disturbances were fresh in the mind.

Accordingly, most of the stores were fire-resistant in their materials, and all made provision for defence. The perimeter walls of the Duke of Cornwall's Barracks contained rifle slits covering the road to Bodmin. Fulljames said of the Gloucester Barracks that 'they are so arranged as to be capable of any amount of defence with small arms, and from the

[8] PRO HO51/121.

flat roofs with guns', and quoted a price for fitting 'ball-proof blinds or shutters' to the windows.[9]

However, despite the undoubted priority placed on functional security, the colourful architecture of the militia's new stores remained within the late eighteenth-century Romantic tradition, of 'picturesque values (that is, architecture as scenery) and associationist aesthetics (that is, architecture as embedded memory)'.[10] Their scenic qualities afforded a dramatic backdrop to the inspections and parades which fostered pride in the local militia, helped fill the counties' quotas and provided a focus for enlistment to the ancient 'constitutional force'. Their embedded memory of medieval castles left no one in doubt as to the building's serious intent: to keep secure the auxiliaries' arms and equipment, and to deter potential insurgents. This example would be taken up again by the War Office twenty years later for the armouries of the localization depots, which combined similar practical and symbolic functions.

Accommodation in the Royal Commission forts

Although reforming the militia was the immediate response to the renewal of invasion fears, the more effective but slower and much more costly reaction was to update the country's coastal batteries and dockyard defences. These fortifications – the later ones popularly derided as 'Palmerston's Follies' – have been the subject of considerable analysis in recent years. The concern here is with the particular way in which the relevant military engineers dealt with the problem of accommodating their inhabitants, the gunners and the defensive garrison.

We have seen how, in the later eighteenth century, Ordnance engineers stopped building domestic-style barracks within the ramparts in forts because they had become vulnerable to higher-angle artillery fire, and provided instead safer, bomb-proof casemates under earthworks. During the nineteenth century, such accommodation casemates were assigned a more active role in close defence or as a 'keep of last resort' should the ramparts be breached. By the 1850s, barracks had become a key ingredient in fortifications theory.

In the re-crystallization of nation States following the fall of Napoleon, fortification theory on the Continent developed away from the old angle-bastion system developed in early-sixteenth-century Italy towards separate or detached works with a polygonal outline. Within them, military engineers increasingly tried to distinguish between offensive artillery fire towards an approaching enemy army, and lighter close defensive fire which could be used against a besieging force. The result was often a detached, polygonal earthwork, with long sides at oblique angles towards the front, where artillery pieces could be concentrated, and a straight or canted gorge, the rear part, protected by a self-defensible blockhouse containing the barracks. Some of the Napoleonic defences, like the batteries on the Shannon crossings in Ireland, or Fort Pitt, had already been provided with casemated barracks which doubled as a blockhouse or gun tower. During the mid-nineteenth century, with much more attention and money being devoted to coastal defence, barracks became drawn into fortification theory, fulfilling roles both as independent, fortified structures and as integral parts of larger forts.

An early instance of the increasing crossover between barrack and fort design was the barracks fort built in 1842–5 for the Royal Marines detachment which protected and policed the Pembroke Naval Dockyard (see Figure 135). The Royal Engineer who published a description of the work described it as a 'loop-holed barracks intended as a Keep for a Square Fort'. It was square with chamfered corners, surrounded by a revetted ditch which was crossed by a bridge. The outside walls were pierced only by two storeys of closely spaced musket loops. The internal elevations to the square courtyard were quite domestic in character, however, and the barracks had a conventional structure of timber floors and a slated roof. Although large water tanks and a 104-barrel powder magazine were provided in the basement as if to withstand a seige, it had little capacity to endure an artillery attack.[11]

Several other forts and barracks were built during the 1850s which show evidence of a process of continued reassessment and rearrangement of

---

[9] Gloucester County Record Office, *Letter to the Lieutenancy*, 8 March 1854.
[10] J.M. Crook, *The Dilemma of Style* (London 1989), p.13.
[11] W. Faris, 'Description of a Loop-holed Barrack', *Professional Papers of the Royal Engineers*, **8** (1845), pp.39–41.

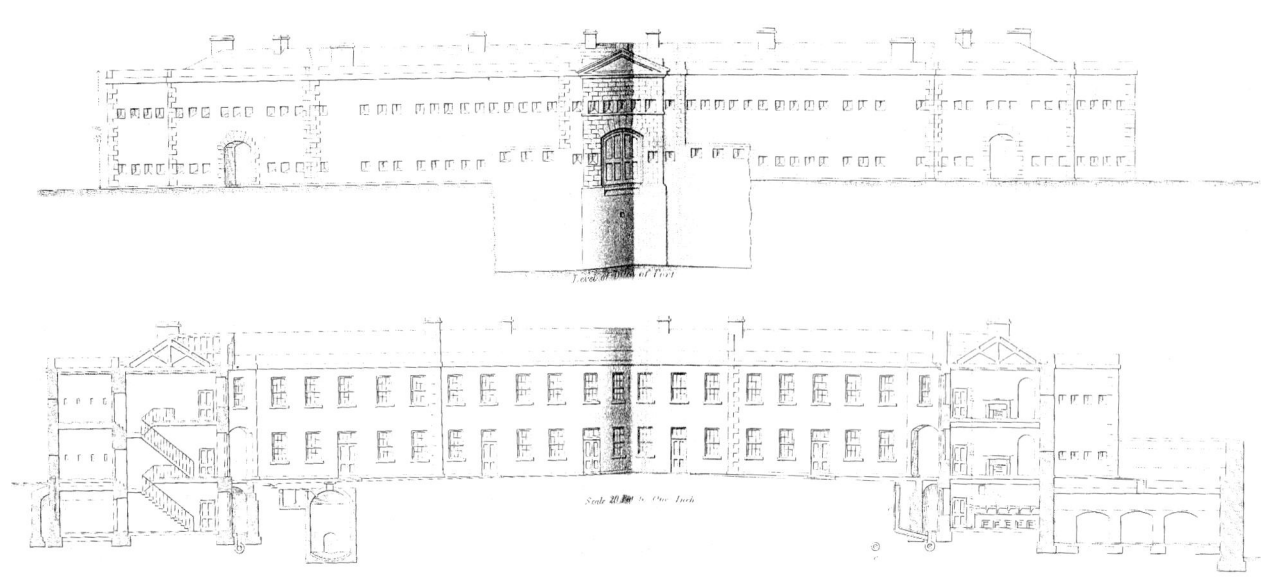

Figure 135 The kitchens, stores and some of the soldiers' barrack rooms were accommodated in the basement. The drawings show (top) the outside elevation of the entrance front and (below) a section through the barracks with the courtyard elevation of the officers' quarters.

fortress design, and of the role which the barracks were expected to fulfil. The first true polygonal work in Britain was Shornmeade Fort, by the Thames estuary, which was completed in the 1853 in response to the second panic. It had barracks in casemates to the two sides to the rear, and guns mounted on the three sides facing the front. Another work from the same period was the battery at Fort Victoria, on the Isle of Wight. It was arrow-shaped, pointing over the Solent, with casemates for the artillery facing out to sea, and as accommodation for the gunners in the gorge at the rear to protect the landward side. The group of 13 forts and batteries designed and built from 1853 to protect the Channel Islands by Captain (later Major) Sir William Drummond Jervois included several polygonal works which incorporated a large, secure barracks or 'keep of last resort' in the gorge, for the infantry garrison. Jervois was to become the most important influence on British fortification design during this key period. This use of the barracks was a characteristic element in many of the forts designed under him.

Other crossovers between fort and barrack design were being developed and built during these years. From 1856, a new transit barracks for a thousand men was erected inside the ditch of the Gosport Lines, which protected the western approach to Portsmouth. Because of its exposed situation so close to the ramparts, an attempt was made to render the new St George's Barracks 'bomb-proof' against high-angle mortar attack, and it had a parapetted flat roof intended to be filled with earth (in fact, the walls cracked when the roof began to be loaded, and the plan had to be abandoned). The long, two-storey soldiers' lodging was sunk half below the ground, with access to the rooms provided from a deep, cast-iron veranda which extended all along the front (see Figure 136) – a feature that convinced even Pevsner that the barracks had been built in Gosport, instead of one of the colonies in the tropics, by mistake. This appears to be a long-standing misconception. The infantry barracks at Aldershot, with their high, iron roofs for wet-weather drill, were described by one occupant as: 'an exotic edifice of iron pillars and verandahs facing north, that had been designed, it was said, for some swamp or jungle in Jamaica, and by a typically imaginative, if erratic gesture of the nineteenth century War Office, had been erected here instead'.[12]

A similar though more heavily constructed type of

[12] O. Sitwell, *Great Morning* (London 1949), p.119.

Figure 136 The deep veranda at St George's Barracks, Gosport, doubled as a covered area for drill.

bomb-proof quarters was built by Jervois in 1860 for officers' accommodation in the Citadel at the Western Heights in Dover (see Figure 137). This unusual hybrid was fortified to the extent of having a 5-foot (1.5-metre) bomb-proof layer of earth on the roof, and strong stone walls at either end. But the buildings' role presumably precluded a fully fortified architecture, since the front and rear, though solidly built, were conventional elevations in a heavy Tudor style. While the rest of the garrison lived down below in high, vaulted casemates looking out onto the ditch around the Citadel, their officers enjoyed the questionable privilege of the most exposed situation on the entire hill.

Military engineers like Jervois had to review their theories of the design and disposition of fortifications in 1858, when William Armstrong produced his new rifled artillery gun, whose vastly extended range changed the whole basis on which defensive works were planned. That year, work had begun on three forts to close the 'Gosport Advanced Line' and extend further outwards the defences around Portsmouth Dockyard. Forts Grange, Rowner and Brockhurst were polygonal works with a four-sided rampart containing casemates for barracks and stores, with open gun emplacements

Figure 137 The defensible officers' quarters at The Citadel on Dover Western Heights.

for the artillery on top (see Figures 138, page 99, 139 and 140). The close defence of the fort was organized around a circular, brick keep at the centre of the canted, brick gorge across the back and overlooking both the rear and the interior of the fort. The garrison of 300 men lived in the rampart casemates, and the master gunner in one of the flanks. The commanding officer had his quarters in

Figure 139 Interior of one of the rampart casemates for the garrison at Fort Brockhurst. Each one was for 14 men.

the north end of the gorge, and senior NCOs, officers and the hospital were in the keep, within casemates radiating off a small, central courtyard.[13]

The recommendations of the 1859 Royal Commission, though circumscribed by Parliament, resulted in 'a prodigality of fortress building unmatched in the British Isles'.[14] Major Jervois, by now Assistant Inspector General of Fortifications, was the Secretary to the Commission, and the major influence on its recommendations. His intention was that the new forts should be quick to build, and defensible by small militia garrisons, aided by a core of Royal Artillery gunners, to avoid tying down the field army in the event of a French invasion. Consequently, there were no casemates within the ramparts, one of the differences from the earlier forts of the Gosport Lines, which enabled work on the main earthworks and artillery positions to progress more rapidly. Rather than being split between the ramparts and the keep, therefore, the whole of the garrison was housed together in a large, brick, self-defensible barrack in the gorge.

This more sophisticated integration of the garrison accommodation with the defence of the fort took various forms, which can be appreciated in the surviving forts along the ridge of Portsdown Hill above Portsmouth. They were designed by Captain (later Sir) William Crossman, with the architect at the War Office, Ingress Bell. At Forts Wallington (see Figure 140) and Purbrook (see Figure 141), for instance, the two-storey casemated barracks extended across the gorge, which was canted sharply inward, and formed part of a huge, triangular redan projecting out to the rear, enclosing a small courtyard. At Fort Southwick, further along the ridge, the barracks across the gorge were canted outwards, and a pair of horns or demi-bastions extended from the back to provide lateral defensive fire.

The development of the use of fortified accommodation, as well the inventiveness of British military engineers during the 1850s and 1860s, can be illustrated by another of Jervois's constructions, the Golden Hill Barracks fort, on the Isle of Wight (see Figure 142). This hexagonal work fulfilled a similar purpose to the Marines' barracks at Pembroke, in this case providing a secure home for the gunners who manned the various batteries along the western tip of the island, facing the Solent. In contrast to the Pembroke Barracks, however, Golden Hill was casemated throughout, with a veranda on the inside for access to the upper storey. It was surrounded by a huge rampart to the same height as the roof, on which were mounted artillery pieces at the six corners. With a ditch covered by caponiers on alternate corners, the barracks were much more secure, and presented a more formidable obstacle to an approaching enemy.[15]

The overlap between fortification theory and barracks design during the 1850s and 1860s is further evinced in another much larger complex associated with the protection of Portsmouth. Both the mid-eighteenth-century Marines' barracks at Chatham and Stonehouse were extended in the early 1860s. The Portsmouth Marines Division had moved out of the old Clarence Barracks ten years earlier, exchanging it for the army's Napoleonic hospital at Gosport (later HMS *Forton*, and now a further education college), which was converted, and a grand new officers' quarters and mess was built by Captain Henry James RE, then the resident engineer in the dockyard.[16] The Royal Marines Artillery Regiment was at this time based at Fort Cumberland, but a new barracks was planned for them jointly by the Admiralty and the War Office, to

[13] EH Map Room WD766, 771, *Plan of Fort Grange*.
[14] Saunders (1989), p.175.
[15] PRO WORK43/258-268, *Defensible barracks, Golden Hill*, 22 August 1864.

[16] H. James, 'Additions to the barracks at Forton', *Professional Papers of the Royal Engineers* (1851), paper 7, pp.101–5.

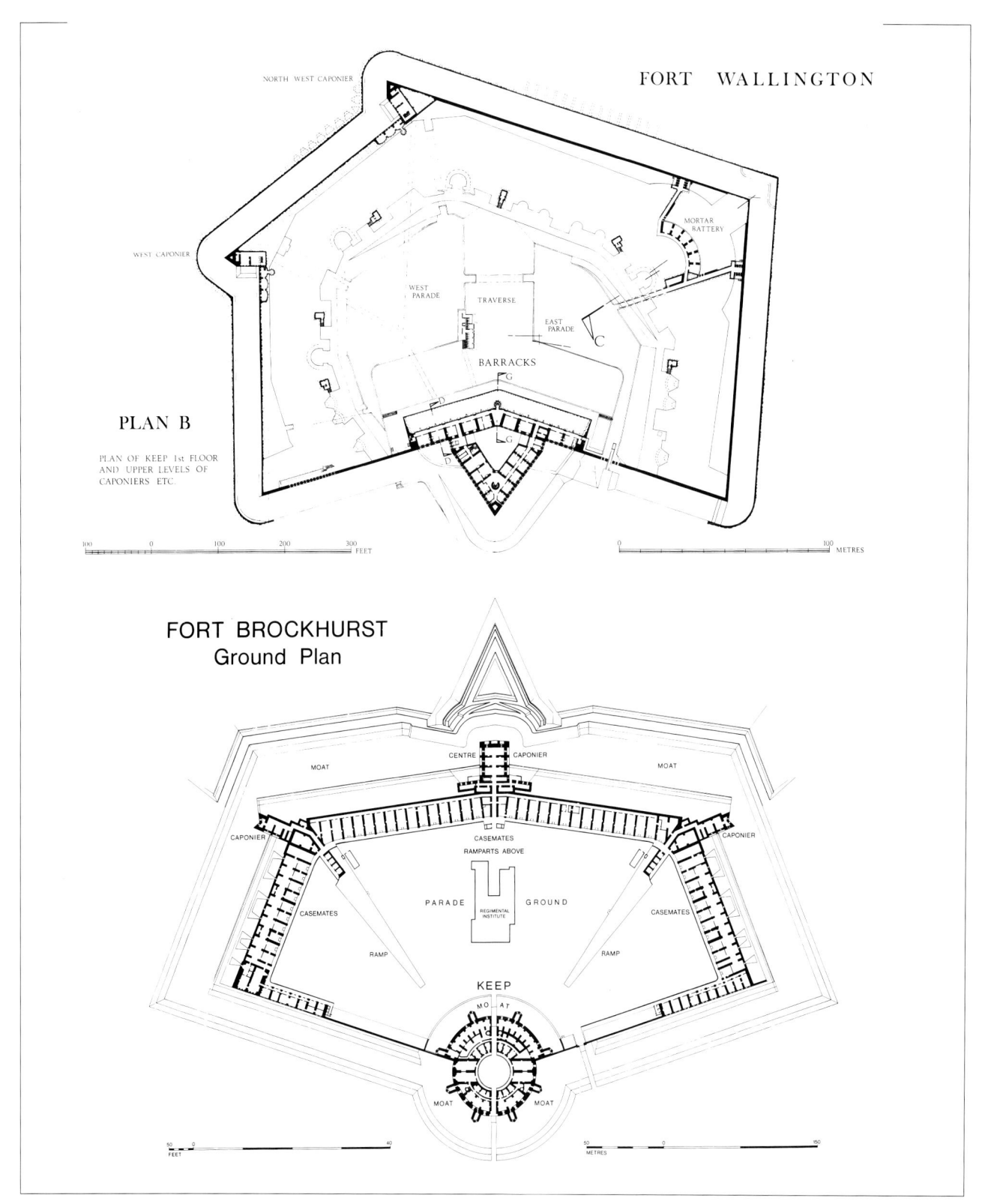

Figure 140 Plans of Fort Wallington and Fort Brockhurst. The keep at Fort Brockhurst (see fig. 138), contained quarters for married soldiers and sergeants, the guardhouse and stores. The barracks in the gorge at Fort Wallington (1861–74) accommodated the 168-man garrison and eight officers, in contrast to the earlier plan at Brockhurst.

Figure 141 Fort Purbrook casemates. Superior ranks had the upper casemates, and the ordinary soldiers, the NCOs, infirmary and stores occupied the lower levels.

Figure 142 The internal courtyard at Golden Hill Fort, with the barrack-room access veranda.

occupy an empty section of shoreline further up the coast at Eastney – in the words of the 1859 Royal Commission, 'to form a defensible post for troops employed in opposing a landing'.[17]

The landward defences of the barracks were provided by a loop-holed wall which continued all round, but to the front, on the shoreline, the wall was connected to a pair of small batteries, Eastney East and West, which occupied the sites of much earlier batteries. They were connected, and the front of the barracks closed, by a raised bank set back from the beach.[18]

Eastney Barracks (see Figure 143) was the responsibility of the head of the Admiralty Works Department, Colonel Greene RE, and his civilian assistant, William Scamp, working in co-operation with Jervois. Greene and Scamp were responsible for the contemporary extension of Stonehouse Marines Barracks, as well as a number of important new buildings in the naval yards, including the ground-breaking Sheerness Boatstore. The new barracks was built between 1862 and 1867, the date at which the Marines Artillery marched down the road from Fort Cumberland. The soldiers' accommodation was a very long range facing the sea. It was made up of seven identical sections, each with a central stair with NCOs' rooms and washrooms off, flanked by cross-lit dormitories for 24 men. The sergeants'

messes, library, kitchens and separate dining rooms were in the basement. As with Denison's Woolwich Barracks, this represented a much more progressive arrangement than was to be found in contemporary army barracks, especially in separating the eating and sleeping rooms of the soldiers.

Eastney repeated the layout of all the previous new Marines' barracks, at Chatham, Stonehouse and Woolwich, the officers' accommodation being in detached wings at either side. The field officers' residence to the east was, like the Marines' barracks of a century before, barely distinguishable from contemporary civilian terraces. The officers' mess at the opposite end of the parade ground was probably at this time the most imposing and architecturally refined in the kingdom (see Figure 144). The central section was of Portland stone, with the entrance, on the *piano nobile*, approached by a grand, imperial stair.[19] Continuing the trend of the new mess at Forton, which had included an orchestra platform in an alcove on the main stairs, the Eastney mess provided an august setting for regimental ceremonies and ritual. The central section was divided laterally by a full-height central stair hall extending the whole depth of the building, with a dignified staircase which rose in two flights to the upper dining room. Eastney was the first of the seriously grandiloquent quarters which the British officer class built for itself during the second half of

[17] PRO ZHC1/25577, *Report of the Royal Commission to consider the Defences of the United Kingdom*, 1859.

[18] RM Museum ACQ 467/76 (A), *Plan of defensible wall and batteries*.

[19] RM Museum ACQP/61/18/CA, *RM Artillery barracks, Eastney*, July 1863.

Figure 143 The Marines barracks at Eastney consisted of seven standard sections forming one prodigious range.

the nineteenth century, in which the navy always outdid the army. Today, it is open to visitors as the Marines' museum.

The various works associated with the 1859 Royal Commission represent a significant point in the continuing evolution of coastal defence and fortification theory. Many of the forts, batteries and barracks built at this time combined artillery works with secure, defensible garrison accommodation in a variety of comparatively sophisticated ways. By 1869, however, the American Civil War had demonstrated the susceptibility of masonry defences to rifled artillery, and the relative value of earth fieldworks. The brick, casemated keeps of the Royal Commission forts were as likely to be vulnerable to artillery fire as the old stone castles of the medieval period found themselves after the 'artillery revolution' of the mid-fifteenth century. With few exceptions, they proved to be 'the last self-defensible combination of barracks and battery to be built in Britain'.[20] Similarly, the concept of the defensible barracks was not revived for later military accommodation, either for coastal defence or in the context of the army's declining civil order responsibilities.

Figure 144 The grand approach to the entrance of the Eastney officers' mess.

[20] Saunders (1989), p.188.

British Barracks 1600–1914

Figure 145 Eastney Marines Barracks was protected by a landward wall and small batteries to the front, and had its own water tower.

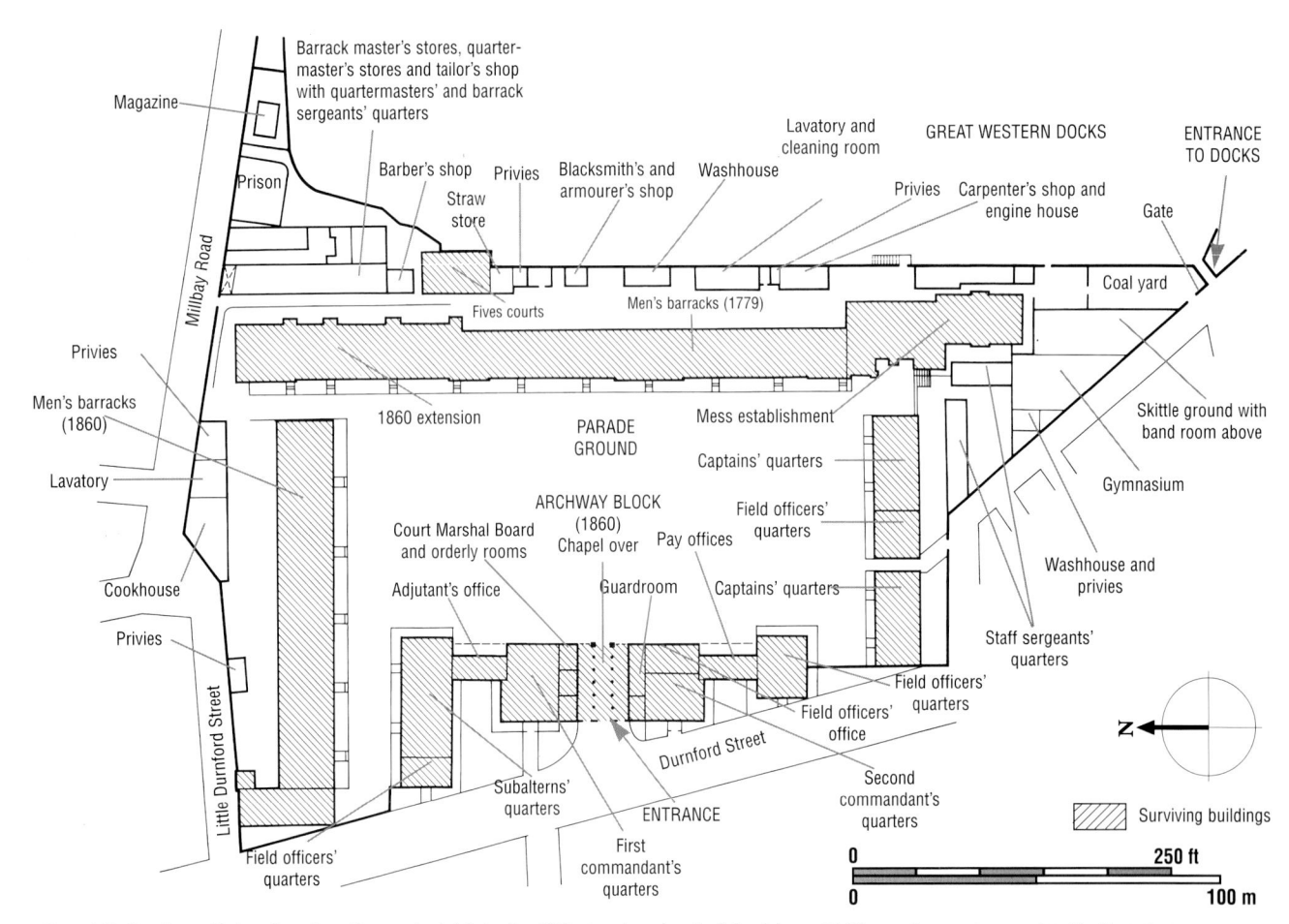

Figure 146 Stonehouse Marines Barracks as it was extended during the 1860s, based on plans by Colonel James RE. The parade ground was enclosed by the archway block, containing senior officers' quarters and offices, and more new quarters were added to the north end. Figure 43, page 51, shows the 1770s barracks.

Figure 147 The handsome, new entrance range in the Archway Block at Stonehouse. Apparently influenced by William Kent's Horse Guards, it was designed under Colonel Geoffrey Greene RE, the Director of the Admiralty Works Department.

Chapter Eight
1872–1914: Localization and the 'Great Camps'

During the last quarter of the nineteenth century, British policy towards the scale and distribution of military accommodation underwent three sharp changes in direction, as military and civil authorities struggled to recruit and train an army appropriate to the country's imperial status. Whilst barracks never occupied the public mind in the way they had during the 1850s, the manner in which the army – and also, for the first time, the navy – was housed became a national issue, closely related to the problem of ruling an expanding global empire with voluntary forces in a period of rising prosperity.

In this context, a chronic gap remained between the growing manpower needs of the army and the number of men coming forward to volunteer. The reforms of the home forces that the Liberal Secretary of State for War, Edward Cardwell, initiated in 1872 were aimed at the recruitment problem, but despite these changes, service life remained unappealing to the great majority, and although living conditions improved, the public status of soldiers remained low.

Army reform remained a major political issue for late Victorian and Edwardian Governments, and one that was intensified by military failure in the Boer War. Secretaries of State from Cardwell to the Liberal Richard Haldane proposed different solutions, reflected in periodic reversals of the country's barrack-building programme. The resolution by Haldane of many of these problems during the ten years before the First World War was therefore a considerable achievement, leading to the successful deployment of the British Expeditionary Force in France in 1914.

Figure 148 Recruiting sergeants outside a pub in Westminster.

The localization of the home forces

When Edward Cardwell was given the War Office in 1868, his immediate policy goal was to reduce the army estimates. However, the military successes of the Prussian Army during the unification of Germany, between 1864 and 1871, had suggested the idea of localizing units in a particular area, the system by which Bismark's conscripts were organized. Army reformers in Britain urged that the training of new recruits should also be improved, and that closer links might be forged between regular and auxiliary units, so that the militia could

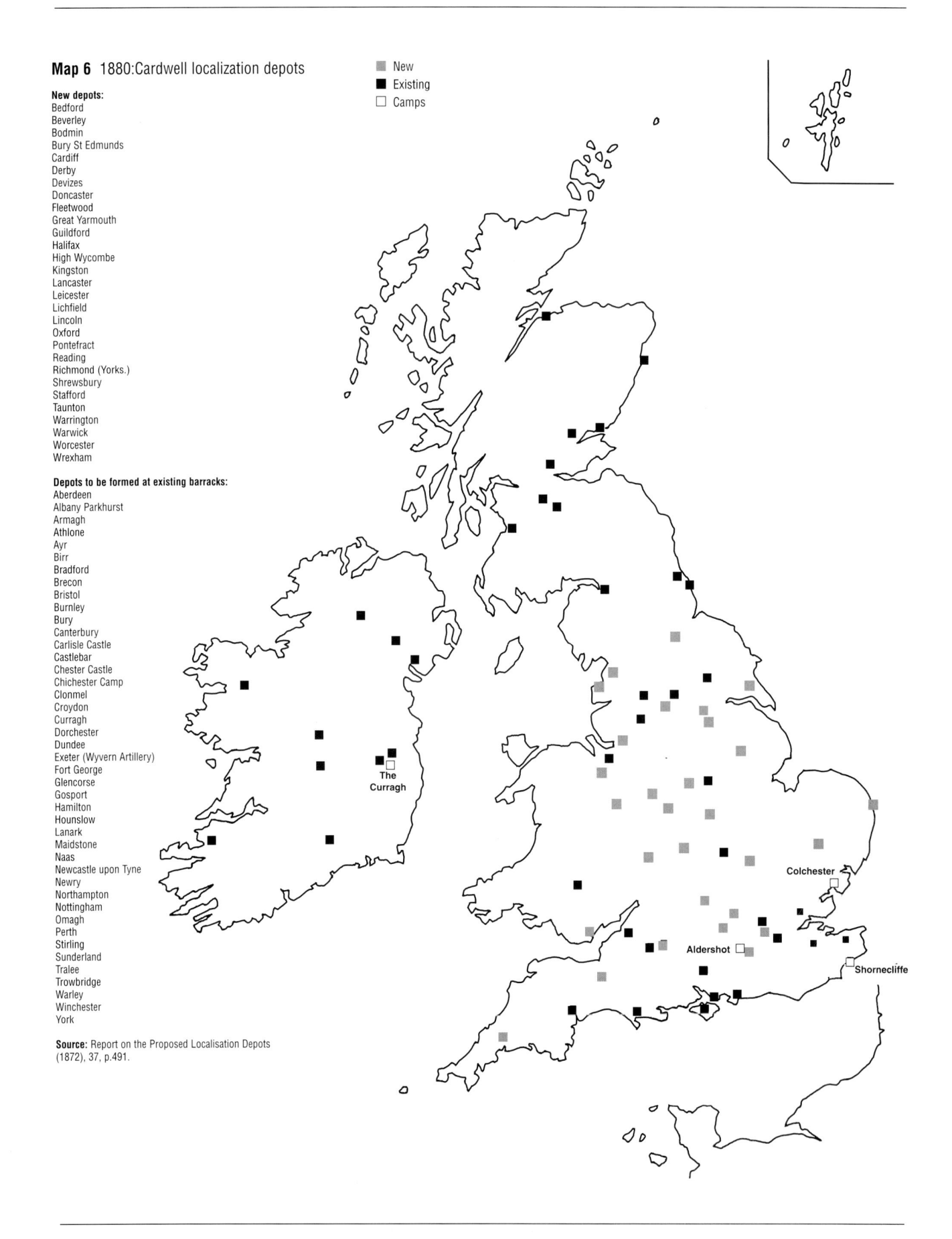

Map 6 1880:Cardwell localization depots

■ New
■ Existing
□ Camps

New depots:
Bedford
Beverley
Bodmin
Bury St Edmunds
Cardiff
Derby
Devizes
Doncaster
Fleetwood
Great Yarmouth
Guildford
Halifax
High Wycombe
Kingston
Lancaster
Leicester
Lichfield
Lincoln
Oxford
Pontefract
Reading
Richmond (Yorks.)
Shrewsbury
Stafford
Taunton
Warrington
Warwick
Worcester
Wrexham

Depots to be formed at existing barracks:
Aberdeen
Albany Parkhurst
Armagh
Athlone
Ayr
Birr
Bradford
Brecon
Bristol
Burnley
Bury
Canterbury
Carlisle Castle
Castlebar
Chester Castle
Chichester Camp
Clonmel
Croydon
Curragh
Dorchester
Dundee
Exeter (Wyvern Artillery)
Fort George
Glencorse
Gosport
Hamilton
Hounslow
Lanark
Maidstone
Naas
Newcastle upon Tyne
Newry
Northampton
Nottingham
Omagh
Perth
Stirling
Sunderland
Tralee
Trowbridge
Warley
Winchester
York

Source: Report on the Proposed Localisation Depots (1872), 37, p.491.

act as a more effective reserve.[1] Cardwell addressed these issues through the Military Localisation Bill, which he introduced to Parliament in February 1872. At its heart was a redistribution of the home forces to depots, each centred in an area populous enough to sustain a brigade. Regular and militia battalions were to be fused into territorial regiments based on the depots. Within these areas, it was hoped that formal bonds between the regular, auxiliary and volunteer units would develop, enhanced by 'ties of kindred and locality', making army service a more accessible and attractive career choice.

To this end, Cardwell proposed dividing Britain and Ireland into 66 districts for infantry regiments, 12 for artillery and 2 for cavalry. The depot was at the heart of each, forming a combined home, training ground and recruitment centre. The ideal was that it would become the permanent base for two linked line battalions, one of which would serve abroad while the other remained at home, and for two associated militia battalions and a unit of volunteers. Two companies of each of the regular battalions would stay permanently at the depot, which would become the regimental home and administrative centre, where pay would be centralized, arms, clothing and accoutrements stored, to which new recruits would be attracted, and where they could be given a proper training.

Over half the towns chosen as the centres of the new recruiting areas already had long-established barracks, like Exeter, Canterbury, Stirling and Naas, and these were adapted and extended to form depots. A small number, such as Warley in Essex and Hamilton in the Borders, were selected as double depots, accommodating two of the new brigades. The old King's House Barracks at Winchester became the home to two brigades of the four battalions of the 60th Foot, and two more of the Rifle Brigades' four battalions. Extra land was acquired at Hounslow Cavalry Barracks, which served as the Middlesex and Metropolitan depots. In Cornwall and Dorset, the militia barracks were taken over to create the depots at Bodmin and Dorchester.[2]

The depots at these existing barracks were the most quickly established, but those at completely new sites were much slower to realize, and several took the best part of ten years to build.[3] By 1880, 22 new depots had been built in England, and 15 existing barracks had been extended, with another 13 in Scotland. Many were in towns which had previously had little experience of a large, permanent military presence, and news of the impending arrival of the barracks was not necessarily greeted with enthusiasm. The University of Oxford in particular made a great fuss about the depot at Cowley, though without success. There has been little analysis of the impact of the erection of barracks and the arrival of several hundred young soldiers on small, peaceful country towns such as Bury St Edmunds, Devizes, Worcester, or Richmond in Yorkshire (only later to become a full-blown military town, with the formation of the camp at Catterick), but it must have been considerable.

Such a large building programme could not be financed from the annual army estimates. Instead, Cardwell raised a Treasury loan of £3.5 million, to be repaid over thirty years: £1.6 million was earmarked for the depots and armoury stores, and £1 million to replace quarters which had been transferred to the depots, and for training barracks for the militia; £500,000 was allocated for the purchase of land, and for a tactical training ground, and the rest was for stores and contingencies.[4]

The Act meant a sharply increased workload for the department of the Inspector General of Fortifications. Two new Assistant Directors of Works for Barracks were appointed, Lieutenant Colonel E.C. Gordon and Lieutenant Colonel P. Ravenhill, under the Deputy Director of Works for Barracks, Colonel C.B. Ewart (see Appendix A, page 199). However, the detailed architectural and planning work was carried out by the Director of the Design Branch, Major H.C. Seddon, who was assisted by a civilian architect at the head of a team of draughtsmen.

Seddon worked out a series of standard categories

---

[1] B. Bond, 'The Prelude to the Cardwell Reforms, 1856–68', *Royal United Services Gazette*, **106** (May 1961).
[2] Parliamentary Papers (House of Commons), 1875, *xliii, Returns related to Depot Centres (Army)*, p.477. The first fully constituted depots were Carlisle, County Durham (initially at Sunderland), West Riding (provisionally at Bradford), Burnley, Ashton-under-Lyne, Bury, Northampton, Great Yarmouth, Warley, Brecon, Exeter, Bristol, Winchester, Chichester, Canterbury, Hounslow, Maidstone, Aberdeen, Perth, Stirling, Hamilton, Ayr, Naas and Tralee, along with new barracks at Cardiff, Bodmin, Dorchester and Inverness.
[3] Parliamentary Papers (House of Commons), 1874, *xxxvi, Return showing the number of situations of Brigade Depots*, p.689.
[4] Military Forces Localisation (Expenses) Bill, 1872, *iii*, p.215.

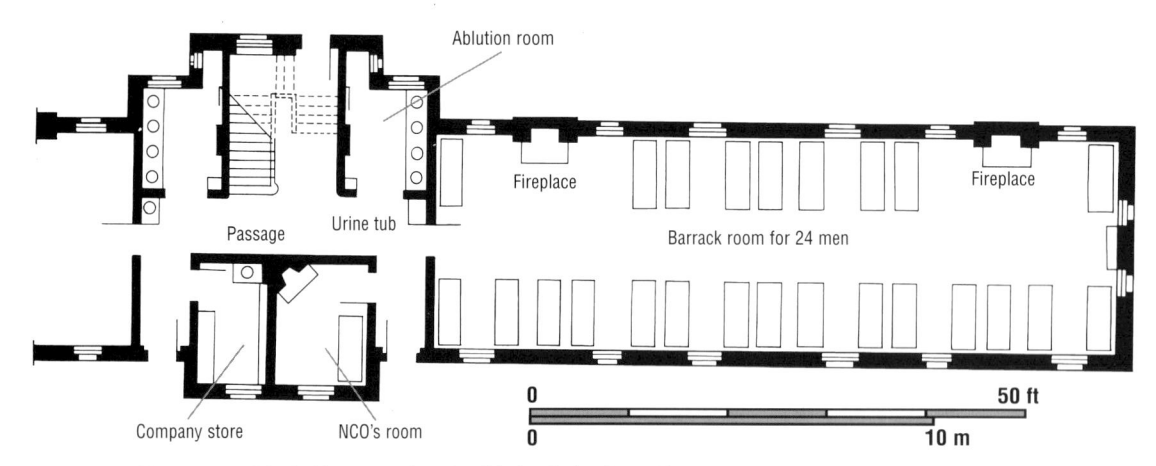

Figure 149 The internal layout of one of the double-company barracks of the localization depots. These dormitories were typical of British barracks in the second half of the nineteenth century. The larger barrack blocks, such as those at Devizes and Hounslow, or the Peninsula Barracks at Winchester, were composed of aggregates of these standard rooms.

or 'Types', building on those established by Burgoyne in his synopsis of the 1850s (see page 128). The Guards' depot at Caterham, which was the largest depot in the country, was the home barracks of four regiments, each of three battalions (the only Type I). Winchester was a triple depot (a Type II); Lichfield, Preston and Pontefract were double depots (Type III), and all the single depots were Type IV. The type plans (see Figure 149) and elevations were sent out to the local Commanding Royal Engineer officers in the districts, who made alterations according to the situation of their depot and the local building materials. These were approved or amended by Seddon, and sent back.[5] The War Office attempted to limit the turnover through foreign postings of the CRE officers responsible – an ongoing problem which affected the work of the Royal Engineers – and men were in general left to get on with the implementation of the approved plan for the decade which most took to build.

Seddon's system resulted in much greater local variation than might have been expected from a national scheme of this sort. In terms of materials, the great majority were built of red brick, decorated by bands of yellow brick or terracotta (see Figure 151). But in areas with a stone tradition, such as Oxfordshire or the West Country, masonry was used. The depots in Oxford and Bodmin were both built from local stone. There was also scope for localization of the architecture. The 'keep' or armoury at Dorchester was an unusually realistic interpretation of a medieval castle, by the army's standards, which must have been in response to local sensibilities over the historic character of the town. In Scotland, the Royal Engineers in Edinburgh evolved a strongly Highland style for the Cameron Barracks at Inverness (see Figure 152), which was approved by Seddon. The privates' quarters, for instance, had crow-stepped end gables and eave dormers, corner bartizans, conical towers, and other favourite elements of the Scottish Baronial idiom.[6]

Figure 150 Hardinge Block, Hounslow. One of the largest Cardwell barracks was built at Hounslow, which was expanded to form one of the new depots.

[5] PRO WO33/233 A738, *Report of the Commission to inquire into the employment of Royal Engineers in the construction etc of Barracks*, 1902, Minutes of evidence of Ingress Bell, November 1901, pp.39–40.

[6] Scottish National Record Office RHP 41374-41392, *Plans of Cameron barracks, Inverness*.

1872–1914: Localization and the 'Great Camps'

Figure 151 Quarters at the Le Marchant Barracks, Devizes, the Wiltshire localization depot.

The typical disposition of the buildings at the new depots differed markedly from the formal layouts of earlier barracks. In particular, they abandoned the bilateral symmetry and parade-centred layout which had dominated British barracks planning since the reform of the Ordnance Board in the early eighteenth century. Instead, more functional arrangements were preferred, the disposition of the various buildings dictated by the internal logistics of depot life. The Gibraltar Barracks in Bury St Edmunds provides an example (see Figure 153). It was authorized in February 1876, and was completed in May 1878, for an actual cost of £47,295, just a little over the estimate, but close to the average cost of the localization depots of £200 per man.

The loan for the Localisation Act included money for a secure armoury, magazine and store in each district, to safeguard the arms of the regular troops, militia and volunteers. These developed the storehouse concept of the 1853 Militia Act, discussed in Chapter 7, though with less frivolous architectural results, and in some areas, such as at Bodmin (see Figure 154), the militia store doubled up as the store

Figure 152 Cameron Barracks, Inverness, with its Scottish Baronial detail, provides the most extreme example of how localization depots could adopt local styles, but the plan is still based on that shown in Figure 149 (page 170).

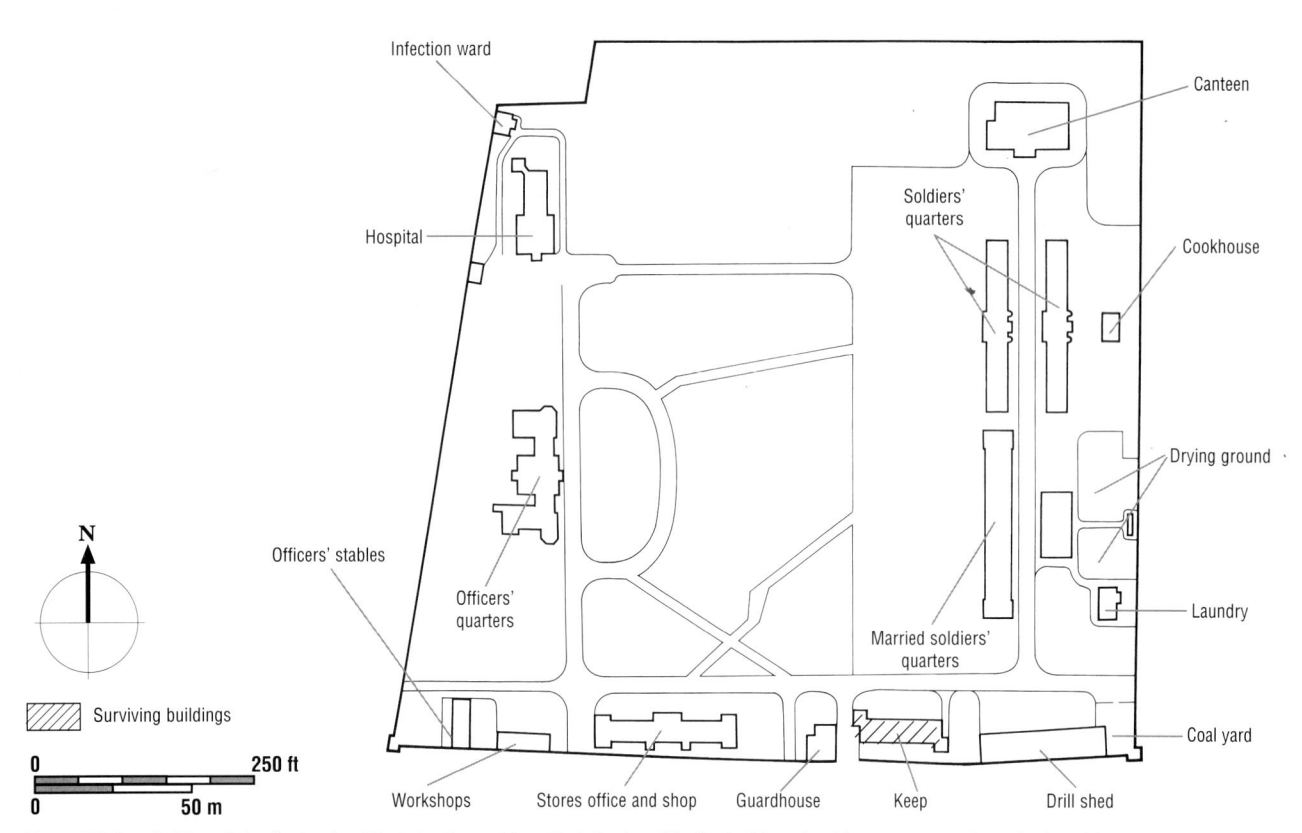

Figure 153 Bury St Edmunds localization depot illustrates the non-hierarchical planning of the Cardwell barracks. A huge armoury, or keep, dominated the entrance, with the soldiers' barracks to one side of the parade ground behind. Redrawn from the original plan of 1880.

for the depot. These armouries were usually referred to as the 'keep', in reference to their commanding and impenetrable aspect. All occupied the dominant position at the depot, beside or astride the entrance, but there were several variations: one, for example, the Jellalabad Barracks in Taunton, consisted of a square tower with a central archway leading into the parade ground, like a barbican; another had offices or officers' quarters attached to the sides, as at Worcester (see Figure 155) and Bedford;[7] a third was free-standing, and set beside the main entrance, with a veranda against the guardhouse. Examples of these survive at the former Stoughton Barracks in Guildford, and at Brock Barracks in Reading.[8]

These 'keeps' became the most memorable physical expression of the Cardwell era and the hopes of the localization reforms for the future of the army. They were the only part of the depots to have an overtly military flavour to their architecture, reflecting their combined role as a secure, fire-proof arms store with a more symbolic expression of strength and invulnerability. Explicitly defensible, they continued the medieval imagery adopted by the 1850s militia stores, with crenellations and machicolations, towers and turrets – even if these were only architectural codes and served to conceal the stairs and a water tank. Internally, they had a non-flammable iron frame, with guardrooms, cells and the depot fire engine on the ground floor, and stores above, filled with shelves of uniforms and equipment for issue to recruits or militiamen, racks of rifles and a magazine. The keep at Bury held stands of arms and clothing for 3,024 men.[9]

The average depots contained 230 privates and NCOs, 11 officers with stabling for six officers' horses, 30 married men, and a 28-bed hospital. The privates' barracks were grouped either end-to-end or in parallel rows. The typical two-storey type had four dormitories either side of a central stair, (see

---

[7] PRO WORK43/405, *Plan of Bedford Brigade Depot*, February 1878.
[8] EH Plans Room Drawer G, *Guildford Brigade Depot*, 13 November 1874.
[9] PRO WORK43/689, *Plan of Bury St Edmunds Brigade Depot*.

1872–1914: Localization and the 'Great Camps'

Figure 154 This 1920s view of the depot at Bodmin, with the 1850s armoury in the top left corner, shows two rows of infantrymen's barracks to the rear of the married quarters (now demolished) and the sergeants' mess to their left.

Figure 149) similar to the plan pioneered at the 1860s Marines' barracks at Eastney (see Figure 143 page 163). Each dormitory held 28 men, or an eighth of the rank and file which made up the battalion complement; the volume of the rooms was calculated on an allowance of 750 cubic feet (21.2 cubic metres) each. They were heated by two open fireplaces, in the rear and end walls. Opening off the central stairs were ablution rooms with a night urinal at the back, and NCOs' rooms at the front, with a side window from which the company sergeant could keep an eye on his charges. The elevations were decorated by a pediment or blind tympanum over the entrance, with the night privies showing as shallow bays at the rear.

There were still no separate dining rooms, despite the persistent recommendations of reformers for the previous thirty years that soldiers' living and eating quarters should be separate. The men collected their food from the kitchens and ate it at tables in the dormitories. Washrooms and latrines with water closets were nearby. The officers' quarters were distinguished by a more lavish application of terracotta or yellow brick. The mess room had a deep bay window giving a view over the parade

Figure 155 A number of variations on standard keep designs were produced by Major Seddon's Designs Branch, including these from the depots at Inverness (top), Hounslow and Worcester, the latter flanked by offices and officers' quarters. The interiors, with concrete floors supported on iron columns, each contained a powder room and armaments store above cells and a guardroom.

Figure 156 The Britannia Barracks in Norwich was the most elaborate and decorative of the depots, and an unusual example of Queen Anne institutional architecture. A more historically aware architect would have been conscious of the incongruity of this style for an English barracks.

square. Sergeants had a separate mess, and private soldiers had the use of the institute, where billiard tables, a reading room, bar and rooms for lectures were intended to keep them from drinking outside the barracks by offering them congenial pleasures in innocuous surroundings. The other principal buildings – the hospital, the quartermaster's quarters and store, the drill shed, canteen and ancillary buildings – were similarly distributed around the square, each, according to the War Office architect, Ingress Bell, 'falling into due subordination and being severally distinguished by appropriate and characteristic treatment'.[10]

In architectural terms, the most interesting of the barracks which followed the Localisation Act was at Norwich, built in 1886, several years after the others, on the crest of a hill overlooking the city. Whilst allowing for the due subordination of the several components, the designer of the new Britannia Barracks reassembled them to create a single more complex and sophisticated composition, enriched by an expensive application of decorative brick and tilework in the Queen Anne style (see Figure 156). The guardhouse and main entrance were situated at one end, next to the armoury keep, with the strongly articulated range continuing along through the offices, stores, officers' quarters and mess, and ending at the opposite end in a tall, square clock tower.

The depot hospital was in the same style. Under the Cardwell reforms, the regimental hospital system that had existed from the seventeenth century was phased out and replaced by one based on the localization districts. Seddon's standard depot hospital had an administrative block with waiting rooms, a surgery and orderly rooms, attached to a single pavilion-plan ward containing about twelve beds on both floors. The Norwich hospital was of this type but, disguised by an overlay of terracotta and pilasters, it achieved an irregular and Picturesque appearance. The corner sanitary annexe, for instance – leitmotif of the pavilion concept – formed an octagonal tower with a leaded Jacobean cap.[11]

On stylistic grounds, the Britannia Barracks might be attributed to J.J. Stevenson or Norman Shaw, and neither would be dishonoured. The plans of the hospital were signed by Colonel Edward Bland RE and Major A.G. Clayton RE, and by the local building contractors, Kirk and Randall. The contemporary military hospital at Colchester, where Bland was based, was in the same Queen Anne style, reinforcing the impression that this was the work of the local Royal Engineers' office. One of the last depots to be built, Norwich is one of the small number of barracks which should be included among the best institutional architecture of its day.

If localization was subsequently unable to resolve the recruitment shortfall that bedevilled the army, this had more to do with relative pay levels at a time of buoyant labour demand. As with the rest of Cardwell's reforms, such as the abolition of purchase and the introduction of short service enlistment, localization failed to enhance the status of the ordinary soldier, and his prospects of finding a job when he left the army remained bleak, unenhanced by his experience of soldiering. However, connections between particular regiments and their recruiting regions were forged, especially of those given county designations, which did help to strengthen local regimental solidarity. An impressive amount of new accommodation was built, with beds for 13,350 single men, 2,014 married soldiers and 542 officers, stabling for 1,118 horses, and 977 hospital beds. In providing a programme for the implementation of the sanitary

---

[10] Bell (1880), pp.19–25. This paper included a full consideration of the planning and design of the depots.
[11] PRO WORK43/692, *Norwich Regimental Depot Hospital*.

reforms, moreover, localization was much more effective than piecemeal improvements to individual barracks had been. These benefits were reflected in the Army Sanitary Commission's statistics by 1876, when the death rate among the home army had fallen by more than a half since the 1850s, to 8.4 per thousand. By 1897 the rate had fallen again to 3.42 per thousand.

The Stanhope Memorandum

In localizing the home forces, Cardwell had carried through a major overhaul of the country's military geography. As Map 6 (page 168) shows, it reversed the twenty-year policy of concentration represented by the camps, as well as the post-Waterloo strategy of siting barracks according to the dictates of maintaining civil order. Localization had dispersed the army and reserve to parts of the country that barracks had never previously reached. In attempting to attract recruits, strengthen the reserve and improve training, it reflected the urgent manpower needs of the imperial armed forces, and the increasing variety and complexity of modern soldiering. In January 1888, the Government delineated the strategic priorities for the army for the first time, in a memorandum by the Secretary of State for War, Edward Stanhope. Supporting the civil power was still considered the number one role for the standing army; it was followed by protecting India and other overseas garrisons, maintaining an auxiliary reserve for the defence of the homeland, and lastly, the ability to dispatch an expeditionary force of two army corps across the Channel in the unlikely event of a Continental commitment.

In fact, this sequence was already outdated. Stanhope's first priority, which had dominated barracks construction since the French Revolution, had diminished. As indicated in Chapter Five, rising social standards and political reform, combined with the expansion of a civil police force and a national railway network, had greatly lightened the army's civil order responsibilities. In the late Victorian period, the principal reason for the use of troops within the country was to control political violence – the Fenian disturbances justified a continued presence in Ireland – and, with greater frequency, labour disputes. Between 1869 and 1910, soldiers were called out on just 24 occasions.

In the two decades preceding the First World War, both parties in Government followed a 'Blue Water' policy for the defence of the realm, based on the domination of the home seas by the Royal Navy, and they resisted pressure to close the army's recruitment gap by instituting conscription. However, frequent colonial expeditions and, to a much larger extent than had been expected, the Second Boer War made heavy demands on the army. With awareness slowly dawning of the possibility of another European war, the need for facilities to recruit, house, train and exercise greater numbers in larger units became the predominant factors affecting barracks, in both their planning and geography.

Refinancing barracks under the Military Loans system

Despite the impact of the localization programme, the country's barracks estate included many which were getting on for 200 years old, such as Berwick-upon-Tweed, the appropriately named Shambles in Galway and, most significantly, the large Royal Barracks in Dublin, usually overcrowded, and with chronic drainage and sanitation problems. In 1879 there was an outbreak of enteric fever in the officers' quarters. Ten years later, another epidemic led to the recall of the Army Sanitary Commission, and it produced a report severely critical of the state of the barracks and living conditions within it. Commenting to a Parliamentary Select Committee in 1888, the Inspector General of Fortifications, Sir Lothian Nicholson, agreed that the country's barracks were in good condition in general, but that some of them were in such a bad state that they needed rebuilding. He cited the Dublin barracks, as well as those for the cavalry at Burnley, Leeds and Regent's Park, and claimed that Galway was 'almost a disgrace to the nation'. Nicholson maintained that chronic underfunding for army accommodation was at the heart of the problem, because the annual estimates were always pared down by Parliament to an inadequate level. Buildings with an anticipated

Women in a man's world

Married quarters at Regents Park Barracks.

The army distrusted the presence of women, and always tried to discourage soldiers from marrying. From 1685, they were only permitted to marry with their commanding officer's permission. The number of married soldiers was restricted to 6 per cent of the establishment, about four or five wives in each company. The position of wives and their families not 'on the strength' was highly insecure, and was especially so when units were sent overseas. Then, the women who had come to be dependent on the regiment were left behind, often with little choice between living off the parish or on the street.

The position of women was little improved when the army gradually moved into permanent quarters. Under the 'corner system', married soldiers inhabited a lightly screened end of the barrack room, usually that furthest from the door. Here, every aspect of raising the family took place short of childbirth – a sordid and coarsening arrangement that only impinged gradually on the Victorian consciousness. 'Old soldiers told [in the 1890s, apparently with some relish] how they had seen a pure girl brought straight from the marriage service to the barrack room corner, and the tremor of mortal shame that overwhelmed her' (A.E. Sullivan, 'Married quarters, a retrospect', *The Army Quarterly, lxiii*, 1951–2, p.115).

The army began to accept more responsibility from the 1850s, though it did not produce any great increase in comfort. In most married quarters, the embarrassment of sharing a barrack room with single soldiers was replaced by that of sharing one with other married soldiers, in similarly open or crowded conditions. Married soldiers' huts at Aldershot were occupied by five or six families with no more privacy than they had enjoyed within the barracks. Model married quarters like that at Hounslow (see figs. 121 and 122, page 146) were the exception, and even these only provided a single room, below the standards of philanthropic urban housing.

Army policy in allowing women into barracks has been described as 'an attempt to maximise the benefits accruing to the regiment from the presence of a small number of women, without disturbing the men's primary allegiance to the regiment' (Trustram, 1984, p.68). In return for being tolerated, women on the strength in barracks were expected to contribute to servicing the regiment through a number of domestic roles, principally washing, cleaning, sewing and later, in the nineteenth century, nursing and teaching.

These were duties also carried out by men, and their allocation to women, whether or not they were paid, depended on the attitude of regimental commanding officers. Washhouses were built at barracks from the 1830s, but only later were drying houses provided, and in wet weather, laundry had to be suspended, dripping, among the beds. NCOs' wives tended to be given more gentle tasks such as employment as nurses in hospitals, or as the schoolmistresses who instructed the children of the married soldiers in the infant school. Married quarters and regimental education both contributed to the formation of the service family, which, by the end of the century, the army was coming to appreciate and foster for its stability and understanding of service ideals and customs, and as a valuable source of recruits.

lifespan of a hundred years could not be adequately funded by yearly allocations.[12]

Pressed by the Army Sanitary Commission and the Inspector General, Stanhope instigated what was to be the first of a series of Acts to re-finance construction and accelerate repairs. Instead of an annual sum, the Government returned to the system used for the localization depots, and asked Parliament to grant a large loan, to pay for some new barracks and for improvements to raise the living standards in existing ones (see Figures 157 and 158). The 1890 Barracks Act raised a loan of £4.1 million. Roughly half was to complete the reconstruction in permanent materials of the 'great camps' at Aldershot, Shorncliffe, Colchester and the Curragh, and of the overcrowded huts on Woolwich Common. Priority was given to improvements to the Royal Barracks in Dublin – where the magnificent centrepiece to the Royal Square was pointlessly demolished and the corners of the neighbouring courtyards knocked out, to improve the flow of air and disperse any lurking 'miasmas' – to Dover Castle, where the worst casemates were to be given up, and to Enniskillen, Leeds and Regent's Park Barracks. New quarters were ordered for Belfast, Dublin, Portsmouth and within the Plymouth Citadel, as well as Malta, Gibraltar and the Cape, and married soldiers' apartments were to be provided at various other stations.[13] Map 7 shows the main barracks and depots in 1899.

The sudden availability of capital for new buildings seems to have released a strongly repressed desire for architectural expression on the part of the Royal Engineers. A brief series of large and richly ornamental barracks was built in Britain and in the colonies which exploited the sudden change from parsimony to generosity. These included the Free-Renaissance-style Grangegorman (now McKee) Barracks in Dublin and a large, Italianate barracks in Malta, new quarters for the garrisons at Plymouth and Portsmouth, and a replacement for the Winchester depot, which was destroyed by fire in 1894.

---

[12] Parliamentary Papers (House of Commons), 1888, *viii*, *Report of the Select Committee of the House of Commons on the Army Estimates*, p.763.
[13] PRO WO33/A50, *Proposed expenditure under the Barracks Bill*, 6 May 1890; Parliamentary Papers (House of Commons), 1900 (52), *xlviii*, *Estimates of Expenditure under the Barracks Act of 1890*.

Map 7 Barracks first built with the Military and Naval Loans before the First World War

Infantry:
Aberdeen
Aldershot
Armagh
Athlone
Ayr
Bedford
Belfast
Berwick-upon-Tweed
Beverley
Birr
Bodmin
Bradford
Brecon
Bristol
Bury
Bury St Edmunds
Canterbury
Cardiff
Carlisle Castle
Castlebar
Caterham
Chatham
Chester Castle
Chichester Camp
Clonmel
Colchester
Curragh
Derby
Devizes
Doncaster
Dorchester
Dover Castle and Western Heights
Dublin
Dundee
Durham
Edinburgh
Exeter
Fleetwood
Fort George
Galway
Glasgow Mill Hill
Glencorse
Guildford
Halifax
Hamilton
Hounslow
Inverness
Kingston
Lanark
Lancaster
Leicester
Lichfield
Lincoln
Maidstone
Naas
Newcastle upon Tyne
Newry
Northampton
Norwich
Nottingham
Omagh
Oxford
Perth
Plymouth
Pontefract
Portsmouth
Preston
Reading
Richmond (Yorks.)
Salisbury Plain (Tidworth)
Shrewsbury
Stafford
Stirling Castle
Sunderland
Taunton
Tralee
Trowbridge
Warley
Warrington
Warwick
Winchester
Wolverhampton
Woolwich
Worcester
Wrexham
York

Cavalry:
Aldershot
Ballincollig
Belfast
Canterbury
Colchester
Curragh
Dublin
Dunkalk
Edinburgh
Glasgow
Hounslow
London and Windsor
Leeds
Newbridge
Salisbury Plain (Tidworth)
Seaforth
Shornecliffe
York

Artillery:
Aldershot
Bristol
Cahir
Christchurch
Clonmel
Colchester
Curragh
Dorchester
Exeter
Hilsea
Ipswich
Newbridge
Newcastle upon Tyne
Salisbury Plain (Tidworth)
Shornecliffe
London – St John's Wood
Weedon Bec
Woking
Woolwich

Naval barracks:
Chatham
Devonport
Portsmouth

Marines barracks:
Chatham
Deal
Eastney
Gosport
Plymouth

Source: Report of the Committee on Barracks Accommodation (1900), PRO WO33/175.

Legend:
- Army Camps
- New Army Barracks
- New Naval Barracks
- ■ Existing Infantry Barracks
- ▶ Existing Cavalry Barracks
- ♦ Existing Artillery Barracks
- ● Existing Marines Barracks

1872–1914: Localization and the 'Great Camps'

Figure 157 One of the two surviving huts, Oudenarde Barracks, Marlborough Lines, Aldershot, which housed 24 men each. They are the only remaining Victorian military accommodation at Aldershot to have survived the 1960s clearance, and now house the Aldershot Military Museum, including a reconstructed interior.

The new barracks intended for the garrison of the Citadel at Plymouth were to replace those of the late-seventeenth century for the artillery and garrison described in Chapter One, although the large Governor's House, the Great Store and the chapel remained. As with the new barracks which were erected within the Tower of London and at Dover Castle in the 1850s (see Figures 102 and 103, pages 128–9), the new buildings were designed to respect their historic context, by adopting a style considered harmonious with de Gomme's fort (see Figure 159). The attitude of the Victorian War Office to their own historic estate was intimated by Ingress Bell, who headed the civilian draughtsmen in the Design Branch from 1890, and who was responsible for the officers' mess: 'The citadel at Plymouth being an historical place, the buildings were allowed to be

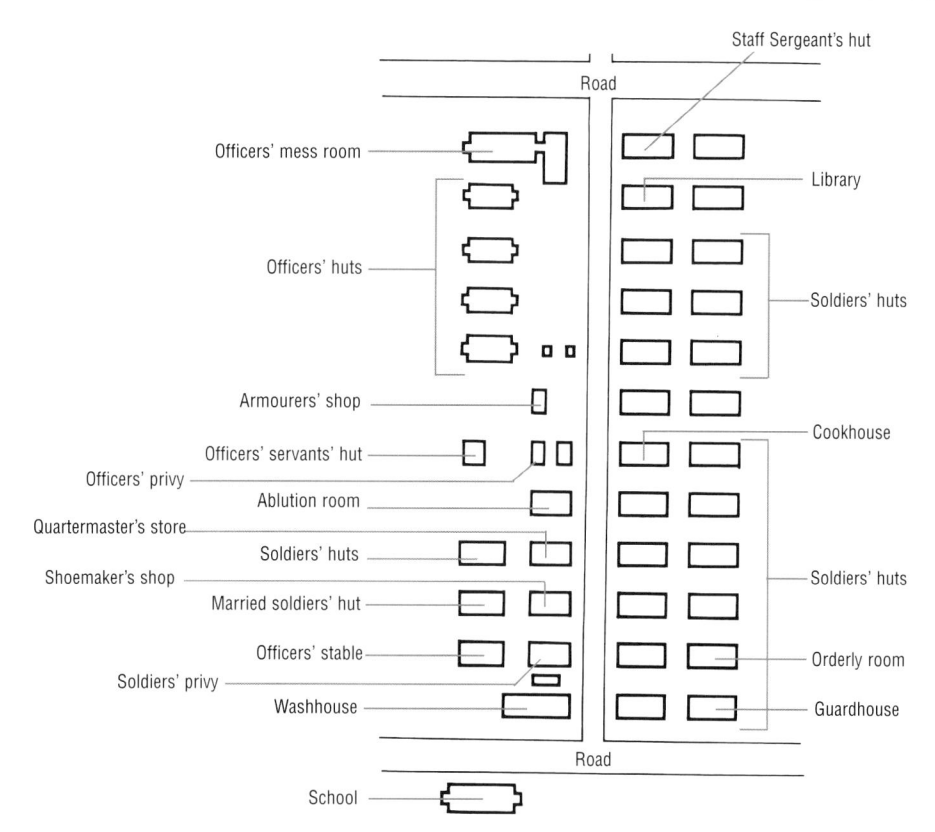

Figure 158 Aldershot huts laid out on the company system, showing the neat lines of soldiers' huts separated by a road from those of the officers, married soldiers, and the various workshops and stores. The Marlborough Lines replaced the South Camp from 1881. The North Camp was replaced by T-shaped huts of the Stanhope Lines.

Figure 159 The separate canteen at The Citadel, an early example enabling soldiers to eat outside their rooms.

treated on a somewhat more liberal scale than the ordinary run of [barracks].'[14] This is most apparent in the soldiers' quarters, which backed directly onto the ramparts and were the work of the architect T. Rogers Kitsell (see Figure 160). They were composed of four of the standard depot-type barracks (see Figure 174, page 193), joined end to end, with the outer pair rotated forward to form the wings of a wide quadrangle. In deference to its situation, Kitsell clothed it in a slightly anachronistic early seventeenth-century dress, with mullioned windows and a few simple Renaissance details, and placed the recreation and reading rooms in a gabled, E-plan section at the centre.[15]

It is clear from the barracks at both Norwich and Plymouth that the response of the Design Branch to more demanding sites or more liberal finances was to use surface decoration and skilful disposition to disguise the employment of units of a standard size. The same approach was again followed in 1894 after the old King's House Barracks in Winchester was gutted by a great fire. The King's House had been one of two new royal palaces commissioned by Charles II from Christopher Wren. However, work was summarily cancelled by James II when he took the throne, with new stone on the way to the site being diverted to the house of a courtier. The shell stood empty and unused for years, until it was taken over and adapted for French prisoners during the Seven Years War, and later for the American War. It was ultimately fitted out for barracks by the Barracks Department, as we have seen, in the late 1790s. Additional facilities, including an officers' quarters, school, chapel, militia store and canteen, were constructed from the 1850s on ground to the north, which was known as the Lower Barracks, and localization turned the whole complex into the second largest depot in Britain.

After the fire, the Inspector General of Fortifications sent his architect, Ingress Bell, down to Winchester to have a look at the ruins and see what could be done. Bell concluded that the best thing was to pull it down and start again – 'all the little rooms built intercommunicating at the time of Charles II would not do for our modern barracks' – but to try to incorporate as much of the old stonework as possible: 'the pediments and Corinthian columns and other things which were unharmed in the old buildings were to be re-used ... and consequently something in the character of Sir Christopher Wren's work was to

[14] PRO WO33/233 A758, *Report of the Commission to Inquire into the Employment of Royal Engineers in the Construction etc of Barracks*, p.41.
[15] *The Builder* (1898), **75**, pp.104–5.

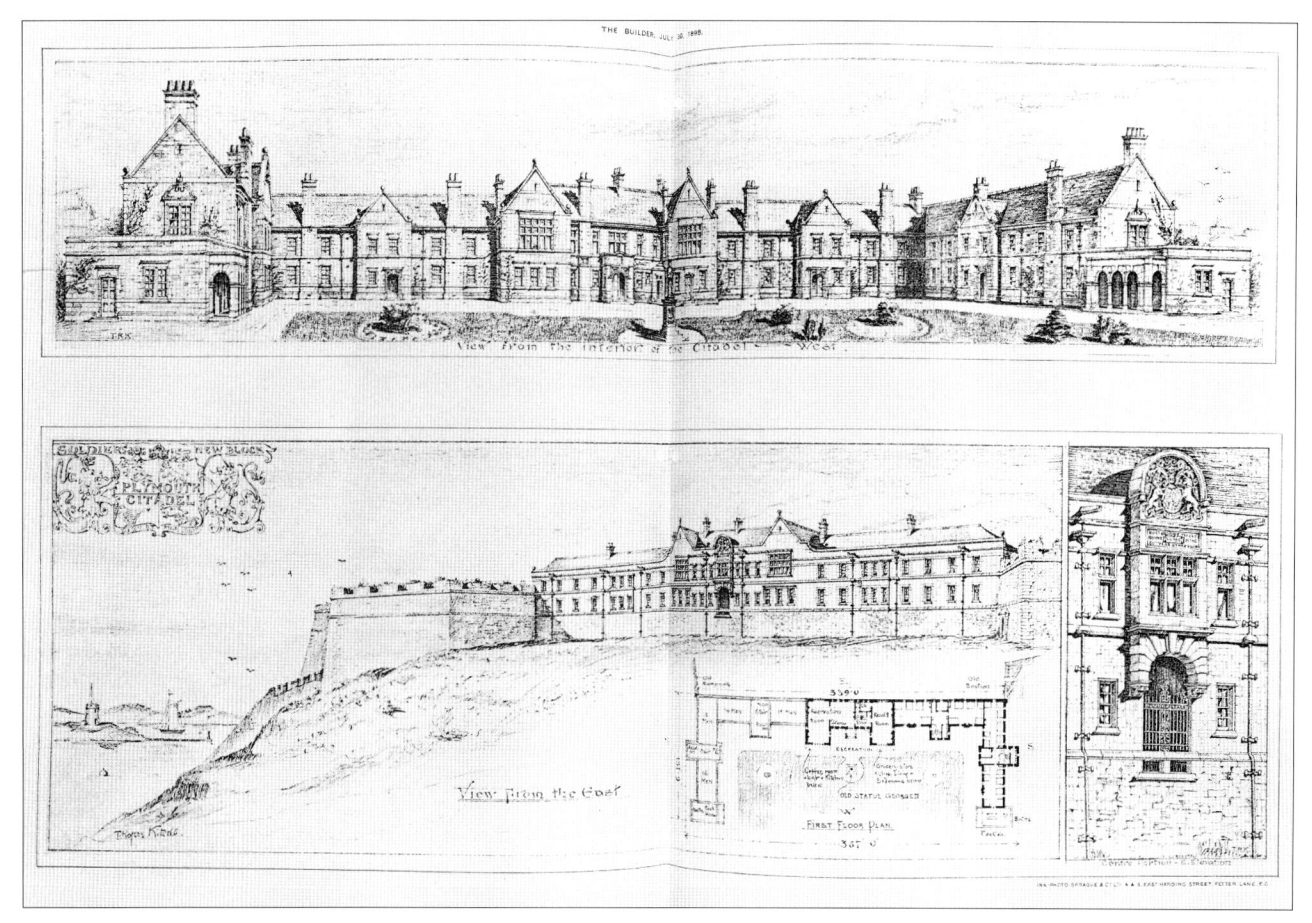

Figure 160 T. Rogers Kitsell's plans for the new garrision quarters at The Citadel, as illustrated in *The Builder*.

be given to the new block'.[16]

Bell's new Peninsula Barracks (see Figure 161) formed three unconnected sides to a wide quadrangle, closed by the mid-nineteenth-century officers' mess to the south which had survived the fire. The two main barrack blocks to the west and north included imposing porticoes with giant-order Corinthian columns, used as they had been when forming the central feature of Wren's palace, and late seventeenth-century Portland stone window sills, door jambs and dressings were worked into the new walls. In terms of planning, however, Bell did little more than his colleague at Plymouth, and behind the Wrenish livery of bright red brick and white dressings, the barracks are again the standard dormitory types used for the depots.[17]

There is some irony that Wren's stonework, carved at a time of profound political opposition to the very existence of a standing army, should end up in a barracks, and moreover at such a palatial, autocratic one as this. The Peninsula Barracks is one of the few from the high imperial years where a visitor might apprehend the ghosts of an army which then controlled the largest empire the world has ever known (see Figure 162).

A third example of the free spending and consequent lavish design which the Barracks Act released was the new quarters built for infantry and artillery in Portsmouth from the late 1880s (see Figure 163). Apart from the partly rebuilt Hilsea Barracks, and the numerous forts and batteries surrounding the dockyard town, the garrison, local artillery and transit regiments passing through

---

[16] PRO WO33/233 A758, *Report of the Commission to Inquire into the Employment of Royal Engineers in the Construction etc of Barracks*, p.42.
[17] PRO WO32/18419.

Figure 161 Wren's unfinished royal palace was used as barracks from the 1790s. Much of the stonework was re-used after it was destroyed by fire.

Portsmouth all still had to be lodged in an agglomeration of antiquated quarters in a tight corner of the old town, up against the remains of the dockyard ramparts. These included the old Four House and Clarence Barracks, Colewort Barracks (a decayed conversion dating from the late eighteenth century), the Cambridge Barracks and the Anglesey Transit Barracks which were built on the eve of the Crimean War. In one of the periodic rearrangements made between the Admiralty and the War Office, Anglesey was incorporated into the first seamen's barracks; Clarence and Four House were demolished, and by infilling the old Lines, a large, new site was created in the heart of the town.

The new Victoria Barracks had already been commenced in 1880, by convict labour, for an infantry regiment. Following the Barracks Act, the new Clarence Barracks was begun in 1890, by private contractors, for six garrison battalions of the Royal Artillery.[18] They were designed under the Assistant Inspector General of Fortifications responsible for barracks, Colonel Philip Ravenhill, and his successor, from 1882, Colonel R.N. Dawson-Scott. The latter's signature is on the drawing of the officers' quarters, but it is not known if a civilian architect, such as Bell, was also involved. In any case, the buildings were an astonishing change from the standard, utilitarian types of the localization programme.

The Clarence officers' quarters, for instance, were a highly Picturesque, free-style composition, very un-English, which included a central clock tower, stairs in detached, conical turrets, and a billiard room in a sort of Great Hall at the back (see Figure 164, page 100). It was built in 1886, and transferred to the Victoria Barracks when new officers' quarters were provided at Clarence. Sadly for Portsmouth, and for posterity, both Victoria and Clarence were damaged in the war, and the site was subsequently cleared to make way for post-war development. The only part which survives is the former regimental institute, now the City Museum, an even more exotic confection than the officers' lodgings, which was apparently inspired – rather disloyally – by the architecture of seventeenth-century France (see Figure 165).

---

[18] PRO WORK41/620, *Clarence Barracks, Portsmouth.*

The Salisbury Plain manoeuvring ground

Once accustomed to the use of loans for military works, the Conservative Governments of the 1890s resorted to them repeatedly to finance the expansions of both military and naval spending. Between 1897 and 1901, three more Military Works Acts were passed, authorizing substantial spending under the four headings of 'defence works', 'barracks services', 'artillery ranges' and 'staff and contingencies'. The first was for £5.4 million, over half of it for the completion of earlier works begun after the Barracks Act. Under Lord Lansdowne, the Secretary of State, there was also a change in spending policy, since the money was no longer used solely to put the great camps into a satisfactory condition and remedy the worst defects of the older barracks. One of the persistent criticisms of the Cardwell changes was that localization involved dispersion, at a time when there were increasing calls for troops to be quartered in corps of a division to improve the opportunities for large-scale training. Accordingly, the 1897 Military Works Act included £600,000 for the purchase of 42,000 acres (16,996.8 hectares) of Salisbury Plain, which was effected by the Military Manoeuvres Act the following year.

But with the size of the army rising to meet the demands of the fighting in South Africa, more new accommodation was also needed. Between 1897/8 and 1899/1900, the strength of the army at home rose from 117,000 officers and men to 132,000. Lansdowne's second Military Works Act in 1899 provided a further £4 million, which included £2.8 million for barracks. The money was spent partly on expanding the camps at Colchester and the Curragh, and also for a completely new camp on the edge of the newly acquired manoeuvring ground, at the tiny village of Tidworth on the border between Hampshire and Wiltshire.

These new quarters marked a return to the strict use of departmental types, after the historicist indulgences of the early 1890s. Under the Deputy Inspector General of Fortifications, Colonel C.M. Watson, the Design Branch of the War Office had

Figure 162 Soldiers on parade at Peninsula Barracks, photographed just before the First World War.

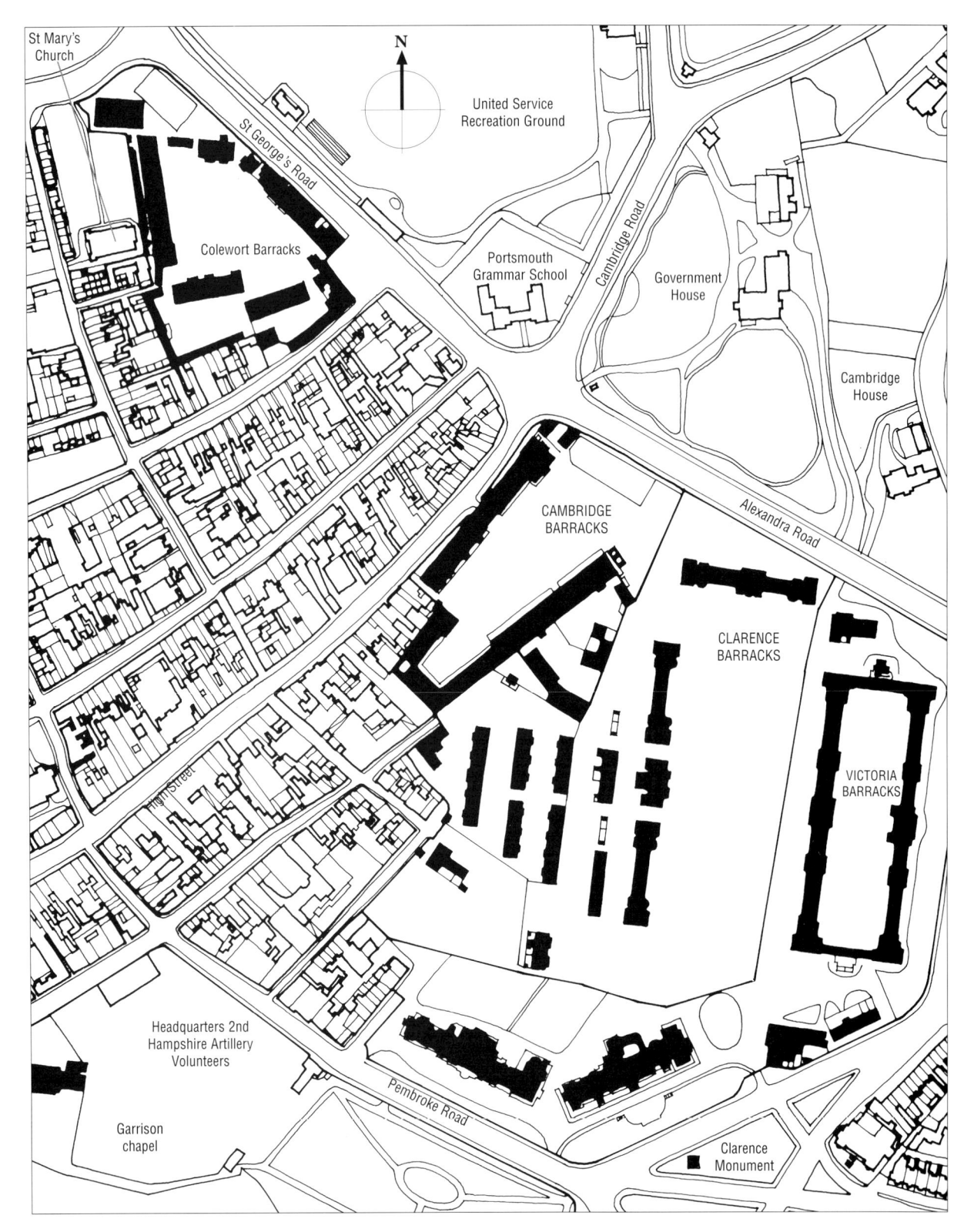

Figure 163 Military accommodation in Portsmouth was reorganized during the 1880s, when the old ramparts round the dockyard were filled in. The map, redrawn from the 1890 Ordnance Survey, shows the huge, new Clarence and Victoria Barracks, the Cambridge Barracks just to the north, with their C-shaped former warehouses, and the eighteenth-century Colewort Barracks, set apart towards the old Gunwharf.

continued to develop these to suit the rising standards which were expected for living accommodation, and the changes to the scale of military quarters to allow corps-level concentrations. More regular block plans were established based on a regular grid, in which different combinations could be deployed, according to the size of the station and its site. Two types were erected according to this programme at Colchester, the single-company block type for Sobraon Barracks, and the half-battalion type for Goojerat, as well as at the new Keane and Gough Barracks at the Curragh. The most complete exposition of modern barracks planning, however, was at Tidworth, where an open, green-field site presented few restrictions on layout.

The head of the Design Branch, Major E.H. Hemmings, explained the brief rules guiding barracks layout to the Royal Engineers' school at Chatham in 1900. They were thoroughly pragmatic. The parade for drawing up a battalion needed to be 100 by 150 yards (91.4 by 137.2 metres) square, and adjoining the drill hall. The barracks accommodation, with associated cookhouses, washhouses, latrines and dining rooms – the latter an innovation of the late 1890s – occupied separate areas from the married men's quarters, with a laundry and drying ground for the traditional occupations of the soldiers' wives. The CO and the officers should enjoy 'the best available frontage, if possible on a private road not used as a thoroughfare by the men, and with their stables conveniently placed'. The regimental sergeant major should be near the guardhouse, which was beside the entrance and overlooking the parade; the sergeants' mess was an important building convenient to the men's quarters, as were the recreational establishments, canteen, fives courts or shooting gallery. No other considerations were required than 'easy approach, simple drainage, general symmetry and free access of air and sunshine'.[19] The British approach to barracks planning remained free of any intellectual or social dogmatism and was firmly pragmatic.

Figure 165 The former Institute at the Clarence Barracks, Portsmouth.

Tidworth was intended to house eight battalions of infantry, plus units of the Royal Engineers, Army Service Corps and the necessary garrison accessories (see Figure 166). Its anticipated cost was £1.6 million. Each battalion unit was of the standard type pioneered at Goojerat. Long barrack blocks for two companies were divided into eight rooms, each for 12 men, which were easier to heat than the long, 24-man dormitories of the depots had been. The rooms were connected by an external passage forming a full-length veranda, leading to sets of stairs built between the veranda and two free-standing, square towers which contained the NCOs' rooms and the company stores (see Figures 167 and 168). Pairs of parallel barrack blocks were linked by covered ways to a separate dining room, and between the two dining rooms was a central washhouse. The H-shaped unit thus formed held a half-battalion of 32 companies. A second matching block formed a full battalion, with its own officers' mess and quarters (see Figure 169), guardhouse, quartermaster's store, drill shed, sergeants' mess, canteen and stables. Named after battles in India and Afghanistan – Aliwal, Assaye, Bhurtpore, Candahar, Delhi, Jellalabad, Lucknow and Meanee – the eight units built at Tidworth followed the curve of the valley. Whilst this meant that individual barracks fell short of Hemmings's ideal of being aligned north–south so that sunlight could penetrate both sides of the rooms, his strictures on

---

[19] Hemmings (1900), p.52.

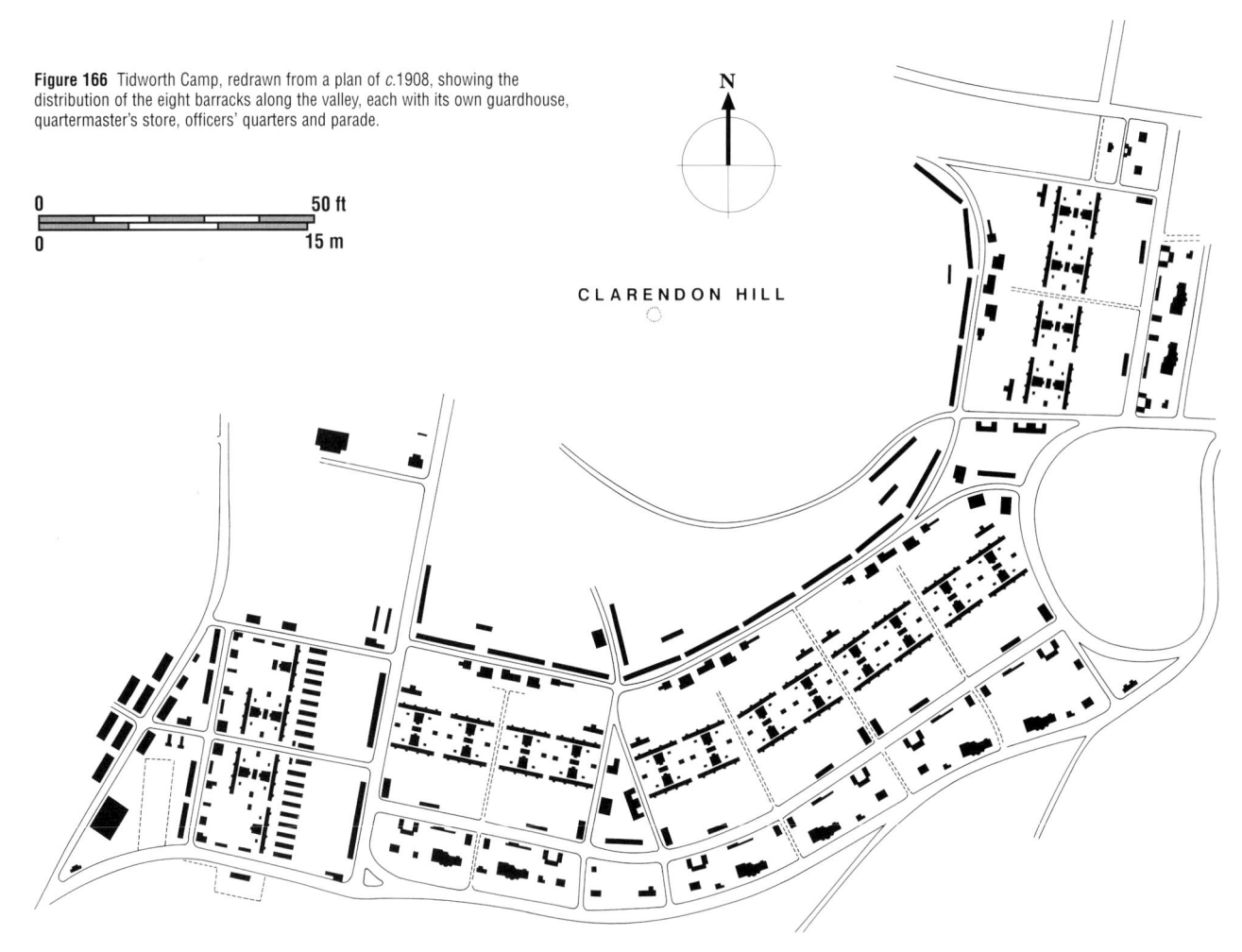

Figure 166 Tidworth Camp, redrawn from a plan of c.1908, showing the distribution of the eight barracks along the valley, each with its own guardhouse, quartermaster's store, officers' quarters and parade.

the quality of drainage were met admirably. Other buildings which were provided at brigade level included the institutes, riding schools, married quarters, hospital and school. A large garrison church was built in 1914, a late Gothic Revival building constructed from terracotta on a steel frame, by C.E. Ponting, who was the Diocesan Surveyor for Wiltshire.

Reversals and confusion in barracks policy

The expansion of barracks space represented by Tidworth and the other new permanent quarters was slow in coming. In 1900 and 1901, the middle years of the Second Boer War, a Committee investigated barracks accommodation in the light of developments since the 1899 Act and continued growth in the army's establishment. It reported that a home establishment of 87 infantry battalions was required, out of a total strength of 12 Guards regiments and 158 of the line. More new quarters were urgently needed at home for the cavalry, which numbered three Household Guards and 18 line regiments. There were 13 battalions of Horse Artillery and 84 of Field Artillery for whom quarters had to be found, apart from the 39 companies of the Royal Garrison Artillery occupying dockyard defences and coastal batteries. New infantry barracks were needed in London for five battalions, partly to replace Windsor, which was in a dangerous condition, and in the North-West Division. New quarters for the cavalry were proposed for Edinburgh, with the Napoleonic Piers Hill Cavalry Barracks given over to the Artillery. In Ireland,

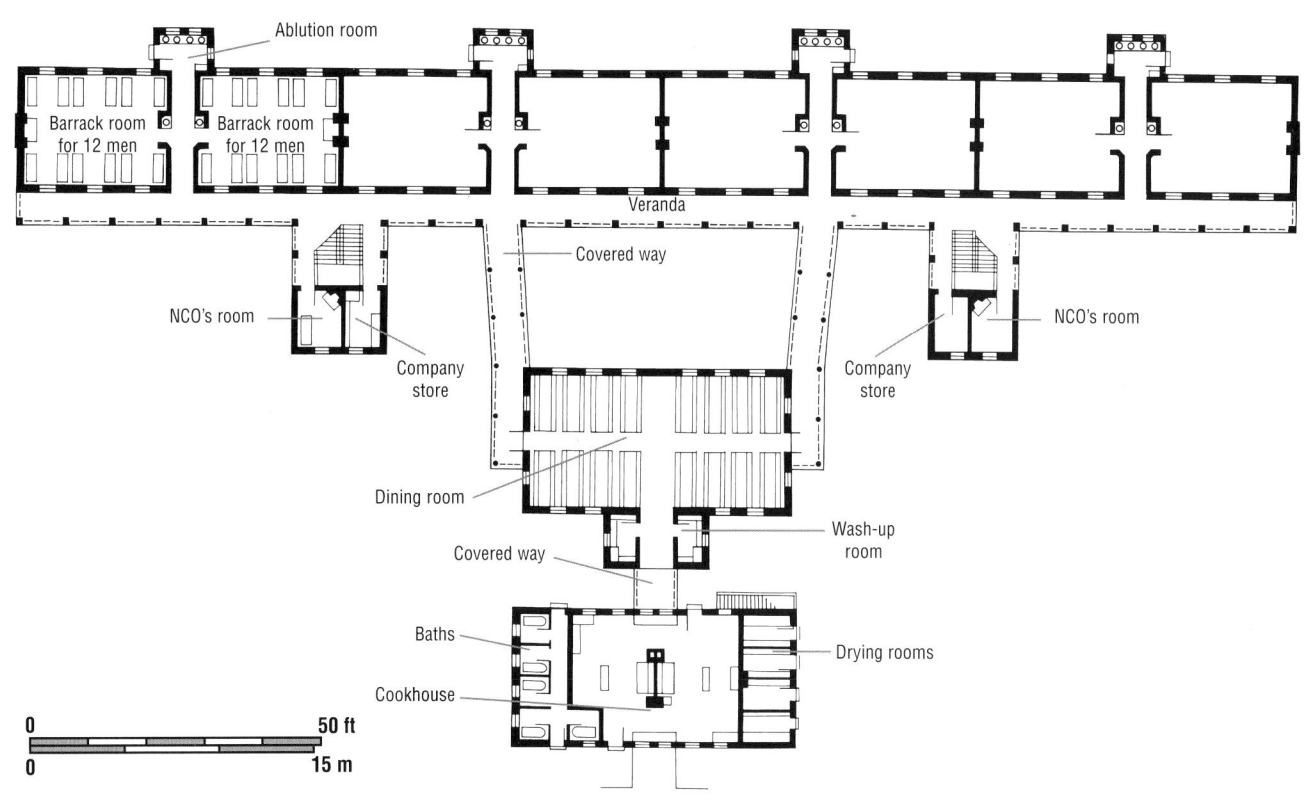

Figure 167 Standard site plans for a brigade of infantry. Similar plans were used at Colchester, the Curragh and Tidworth.

Dundalk was to be closed down.[20]

Accordingly, Lord Lansdowne's successor from 1900, St John Brodrick, proposed a third Military Works Act, which was passed in 1901, this time for a loan for £6.3 million. Barracks again accounted for the greatest part, £4.2 million. Further large camps were planned at Bulford, off Salisbury Plain, and at Stobbs, in Scotland. The largest part of the loan was for Aldershot, Kildare, Lichfield, Salisbury Plain and Shorncliffe, and for extra accommodation at the other large camps. Under this Act, the wartime expedient of 'temporary' timber huts – the final eradication of which had been one of the prime aims behind the acceptance of the loans system under the first Barracks Act – were once again resorted to.

This high level of expenditure, which by March 1903 had reached £3 million on barracks, out of almost £10 million, took place in the context of continued attempts by Balfour's Government to achieve an acceptable reform of the shape and structure of the

Figure 168 Jellalabad Barracks, Tidworth. Separate barrack rooms were accessed by a two-storey walkway. (Fig. 167 shows the standard plan of this building).

army, and to prevent further rises in its size and cost. Later in the year, Brodrick, his scheme for an army of six corps discredited, was replaced as Secretary of State by a long-term proponent of army reform, Hugh Arnold-Forster. However, his own elaborate schemes similarly failed to find much political support. In 1905, the Conservatives lost power, and the following spring, in April 1906, the

[20] PRO WO33/175 A647, *Report of the Commission on Barracks Accommodation*, 1900.

Figure 169 Officers' quarters at Aldershot. These were a widely built type, and other examples can be found at Tidworth and Colchester.

whole programme of loans was cancelled by the new Liberal Secretary of State, Richard Haldane.[21] The camps intended for Scotland and Salisbury Plain were cancelled, and the large cavalry barracks in Norwich, for which Arnold-Forster had laid the foundation stone, was abandoned in order to fulfil the Liberals' commitment to reduce their predecessors' inflated military budget. By this time, £9 million had been consumed out of a total of £13.5 million made available under the military loans heading of 'barracks services'. The balance of £4.5 million was never spent.[22]

Barracks under civilian administration

The protracted search for a politically acceptable reform of the army undertaken by successive Conservative administrations was paralleled by a series of inquiries into the possible options by the political 'fixer' Lord Esher. His widespread investigations into army administration included a report, published in 1902, into the perceived overstretching of the Corps of Royal Engineers through their multifarious quasi-civilian activities at home, to the detriment of their wartime effectiveness. Esher recommended that the War Office staff of engineers be replaced by a new body, headed by a Director of Works equivalent to the Inspector General for Fortifications, with four principal architects, two of whom should be civilians. These would have responsibility for all War Department buildings and land except fortifications.[23]

The appearance of Esher's General Reports in early 1904 led to the formation of an Army Council and General Staff, as well as the decentralization of various executive duties from the War Office, which included barracks. In the end, despite the opposition of the Royal Engineers, a wholly civilian Barrack Construction Department was formed, in February 1904, under a Director of Barracks Construction, to take charge of all home military quarters outside of fortifications. The Royal Engineers thereby lost the traditional responsibility for barracks which they had exercised since the seventeenth century, although they continued to oversee quarters at foreign stations and the colonies.

The architect chosen as the new director was Harry Bell Measures. The experience which presumably recommended him was acquired in designing model homes for working men in London and Birmingham, called 'Rowton Houses'. Measures completely rethought the spatial considerations of barracks and abandoned the long-entrenched principles of subdivision and separation of the various elements and functions. He also brought a vigorous and colourful – if not necessarily measured – sense of composition to the becalmed 'Type' architecture of the old Design Branch.

Measures's first project was the new cavalry barracks in Norwich. His proposal consisted of a five-storey, C-shaped block, in which all the ancillary and recreational functions were congregated together on the ground floor and in the covered courtyard. Above, the four troops of a squadron were housed within a single floor, each with its own separate access. The stables were in separate ranges parallel to each side, and the quarters of the higher ranks in suitable detached buildings. An enthusiast for this new barracks architecture after the dullness of the Royal

---

[21] Spiers (1980), p.10.
[22] Watson (1954), pp.164–71.
[23] PRO WO33/233 A758, *Report of the Committee to Inquire into the Employment of Royal Engineers in the Construction etc. of Barracks*, 1902. From a conservation standpoint, it is interesting to note that the report recognized that certain sites such as the Tower and Edinburgh Castle were of 'great historical value', and recommended their transfer from the War Office to the Office of Works.

Figure 170 Redford Barracks, Edinburgh, showing the cavalry officers' mess and quarters (above), and the infantry barracks centre block and north-east wing (right).

Engineers' approach to the subject, the Secretary of State, Arnold-Forster, laid the foundation stone in October 1905. Six months later, it was cancelled by his successor, Richard Haldane, and work was abandoned.[24]

Measures had more luck with the long-planned Redford Barracks at Edinburgh, which was begun in 1909 and completed in 1915 (see Figure 170). This enormous complex, the largest permanent military quarters erected north of the border since the completion of Skinner's Fort George in the mid-eighteenth century, contained both cavalry and infantry barracks – the former planned similarly to the aborted Norwich station – and butterfly-plan officers' quarters and mess. Stylistically, Measures threw much of the vocabulary of Free Imperial Baroque into a lively and highly eclectic design, with polychromatic effects in brick and stone. Much the same approach was taken for the huge new cadets' accommodation at Sandhurst New College, built at the same time. These enormous piles represent the culmination of a brief but luxuriant flowering of richly decorated military quarters, corresponding to changes in the financing and administration of barracks construction.

The first sailors' barracks

By the 1850s, the Admiralty's traditional manning practice – raising or pressing a crew when a ship was to sail, and dismissing it when it returned – was becoming inefficient and wasteful. The revolution in the construction, propulsion and arming of the Royal

---

[24] Arnold-Forster (1906), pp.297–301.

Navy's ships from the mid-nineteenth century produced corresponding changes in their manpower requirements. There was an increasing demand for skilled and specialized ratings, who could not so easily be rounded up ashore or casually laid off at the end of a journey and lost to the merchant fleet. Long Term Service for ten years was therefore introduced for naval ratings in 1853, and as with the European armies of the early seventeenth century, the requirement of higher levels of technical accomplishment leading to the retention of a long-term or standing force resulted in the construction of barracks, where seamen could train and maintain their proficiency.

Accommodation for sailors who were neither at sea nor on leave was traditionally provided in old vessels moored near the dockyard, known as 'hulks'. Dockyard hands and their families had lived in hulks since the late sixteenth century. After the loss of the American colonies, they were used as a depository for prisoners of war, and this use expanded greatly in the early nineteenth century for French prisoners of war and for convicts, like Dickens's Magwich, awaiting transportation to Australia. In 1841, estuarine hulks provided a miserable home for 3,625 convicts.[25]

Their use as prisons declined after a condemnatory report on those at Woolwich in 1847, and they were given up ten years later, but they continued to be used by the Royal Navy. At Portsmouth, the depot hulks in which the naval reserve was quartered at the end of the nineteenth century were over a hundred years old, though they had a bright, ship-shape appearance. The gun ports were replaced by rather quaint casement windows, and a corrugated-iron roof covered the decks. Inside, however, conditions were cramped. Dark, dank and insanitary, not long after the practice had been abandoned for convicts, quartering sailors in hulks was criticized by Admiral Sir Charles Napier. Urging their replacement by dockyard barracks, in 1859 Napier wrote: 'I think these hulks are the curse of the navy.'[26]

Five years later, plans were drawn up for a seamen's barracks at Devonport, but nothing came of them.

Work was finally started in 1879 at Devonport, on land adjoining the Keyham Steam Extension to the north of the seventeenth-century dockyard, adjoining what would later become the Dreadnought yard.[27] Ten years later, complementary barracks were also begun at Portsmouth, and at the end of the century at Chatham.

It is unclear who held direct responsibility for the planning and design of these large complexes. The Director of Works at the Admiralty, C. Pasley, submitted a plan for a suitable 'type' for the accommodation in 1879, whilst some Plymouth local histories credit the first phase to Sir John Jackson, the civil engineer responsible for the dockyard extension. The resident Superintendent Engineer at Devonport, Lieutenant Colonel Percy Smith RE, exercised detailed control, and a similar arrangement to that of the Inspector General of Fortifications' department and local Commanding Royal Engineers officers probably pertained. In 1890, Major General Sir Henry Pilkington RE, who had been the Superintendent Officer at Chatham, took over as Director of Engineering, and he was Engineer-in-Chief of the Naval Loan Works Department from 1894, with responsibility for the extension of the first phase from 1898. A plan of the site in 1884 was signed 'JWS', probably Major Johnson William Savage RE.[28] The later extensions were supervised at Devonport by Major Monro Wilson, Admiralty Civil Engineer, acting for Major E.R. Kenyon RE, Superintending Engineer of Devonport Dockyard.[29]

Keyham Barracks, as it was initially called, was built in three phases. The first accommodation consisted of an H-shaped pair of ratings' blocks, similar in outline to a pavilion-plan hospital ward, and anticipating the layout of Goojerat and Tidworth army barracks. They were named Hawkins and Boscawen, and were occupied by 1889 (see Figures 171 and 174) but demolished in the 1960s.[30] Each contained a large, open dormitory the whole length of the building, heated by stoves, with space to hang 125 hammocks on all four floors (see Figure 172, page 101). The blocks were connected to

---

[25] W. Branch Johnson, *The English Prison Hulk* (London 1970).
[26] Dwyer (1960), p.12.
[27] PRO ADM116/727, *Admiralty Letters* 14, 18 January 1880.
[28] PRO WORK41/561 *Keyham Seaman's Barracks*. This information was kindly supplied by Roger Bowdler and Jonathan Coad.
[29] *Naval and Military Record*, 17 February 1898 and 3 May 1900.
[30] EH Plans Room, *Keyham barracks*.

1872–1914: Localization and the 'Great Camps'

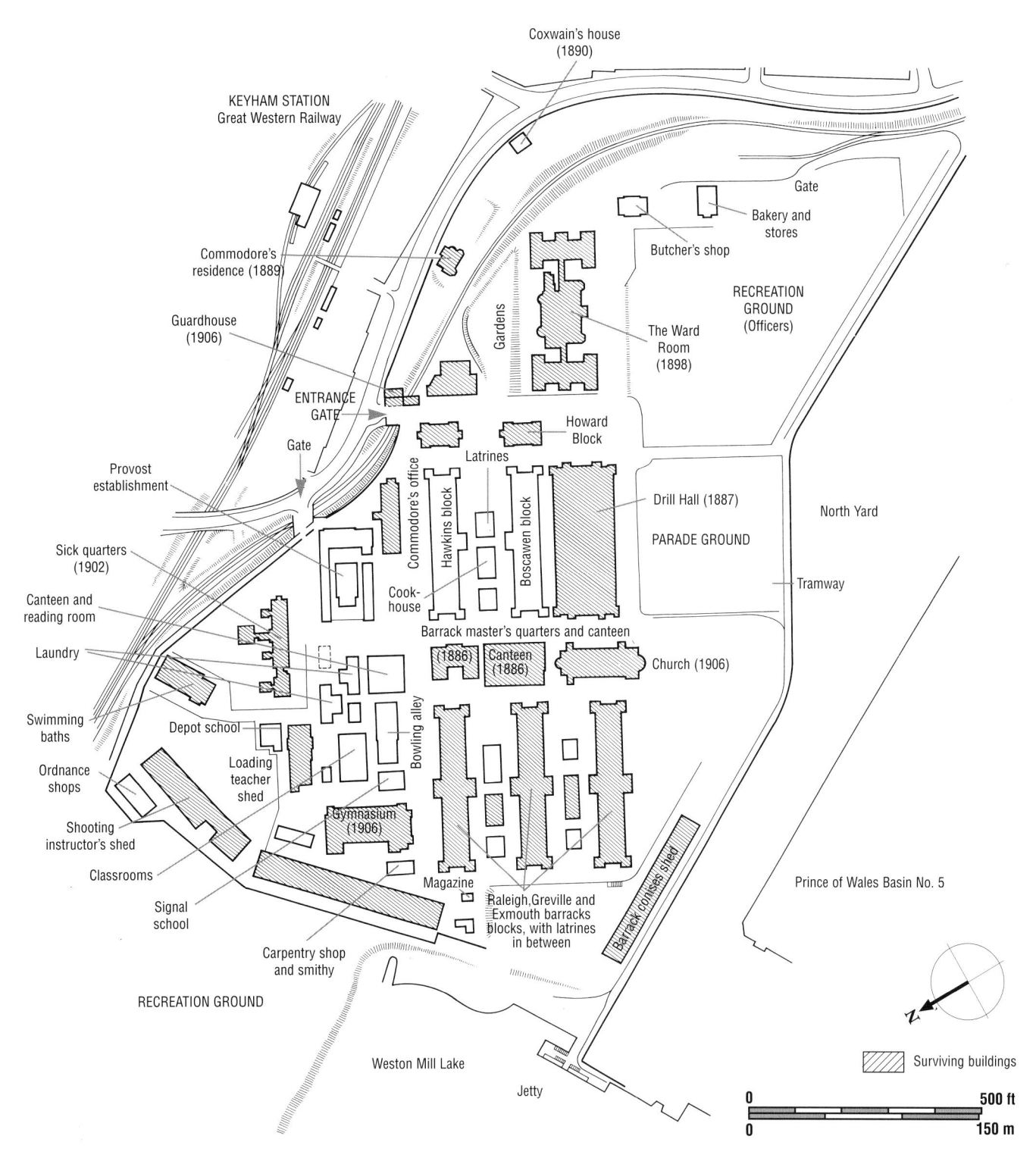

Figure 171 Keyham Barracks (later HMS *Drake*), Devonport, redrawn from a plan of *c.*1907. The two original barracks – Hawkins and Boscawen – are shown, with their respective officers' quarters at one end. These were succeeded by the great wardroom with its linked quarters, and the Raleigh, Exmouth and Greville Blocks for ratings.

Figure 173 The middle wardroom of HMS *Drake*, linked by bridges to officers' quarters each side, its grandiloquent architecture crisply cut out in carefully detailed limestone.

a central cookhouse and latrine block, in the same manner as at Tidworth. To one side were two officers' barracks (now used as offices), on the other side the quarters and office of the barrack master (later a theatre), and to the south stood a large, covered drill hall. The commandant's lodging, now called Drake House, was built in 1887.[31] In 1896, a large guardhouse was completed beside the entrance, topped by a campanile clock tower with a semaphore on top (see Figure 175). These barracks formed the steam reserve depot, and were occupied by men returning at the end of their leave, waiting to be drafted as crews for ships being newly commissioned.

The second phase was begun in 1898 with two further identical barracks, Raleigh and Grenville, and a very grandiose pile for officers' quarters and mess. The evolution of these buildings shows a progressive increase in the scale and self-importance of the officers' allocation at Keyham. The earliest known plan, from 1878, shows eight parallel barrack blocks, each with a small building for the officers at one end and a separate mess. Two of these were built before the plans were changed, and still survive.[32] After 1885, this approach was abandoned, and the officers were all brought together in a single, large range. As built, this consisted of a central wardroom with a domed belvedere, linked by bridges to flanking quarters containing 'cabins' for 106 officers (see Figure 173).

A fifth sailors' barracks, Exmouth, was added in the third phase, concluded in 1907, which included a doubling of the size of the drill shed, further buildings for training and education, a gym and a large church – one of four virtually identical naval churches built at Keyham (the only one in stone), Chatham and at the marines' barracks at Deal and Eastney.[33] The total capacity at Keyham of 4,895 men was divided between the captain, 118 officers, 84 warrant officers, 388 chief petty officers, 520 1st and 2nd class petty officers and 3,360 seamen and stokers, with 52 NCO marines, 336 marines and 36 domestics.[34]

Despite the uncertainty over the authorship of the plan and the architecture of the buildings, and a phased construction over almost thirty years, the design and detailing remained remarkably consistent. HMS *Drake* was on a similar scale to the army's 'great camps' like Tidworth and Colchester, but architecturally it was in a different dimension. The whole complex, from the clock tower to the latrines, was built of grey Plymouth limestone. Stylistically it was in that hybrid late nineteenth-

---

[31] *Naval and Military Record*, 6 June 1889, p.4.
[32] EH Plans Room, 8718 HF 9/8/1878, *Preliminary block plan; Military and Naval Record*, 17 February 1898, p.7.
[33] PSA Collection, RCHME Swindon, PLM/285-303.
[34] PRO WORK41/100.

century grammar known as Free Classicism, including Italian and Domestic Revival details, although on a scale that was far from domestic. Indeed, the size of the officers' range, raised on its rusticated basement and topped by the dome, foreshadowed the grandiloquence of Imperial Baroque, and the even less restrained work for the War Office of Harry Measures. It became known as HMS *Drake* in 1934.[35]

The naval barracks at Chatham and Portsmouth were architecturally similar to Keyham, though they were less richly executed, and both were built of brick. At Portsmouth, land so close to the dockyard on the scale required for a barracks was unobtainable. HMS *Victory* (later renamed HMS *Nelson* to avoid confusion with Nelson's nearby flagship) had to be adapted from the Anglesey Infantry Barracks dating from the Crimean War, which was vacated by the army in favour of the Victoria Barracks in the 1890s. Work began in 1888, and it was opened in 1903 for 4,000 men.[36]

Before their transfer to permanent quarters, seamen and officers at Chatham lived in the hulk HMS *Pembroke*, engine room ratings were housed in HMS *Adelaide*, while HMS *Algiers* was home to artisans and the Royal Marines. In 1897, all were marched out and up the road to HMS *Pembroke*, the new 'stone frigate'. The barracks were built on a long, narrow site on the side of a hill, on two levels. In terms of architecture, they were very close to their precursor at Devonport, though with more Arts and Crafts-style detailing to elements like the iron lamps and rain hoppers.[37] On the upper level, the four barrack blocks were arranged in parallel pairs, with separate canteens, ablution bays and central washhouses between. The magnificent wardroom for the officers with their flanking quarters, as at Devonport and Portsmouth, formed a fifth range overlooking the Commodore's House and the huge, new steam dockyard taking shape on St Mary's Island below. On the lower level immediately to the north were the dining room, a gymnasium, the swimming pool and an enormous drill shed.

Figure 174 HMS *Drake*. One of the four remaining seamen's barracks.

The construction of the three great naval barracks at the principal home bases coincided with accelerating naval competition, initially with France but later with Germany. This was effected through a massive investment in the navy and its shoreside facilities, financed by a series of Naval Loans, resulting in the development of warships of a size, speed and fighting power hitherto undreamt of. During the period of the erection of Keyham Barracks, Devonport Dockyard built 17 battleships, including five Dreadnoughts and 14 cruisers. By

Figure 175 HMS *Drake*. The entrance is dominated by the elaborate architecture of the tower, on top of which stood a semaphore for communication with the Admiralty.

---

[35] Brimacombe (1992), pp.20–6.
[36] Dwyer (1960), p.13.

[37] In the 1923 *Who's Who in British Architecture*, Francis Agutter laid claim to responsibility for designing HMS *Pembroke*, but the connection has not been substantiated elsewhere.

1914, on the eve of the war, it had expanded to become the largest naval dockyard in Europe. Today, with the men gone, the ships scrapped or sunk, and the yard's future still unclear, its barracks can still be seen to embody the Royal Navy at the height of its imperial pomp.

Postscript

Figure 176 An army camp being erected by volunteer soldiers in 1914.

'... on occasion a lecturer would give us a discourse on Cavalry Charges in the Coming War. He would tell us that he hoped it would constitute no breach of trust if he informed us in strictest confidence that the authorities knew that a war was drawing near on the Continent, that we should become involved in it, and that it would be a Cavalry War. At last the Horse would, thank God, come into its own ...' [1]

But it wasn't to be a cavalry war. It was a machine gun war. The horse's day had already passed. The grand, new cavalry barracks at Edinburgh was the last of its type. Admiring the splendid ranges at Redford, at Winchester, at HMS *Drake* or the New College at Sandhurst, words like 'imperial' or 'grandiloquent' come to mind – followed by 'hubris'. If the military architecture of the late Victorian and Edwardian years revealed the satisfaction of the army and navy with its recent military experience and likely future prospects, that which followed reflected the very different reality of twentieth-century war.

In August 1914, the home barracks had room for 174,800 men. By the end of the year, about eight times that number had responded to Kitchener's call

---

[1] Osbert Sitwell, *Great Morning* (London 1949), p.123.

Figure 177 The officers' mess at the former Royal Naval Air Service base at Mount Batten, Plymouth. It is typical of the neo-Georgian style favoured for barracks in the inter-war period, the great majority of which were built on air bases.

and, as in 1792, the available quarters were swamped. Echoing the complaints of the soldiers in Kent in that earlier crisis, recruits marched out of Fulwood Barracks heading for Preston Station, protesting: 'No Food, No Shelter, No Money.'[2] The Cardwell depots were overwhelmed, with six of them containing over 2,000 men, many times the normal capacity of around 350. Building permanent quarters for the New Army was not an immediate option, so billeting, canvas and hutment camps were adopted (see Figure 176). Billeting peaked over Christmas, though it continued throughout the war, tents were being phased out by the following year, but camps of huts provided the majority of barracks accommodation for the remainder of the war, and Captain P.N. Nissen's proposal for his eponymous arched, corrugated-iron hut in 1916 provided a rapidly built unit for assembling the camps. Bovington Camp in Dorset (later the home station of the Royal Armoured Corps) started out as a militia camp and training area which, by late 1914, contained 12,000 men living in tents. These were gradually replaced by huts, laid out in battalion lines, the following year. Catterick Camp, near Richmond in Yorkshire, became one of the largest New Army bases, with room for 40,000 men by 1915, and also became established on a permanent basis.

Most of the camps were given up after demobilization, and with the exception of the slow conversion of cavalry barracks as the army mechanized, the inter-war years were a period of retrenchment for the army (see Figure 177). The return to pressed expediency as war loomed again meant that the pre-1914 barracks, supplemented by encampments of huts, continued to form the basis for the army's accommodation throughout the Second World War.

Overhauling this ageing estate finally began in the 1960s, as post-empire Britain reassessed its armed forces' priorities in the light of the Cold War and membership of NATO. Many older barracks were vacated and demolished as the country's military geography shifted once again, and its barracks estate was rationalized and concentrated into fewer, larger centres. All the old civil order barracks in towns like Manchester and Birmingham were swept away, as were most of those planned by Napier, such as Bury and Bristol. The abandonment of the Cardwell system meant that barracks in towns like Bodmin and Oxford were no longer needed. When coastal defence ended in 1956, so did Dover Castle's strategic importance, and the large barracks within the castle and overlooking the Grand Shaft were flattened without thought to their historic value, or potential reuse. The mid-eighteenth-century Ordnance and Marines barracks in Chatham were also demolished, and almost all of the spectacular Victoria and Clarence Barracks in Portsmouth was cleared.

The services' accommodation was reorganized from 1963 under the Ministry for Public Buildings and Works, using its own staff and various private architectural partnerships. All but two of the brick huts at Aldershot were demolished, as well as the once-innovative permanent barracks, and replaced by more up-to-date quarters by the Ministry, working with the Building Design Partnership. The two prize-winning London barracks at Chelsea and Knightsbridge were knocked down and rebuilt, the latter by Sir Basil Spence with a controversial tower-block design. The timber quarters in Maidstone were replaced by a new Invicta Barracks, built using the CLASP and NENK building systems. The celebrated Richard Poulson had plenty of work from the Ministry, at Catterick, Bisley and elsewhere.

---

[2] I. Becket and K. Simpson, *A Nation in Arms* (Manchester 1985), p.166.

Postscript

Figure 178 Hillsborough Barracks in Sheffield has now been converted into a supermarket.

The end of the Cold War obliged the Ministry of Defence to undertake further evaluations of the British Forces accommodation needs, leading to further withdrawals and some closures of long occupied sites. It has also become vitally important for the military to retain personnel, which has meant keeping pace with their greater expectations of comfort. This is reflected in the improved standard of new 'junior ranks single living accommodation' – the 'barracks' of the 1990s, and the increasing recognition of the continued benefit provided by traditional barrack accommodation if it is upgraded to current standards. Far greater care is now exercised in the repair and adaption of the nation's military heritage by the Ministry of Defence, and many of the important historic sites covered in this book, such as the Royal Military Academy at Sandhurst, the Royal Marine Barracks at Stonehouse and the Royal School of Military Engineering at Brompton are the subjects of major refurbishment projects.

Attitudes towards reuse have also matured enormously since the 1960s, partly as a result of the success in finding new and viable uses for obsolete

Figure 179 The successful conversion of Peninsula Barracks in Winchester to housing has been spearheaded by local architect Huw Thomas, who campaigned for its preservation. This is one of the Edwardian barrack blocks in the Lower Barracks.

industrial buildings. Hillsborough in Sheffield was one of the first barracks to be preserved and given a new lease of life, as a supermarket and offices (see Figure 178). Conversion to housing raises fewer issues, either in terms of the scale of alteration to the fabric or the appropriateness of the new use – basically, a change from military to civilian occupation – and in the last few years, the number of barracks adaptations has grown.

In Dublin, the former Beggars Bush Barracks is now one of the most sought after pieces of real estate in the city, partly because the bastion walls offer the sort of security that wealthy Dubliners without a sense of irony find attractive. The Stoughton Localisation Depot in Guildford has similar advantages. In this case, reuse was preferred by the developer despite the barracks not being listed. It is now marketed as Cardwell Village. Conversion of the Royal Herbert Hospital in Woolwich has removed all the *ad hoc* accretions that mar many fine medical buildings. In passing from military to civilian use, the Eastney Marines Barracks, the Peninsula Barracks in Winchester and the naval hospitals at Stonehouse and Great Yarmouth have all benefited from major repair programmes without unnecessary compromise to their historic character.

Indeed, in the case of the Peninsula Barracks at Winchester (see Figure 179), one could say that change and adaptation *were* the historic character of the site. Once a royal palace-to-be, later a prisoner of war camp for the French, then a barracks for a century, it is now to be returned to its original purpose – providing quality family accommodation.

Appendix A
Departments and Senior Officers Responsible for Barracks

Chief Engineer of the Board of Ordnance

1660	Colonel Sir Charles Lloyd
1661	Sir Bernard de Gomme
1661	Colonel Sir Godfrey Lloyd
1685–1702	Colonel Sir Martin Beckman
1711	Brigadier Michael Richards
1714	Major General John Armstrong (Engineers formed into corps.)
1742–51	Colonel Thomas Lascelles
1757	Colonel William Skinner
1781	Colonel James Bramham
1786	Major General Sir William Green
1802	Post of Chief Engineer abolished, to be replaced by **Inspector General of Fortifications**.

Barracks Department

1792	**Barracks Department** created under Secretary at War, headed by **Barrack Master General**.
1792–1804	Colonel Oliver DeLancey (formerly Deputy Adjutant General)
1804–6	Major General G. Hewett
1806	Barracks Department replaced by **Barracks Board**, headed by three commissioners.
1817	Barracks Board and commissioners replaced by **Controller of Barracks**. This post abolished in 1822, when barracks were returned to the **Board of Ordnance** under the **Inspector General of Fortifications**.

Inspector General of Fortifications

1802	Lieutenant General Robert Morse
1811	Lieutenant General Gother Mann
1830	Major General Sir Alexander Bryce
1832	Major General Robert Pilkington
1834	Major General Sir Frederick Mulcaster
1845	Major General Sir John Burgoyne
1855	Post of Master General and Board of Ordnance abolished. Inspector General of Fortifications placed under the War Office.

Inspector General of Engineers and Director of Works

1862	Inspector General of Fortifications henceforth known both as **Inspector General of Engineers** (under the Commander-in-Chief and responsible for command and discipline of the corps) and **Director of Works** (under the Secretary of State for War in the War Office, and controlling building work). Two **Assistant Directors of Works** appointed: one for fortifications and the other for barracks.
1862	General Sir John Burgoyne
1868	Major General Edward Frome
1869	Major General Sir John William Gordon (Inspector General only)
1870	Title of **Inspector General of Fortifications** revived.
1870	Major General Sir Frederick Chapman

1875	Major General Sir Lintorn Simmons
1880	Major General Thomas Gallway
1882	Major General Sir Andrew Clarke
1886	Lieutenant General Lothian Nicholson
1886	The two titles amalgamated within the Horse Guards as **Inspector General of Royal Engineers.**
1888	Title Director of Works dropped. **Deputy Inspector General for Barracks and Civil Holdings** appointed.

Deputy Inspector General of Fortifications (Barracks)

1862	Captain Edward Belfield
1867	Lieutenant Colonel Thomas Murray
1872	Colonel Charles B. Ewart
1877	Colonel Philip Ravenhill
1882	Colonel R.N. Dawson-Scott
1887	Colonel H. Locock
1896	Colonel C.M. Watson

Assistant Directors of Works (Barracks)

1873	**Assistant Directors of Works (Barracks)** appointed following passage of Localisation Act.
1873	Lieutenant Colonel Edward Gordon and Lieutenant Colonel Philip Ravenhill, with Major H.C. Seddon in charge of **Design Branch**, preparing plans for the new depots, with civilian drafting staff.
1876	Lieutenant Colonel G.E. Walker
1877	Colonel G. Graham
1881	Lieutenant Colonel R.N. Dawson-Scott
1881	Major H. Locock
1883	Major W. Salmond
1884	Colonel C.J. Moysey
1887	Lieutenant Colonel G.E. Grover
1890	Major C.M. Watson
1896	Lieutenant Colonel N.M. Lake

1904	Positions of Inspector General, Deputy and Assistant Inspector General of Fortifications abolished, and replaced by **Director of Fortifications and Works**, under a military member of the Army Council, responsible for works to existing barracks, and construction of new works abroad.

Director of Barrack Construction

1904	Civilian **Barrack Construction Department** created, headed by **Director of Barrack Construction**, under a civil member of the Army Council, responsible for new works at home.
1904	Harry B. Measures (RIBA)

Source: The History of the Corps of Royal Engineers (Chatham 1880), **vii**, pp.94–8, and *The History of the Corps of Royal Engineers* (Chatham 1954), **viii**, 131–72.

The Chief Engineer was answerable to the Surveyor General, who with the exception of Marlborough was not so frequently involved in fort and barracks design (see Barker, 1993).

Appendix B
Ranks and Roles in Infantry, Cavalry and Horse Artillery Units in 1857

Battalion of Infantry

1,000 strong, 10 companies

1	Lieutenant Colonel
2	Majors
12	Lieutenants
8	Ensigns

Staff:
1	Sergeant Major
1	Quartermaster
1	Paymaster Sergeant
1	Armourer Sergeant
1	Schoolmaster
1	Hospital Sergeant
1	Orderly Room Clerk
1	Band Sergeant
50	Pay and Company Sergeants

Drummers:
1	Drum Major
20	Drummers

Rank and file:
50	Corporals
950	Privates

Total: 39 officers, 1,097 men

Regiment of Cavalry

Home establishment: 6 troops

1	Lieutenant Colonel
1	Surgeon
1	Assistant Surgeon
1	Veterinary Surgeon
1	Riding Master
1	Paymaster

Staff sergeants:
1	Regimental Sergeant Major
1	Paymaster Sergeant
1	Sergeant Saddler
1	Farrier Major
1	Sergeant Armourer
1	Hospital Sergeant
1	Orderly Room Clerk
18	Sergeants
1	Band Sergeant

Trumpeters:
1	Trumpet Major
6	Trumpeters

Rank and file:
6	Farriers
18	Corporals
304	Privates

Total: 27 officers, 362 men
Horses: 50 officers, 271 troops

9-Pounder Troop of Horse Artillery

2   Captains
3   Lieutenants

Staff:
1   Assistant surgeon
1   Veterinary surgeon

Staff Sergeants, etc.:
1   Sergeant Major
1   Quartermaster General
1   Farrier General
1   Hospital Sergeant
1   Orderly Room Clerk
8   Sergeants
2   Trumpeters

Rank and file:
11   Artificers
12   Corporals
160   Privates

Total: 7 officers, 198 men

Horses:
11   Officers
154   Troop
6   Guns and limbers
8   Ammunition waggons
1   Spare gun carriage
1   Forge waggon
1   Store waggon
1   Store cart

Source: Parliamentary Papers (House of Commons) 1857–8, *xxxvii, Correspondence relating to barracks*, p.145.

Acknowledgements

James Douet

This book grew out of a joint commitment by English Heritage and the Ministry of Defence to publish research which they commissioned to substantiate the need for protection of barracks of national historical importance. Credit for this is due to Dr Martin Cherry, the head of the Listing Team at English Heritage, and to Tony Whitehead, Principal Conservation Architect at the Defence Estate Organisation. Helen Bostock and Obode Ebuehi of the Listing Team helped carry through the project, and thanks are also due to Sylvia Archer. The staff at the following institutions have been particularly helpful with information: the National Army Museum Library, the Royal Engineers Library, the Royal Marines Museum Library, the Aldershot Military Museum, the Prince Consort's Library, and Portsmouth City Museum and Record Office.

Individuals for whose assistance and advice I am indebted include: Lieutenant Colonel Ahern, Roger Bowdler, Captain Ian Carlile, Jonathan Coad, Ray Cooney, Mairead Dunlevy, Patrick Gannon, Ian MacIvor, Debbie Mays, Edward McParland, Harriet Richardson, Glenn Steppler, Ian Stuart, Major W.H. White, A. Wright and Commandant Peter Young. I am also indebted to Kathryn Morrison for showing me a draft of her chapter, 'The Hospitals of the Armed Forces' (3rd draft, February 1994), of the Royal Commission for Historical Monuments in England's unpublished 'Hospitals and Asylums in England, 1660–1948'. Thanks are due to Sue Goodman of Clews Associates for drawing the perspective illustrations, the maps and redrawing the barrack plans by Colonel James. I am also grateful to Philip Judge for finalizing many of the drawings and for his work on other illustrations. Thanks are also due to the many property managers at different barracks who courteously showed me around their estates.

Anthony Peers undertook some of the original research, notably on the militia storehouses. Professor John R. Breihan, Dr Tony Hayter and Patricia Douet generously waded through various early texts and offered helpful suggestions, as did Professor Andrew Saint with the completed manuscript. Andrew Saunders has done much more than provide an important opening chapter, and I am grateful to him for his kindness and forebearance towards a newcomer in a field which he commands.

Most of all, I must acknowledge the help of Jeremy Lake, who has the lion's share of the credit for this book. Tirelessly tolerant and always looking for ways in which to improve the final work, my thanks go most of all to him.

Andrew Saunders

I am grateful to the Stichting Menno van Coehoorn for access to its library, and in particular for the assistance of Dr D.C. Leegwater. Esther Godfrey of Historic Royal Palaces advised on drawings of Hampton Court Palace Barracks. Finally, my thanks are due to James Douet for reading the chapter in draft and for his helpful comments, and to Jeremy Lake of English Heritage for his continuing involvement with the project and his sound editorial discipline.

Illustrations

Maps 1–7 by Sue Goodman.
Unless otherwise stated, photographs were taken by James Douet and Jeremy Lake.

Figures

1	Redrawn from original in British Library (Philip Judge).
2	BL King's MS 45, f.23.

Figures (contd.)

3	PRO MPF262.
4	The Provost & Fellows of Worcester College, Oxford.
5	Forsvarets Bygningstjenestes Historiske Tegningsarchiv, Copenhagen.
6	National Maritime Museum P42, f.17.
7	Andrew Saunders.
8	Rochester Guildhall Museum.
9	Crown Copyright. Reproduced by permission of Historic Royal Palaces.
10	BL King's MS, f.36.
11	MoD.
12	BL King's MS, f.12.
13	BL King's MS, f.25.
14	Crown Copyright. Reproduced by permission of Historic Scotland.
15	BL King's Top. Coll. XXXII, 47-f.
16	English Heritage Photographic Library.
17	English Heritage Photographic Library.
18	BL King's Top. Coll. XVIII, 58c.
19	Crown Copyright. Reproduced by permission of The Trustees of the National Library of Scotland.
20	Crown Copyright. Reproduced by permission of Historic Scotland.
21	Crown Copyright. Reproduced by permission of The Trustees of the National Library of Scotland.
22	English Heritage Photographic Library.
24	BL King's MS 45, f.49.
27	Redrawn from original (Sue Goodman/ Philip Judge).
28	Dublin National Library.
31–3	Yale Centre for British Art.
34	Crown Copyright. Reproduced by permission of The Trustees of the National Library of Scotland.
35 & 36	RCHMS.
37	Crown Copyright. Reproduced by permission of The Trustees of the National Library of Scotland.
38	BL K Top 40-86-dd.
39	PRO ADM140/120.
40	Royal Marines Museum.
41	Redrawn from original (Sue Goodman/ Philip Judge).
42	Royal Marines Museum.
43	Perspective reconstruction by Sue Goodman
44	PRO ADM140/307.
45	PRO ADM140/120.
46	PRO WO55/2269/8.
47	Exeter Archaeology.
48	BL K Top 27-7-d-3.
49	BL K Top 26-6-b.
51	PRO WO78/1281.
52	Illustrated London News.
54	Redrawn from original drawing in PRO HO4220 (Sue Goodman).
55	Perspective reconstruction by Sue Goodman. Redrawn from original drawing in PSA CTR/472 (Philip Judge).
56	BL K Top 27-7-uu.
57	Paul Jones.
58	Redrawn from original (Sue Goodman/ Philip Judge).
59	Redrawn from original (Sue Goodman/ Philip Judge).
60	Perspective reconstruction by Sue Goodman.
61–3	Eric Berry.
64	MoD.
68	Redrawn from original (Sue Goodman/ Philip Judge).
69	Cornwall Archaeological Unit.
70	Plan redrawn from original in PRO WO55 (Philip Judge).
71	Redrawn from original (Sue Goodman/ Philip Judge).
72	Courtesy of the Director, National Army Museum, London.
73	MoD.
74	Redrawn from original (Sue Goodman/ Philip Judge).
75	Eric Berry.
76	Redrawn from original (Sue Goodman/ Philip Judge).

Acknowledgements

78	Dover Museum.	134	The Builder.
80	Redrawn from original (Sue Goodman/Philip Judge).	135	Redrawn from original in Professional Papers of the Royal Engineers (Philip Judge).
85	BL K Top 26-8-a.	137–9	English Heritage Photographic Library.
88	Yale Centre for British Art.	140	English Heritage Plans Room.
90	PRO HO55/951.	145	Redrawn from original (Sue Goodman/Philip Judge).
91	Redrawn from original (Sue Goodman/Philip Judge).	147	Eric Berry.
92	Perspective reconstruction by Sue Goodman.	148	Bridgeman Art Library.
95–7	Illustrated London News.	149	Redrawn from Scott-Moncrief (1895), Plate III (Philip Judge).
98 & 99	MoD.	150	MoD.
100	Professional Papers of the Royal Engineers, 19 (1837).	152	RCHMS.
101	Royal Marines Museum.	153	Redrawn from original in PRO WORK43/689 (Philip Judge).
102	Illustrated London News.	154	MoD.
103	English Heritage Photographic Library.	155	MoD.
104 & 105	Illustrated London News. Fig. 105 redrawn from original (Sue Goodman/Philip Judge).	158	Redrawn from Scott-Moncrief (1895), Plate I (Sue Goodman/Philip Judge).
106	Redrawn from original (Sue Goodman/Philip Judge).	159	Eric Berry.
107	RCHME.	160	The Builder.
110	Aldershot Military Museum.	161	Hampshire Record Office, 138M84W/b
111	The Trustees of the Imperial War Museum, London, Q71157.	162	Huw Thomas and RCHME
113	Courtesy of the Director, National Army Museum, London.	163	Redrawn from OS Map, 1890 (Sue Goodman).
114–17	MoD.	164	Portsmouth City Museum.
119	Redrawn from original (Sue Goodman/Philip Judge).	165	PRO WORK43/474.
120	MoD.	166 & 167	Redrawn from originals in possession of MoD (Philip Judge).
121	PRO WORK43/1408.	168	MoD.
122	MoD.	169	MoD.
123	Illustrated London News.	170	RCHMS.
125	MoD.	171	Redrawn from original in possession of MoD (Sue Goodman/Philip Judge).
126	Journal of the United Services Institute.	172	English Heritage Plans Room.
127	Perspective reconstruction by Sue Goodman.	173	Eric Berry.
129	Gloucestershire County Record Office.	174	Eric Berry.
130	Cirencester Barracks D2593/2/114 GRO, Astam Design Partnership	175	Eric Berry.
		176	The Trustees of the Imperial War Museum, London, Q53364.
131	Gloucester Barracks D2593/2/109 GRO, Astam Design Partnership	177	Eric Berry.
		178	Mike Williams.
132	The Builder.	179	Huw Thomas

Boxes

Drill and the barracks square: Illustrated London News.

The architecture of military education: MoD (Sandhurst) and Clews Architects.

Military hospitals: MoD (Stonehouse) and Clews Architects.

Women in a man's world: Illustrated London News.

Select Bibliography

The following list includes the principal books and papers which deal specifically with barracks, but excludes less relevant texts, as well as the parliamentary papers, reports, and other primary material cited in full in the footnotes.

Anglesey, Marquess of (1975) *A History of the British Cavalry, 1851-1871*, **2** (London)

Arnold-Forster, H.O. (1906) *The Army in 1906: A Policy and a Vindication* (London)

Barker, J. (1984) *Christchurch Barracks*, Bournemouth Local Studies Publications

Barker, N. (1993) 'The Building Practice of the English Board of Ordnance, 1680–1720', in Bold, J. and Chaney, E. (eds) *English Architecture: Public and Private* (London), pp.199–214

Barrett, C.R.B. (1912) 'Early Cavalry Barracks in Great Britain', *The Cavalry Journal*, 26, pp.161–77

Bartlett, T. and Jeffery, K. (eds) (1996) *A Military History of Ireland* (Cambridge)

Becket, I. (1991) *The Amateur Military Tradition, 1558–1945* (Manchester)

Bell, I.E. (1880) 'The Modern Barrack, its Plan and Construction', paper read to RIBA, 15 November

Blumberg, H. and Field, C. (1935) *Random Records of the Royal Marines* (Portsmouth)

Breihan, J. (1989) 'Barracks in Dorset during the French Revolutionary and Napoleonic Wars', *Proceedings of the Dorset Natural History and Archaeological Society*, **3**, pp.9–14

Breihan, J. (1990a) 'Army Barracks in the North East in the Era of the French Revolution', *Archaeologia Aeliana*, 5th series, **18**, pp.165–76

Breihan, J. (1990b) 'Army Barracks in Devon during the French Revolutionary and Napoleonic Wars', *Proceedings of the Devon Association for the Advancement of Science and Literature*, **122**, pp.133–58

Breihan, J. and Caplan, C. (1992) 'Jane Austen and the Militia', *Persuasions*, **14**, pp.16–26

Brimacombe, P. (1992) *The History of HMS Drake* (Plymouth)

Chandler, D. and Becket, I. (eds) (1994) *The Oxford Illustrated History of the British Army* (Oxford)

Childerhouse, T. (1990) *Military Aldershot: The First Fifty Years* (London)

Childs, J. (1976) *The Army of Charles II* (Manchester)

Childs, J. (1980) *The Army, James II, and the Glorious Revolution* (Manchester)

Childs, J. (1987) *The Army of William III, 1689–1702* (Manchester)

Clode, C.M. (1869) *The Military Forces of the Crown, Their Administration and Government* (London)

Coad, J. (1989) *The Royal Dockyards, 1690–1850* (Aldershot)

Coad, J. (1995) *Dover Castle* (London)

Select Bibliography

Coad, J. and Lewis, P. (1982) 'The Later Fortifications of Dover', *Post-Medieval Archaeology*, **16**, pp.141–200

Cole, H.N. (1980) *The Story of Aldershot* (Aldershot)

Colley, L. (1993) *Britons: Forging the Nation, 1807–37* (London)

Colvin, H. (1995) *A Biographical Dictionary of British Architects*, 3rd edn (London)

Colvin, H. (ed.) (1963–82) *The History of the King's Works*, 6 vols (London)

Dallemagne, François (1990) *Les Casernes Françaises* (Paris)

Denison, W. (1848) 'Observations on Barracks, and on the Moral Condition of the Soldier', *Royal Engineer Corps Papers*, paper 25, pp.247–61

Dietz, P. (1986) *Garrison: Ten Military Towns* (London)

Dwyer, D.J. (1960) *A History of the Royal Navy Barracks, Portsmouth* (Portsmouth)

Emsworth, E.A.L. (1952) *The Army Gymnastic Staff* (Aldershot)

Fortesque, J.W. (1905) *A History of the British Army, 1783–1802* (London)

Graham, C.A.L. (1962) *The Story of the Royal Regiment of Artillery* (Woolwich)

Grierson, J.M. (1900) *Scarlet into Khaki* (London)

Harries-Jenkins, G. (1977) *The Army in Victorian Society* (London)

Hefferson, M. (1968) 'The Barracks and Posts of Ireland, 14: Collins Barracks, Dublin', *An Cosantoir* (February), pp.129–36

Hemmings, E.H. (1900) 'Progress in Barrack Design', *Professional Papers of the Royal Engineers*, paper 2, pp.41–68

Hewlings, R. (1993) 'Hawksmoor's Brave Designs for the Police', in Bold, J. and Chaney, E. (eds) *English Architecture: Public and Private* (London), pp.215–29

Houlding, J.A. (1981) *Fit for Service* (Oxford)

James, Colonel. (1858–67) *Plans of the Barracks of England and Ireland*, Topographical Department of the War Office (London)

Jones, C. (1980) 'The Military Revolution and the Professionalism of the French Army under the Ancien Regime', in Roger, C. (1995) *The Military Revolution Debate: Readings on the Transformation of Early Modern Europe* (London), pp.149–68

Kerrigan, P. (1985) 'Garrisons and Barracks in the Irish Midlands', *Journal of the Old Athlone Society*, **2**, pp.100–6

Kerrigan, P. (1995) *Castles and Fortifications of Ireland, 1485–1945* (Cork)

Lowe, J.A. (ed.) (1990) *Records of the Portsmouth Division of the Royal Marines*, Portsmouth Record Series (Portsmouth)

MacIvor, I. (1967) *The Fortifications of Berwick-on-Tweed* (London)

MacIvor, I. (1976) 'Fort George, Inverness-shire, Parts I and II', *Country Life*, pp.410–13 and 478–80

MacIvor, I. (1993) *Edinburgh Castle* (London)

MacLaren, A. (1865) 'Military Gymnasia', *Journal of the United Services Institute*, **8**, pp.217–30

Magrath, P. (1992) 'Fort Cumberland, 1747–1850', *Portsmouth Papers*, 60, p.15

Mallett, M.E. and Hale, J.R. (1984) *The Military Organisation of a Renaissance State: Venice c1400 to 1617* (Cambridge)

McGuffie, T.H. (1964) *Rank and File: The Common Soldier at Peace and War 1642–1914* (London)

Select Bibliography

McParland, E. (1995) 'The Office of the Surveyor General in Ireland in the Eighteenth Century', *Architectural History*, **38**, pp.91–101

O'Donnell, P.D. (1973) 'The Barracks and Posts of Ireland, 21: Collins Barracks, Dublin', part 3, *An Cosantoir* (February), pp.48–52

O'Donnell, P.D. (1981) 'Dublin's Military Barracks', *An Cosantoir* (March and April), pp.73–7

Parker, G. (1971) *The Army of Flanders and the Spanish Road 1567–1659* (Cambridge)

Parnell, G. (1993) *The Tower of London* (London)

Pasley, C.W. (1862) *Practical Architecture: A Course for Junior Officers of the Royal Engineers*, 2nd edn (first published c.1825) (Chatham)

Porter, W. (1889) *History of the Corps of Royal Engineers*, **2** (London)

Rose, M. (1935) *The Story of the Royal Marines: Lectures for Recruits*, 7th edn (Portsmouth)

Rowe, J. (1988) 'The Cavalry Barracks at Barnstaple', *Devon and Cornwall Notes and Queries*, **36**, pp.121–7

Saunders, A.D. (1960) 'Tilbury Fort and the Development of Artillery Fortification in the Thames Estuary', *Antiquaries Journal*, **40**, pp.152–74

Saunders, A.D. (1967) *Upnor Castle* (London)

Saunders, A.D. (1985) *Tilbury Fort* (London)

Saunders, A.D. (1989) *Fortress Britain: Artillery Fortification in the British Isles and Ireland* (Liphook)

Schwoerer, L. (1974) *No Standing Armies!* (Baltimore)

Scott-Moncrief, P. (1895) 'The Design of Soldiers' Barracks', *Professional Papers of the Royal Engineers*, paper 7, pp.125–36

Scouller, R.E. (1953) 'Quarters and Barracks', *Journal of the United Services Institute*, **98**, pp.91–4

Skelley, A.R. (1977) *The Victorian Army at Home* (London)

Smyth, C. (1961) *Sandhurst: The History of the RMA Woolwich, RMC Sandhurst, RMA Sandhurst, 1741–1961* (London)

Spiers, E.M. (1980) *The Army and Society, 1815–1914* (London)

Spiers, E.M. (1992) *The Late Victorian Army* (Manchester)

Stell, G. (1973) 'Highland Garrisons 1717–23: Bernera Barracks', *Post-Medieval Archaeology*, **7**, pp.20–30

Strachan, H. (1984) *Wellington's Legacy: The Reform of the British Army, 1830–54* (Manchester)

Tabraham, C. and Grove, D. (1995) *Fortress Scotland and the Jacobites* (London)

Tomlinson, H.C. (1979) *Guns and Government: The Ordnance Office under the Later Stuarts* (London)

Trustram, M. (1984) *Women of the Regiment: Marriage and the Victorian Army* (Cambridge)

Walton, C. (1894) *The History of the British Standing Army 1660–1700* (London)

Watson, C.M. (1954) *The History of the Corps of Royal Engineers*, **3** (Chatham)

Watson-Smyth, M., et al. (1993) *SAVE Britain's Heritage: Deserted Bastions, Historic Naval and Military Architecture* (London)

Weiler, J. (1987) 'Army Architects: The Royal Engineers and the Development of Building Technology in the Nineteenth Century', unpublished PhD thesis, Institute for Advanced Architectural Studies, University of York

Index

Page numbers in *italics* refer to illustrations and to colour plates. Locations listed on the map pages have not been indexed.

Aberdeen, infantry barracks 71, 80
Admiralty Works Department 121
Albany Barracks, Isle of Wight 105
Aldershot Camp xii, xvi, xviii, 129,
    130–4, *130*, 187, 196
  churches 135
  drill sheds 156, 158
  Fox Gymnasium 145, 146–7, *147*
  Marlborough Lines (South Camp) 130, *131*, *179*
  married quarters 177
  Stanhope Lines (North Camp) 130, *131*, *179*
  Wellington Lines 131–4, *132*, 133, 140–1
American War of Independence 38, 46, 180
Anglesey Infantry Barracks *see under* Portsmouth
Antwerp (Belgium) 4
Archer, Major John 48
architecture (specific types of buildings, rooms or features) *see* artillery regiments, barracks; billiard rooms; canteens; cavalry barracks; chapels and churches; circular plans; cookhouses; dining rooms; drill training and drill premises; fives courts; forage barns; governors' houses; guardhouses; gymnasiums; hospitals; infantry barracks; iron; 'keeps'; kitchens; latrines and privies; laundries; libraries; married quarters; militia storehouses; naval barracks; officers' accommodation; parade grounds; pavilion plan; prefabricated buildings; polygonal buildings; riding schools; schools; stables; storehouses; straw stores; sutlers' houses and sutleries; verandas; washhouses
Arklow 104
armouries *see* keeps; militia storehouses
Army Sanitary Commission 139–41, 144–9, 175, 177
Army Service Corps 185
Arnold-Forster, Hugh 187, 188, 189

artillery regiments 2, 10, 54
  barracks/accommodation for gunners and artillerymen 21, 23, *25*,
    44, 48, 54, 61, 68, 70, 83,
    84–8, 112, 117, 133, 137–8,
    160, 178
  at localization depots 169
Ashford 73, 74
Aston-under-Lyne 112
Athlone 33, 86, 91
auxiliary (volunteer) units 35, 151–7,
  167, 169, 171, 175; *and see* militia
Ayr, cavalry and infantry barracks 7, 71, 80, 87

Baillie, Col. 71
Balaclava (Crimea), camp 127, *135*
Ballinrobe 104
Banagher, fort 6
Bantry 7
baraque (Fr.) 1, 3
Barn Rock 74
Barnet, militia storehouse 153
Barnsley 112
Barnstaple 71, 77
barraca (Sp.) 1, 82
Barrack Construction Department 188
Barrack Master General 68, 93, 106, 199
Barrack Masters 33, 49–50, 76, 78–9
Barracks Accommodation Report (1855) 128–9
Barracks Act (1890) 177, 181, 182
Barracks Board 29, 34, 106, 109
Barracks Department 68–83, 89, 91–4,
  104, 105, 106, 139, 140, 180, 199
Battle, hutment camp 93
Bedford, loc. depot 172
beds and bedding 4, 9, 11, 23, 25,
  26, 28, 33, 50, 76, 79, 106, *118*
Beggars Bush Barracks *see under* Dublin
Belfast 140, 177
Bell, Ingress, architect 127, 160,
  174, 179, 180–1

211

Bentham, Sir Samuel 51, 118
Bernera 21, *22*, 28
Berwick-upon-Tweed 5, 13, 16, *19*, 20,
    26, 27, 28, 35, 42, 68, 104, 140, 175
Bethune (France) 4
Bexhill, hutment camp 82, 93
billeting system xiii, xvi, 2, 5, 7,
    14–17, 34, 35, 37–9, 40–1, 42,
    43, 45, 48, 49, 51, 60, 62, 67,
    73, 74, 93, 94, 105, 196
billiard rooms *100*, 174, 182
Birmingham 62, 104, 111, 196
Bisley Camp 196
Blackness Castle 68
blockhouses 5, 85
Bodley, Sir Josias 6
Bodmin
  loc. depot 169, 170, 171, *173*, 196
  Duke of Cornwall's Militia
    Barracks 155, 156
Boer War (Second) 175, 183, 186
bomb-proof barracks, within
    fortifications 54–6, *and see*
    casemates
Bovington Camp 196
Bradford 112
Brandreth, Capt. Henry 120, 121
Brecon, ordinance depot and barracks 104, 112
Breda (Netherlands) 4
Brest (France) 4
Bridport, cavalry barracks 71
Brighouse 112
Brighton 69, 73, 104, 111
  Royal Pavilion 33
Bristol 35, 37, 69, 71, 73, 104, 112, 196
British School of Gunnery *see under* Shoeburyness
Brodrick, St John 187
Brompton Artillery Barracks *see under* Chatham
Broughty 5
Brunel, Isambard Kingdom 134, 143
Building Design Partnership 196
Bulford Camp 187
Burgh, Capt. Thomas 29, 30, 32
Burgoyne, Col. (Gen.) Sir John 106,
    128–9, 151, 170
Burnley 110, 175
Bury, Lancashire 112, *114*, 196
Bury St Edmunds, Gibraltar Barracks
  loc. depot 169, 171, 172, *172*
Butterfield, William, architect 119

Cahir 91
Calais (France), garrison 5
Cambridge Barracks *see under* Portsmouth
Cambridge Infantry Barracks *see under* Woolwich
'camp measurer' 3
camps 183, 187–8, *195*
canteens 27, 89, 128, 134, 138,
    174, *180*, 185, 193
Canterbury 69, 73, 86, 104, 169
Cape of Good Hope 177
Cardew, Major Gen. 123
Cardwell, Edward, and Reforms xii,
    xiv, 167, 169, 172, 174, 175,
    183, 196
Carlisle 42, 68
  Castle 21, 74, 104, 110–11
Carrickfergus 33
casemates 23, 54, *55*, 56, 85–6, 89,
    118, 141, 157, 158, 159, 160,
    160, *162*, 163
Castlebar 86, 104
Caterham, Guards depot 119, 170
Catterick Camp 169, 196
cavalry barracks (stations) 7, 15,
    30, 32, 33, 34, 43, 60, 61, 62–6,
    69–71, 73, 81, 82, 91, 104, 107,
    108, 110, 111, 112, 114, 117, 128–9,
    133, 136–7, 140, 141, 144, 147,
    148–9, 178, 186, 189, 195, 196
  Barracks Department 76, 77–81
  hutment camps 74, 75, 76
  localization depots 169
cavalry regiments xv, 30, 201
Chambers, Sir William, architect 57, 58
Channel Islands, forts and batteries
    116, 158
chapels and churches 10, 27, 44,
    56, 87, 111, 119, *120*, *134*,
    136, 144, 186, 192
  pre-fabricated 135, *135*
Charles II 7, 9, 180
Chartism xii, 109, 110, 111, 112, 114
Chatham 68, 104, 111
  Brompton Artillery Barracks 84, 86–7, *86*, *87*,
    106, 140, 145, 146, *148*, 196, 197
  HMS *Pembroke* naval barracks 190, 193
  Infantry Barracks (now Kitchener Barracks)
    45, 47–8, *47*, 118, 119, *120*, 140

Lines 47
pubs for billeting 38
Royal Marines Barracks 46, 48, 51, *54*, 118, 160, 196
St Mary's Casemates 85–6, 119, *119*, 140, 141
School of Military Engineering 125, *125*
see also Fort Pitt
Chelmsford 72, 73, 74, 77, 81, 104
  militia storehouse 153
Chelsea *see under* London
Chester 42, 68
  Castle 21, 35, 104
Chester-le-Street 73
Chichester 82, *83*
Christchurch, cavalry barracks 77, 78
churches *see* chapels and churches
circular plans 138–9
Cirencester, militia storehouse *152*, 153, *153*, *154*, 155
civilian administration of barracks 188–9
civil order and unrest xii, xiii, 35, 37, 41, 60–6, 103, 104, 109–12, 175
Civil War (English) 7, 9
Clarence Barracks *see under* Portsmouth
Clonmel 86, 104
Coade stone 87, *88*
Coast Guard 104
coastal batteries (defences; garrisons) 35, 83, 84, 104, 151, 157, 163, 186, 196
Colchester 72, 73, 74, 77, 104
  Camp 134, *134*, 135, *135*, 136, 137, 177, 183
  Goojerat Barracks 185, *188*, 190
  Le Cateau Cavalry Barracks 136–7, *137*
  military hospital 174
  militia storehouse 153
  Sobraon Barracks 185
  timber barracks 81
Colewort Barracks *see under* Portsmouth
cookhouses 51, 78, 80, *81*, 89, 118, 130, 138, 185; *see also* kitchens
cooking facilities 3, 4, 9, 17, 20, 25, 33, 51, 76; *see also* cookhouses; kitchens
Copenhagen (Denmark), Nybodn 4; *see also* Kastellet
Copland, Alexander 76, 77, 82, 105, 125
Corgarff, tower-house 21
Cork 33, 34, 91, 104

Corkbeg 6
Corneille, Rudolph 26
Cornwall, 'duty area' 35
Coventry 63, 111, 104, 140
Cowley, Oxford, loc. depot 169, 170, 196
Crimean War xii, xiii, 123, 127, 134
Cromwell, Oliver 2, 6, 39, 40
Crossman, Sir William 160
Croydon, timber barracks 81
Curragh of Kildare, Camp 129, 136, *136*, 177, 183, 187
  Keane and Gough Barracks 185

D'Arcy, Lt Col. R. 86
Darmstadt (Prussia) 32
Dawson-Scott, Col. R.N. 182
Deal 74, 104
  Castle 5
  cavalry barracks 77
  cookhouse *81*
  hospital 142
  infantry barracks 71, 80, *80*
Debbeig, Capt. Hugh 47
Deepcut, church 135, *135*
de Gomme, Sir Bernard 9–13, *10*, 23, 25, 116
DeLancey, Col. Oliver 62–6, 68–9, 71, 73–4, 76, 77, 93–4, 106
Denison, Capt. Sir William 121–3, 141
depots, Ordnance 104, *104*; *see also* hospitals; localization depots
Derby, ordinance depot 104
Design Branch (of the War Office) 169, 179, 180, 183, 185
Desmaretz, Capt. John Peter, architect 47
Devizes, Le Marchant Barracks loc. depot 169, *171*
Devon
  cavalry barracks 69
  'duty area' 35
  huts 82
  militia storehouses 152
Devonport 73, 111, 116
  Dockyard 85, 193–4
  Keyham Barracks 190–2, 193
    as HMS *Drake 101*, 143, 192–3, *192*, *193*
  Lines and 'Squares' 45, 48, 62, 97
  Raglan Infantry Barracks 121, 141
Dewsbury 112
dining rooms xiv, 162, 173, 185, 193

Disbanding Act (1679) 14
discipline and punishment xvi, 37, 115
dockyards 13, 43, 45–6, 60, 121,
    151, 157, 186
Dorchester 69, 72
  loc. depot 169
  'keep' or armoury 169, 170
  Marabout Cavalry Barracks *71*, 111
  riding school 80
Dorset 69
Dover 83
  Castle 23, *25*, 28, 68, 104, 196
    barracks (1850s) *129*
    casemates 177
    Cliff Casemates 118, 141
    Keep Yard Barracks 118, *141*
    Western Heights 86, 88–90
    The Citadel 159, *159*
    Drop Redoubt 88–9, *90*, 118
    Grand Shaft 90, *90*
dragoons 30, 33, 104, 111
drill training and drill premises
    xvi, 34, 36–7, 51, 122
  drill halls and sheds 153, 156, *156*, 174, 185,
    192, 193
Drogheda 33
Drumgoff, Wicklow *92*
Drury, Capt. Theodore 18
Dublin 34, 116
  Arbour Hill Prison 140
  Beggars Bush Barracks 111, *111*,
    114, 198
  Grand (Royal; Collins) Barracks
    29–33, *31*, *32*, 35, 104, 119, 140, 175, 177
  Grangegorman (McKee) Barracks 177
  Linen Hall 140
  Phoenix Park exercise ground 34
  Portobello Barracks 91
  Richmond Infantry Barracks 91
  Royal Hospital, Kilmainham *30*, 142
Dubois, Nicholas, architect 56
Dumbarton Castle 68
Dunbar 76
Duncannon Fort 6
Dundalk 104, 187
Dundas, David 36
Dundas, Henry, Secretary of State
    62, 63
Dundas, William 48
Dundee 71, 80

Durham 68
Dymchurch, redoubts 85

earth fieldworks 163
Eastbourne, redoubts 85
East India Company 119
Eastney Marines Barracks 162–3,
    163, *164*, 198
Edinburgh
  Castle xiii, 5, 18–19, 23, 42, 68, 87
  New Barracks (Castle) 69, *69*, 71,
    104, 116
  Piers Hill Cavalry Barracks 186
  Redford Barracks 189, *189*, 195
education, of soldiers 119, 123, 124–5
Elizabeth I 4, 5
encampments (marching camps;
    siegeworks) 2–3, *3*
Enniskillen 177
Esher, Lord 188
Ewart, Col. C.B. 169
Exeter 74, 116
  cavalry station 69, 71, 104
  depot 169
  forage barn or straw store *78*
  Higher Barracks 79, *79*
  hospital 79, *80*
  riding school 80
  Wyvern Artillery Barracks 86,
    87, *88*

Fenham Artillery Barracks *see*
    Newcastle upon Tyne
Fermoy 91
Field Artillery 68, 186
Finsbury *see* London
First World War 195–6, *195*
fives courts 119–20, 123, 134, 185
Folkestone 104
Foot Artillery 87
Foot Guards (Grenadier and
    Coldstream) 7, 9, *13*, 16, 26, 56,
    57–8, *57*, 62, 111
forage barns 78, *78*, 107
Fort Augustus 21, 23, *24*, 27, 68
Fort Blaugaret (Netherlands) 9
Fort Brockhurst *99*, 159, *160*, *161*
Fort Charles *see* Ringcurran
Fort Charlotte, Shetland 56, 68
Fort Cumberland 43–4, 54, 74, 104, 160

Fort de Bescou 4
Fort Frederick (Netherlands) 9
Fort George, Ardersier 43–4, *45*, 68, *96*, 118, 141
Fort George, Guernsey 56
Fort Grange 159
Fort Henderick (Netherlands) 9
Fort Monkton 56, 74
Fort Oranje (Netherlands) 4, 9
Fort Pitt 85, 157
Fort Purbrook 160, *162*
Fort Rowner 159
forts xii, 21, 67, 69, 84, 157–65
  Henrician 5, 84
Fort Southwick 160
Fort Townshend, Newfoundland 44
Fort Victoria, Isle of Wight 158
Fort Wallington 160, *161*
Fort William 19–20, 68
Foster, Major T. 114
Four House Barracks *see under* Portsmouth
Fowke, Capt. Francis 121, *133*, 134
Foxford 104
France 125, 130, 142, 151, 182, 193
  barracks xiii, 3–4, 17, 94
  central corridor 21
  French Revolutionary and Napoleonic Wars, effects of 67–94, 104
  standing army 2, 17
fuel supply 23, 25, 76, 118
Fulford Barracks *see* York
Fulljames, Thomas, architect 155, 156–7
Fulwood Barracks *see* Preston
furniture and fittings 23–6, 33, 49, 50, 76, 78–9; *see also* beds and bedding; heating; lighting

Galton, Capt. Douglas xv, 139, 143, *143*, 144, *145*, 148
Galway, Shambles barracks 33, 139, 175; *see also* St Augustine's Fort
Geldern (Netherlands) 3
George Town (West Indies) 120, *121*
Gibraltar xviii, 177
Gibson, William, architect 34
Glasgow
  artillery 104
  hutment camp 74
  infantry barracks 71, 80, 87, 116
Gloucester 69, 71

militia storehouse (Barracks) 153, *154*, 156–7
Goddard, Henry, architect 155
Golden Hill Fort barracks, Isle of Wight 160, *162*
Goojerat Barracks *see under* Colchester
Gordon, Lt Col. E.C. 169
Gordon Riots 56
Gosport 74
  Marines Barracks (later HMS *Forton* and HMS *St Vincent* 49, 121, 142, 160, *162*)
  forts of the Lines 159–60
  St George's Barracks 141, 158, *159*
  see also Fort Brockhurst; Fort Grange; Fort Monkton; Fort Rowner; Haslar Naval Hospital
governors' houses 7, 10, *16*, 19, 21, 26, 27, 44
Grantham, militia storehouse 155
Gravesend, timber huts 84
Great Yarmouth 74
  ordinance depot 104
  naval hospital 142, 198
Green, Gen. William 84
Greene, Col. Geoffrey 121, 162, *165*
Grenoble (France) 4
Grol (Netherlands) 3
guardhouses 16, 48, 88, *89*, 109, 185
Guards regiments xiv, 7–8, 17, 56–7, 74, 106–9, 119, 147–9, 186; *see also* Foot Guards; Horse Guards; Household Guards; Life Guards
Guernsey 13, 68, 74, 103, 104
Guildford 73
  Stoughton Barracks depot 172, 198
gymnasiums 141, 145–7, *147*, *148*, 192, 193

Haddington 76
Haldane, Richard xiv, 167, 188, 189
Halifax 112
Hamilton 69, 87
  depot 169
Hampton Court Guards barracks 9, *13*, 16, 26, 56, 68, 74
Hardinge, Lord 129–30
Hardwick, Philip, architect 108–9, 135
Harwich 85, 104
Haslar Naval Hospital 142
Hawksmoor, Nicholas, architect 20, 26
heating 9, 20, 118, 122, 123, 139, 141, 144–5
Hemmings, Major E.H. 185
Henry VIII 5

Herbert, Sydney 139, 144, 145
Hewett, Major Gen. George 106
Hilsea Barracks *see under* Portsmouth
HMS *Drake see under* Devonport
HMS *Nelson see under* Portsmouth
HMS *Pembroke see under* Chatham
HMS *Victory see under* Portsmouth
Holl, Edward, architect 51
Horfield barracks 112
Horse Artillery 68, 186, 202
Horse Guards 7, 16, 73, 103–4, 110,
    116, 119, 120, 127, 128–9
Horseshoe Barracks *see under*
    Shoeburyness
Horsham hutment camp 73, 82
hospitals *30*, 69, 76, 79, 114, 134, *134*,
    138, 139, 140, 142–3, *144*, *145*, 198
    at localization depots 172, 174
Hounslow 63, 111, 119
    Cavalry Barracks 79, 144, *144*
    Hardinge Block depot 169, *170*, *173*
    hospital 143, *144*, 145
    keep 153
    married quarters 145, *146*, 177
Household Guards 111, 186
Howick, Lord 116, 118, 119, 120
Hull 16, 68, 74
    Citadel 104
    magazine 104
Hulme Barracks *see* Manchester
Hurst Castle 74
hutment camps 74, *75*, 76, 77, 82–3,
    93, 104, 196
Hythe 74, 104

infantry barracks 7, *15*, 30, 33, 34,
    44, 61, 68, 70–6 *passim*, 80–1, 82,
    91, 108, 111, 112, 114, 117, 128–9,
    133, 147, 158, 178, 186, *187*, 189
    at dockyards 47–8
    localization depots 169
infantry regiments xv, 30, 201
Inglis, Capt. T. 138 9
Inspector General of Fortifications
    (post of) 84, 169, 199
    Deputy 200
Invalid Companies 35, 46
Inverlochy (Fort William) 7, *8*, 18
Inverness 7, 21, 23, 28, 43
    Cameron Barracks depot 170, *171*, *173*

Inversnaid 21, *22*
Invicta Barracks *see* Maidstone
Ipswich 69, 71, 73, 74, 77, 86, 104, 111
    Artillery Barracks 87
    Suffolk Militia barracks *155*
Ireland xiii, xviii, 2, 5–7, 13,
    15, 17, 18, 29–35, 68, 85, 86, 104, 112,
    116, 117, 140, 175
    billeting 37, 105
    cavalry regiments 104
    furniture and fittings 23, 25–6, 33
    localization depots 169
    Napoleonic Wars 90–1
    Ordnance organization 23
    'redoubts' 21
    training camp 135–6
    washing facilities 116
Irish Board of Ordnance 29, 34
iron (structural use of) 120, 121, 133, 135, 137,
    137, 158, 172, *173*, 193, 196
Isle of Wight *see* Albany Barracks;
    Fort Victoria; Golden Hill Fort barracks
Isles of Scilly 7, 27, 68, 104;
    see also St Mary's; Tresco

Jackson, Sir John 190
Jacobites 2, 18, 20, 21, 22, 44
James, Capt. Sir Henry 121, 160
James II 14, 16, 40
Jennings, Joseph, architect 155
Jersey 68, 74, 86, 103, 104
Jervois, Maj. Sir William Drummond
    158, 159, 160, 162
Johnson, James, architect 60, 63,
    76, 77, *99*, 148

Kastellet, Copenhagen (Denmark) 9,
    11, *95*
Keene, Henry, architect 34
'keeps' (depot armouries) *115*, 170, 172, *173*
Kent 67, 68
Kent, William, architect 56
Keyham Barracks (later HMS *Drake*)
    see Devonport
Kilchurn Castle 18, *18*
Kildare *see* Curragh of Kildare
Kiliwhimen, Great Glen 21, *22*
Kilkenny 33
Kilmainham *see under* Dublin
King Charles's Castle 7

Kinsale 34
  Castle Park Fort 6
  see also Ringcurran
Kirk and Randall, building
  contractors 174
kitchens 5, 79, 80–1, 123, 128, 141
Kitsell, T. Rogers, architect 180, *181*

Laffan, Capt. R.M. 131
Landguard Fort, Suffolk 23, *55*,
  68, 104
Lansdowne, Lord 183
latrines and privies (bog-houses;
  'necessaries'; night urinals)
    11, 17, 18, 21, 27, 78, 89, 118,
    137, 139, 140, 141, 144, 173, 185
Lauder 5
laundries (and drying houses) 56, 123,
  141, 185
Le Cateau Cavalry Barracks *see*
  Colchester
Leeds, cavalry barracks 110, 116, 177
Le Havre (France) 4
Leicester, cavalry station 69
Leith 7, 36
Lerwick fort 13
Libourne (France), riding school 33
libraries (and reading rooms) 118–19, *119*, 123,
  133, 134, 138, 141, 144
Lichfield 170, 187
Life Guards 7, 56, 60, 104, 149
lighting 25, 118, 139
Lilly, Col. Christian, survey 5, 17–18, 23, 26
Limerick (Ireland) 29, 33, 34, 91
Lincoln
  cavalry station 69, 71
  militia storehouse 155, *155*
  ordinance depot 104
Lines, of bastioned earthworks 45, 47
Liverpool 68, 104, 112
localization, of the home forces
  167–75, 183
localization depots *115*, 145, 157,
  168, 169–75, *170*, 180, 196
London
  Bloomsbury, drill hall 153
  Chelsea Hospital *30*, 142
  Chelsea Infantry Barracks 147–8, 196
  Chelsea Royal Military Asylum 76
  Deptford 104
  Finsbury, Royal London Militia
    Depot 155
  Horse Guards building 56, *57*, 104
  Hyde Park barracks 8, 56, *57*, *99*
  infantry barracks 186
  Kensington Palace, Guards'
    barracks 56, 68, 74
  Kew Guards' barracks 74
  Knightsbridge, Foot Guards'
    barracks 62, 109
  Knightsbridge (Life Guards
    Cavalry) Barracks 60, 62,
    68, 74, 76, 104, 109, 111
    rebuilt by Wood 148–9, *149*
    rebuilt by Spence 196
  Portman Street Barracks 105, 111, *118*, 140
  Regent's Park Barracks xiv, 106–7, *107*, 109,
    111, 118, 175, *176*, 177
  St George's Barracks 108, 111, 118
  St James's 56
  St James's Park 56, *98*
  St John's Wood artillery barracks *36*, 107–8
  Savoy Palace 56, 57–8
  Somerset House 56
  Southwark barracks 8
  Tower of London 5, 56, 68, 111
    'Irish Barracks' 8, 28
    New Guard Room 25
    Royal Palace 8
    Waterloo Barracks *128*
  water supply 116
  Wellington Barracks (Westminster
    Guards Barracks) xiv, 108–9,
    108, 111, 119
  Whitehall 8, 16
  see also Hampton Court; Woolwich
Longford 86
Loughborough 112
Low Countries 3–4, 26, 29, 34
Lugarde, Lt Col. 136

Macclesfield, militia barracks 155
MacLaren, Archibald 145
Maidstone
  Invicta Barracks 196
  timber-framed cavalry station
    81–2, *81*, 104, 196
Maker Heights, Plymouth 46, *84*, 85, *85*
Malta xviii, 177
Manchester 112

Hulme Barracks (cavalry) 62, *64*,
    79, 92, 104, 111, 141, 196
Mann, Gen. Gother 106
Mansfield 112
Marabout Cavalry Barracks *see* Dorchester
marching camps *see* encampments
Marchwood, magazine 104
Margate 104
Marlborough, Duke of 17, 26, 40
married quarters xv, 123, 128, 139,
    141, 144, *144*, 145, *146*, 176–7,
    177, 185
Martello towers 84, 85, 104
Master General of the Ordnance 68, 106
mathematical tiles 105, *105*
Maurice, Prince of Nassau 2, 4, 36
Measures, Harry Bell, architect
    188, 189
Metropolitan Improvements 106–9
Middlesex, militia storehouses 152–3
Milford Haven 104
Military Loans system 175, 177–82,
    187, 188
Military Localisation Act (1872) 169
Military Manoeuvres Act (1898) 183
military units xv–xvi, 9, 30, 32
Military Works Acts 183, 187
militia 5, 38, 41, 46, 67, 68, 74, 130,
    151–7, 167, 169, 171
Militia Acts 152, 156, 171
militia storehouses 152–7, 171
Ministry for Public Buildings and
    Works 196
Modbury 71, 77
Montpellier (France) 4, 17
Moore, Sir Jonas 8
Morgan, James, architect 107 n.13, 147
Morpeth 73
Morse, Lt Gen. Robert 84
Mullingar 91
Musselburgh 76
Mutiny Acts (and Bill) 16, 17, 37, 41, 42, 93
Myers, Christopher, architect 34

Naas 91, 118, 169
Napier, Admiral Sir Charles 190, 196
Napier, Major Gen. Sir Charles 111–14, 119
Nash, John, architect 106–8, 109, 138
naval barracks xiv, 189–94
naval dockyards *see* dockyards

Navan 33
Navy Board 49, 50, 51, 120
Navy Yard 12
Neill, Thomas 77, 82
Nenagh 33
Netherlands, barracks and forts 3–4, 6, 9
Nevin, Charles, architect 63
Newbridge 104
Newcastle under Lyme, militia barracks 155, *155*
Newcastle upon Tyne 73
    Fenham Artillery Barracks 86,
        87–8, *89*, 104
Newport 112
Nicholson, Sir Lothian 175
Nieuport (France) 4
Nightingale, Florence 127, 139, 143
Nissen hut 196
Northampton
    cavalry barracks 69, 71, 87
    ordinance depot 104
    militia barracks 152
Northern District 68, 111–12, *113*
North Shields 68
Norwich 73, 74
    Britannia Barracks depot 174, *174*, 180
    Cavalry Barracks 63, *65*
    hospital 174
    new cavalry barracks abandoned 188–9
Nottingham, cavalry barracks 62, 104, 111

Office of Works 94
officer's accommodation xvi, 6, 13,
    17, 18, 21, 23, 32, 44, 47, 48, 50,
    51, 59, 60, 62, 63, *64*, *65*, 76, 77,
    79, 80, 81–2, *81*, 87, 89, 91, *100*,
    107, 114, *116*, 129, 133, *133*,
    136, *137*, 159, *159*, 162, *188*,
    192, 193
at localization depots 173
Ommanney, Sir Frederick 125
Ord, Colonel 112
Ordnance Board 45, 47, 48, 51, 54,
    55, 56, 58, 67, 68, 69, 70,
    74, 83–9, 91, 94, 105–6, 108,
    109, 110–11, 116, 127, 199
Ordnance Department 34
Ordnance depots 104, *104*
Ordnance Office 8, 9, 16, 18, 19,
    20, 21, 23, 25, 26–7
Oxford *see* Cowley

Palmerston, Lord 103, 127, 139,
  151, 152, 156
Panmure, Lord 128, 139
Papillon, David 7
parade grounds (or squares) xvi, 7,
  21, 27, 36–7, 44, 60, 114, 185
  for the militia 152, 153, 155
Parkhurst, Isle of Wight 74, 76, 77
  Depot 105, *105*
Parsonstown Barracks 91, *92*
Pasley, C. W. 84, 190
pavilion plan 13, 17, 20, 21, 32, 62, 86, *99*,
  142–3, *145*, 174
Pembroke
  camp 134
  Naval Dockyard 157, *158*
Pendennis Castle, Cornwall 5, *5*,
  17–18, *18*, 27, 28, 68, 104
Peninsular Barracks *see under*
  Winchester
Pennethorne, Sir James, architect 125
Perth 69, 87, 140
Pett, hutment camp 76
Phillips, Thomas, engineer 20
Pilkington, Major Gen. Sir Henry 190
Pitt, William (the Elder) 46
Pitt, William (the Younger) 60, 62, 69, 92, 93, 94
Plymouth 46, 68, 74, 104
  Citadel 9, 13, *14*, *16*, 26, 28, 46, 104, 140, *141*, 177
    casemates 54, 55
    timber shed (canteen) 27
  Citadel, new barracks 177, 179–80, *180*, *181*
  Dock barracks 45, 46, 48
  dockyard 97
  Fort 6, *6*, 7, 9–10
  Marines barracks *see* Stonehouse
  Royal Naval Air Service base,
    Mount Batten *196*
  see also Devonport; Maker Heights
police barracks 63, *64*
polygonal buildings 88, 157, 158, 159
Pontefract, loc. depot 170
Ponting, C.E., architect 186
Poole 73
Porchester, hutment camp 74
Port Louis (France) 4
ports of embarkation (and return)
  35, 38
Portsmouth xvi, 7, 26, 27, 28, 37, 48,
  68, 104, 111, 177, 181–2, *184*

Anglesey Infantry Barracks 123, 182, 193
barracks at Round Tower and near the Landport
  11
Cambridge Barracks 73, *104*, 182,
  184, *185*
Clarence Marines Barracks 46, 48–9, *49*, *98*, *100*,
  140, 182
Clarence Barracks (begun 1890)
  182, *184*, *185*, 196
coal storage 25
Colewort Barracks 48, 182, *184*
de Gomme barracks (in the vicinity of
  Pembroke Mount) 9, 10–11, *10*, 12, 13
depot hulks 190
Four House Barracks 139, 182
Gun Wharf artillery barracks 23, 48
Hilsea Barracks 45, 48, 68, 181
HMS *Victory* (later HMS *Nelson*)
  naval barracks 190, 193
hospital bedding 25
Lines 182
Portsdown Hill forts 160
Victoria Barracks 181, 182, *184*, 196
  see also Eastney Marines Barracks; Fort
    Cumberland; Fort Purbrook; Fort Southwick;
    Fort Wallington; Gosport
Portumna 33
Poulson, Richard, architect 196
Pownall, Frederick, architect 155
prefabricated buildings
  churches 135, *135*
  hospital 134, 143
Preston
  depot 170
  Fulwood Barracks 112, 114, *115*, *116*,
    119–20, 196
privies *see* latrines and privies
punishment *see* discipline and
  punishment

quartermasters (houses; storerooms)
  2–3, 49, 85

Radipole, cavalry station 74, 77,
  82–3, 104–5
rank, and architecture xv, 2, 13, 27, 47–8, 62,
  122–3, 129
Ravenhill, Col. Philip 169, 182
Reading, Brock Barracks depot 172
Rebecca Riots 112

Redford Barracks *see under* Edinburgh
redoubts 33, 85
Richmond, Yorkshire, loc. depot 169
riding schools 32–3, 59, 62, 80, 108, *108*, 133, *133*, 137
Ringcurran (Fort Charles) 13
Riot Act (1715) 41
Robinson, Sir William 29, *30*
Roborough Down, militia camp 46
Romer, John 24
Romford, timber barracks 81
Roussillon (France) 4
Roxburgh Castle 5–6
Royal Arsenal *see* Woolwich
Royal Artillery 35, 43, 48, 60, 83, 86, 104, 106, 108, 116, 140, 160, 182; *for* Barracks *see* Exeter; Newcastle upon Tyne; Portsmouth; Woolwich
Royal Commissions 27, 28, 139, 140, 141, 145, 151, 160, 163
Royal Engineers xv, xviii, 35, 68, 84, 87, 90, 106, 114, 116, 120–3, 127, 137, 170, 174, 177, 185, 188
Royal Garrison Artillery 186
Royal Herbert Hospital *see under* Woolwich
Royal Irish Constabulary 104
Royal Irish Engineers 91
Royal London Militia Depot *see under* London, Finsbury
Royal Marines 43, 46, 48–53, *54*, 61, 70, 117, 121–2, 157, 160, 162, 178, 193
Royal Marines Artillery Regiment 160, 162
Royal Military Academy *see under* Woolwich
Royal Military Artificers (Royal Sappers and Miners) 87, 106
Royal Military College *see* Sandhurst
Royal Navy *see* naval barracks; Royal Marines
Ruse, Hendrik, engineer 9, *95*
Ruthven 21, *22*, *23*, 28

St Augustine's Fort, Galway 6
St George's Barracks *see* Gosport; London
St Mary's, Isles of Scilly 17, *17*, 28
  Star Castle 7
St Mary's Casemates *see under* Chatham
St Mawes 68
St Nicholas Island 7
Salisbury Plain 183, 187, 188
Salvin, Anthony, architect *129*
Sanders, John, architect 74, 76–7, 106, 125
Sandhurst
  gymnasium 145, 147, *148*
  New College 189, 195
  Royal Military College 76, 124, *124*, 125, 143, 197
Sanitary Commission Report *see* Army Sanitary Commission
sanitation 103, 118, 123, 128, 139–41, 144, 174–5; *see also* latrines and privies; water supplies
Scamp, William 162
Scarborough 68, 71
School of Military Engineering *see under* Chatham
schools (regimental) 119, 123, 136, 137, 144
Scobell, John 77
Scotland xii, 2, 5, 7, *15*, 17, 18–20, 21, 27, 33, 35, 71, 74, 116, 117, 140
  billeting 37, 105
  camps 188
  garrison 103
  localization depots 169
Seaton Sluice 68
Seddon, Major H.C. 169–70, *173*, 174
's-Hertogenbosch (Netherlands) 3, 4
Selsea 74
Seven Years War 38, 45–6, 180
Shannon, River, defences 85, 91, 157
Shaw, Norman, architect 174
Sheerness
  Boatstore 162
  Fort 7, 10, 12–13, *12*, 68, 104
Sheffield 62, 63, 91, 112, 119
  Hillsborough Barracks 197, *197*
Shoeburyness
  British School of Gunnery 137
  Horseshoe Barracks 119, *120*, 137–9, *138*
Shoreham, hutment camp 74
Shornecliffe
  artillery barracks 86
  Camp 134–5, 177, 187
Shornmeade Fort, Thames estuary 158
Shrewsbury, cavalry station 69, 71
Sidney, Sir Philip 3–4
Silverhill, hutment camp 93
Skinner, William 43, 44, 54, *96*

Smith, Sir Charles 120
Smith, Col. Sir Frederick 108, 109, 131
Smith, Lt Col. Percy 190
soldiers' lodgings 5–7
Southampton 71
South Shields 68
Spanish barracks xiii, 3, 4
Spence, Sir Basil, architect 149, 196
stables 32, *44*, 77, 79, 87, *88*, 136–7,
    137, 140, 144, 145
  at hutment camps 82
Stanhope, Edward, Memorandum (1888) 175, 177
Stevenson, J.J., architect 174
Stevin, Simon 2
Steyning, hutment camp 74, 77
Stirling Castle xiii, 19, 68, 140, 169
Stobbs Camp 187
Stockport, militia drill hall *156*
Stonar 68
Stonehouse Marines Barracks 48, 50–1,
    50, *51*, *52–3*, 121, 160, *162*, *164*, *165*, 197
  Naval Hospital 142, *143*, 198
storehouses 10, 26, 27, 44
  of the militia 152–7, 171
straw stores 78, *78*, 107
Street, G.E., architect 119
Sunderland 73, 74, 77, 79, 81, 104, 105, 116
Sussex 67, 74
Sutherland, Sir John 139, 145, 148
sutlers' houses and sutleries 3,
    10, 27, 77
swimming pools 147, 193

Tangier garrison 7
Taunton 71
  Jellalabad Barracks depot 172
Thomas, Huw, architect *197*
Tidworth Camp 183, 185–6, *186*, 187
Tilbury Fort 7, 9–10, *11*, 11–12, 13, 25,
    28, 68
  timber huts 84
timber buildings
  barracks 18, *25*, 81
  churches and chapels *134*, 135,
    135, *136*
  shed (canteen) 27
timber-framed barracks 6, 8, 10, 73, 81–2,
    81, 83, 85, 105–6
timber huts 48, 69, 71, 72, *82*, 84,
    130–1, *131*, *135*, 187; *see also* hutment camps

Tipner, magazine 104
Totnes 71, 77
training camps 129–37, *and see* Aldershot
Tralee (Ireland) 91
Tresco, Isles of Scilly 7
Trowbridge, cavalry barracks 71, 77, 104
Twiss, Lt Col. William 88, 89
Tynemouth Castle 5, 23, 68, 104

Upnor Castle, Kent *20*, 21, 27, 28, 68
Uxbridge, militia storehouse 153

Vauban, Sébastien le Prestre de 17, 32
Venice (Italy) 2
verandas (loggias) 49, 122, 136, 145,
    158, *159*, 160, *162*, 185
Verona (Italy) 2
Victoria Barracks *see under* Portsmouth

Wade, General 41, 42, 43
Wales 116
  barracks 117, 140
  billeting 43
  'duty areas' 35
Wallsend, Roman barracks 1
Walmer Castle, Kent 23, *25*
Ward, Robert 3, *3*
Wareham 71
Warley, East India Company depot 169
  chapel 119
War Office 73, 76, 120, 127, 128,
    147, 156, 157, 160, 167, 170,
    179, 182, 188
washhouses 11, 51, 89, 123, 173, 177, 185
water supplies 116, 118
Waterford 25–6, 33, 34, 86
Waterloo Barracks *see under* London,
  Tower of London
Watson, Col. C.M. 183
Weedon Bec, arms depot 104, *104*
Wellington, Duke of 103, 106, 115, 127, 151
Wellington Barracks *see under* London
Wellington Lines *see under* Aldershot
West Indies 106, 120, *121*
Weymouth 71, 72, 77, *82*; *see also* Radipole
  Barracks
Whitehaven, Barracks Mill 73
Wicklow Mountains, military road and
    barracks 91, *92*
William III (of Orange) 16, 18, 29, 90

Index

Wiltshire, duty area 35
Winchelsea, camp 82
Winchester *40*, 69, 73, 74
  loc. depot 170, 180
  depot (replaced) 177
  King's House Barracks 169
    Lower Barracks 180, *197*
    Peninsular Barracks 180–1, *182*,
      183, *197*, 198
Windsor
  Castle 8
  Foot Guards 111
  Horse Guards' Barracks *72*, 73,
    74, 104, 111, 186
  infantry barracks 80
women xv, 79, 176–7
Wood, Major Gen. Sir Elliot 148–9
Woolwich 104, 141
  Marines Barracks (Cambridge
    Infantry Barracks) 121–2, *122*
  Royal Arsenal 58
  Royal Artillery Barracks 58–9, *58*, *59*,
    60, *60*, 86, 106, 116, 119, 140, 177
  Royal Herbert Hospital 143, *143*, 198
  Royal Military Academy 58, 59, 124–5, *124*, *125*
Worcester, depot 169, 172, *173*
Wren, Sir Christopher, architect *30*, 180, 181, *182*
Wyatt, James, architect 58, 59, 84,
  86, 87, 88, 94, 124–5
Wyatt, Matthew Digby, architect
  119, 147, 148, 149
Wyvern Artillery Barracks *see under*
  Exeter

Yeomanry 67, 103, 110, 152
Yonge, Sir George 62, 63
York, Fulford Barracks cavalry
  station 69, 71, 79, 87, 104